# RAPID FIRE

*Ministry of Defence Pattern Room, ground floor weapons hall* (Courtesy: MoD Pattern Room)

# RAPID FIRE

The Development of
Automatic Cannon, Heavy
Machine Guns and their
Ammunition for Armies,
Navies and Air Forces

# ANTHONY G. WILLIAMS

**Airlife**
England

First published in the UK in 2000
by Airlife Publishing Ltd

This edition published 2003

**British Library Cataloguing-in-Publication Data**
A catalogue record for this book
is available from the British Library

ISBN 1 84037 435 7

Typeset by Servis Filmsetting Ltd, Manchester
Printed in Italy.

For a complete list of all Airlife titles please contact:

# Airlife Publishing Ltd

101 Longden Road, Shrewsbury SY3 9EB, England
Email: airlife@airlifebooks.com
Website: www.airlifebooks.com

# Acknowledgements

THIS BOOK WOULD NOT HAVE BEEN POSSIBLE without the generous co-operation and assistance of Herbert Woodend, the curator, and the staff of the Ministry of Defence Pattern Room, whose unique library and weapon collection was extensively consulted.

Particular thanks are also due to Dr Derek Allsop, for giving permission to use the gun action drawings from his book *Cannons* and for commenting on the text, and to three people who have provided invaluable comments on various drafts of this book: Dr Jean-François Legendre, who contributed to the sections on French, Swiss and Russian developments as well as producing the cartridge drawings in Appendix 3; Ted Bradstreet, who provided much information about German and especially Japanese aircraft armament together with illustrations for Appendix 4; and Dr Emmanuel Gustin, who maintains an excellent website on World War Two fighter armament (http://www.geocities.com/CapeCanaveral/Hangar/8217/).

Others who have provided information and assistance include Ing. Luigi Bodio, John Carlin, John Carrier, Ron Wallace Clarke, Dr J. R. Crittenden Schmitt, Eugene Dvurechenski, Nigel Eastaway of the Russian Aviation Research Trust (RART), Urban Frederickson, Dr Ian Gooderson, Jack Green of the US Naval Historical Centre, Alexei Gretchikhine, Bill Gunston, Henri Hubegger, Hans Häfeli, Robert Hawkinson Jr, Ian Hogg (who generously loaned his extensive photo collection), I. J. Inauen of the Swiss Federal Military Library, Jukka P. Koivusaari, Yasufumi Kunimoto, Peter Labbett, Jakob Lippert, Leo Marriott, Tim Mason, Steve McGregor, Freddy Mead, Robert A. Mellichamp, Jim O'Brien, Keith Painter, Mats Persson, Phillipe Regenstreif, John Salt, Yuji Sasaki, Paul Smith, Peter Smithurst of the Royal Armouries (Leeds) and David Stone.

Thanks are also due to the many companies who have given permission to use their photographic material. The author is particularly grateful to Ernst Jaggi of Oerlikon-Contraves, V. Köhne and Corina Wassner of Mauser-Werke Oberndorf, B. Nardini of Alenia and Denny Petersen of Bofors Weapon Systems (Celsius Corporation)

# Foreword

THE QUESTION ANY AUTHOR IS LIKELY TO BE ASKED (or, indeed, to ask himself) is, 'Why write this book?' In my case the answer goes back to my student days more than thirty years ago, when I first took up competitive rifle shooting. This sparked an interest in the weapons themselves and in the ammunition they used. The interest developed over the years (somewhat patchily, as career demands intervened) and extended to cover the range of military technology – but always with guns and ammunition at the core.

After a while this interest became combined with an enthusiasm for writing and a series of articles for various magazines followed, on such diverse subjects as hunting rifles, military small arms, anti-tank rifles, heavy machine guns, automatic cannon, aircraft armament, naval guns and even battleship design.

The genesis of this book lay in a combination of frustration and opportunity. There is plenty of published information about rifle-calibre machine guns and other infantry weapons, but very little about the larger-calibre automatic guns, even less about their ammunition and virtually nothing about why particular choices of equipment were made or how well they worked in practice. Worse, I soon realised that what little information there was frequently contained major errors (often repeated by authors who borrowed from preceding works). The opportunity came from access to the Ministry of Defence Pattern Room at the Royal Ordnance Factory, Nottingham – a matchless depository of equipment and information.

This book is the result. The scope is admittedly ambitious, covering as it does all heavy automatic weapons (12.7–57mm plus a few others) of every nation throughout the twentieth century, whether used by armies, navies or air forces. I freely admit that despite my best efforts, some errors and omissions are almost inevitable in such a work. If any readers can supply more information it will be gratefully received!

The book may be used as a reference work, as it contains tabulated data for the weapons and ammunition as well as a cartridge identification guide. However, I hope it will be read for more reasons than that. I have tried to give some understanding of the factors which have influenced both the designers of the weapons and the military procurement authorities who acquired them. Gun and ammunition design is usually a struggle to reconcile conflicting requirements while achieving the maximum performance with the minimum size, weight and cost. Sometimes the result is spectacular success, at other times dismal failure. Perhaps most frustrating of all for the designers is to produce a technically flawless weapon system, only to win no sales because the time wasn't right or the military's priorities were elsewhere.

I have enjoyed writing this book; I hope you enjoy reading it.

*Anthony Williams*
*Derbyshire, 1999*

# Contents

# Introduction

THE PERIOD FROM THE MIDDLE OF THE NINETEENTH century to the early years of the twentieth saw a transformation in military firearms. British troops went to the Crimea in 1854 armed with rifles not very different from those of centuries earlier: muzzle loaders, in which the powder, shot and primer were separately loaded, limiting the rate of fire to only a few rounds per minute. Sixty years later they fought in the Great War with bolt-action rifles capable of thirty aimed rounds per minute (rpm). They also had automatic weapons – machine guns – which fired at around 600 rpm. While improvements in engineering and chemicals facilitated the change, these innovations were made possible by one technical development: the advent of the metal cartridge case holding the primer, powder and bullet together.

The first cartridges emerged in the middle of the nineteenth century. Ammunition handling was immediately transformed and loading made much faster, even in the single-shot rifles of the day, as breech-loading became much easier to arrange. The rugged, convenient cartridges were particularly suited to mechanical handling and it was not long before the first machine guns were designed to use them.

Developments in engineering permitted the mass production of cartridges and weapons to standard sizes which were interchangeable. Advances in chemicals led to the replacement of gunpowder, or black powder, by smokeless powders as the standard propellant. The new powders were not only relatively smokeless; their burning characteristics could more easily be adjusted to work efficiently in cartridges with a wide range of calibres and performance levels. This encouraged the development of smaller-calibre weapons, typically reducing the bullet diameter of military rifles from 11–12mm to around 7–8mm or, in some nations, 6.5mm. The new propellants also led to a great increase in muzzle velocities from around 400–500 metres per second (m/s) to 730–850 m/s, giving much greater effective range.

Since the Great War, the development of infantry weapons has been gradual. There were few changes in small arms until the Second World War stimulated the development of greater individual firepower; at first with sub-machine guns, later with assault rifles. The first of these used pistol ammunition to produce a simple, short-range weapon. The second eventually replaced both high-powered rifles and sub-machine guns with a compact, shoulder-fired machine gun firing cartridges intermediate in power between pistol and rifle ammunition.

After that, little altered in weapon and ammunition design until well into the second half of the twentieth century, which has seen a further reduction in the calibre of the standard infantry weapon to around 5.5mm (5.56mm NATO, 5.45mm Russian) with an increase in muzzle velocities to about 900 m/s.

Throughout this period the vast majority of machine guns have been designed to use the same cartridges as those of the standard infantry rifles (thereby referred to as rifle calibre machine guns, or RCMGs). This is partly because these cartridges have been, by definition, of adequate range and effectiveness to deal with enemy infantry, and partly to simplify ammunition production and supply. Only with the introduction of the 5.5mm rifles has there been a tendency to keep at least some infantry machine guns in the older 7.62mm calibre in the interests of adequate long-range performance.

Various descriptions have evolved for machine guns of different types. The light machine gun (LMG), nowadays also sometimes called the squad automatic weapon or light support weapon, uses the same ammunition as the standard rifle and is light enough to be carried and fired by one man. Ammunition is usually contained in a detachable magazine to aid portability. The first such weapon to be successful were the Lewis and Madsen guns of the First World War. Two other famous examples which saw extensive service in the next war, and for some time thereafter, are the Browning automatic rifle (BAR) and the Bren gun. Today's LMGs are generally in 5.5mm calibre.

Preceding the LMG was the medium machine gun (MMG), although it was not called that at the time. Essentially it was a weapon which used rifle-calibre ammunition but was intended for sustained fire. It was therefore tripod-mounted, usually water-cooled, belt-fed and served by several men. The Maxim was the first of these, with the Vickers derived from it being perhaps the most famous example. This remained in British service until the mid-1950s.

The MMG, and the earlier LMGs, were replaced by a different concept, the general-purpose machine gun (GPMG), which again used the standard rifle ammunition. This was developed in Germany in the 1930s as a versatile weapon, air-cooled but with quick-change barrels, belt-fed and used with a bipod in the light role or a tripod where sustained fire was required. The German guns, the MG 34 and MG 42, became famous in the Second World War and inspired many similar weapons which remain in service today, normally in 7.62mm calibre.

From the earliest years there has been a need for some weapons intermediate in power between the standard rifle calibre and field or naval artillery. The reasons for this are many and varied. The original purpose, which is still valid today, was to apply the greater destructive power of explosive shells against light naval craft and army units. Later, the need to destroy vehicles (especially armoured) and aircraft was added to the list. Most of these weapons have been automatic but some of the more portable ones have not. While such weapons have remained important in army and naval applications throughout their existence, their period of major development occurred in the middle years of the twentieth century, especially for aircraft installations. The constant pressure for higher rates of fire for less weight drove aircraft gun designers to produce most of the technical innovations in this field. For the same reason, aircraft guns have tended to be rather like Formula One racing cars: highly tuned and of uncertain reliability.

This book is concerned with the development and history of these heavy weapons and their ammunition; larger in calibre than the standard infantry rifle or machine gun but usually much smaller in size than artillery. The emphasis is very much on weapons which saw service but some important experimental types, and recent developments which have yet to be adopted, are included. However, there is a large number of experimental cartridges and weapons which have had to be omitted for reasons of space.

In general, the calibres considered in this book range from 12.7mm to 57mm. There are some exceptions, however: a few weapons of smaller calibre which are included for the sake of completeness, and a few automatic guns of larger calibre for the sake of comparison. It is a category of gun which has probably seen more, and more varied, technical development than any other, and there is every likelihood that this will continue into the future.

*Rifle-calibre machine gun cartridges compared with .50" Browning (left to right):*

|   |   |   |   |
|---|---|---|---|
| 1 | 6.5mm Arisaka (6.5 × 50SR) | 7 | .30-06 US (7.62 × 63) |
| 2 | 6.5mm Carcano (6.5 × 52) | 8 | .50" Browning for scale |
| 3 | 8mm Lebel (7.92 × 50R) | 9 | 7.62mm NATO (7.62 × 51) |
| 4 | .303" British (7.7 × 56R) | 10 | 7.62mm AK47 (7.62 × 39) |
| 5 | 7.62mm Russian (7.62 × 54R) | 11 | 5.45mm AK74 (5.45 × 39) |
| 6 | 7.92mm Mauser (7.92 × 57) | 12 | 5.56mm NATO (5.56 × 45) |

# *Chapter One*

## THE CARTRIDGE

### CARTRIDGE DESIGN

A CARTRIDGE IS A UNIT OR ROUND OF AMMUNITION consisting of a projectile, propellant to thrust the projectile from the gun, a primer to ignite the pro-pellant and a cartridge case to hold it all together. For as long as it has been used, the cartridge has been the heart of all automatic weapons. It is almost invariably designed first and the gun config-ured around it. This particularly applies to gas- or recoil-operated automatic and semi-automatic weapons because their functioning depends upon the characteristics of the ammunition; not just the size and shape but also the gas pressure and recoil generated. These factors are less significant in exter-nally powered weapons such as chain guns and most rotary cannon, but these form only a minori-ty of the guns in service.

While it is not uncommon for different guns to be designed around the same cartridge, it is therefore rare for a service cannon or HMG (heavy machine gun) to be adapted to fire a new cartridge. The few exceptions are generally concerned with an alteration to the neck diameter of the cartridge case in order to take a projectile with a different calibre. The best-known example of this is probably the German MG 151 aircraft cannon, which com-menced life in the 1930s in 15mm calibre but was increased to 20mm during the Second World War.

Cartridges are designed to achieve particular effects. The official requirement might specify the ability to penetrate a given thickness of armour at a particular range, a maximum time of flight to a given range, or the effectiveness of incendiary or high-explosive projectiles. There will also be a range of other criteria including acceptable levels of accu-racy, consistency, reliability and safety, which will need to be sustained over a wide range of climatic conditions and a long period of time. These only

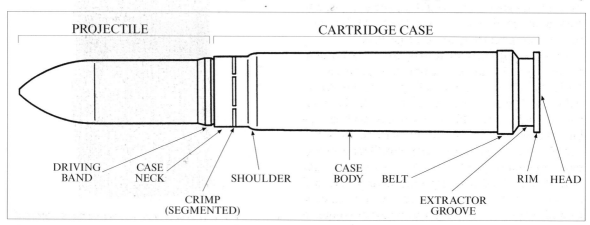

*Elements of a cannon cartridge (drawing courtesy of J-F Legendre)*

partly apply to blank cartridges and not at all to drill or dummy rounds, but these types will not be considered here.

For use in automatic weapons (except in the case of externally powered guns), it almost goes without saying that the ammunition must be able to operate the gun mechanism reliably. This might not be a simple matter given that the projectile weights and propellant powders can vary considerably in different loadings of any particular cartridge, and this can alter the recoil and pressure characteristics accordingly.

## THE PROJECTILE

THE PROJECTILE IS WHAT THE WEAPON IS ALL ABOUT. Everything else – the rest of the cartridge and the gun itself – is concerned with ensuring that the projectile hits the target at the desired velocity. The design of the projectile is therefore the most crucial aspect of ammunition design.

Projectiles are available in a wide variety of types, even ignoring those intended for practice or drill purposes. Service ammunition can be classified into four broad categories: ball, incendiary (I), high-explosive (HE) and armour-piercing (AP), any of which may also be equipped with tracers (T) so that the gunner can observe the accuracy of his shooting. Other common designations are SAP (semi-armour-piercing), TP (target practice), SD (self-destruct), APDS (armour-piercing discarding-sabot) and APFSDS (armour-piercing fin-stabilised discarding-sabot). The terms HV (high or hyper velocity) and SV (super velocity) are sometimes used to designate lightweight projectiles (usually AP). Some manufacturers use their own designations for proprietary types of projectiles.

Cannon projectiles are usually painted according to their type for rapid identification purposes (in HMG projectiles it is normally just the tip that is painted). Colour schemes have varied between nations and military blocs and within such groupings over time, so this is not the place to attempt a complete listing. However, AP projectiles are nowadays commonly painted black and practice ones blue. Reds and yellows frequently indicate chemical contents, either HE, incendiary or tracers. Combined projectiles often have bands of colour to indicate their particular mix of characteristics, so

projectiles can be quite colourful.

Ball ammunition is the simplest and is named after the round lead balls which were the standard small-arms projectiles until the nineteenth century. The name is still applied to standard rifle ammunition, in which the bullet consists of a jacket (originally copper, now a variety of alloys) normally enclosing a lead core. Ball projectiles are not now common in heavy-weapon ammunition as they have limited effect on the target in comparison with more specialised projectiles. Where they do occur, they usually have a predominantly steel core. Most heavy weapon projectiles now in service have armour-piercing, incendiary and/or high explosive capabilities.

The method of projectile construction varies

*Fired 6pdr AP projectile showing driving band engraved by the rifling*

*Crimps and driving bands (from left to right): iron driving band (30 × 170), plastic driving band with two continuous crimps (30 × 165 US experimental), single copper band with two segmented crimps (30 × 165), double copper band with two crimps (30 × 210B)*

considerably. In calibres of up to 15mm it is common to use all-enclosing soft metal jackets as described above, designed to be easily engraved by the barrel rifling, with incendiary and AP as well as ball rounds. Larger calibres use steel projectile bodies fitted with separate driving bands of greater than projectile diameter, which are gripped by the rifling in order to spin the projectile. Spinning the projectile ensures that it remains stable in flight, pointing towards the target, and greatly improves long-range accuracy. Originally driving bands were made of copper (still favoured by the Russians) but this is not strong enough to withstand the shearing effect of the rifling at very high velocities, so soft iron driving bands are used on most Western high-velocity cannon.

After much experimentation US designers have perfected plastic driving bands, first successfully introduced in the 1970s in 30 × 173 calibre for the 30mm GAU-8/A aircraft gun. The advantage of plastic-banded projectiles is that barrel wear is only one-third that caused by metal driving bands. Plastic and iron bands also avoid the problem of 'coppering' – the coating of the bore with copper which has to be cleared from time to time with a 'decoppering' round.

Light-alloy projectile bodies are usually used in APCR (armour-piercing, composite, rigid) shot, in which only the hard central core penetrates the target, the light-alloy body breaking up on impact. Sub-calibre projectiles such as APDS and APFSDS are nowadays commonly encased in plastic sabots.

## ARMOUR-PIERCING SHOT

THE SIMPLEST FORM OF CANNON AP PROJECTILE consists of a pointed steel shot – the military term

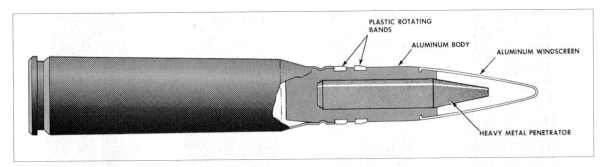

*APCR with DU core, for 30 × 173 GAU-8/A (Courtesy: Aerojet/Ian Hogg)*

'shot' (from the cannon ball era) meaning a solid or very thick-walled projectile without any explosive content. The steel will be hardened, at least at the point, and the shot will have a driving band (see photo on page 11). The best AP performance is obtained with a rather blunt point, so the shot is sometimes given a 'ballistic cap' – a pointed nose cone usually made out of light alloy or thin steel in order to minimise the added weight. Some projectiles were also given a blunt cap of soft steel as this improved penetration against face-hardened armour, leading to designations such as APC (armour-piercing, capped) and APCBC (armour-piercing, capped, ballistic-capped).

This simple type of AP shot was usual in automatic cannon until after the Second World War, when it began to be replaced by more sophisticated composite projectiles. Heavy machine guns have tended to follow a slightly different route, retaining the cupro-nickel bullet jacket of the ball rounds but inserting a hardened steel or tungsten AP core to achieve the desired effect.

The first major improvement in cannon AP performance emerged during the Second World War: the composite rigid shot. This consists of a hard steel or tungsten-alloy core surrounded by a light-alloy sleeve. Tungsten is heavier than steel and better at penetrating armour. When the shot hits the target, the alloy sleeve breaks up and the narrow core penetrates. This type of projectile is still in common use in cannon, particularly in aircraft guns such as the 30mm GAU-8/A. In this and in some other cases the core is of DU (depleted uranium), which adds pyrophoric behind-armour effects after penetration.

When used with tank and anti-tank guns, the composite shot (known during the Second World War as APCR in British service, HVAP – high-velocity armour-piercing – to the Americans and *Panzergranat 40* or *Hartkernmunition* to the Germans) was usually made much lighter than standard. This permitted a higher muzzle velocity and therefore better armour penetration. Such lightweight projectiles are less common in automatic weapons because of the need to match the trajectory of other ammunition types which may be mixed with AP rounds in the same belt, although this is not a factor when the weapon is used for a dedicated anti-armour mission. A current generic designation for this type of ammunition is APHC, for armour-piercing hard core.

The next stage of development of armour-piercing ammunition – the squeeze or taper bore – has not seen service in automatic weapons (although various experimental guns have been made) and therefore will not be discussed in detail. Essentially, it was the same as APCR except that the light sleeve was designed to be squeezed flat against the AP core by a tapered barrel or barrel attachment in order to reduce air resistance and thereby retain the APCR's performance out to a longer range. The main tactical problem is that a taper-bore barrel cannot fire full-calibre ammunition and is therefore very specialised, only seeing service in a few Second World War anti-tank and armoured fighting vehicle (AFV) weapons.

A further improvement was also developed during the Second World War: the APDS shot. This is similar to APCR except that the sleeve (sabot) is designed to break up and fall away as soon as the projectile leaves the barrel, leaving the dense, small-calibre AP core to continue alone. This provides a

*Experimental 40mm APDS projectile*

*APDS components: plastic sabot, tungsten carbide penetrator with aluminium ballistic cap, base cup*

great improvement in the performance of APCR at longer ranges, in terms of both reducing the time of flight to increase hit probability and increasing the impact velocity (and therefore armour penetration), without the practical disadvantages of taper bores. It has accordingly seen widespread post-war use in automatic weapons; in smaller calibres the sleeve is nowadays usually plastic. It is not generally used in aircraft weapons because of the potential damage from bits of discarded sabot hitting the aircraft or being sucked into the engines. 'Sabot diverters' have been designed to try to circumvent this problem, with some success, but they are bulky and heavy.

The most sophisticated type of AP shot is the APFSDS. This was developed as a result of the observation that a long, thin projectile has advantages for AP use, partly because it has less air resistance and therefore does not slow down as much on its way to the target, but also because it can punch through armour more easily. The problem is that there is a limit on the length of projectile which can be stabilised by being spun by barrel rifling: it can be no longer than about five or six times the calibre (an L/D or length/diameter ratio of 5:1 or 6:1). Long, narrow shot therefore have to be stabilised by fins and have sometimes been

*Armour-piercing technology (from left to right): APDS for 20 × 139 with plastic sabot removed, APCR for 20 × 128 with alloy nose-cone and tungsten core removed, APDS for 30 × 170 ( Rarden) with sharply-pointed tungsten core*

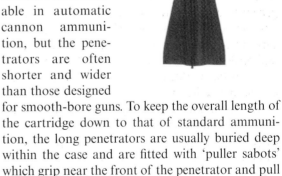

*Sub-calibre 35mm projectiles for Oerlikon-Contraves ammunition:*
*LEFT: FAPDS for air defence. MIDDLE: APDS-T for anti-armour use.*
*RIGHT: APFSDS-T for enhanced anti-armour use (Courtesy: Oerlikon-Contraves)*

called arrow projectiles, notably by the Germans who developed this *Pfeil-geschoss* concept in the Second World War with HE projectiles in order to achieve very long range in large-calibre artillery weapons.

APFSDS penetrators with an L/D ratio of between 10:1 and 20:1 are in common use in smooth-bored tank guns, but less so in automatic weapons because their stability is upset by being spun by the rifling. Muzzle velocities of over 1,000 m/s can result in rotational rates of 100,000 rpm; spinning at these speeds, the slightest deviation from precise symmetry in the construction and location of the penetrator within the sabot will result in it bending out of shape, and the longer and narrower the penetrator, the more difficult that is to control. In these smaller calibres, some degree of rifling is needed (even if confined to a small section near the muzzle) to act as a 'sabot stripper', ensuring that the sabot separates cleanly from the penetrator, but the ideal rifling angle for this is much less than that needed to stabilise conventional projectiles.

These technical difficulties are being overcome, mainly by fitting the sabot with slip rings which reduce the amount of spin provided to the projectile. APFSDS shot is therefore now available in automatic cannon ammunition, but the penetrators are often shorter and wider than those designed for smooth-bore guns. To keep the overall length of the cartridge down to that of standard ammunition, the long penetrators are usually buried deep within the case and are fitted with 'puller sabots' which grip near the front of the penetrator and pull it up the barrel.

Both tungsten alloy and DU are used to make penetrators. DU is easier to work with and delivers more consistent results over a wider range of conditions than tungsten, as well as producing behind-armour pyrophoric effects. However, it has been criticised for creating toxic fumes around the target, with obvious long-term health hazards.

*Sectioned APFSDS 35 × 228 round* (Courtesy: Oerlikon-Contraves)

Figures quoted for the thickness of armour penetrated by particular AP ammunition need to be treated with caution as they are affected by several variables. One is obviously range, as performance reduces in line with velocity (less of an issue with APFSDS which slows down very little even at long range). Another is the type of armour being attacked, some being more resistant than others. The third main variable is the angle at which the shot strikes the armour. Typically, a shot striking at 60° has only 80% of the penetration of one striking at 90°; at 45° this reduces to 66% and at 30° to 45%. Two of these variables are normally dealt with in the standard way of describing penetration, which is to list the thickness penetrated at a given range and striking angle, as in 75mm/500m/60°. An unwelcome complication is that there have been two different conventions for describing striking angle: from the horizontal or from the vertical. A hit perpendicular to the armour surface (the optimum for penetration) is described in NATO terminology as being at 90°, but in the past it has sometimes been described as being at 0°.

## EXPLOSIVE / INCENDIARY SHELLS

THE TERM 'SHELL' IS AGAIN OF ANCIENT ORIGIN AND obvious meaning: a hard outer casing protecting something more vulnerable inside, in this case a high-explosive or incendiary compound. In larger artillery calibres, shells can contain a wide variety of materials including smoke to obscure visibility, starshell for illumination, chemicals, various anti-personnel rounds, and anti-tank sub-munitions (some capable of homing onto their targets) but these need not concern us here.

Cannon shells were originally made by drilling out a cavity of the appropriate shape in a steel shot to take the desired explosive or incendiary compound. This led to a relatively small capacity in smaller calibres, however, so during the Second World War, German technicians perfected the mine shell (*Minengeschoss* or *M-Geschoss*) which was made by stamping and drawing the shell from a thick disc of metal in the same way in which cartridge cases are made. This resulted in a shell with thin but strong walls, with a far larger capacity. It also led to a lighter shell overall (steel being much heavier than explosives), permitting a higher muzzle velocity at the expense of range (as light shells slow down more quickly), which made this innovation particularly suitable for aircraft cannon.

Important but conflicting characteristics of HE fillings are that they must explode as violently as possible to make the most of the restricted quantity of compound that the shell can carry, yet be completely safe over a wide range of temperatures, despite the rough handling the ammunition may receive from the gun mechanism.

Incendiary and even HE projectiles have been used in rifle-calibre ammunition, most notably for .303″ (7.7mm) aircraft guns in the Second World War when the RAF made much use of incendiaries, officially known as the De Wilde after a Belgian inventor but modified by Major Dixon of the War

Office Design Department to remove some short-comings in De Wilde's design. However, such small projectiles are barely able to contain enough chemicals to make the effort worthwhile. The heavy machine gun is really the smallest calibre in which incendiary shells are common, with HE shells being more common in cannon (20+mm) calibres. During the Second World War, it was discovered that adding aluminium dust to HE compounds not

only improved the strength of the explosion but also had an incendiary effect. In consequence, pure incendiary cannon shells became less common.

One specialised form of HE projectile is the HEAT (high-explosive anti-tank) or shaped charge shell. In this, there is a cone-shaped hollow, lined with metal, left at the front of the shell. An instant-acting fuze detonates the HE on the surface of the target. The explosion compresses the metal

*Sectioned German WW2 aircraft gun cartridges (from left to right): 20 × 80RB HE/T-SD for MG-FF, 20 × 80RB HE (M-Geschoss) for MG-FFM, 20 × 82 HE/T-SD for MG 151/20, 20 × 82 HE (M-Geschoss) for MG 151/20, 20 × 82 AP/HE (base fuze) for MG 151/20. Note differences between mechanical (1 and 2) and chemical (3) fuzes. Cartridge 4 is a practice round with a dummy fuze.*

lining to form an elongated high-velocity jet whose tip can be travelling at 8,000–9,000 m/s, with considerable armour-piercing capability. This type of projectile is standard in modern infantry anti-tank weapons and is used in some larger cannon. It was experimentally used in the Second World War in ammunition for German aircraft guns, but has not been generally used in smaller calibres because the effectiveness is largely determined by projectile diameter and is also lessened by being spun by barrel rifling. A rotation of only 150 revolutions per second is sufficient to reduce the penetration by 50%, yet a cannon shell will typically rotate at considerably more. In larger calibres, such as the Obus 'G' (named after the inventor, Gessner) for the French 105mm tank gun, this problem has been reduced by mounting the shaped charge on ball bearings within the case, greatly reducing the spin imparted to the explosive section, but this is not feasible with small-calibre ammunition.

However, the problem has been tackled by careful design of the shape of the HE cone and metal lining – generally a flatter cone is needed – and HEAT ammunition has quite recently become available for automatic cannon. Known as the M789 HEDP (HE dual purpose – anti-personnel as well as anti-armour), it is the standard type of ammunition used in the 30mm M230 chain gun fitted to the AH-64 Apache attack helicopter, in which the angle of the rifling has also been reduced to the minimum level needed to achieve stability. The M789 is capable of penetrating 50mm of steel as well as having a 4m lethal radius against unprotected personnel.

It should be noted that military terminology is not always logical. All projectiles for the 20mm Hispano, including AP, were officially referred to as 'shells' by the RAF.

## COMBINED PROJECTILES

IT IS USUAL FOR PROJECTILES TO COMBINE characteristics in order to maximise the effect on the target. The term 'AP shell' (which should properly be APHE) is used to describe an essentially armour-piercing projectile which also contains some high-explosive (usually only a very small percentage of the projectile weight), intended to detonate once the armour has been penetrated. It is generally only worth doing this in larger calibres, although national practices have varied. In World War Two, for example, British AP shot for tank/anti-tank guns contained no HE, while the German equivalents did.

More of a compromise is the SAP or SAPHE (semi-armour-piercing HE) shell, which is similar to an APHE shell but has thinner walls to provide more space for explosives, thereby losing some AP performance. Because of the necessity for a hard point to both APHE and SAPHE shells, the fuzes are fitted into the base.

A common form of combination adds a tracer element to an HE, incendiary or AP projectile. These usually consist of a pyrotechnic element in the base of the projectile which burns brightly, enabling the trajectory to be followed and the aim corrected as required. These are obviously more effective at night so daytime tracers sometimes utilise a smoke trail. It is usual for the tracers to burn without emitting light for the first part of their travel ('dark trace'), partly to avoid blinding the gunner and partly to conceal the precise location of the gun. An originally unintended side-effect of tracers is psychological: the sight of a stream of tracers heading towards an attacking aircraft can distract the pilot.

Ammunition designations now include 'HE/I' (high-explosive and incendiary) and 'AP/I/T' (armour-piercing incendiary tracer). It is possible for all of the above types to be combined in one multi-purpose projectile but there is obviously the risk that it will not be very effective in any of its tasks. The Norwegian firm Raufoss has been particularly successful in developing multipurpose (MP) ammunition which combines a chemical impact fuze with incendiary and HE elements – and even, in the .50″ calibre version known as the NM140, some AP capability. This type has now been adopted by other countries for a wide range of ammunition, such as the American Olin PGU-28 round for the 20mm M61 series cannon and the British Royal Ordnance MP ammunition for the 30mm Aden. A more recent Raufoss development is the Mk 211 in 12.7mm calibre, which has a pyrophoric zirconium penetrator to ignite flammable material.

## OTHER PROJECTILES

MOST PROJECTILES ARE VARIANTS OR COMBINATIONS of those already described. 'Multiball' rounds have been developed for heavy machine guns as well as infantry rifles. As the name suggests, two or more short projectiles are stacked on top of each other in the cartridge case and all fired at once, with the aim of increasing the hit probability against infantry. These are also known as duplex or triplex loadings, when they have two or three projectiles respectively. The problem is that, being light for their calibre, the projectiles lose velocity and range rather quickly.

A development of this idea is the 'salvo-squeeze-bore'. This consists of a number of funnel-shaped projectiles stacked on top of each other and held together by a plastic sheath. When fired down a taper-bore barrel the projectiles separate and are simultaneously squeezed to a smaller calibre. Each cartridge fired therefore results in a stream of small, high-velocity projectiles. Although extensively tested in .50″ (12.7 mm) calibre by the Americans, who were attracted by its potential for short-range defence against ambushes, it was not adopted.

Some projectiles are designed to break up into a hail of sub-projectiles, either on or immediately before impact with the target. The former are called 'frangible', leading to the 'F' designation. Some of these have been developed for training, to ensure that the projectile breaks up on impact instead of ricocheting a long way into the distance (or, in the case of air-to-ground firing, back off the ground to hit the firing aircraft; a surprisingly high risk). Other uses are more warlike, with the projectiles being intended to break up after penetration to cause more damage within the target. This has also been applied to the APDS principle to create the FAPDS (frangible armour-piercing discarding-sabot), which has a useful capability against aircraft and light armour. A special version of this is NWM De Kruithoorn's FMPDS (frangible missile-piercing discarding-sabot) which is loaded into the 30 × 173 cartridges used in the Goalkeeper naval anti-missile system.

The relative AP performance of the different types of discarding-sabot ammunition can be judged from data quoted for the 25 × 137 NATO

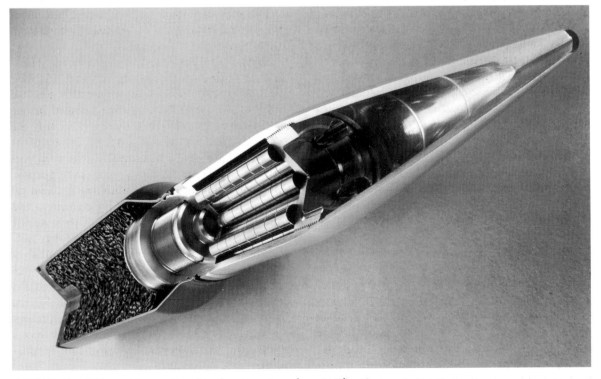

*AHEAD 35 × 228 cartridge, sectioned to show tungsten sub-projectiles* (*Courtesy: Oerlikon-Contraves*)

cartridge (Oerlikon-Contraves production): FAPDS 26mm (at 1,000m/60°) APDS 31mm and APFSDS 37mm.

A unique light cannon variant currently applied to Russian aircraft ammunition for ground-attack purposes is the CC, or cargo-carrying, projectile. This contains sub-projectiles which are discharged from the body of the projectile at a set distance after firing in order to saturate the target area. It is designed to cause significant damage to such targets as aircraft parked in the open, but would also be highly dangerous to any personnel in the area. The version for the $23 \times 115$ cartridge carries $24 \times 2$g sub-projectiles, that for the 30mm guns $28 \times 3.5$g. The $30 \times 165$ loading discharges at between 1,100m and 1,800m after firing, the sub-projectiles forming a cone with an angle of 8°. Total projectile weights and muzzle velocities are similar to that of standard ammunition.

A more sophisticated approach is represented by the Oerlikon AHEAD (advanced hit efficiency and destruction) anti-aircraft/anti-missile ammunition initially offered in $35 \times 228$ calibre. The shell is timed to detonate 25m before it reaches the target, creating a 5m wide pattern of 152 3.3g tungsten sub-projectiles travelling at extremely high velocity due to a combination of the carrier projectile velocity and the force with which the sub-projectiles are ejected. In principle, this is similar to the nineteenth-century shrapnel shell, except that the latter was intended for use against troops and the timing method was considerably less sophisticated.

A rival to AHEAD is the Bofors PFHE (pre-fragmented high-explosive) shell available in 40mm and 57mm calibres as a component of the 3P system (prefragmented, programmable, proximity fuzed). This differs in being an HE shell lined (in 40mm calibre) with 650 tungsten pellets, with detonation normally triggered by a proximity fuze. The effective radius of the exploding 40mm shell is up to 7m against aircraft and 3m against sea-skimming anti-ship missiles.

Rocket-assisted projectiles (RAPs) are used in artillery ammunition to extend the range but as the space required for the rocket reduces the HE capacity by about 50% they are not used in smaller-calibre weapons. However, an AP RAP (with the propellant wrapped around the penetrator) was experimentally developed for the 30mm GAU-8/A aircraft gun in the 1970s and demonstrated the same penetration at 1,800m as the standard APCR could achieve at 1,200m.

Not all projectiles are designed for offence; some shells have contents designed to defend aircraft against missile attack. Some post-war Soviet aircraft cannon are available with chaff-dispensing anti-radar ammunition (PRL-23 in 23mm) and even IR (infra-red) decoy projectiles (IK-23). The $23 \times 115$ version of the IR decoy round ignites about one second after firing and burns for some four seconds. The $30 \times 155$B chaff dispenser projectile produces a cloud of radar-obscuring particles which grows from an initial 7–9m² to a maximum of 14–18m² in area.

## FUZES

THE TRIGGERING OF INCENDIARY COMPOUNDS MAY not be too critical as they burn for a noticeable, albeit short, period of time. HE shells, however, have to be detonated at precisely the correct instant and for this, a fuze is needed.

Every fuze has two distinct requirements. First, it must reliably detonate the explosive filling at the precise instant required. This might be the instant it hits the target, a fraction of a second later, at a pre-set point of its flight, or when it detects the target is close enough (many fuzes are capable of being set to achieve more than one of these). Secondly, it must be completely safe when being handled (or mishandled) and fired. It is not easy to achieve these aims and fuzes are often intricate devices built with the precision of a Swiss watch. They therefore tend to be expensive, which is why they are most common in cannon calibres, where the cost can be justified by the effect.

Fuzes are of several distinct types. The original version, applied to mortar shells in previous centuries, consisted of a length of fuze cord (rope soaked in a flammable compound) which could either be ignited just before firing or be lit by the propellant charge. It was a time fuze, which detonated after the cord had burned through to the filling, and could be adjusted by varying the length of the cord. The same system is still used in fireworks.

The first 'modern' time fuzes, which were used in

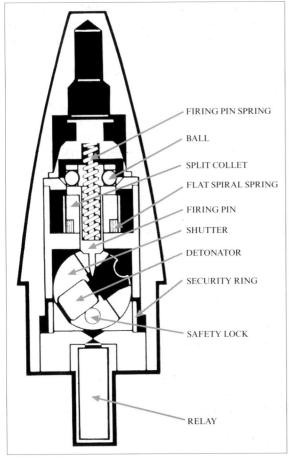

FIRING PIN SPRING

BALL

SPLIT COLLET

FLAT SPIRAL SPRING

FIRING PIN

SHUTTER

DETONATOR

SECURITY RING

SAFETY LOCK

RELAY

*Impact fuze for Rarden 30 × 170 HE-T projectile*
*(Courtesy: Ian Hogg)*

determined by the fire-control computer and set electronically as the projectile leaves the muzzle. An intriguing variation is used in the 20mm OICW infantry weapon currently being developed in the USA; the fuze counts the number of projectile rotations to determine when to detonate the airburst shell.

Contact or impact fuzes may appear simpler to design – the general principle is the same as that used to fire a toy cap gun – but they have their own problems. The main one is to ensure that the shell will detonate at the instant of contact while remaining inert at all other times. Mechanical contact fuzes therefore have elaborate safety measures, which usually involve the detonating mechanism being locked in a safe position by devices which are moved out of the way by the centrifugal force applied to the shell as it is spun by the rifling. One of the earliest contact fuzes specifically designed for aircraft use was the British No. 131 fuze of the Great War, made extremely sensitive in order to achieve detonation when penetrating airship fabric. Somewhat surprisingly the Russians have a modern equivalent for their 30 × 165 ammunition, intended to destroy balloons.

The mechanism is further complicated by the usual requirement that there be a slight delay between contact and detonation. This is in order to achieve a more useful effect against vehicles as it is usually better for the shell to explode inside the target aircraft or vehicle rather than on the surface. This requirement can cause problems: for example, Israeli pilots, in various actions during the 1960s, discovered that their 30mm DEFA cannon fire was ineffective. It transpired that the shells were fitted with long-delay fuzes intended for use against bombers; against fighters, they had passed right through before exploding.

Another problem is concerned with ensuring that the fuzes detonate even when the target is struck a glancing blow. This is a particular problem in AA fire, and despite the best efforts of fuze designers it is difficult to ensure 100% reliability of detonation.

Not all contact fuzes are mechanical. Some, particularly in smaller calibres, use chemicals which detonate on impact. These are far simpler in theory but very difficult to get right in practice, because

both world wars, were a more sophisticated version of the same principle. They contained a powder train which could be adjusted in length by turning the head of the fuze to achieve the required burning time. During the Second World War, Germany made much use of mechanical fuzes which were, in effect, clock timers (the British adopted these halfway through the war). These were much more precise than powder fuzes, being accurate to 0.5% instead of 2%. This was particularly important in anti-aircraft fire, in which time fuzes were set to detonate shells at a specified altitude.

In more recent times, time fuzes, like clocks, are electronic. These fuzes are mainly reserved for larger artillery, but are an essential feature of the Oerlikon AHEAD system in which the time is

there are no mechanical safety devices. The characteristics of the fuze compound and its metal exterior therefore have to be extremely carefully judged to ensure the necessary combination of reliable detonation with safety when mishandled. Put simply, the shell must never detonate when dropped point-down onto a concrete floor, but must always detonate when it hits a target at high velocity. Raufoss multipurpose ammunition uses such fuzes.

Fuzes which are detonated by the close proximity of the target are unsurprisingly known as proximity fuzes, although for security reasons during the Second World War (when they were first introduced) some disinformation was circulated to the effect that their USN code letters – VT – stood for variable time. Initial theoretical work was carried out in the UK in 1939–40, but the concept was transferred to the USA for development and production. These immediately achieved an improvement in AA successes of between three and five times in comparison with timed or contact fuzes. There are various methods of achieving detection but a small radar set is by far the most common in cannon shells, which limits its application to the larger calibres (originally 75mm but now down to about 40mm), partly because of the size of the fuze and partly because smaller shells do not contain enough HE to damage the target at a distance.

Because of the difficulty of detecting other targets against background clutter, proximity fuzes for automatic cannon are used almost exclusively against aircraft or missiles. They can normally be set to detonate at different distances according to the nature of the target or of the environment, with a smaller distance being set when firing at targets close to the ground or sea to ensure that the fuze is not triggered accidentally. In recent years more sophisticated fuzes have been developed to deal with this problem.

Modern electronic fuzes can be extremely versatile, such as the Bofors programmable fuze which forms an essential part of the 3P ammunition already mentioned. As well as the normal proximity function, the fuze can operate in five other modes: gated proximity (fuze only activated close to the target to avoid premature detonation); gated proximity with impact priority (a slight delay in activation to provide the opportunity for a direct hit); time function (for airburst fire to provide a shrapnel effect against surface targets); and two impact functions with variable delay.

The vast majority of fuzes are fitted to the points of projectiles. However, some types of shell make use of base fuzes, as in the case of the SAPHE shells already mentioned. Some fuzes are associated with particular types of shell. For example, mine shells produce few fragments, relying almost entirely on blast and incendiary effects, so need to explode inside the target. They are therefore used with delayed-action contact fuzes. Shells exploded outside the target by proximity fuzes cause most damage by means of fragments and therefore either contain separate pellets (as in the Bofors PFHE) or have a thick case which is designed to break up into fragments of a specified range of sizes.

There is the obvious risk that shells fired at an attacking aircraft might carry on to detonate on landing some distance away, possibly among friends. Contact and proximity-fuzed shells are therefore often fitted with a self-destruct device which detonates the shell after a certain period of time, when it can be presumed to have missed the target. Sometimes this is a function of the fuze, but a simpler system used in smaller calibres is for the propellant to ignite a separate chemical fuze in the base of the shell, a reversion to the original form of time fuze. This may also be achieved by the final stage of a tracer burn.

## PROPELLANTS

THE EARLIEST MACHINE GUN CARTRIDGES WERE designed to use black powder (gunpowder) as a propellant. This is a simple mixture of saltpetre, sulphur and charcoal, and has been used for centuries. It is not ideal as a propellant, however, because of its inefficient burning characteristics and the large quantities of smoke and other residues generated.

Improvements in chemical science in the late nineteenth century led to the development of smokeless powders, the first of these entering service in France in the late 1880s. Other nations soon followed suit, with the British version being known as 'cordite' because it was extruded in fine strings resembling cords, which were bundled together for insertion into the cartridge case.

There are three different types of smokeless propellant, known as single-base, double-base and triple-base. All are based on nitro-cellulose with nitro-glycerine (or equivalent) and nitro-guanidine as other major components in the more complex versions, triple-base including all three. Cordite is a double-base type.

The increasing complexity of the propellants is due to the constant search for the ideal combination of characteristics. These include maximum power for a high muzzle velocity, moderate pressure and temperature to minimise the stresses and erosive effects on the gun, as little fouling and corrosion as possible, and a minimum of smoke and flash at the muzzle. Many of these desiderata are mutually exclusive so each propellant is a compromise. As with other chemical ammunition components, propellants must be insensitive to rough treatment, provide consistent performance over a wide range of climatic environments and be tolerant of storage for long periods in poor conditions.

The performance of a given cartridge depends upon the maximum pressure which the gun is designed to accept. Pistols and shotguns, for example, are usually only intended to work at relatively low pressures while rifles, machine guns and cannon are generally much stronger, so cartridges for them can be loaded to higher pressures and therefore velocities. Not all guns are the same, however, and some can take much higher pressures than others. This is usually determined by the strength of the mechanism which locks the bolt or breechblock to the breech at the instant of firing, as will be discussed in the next chapter.

Propellants today are generally prepared in the form of grains or small pellets. The precise chemical composition, and the size and shape of the grains, will vary from one cartridge to another in order to provide the power and pressure characteristics suited to the gun.

## PRIMERS

PRIMERS ARE OLDER THAN METALLIC CARTRIDGES. The first percussion primer was developed early in the nineteenth century and this invention soon replaced the flintlock in military service. It consisted of a small copper cap containing fulminate of mercury, which produced an intense flash when

*Primer DM64 for 20 × 139 cartridge* (Courtesy: Diehl)
*The firing pin of the gun indents the base of the primer cap (1) and the primer charge is ignited. The flame sets off the igniter charge (2), which in turn initiates burning of the propellant.*

struck with a sharp blow by a hammer or firing pin and thereby ignited the propellant charge.

Many of the early metallic cartridges departed from this arrangement in that the priming compound was contained within the rim of the cartridge case, and fired by the impact of the hammer on the rim. This proved inconvenient because it required the rim to be thin and soft, and also meant that the used case could not be reloaded. The rimfire principle therefore soon fell from favour except in the small inexpensive cartridges still used for target shooting.

Rimfires were superseded by the return of the separate percussion cap, now housed centrally in a cavity, known as the primer pocket, in the head of the case (the cartridges therefore being called 'centrefire'). It was so arranged that when struck, the primer fired into the propellant via a central hole or holes in the cavity. Once fired, the primer could be knocked out of the case, which could then be reloaded. In larger calibres, the primer ignites an intermediate igniter charge.

Little has changed in primer design since then. Fulminate of mercury has been replaced by less corrosive compounds and the precise details of the

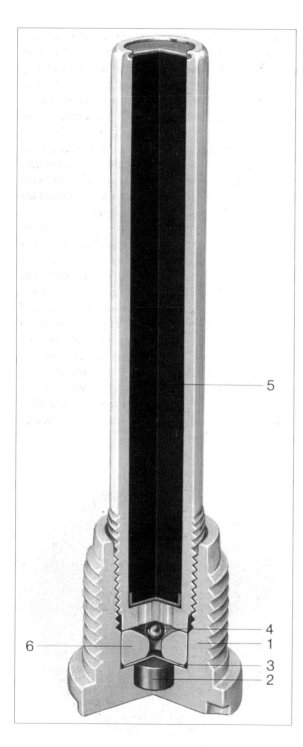

*Primer DM 201 A1 for 40mm Bofors* (Courtesy: Diehl) The firing pin of the gun hits the base of the primer body (1) and deforms it, thus also deforming the base of the primer cap (2). Due to the abrupt compression, the friction- and impact-sensitive priming charge is ignited. The flame penetrates the cover disc (3), presses the valve ball (4) forward and sets off the igniter charge (5) through the three firing holes. The resultant gas pressure presses the valve ball (4) through the blowback channel and back to the valve body (6), thereby sealing the primer against the base. The flame of the igniter charge (5) ignites the propellant in the cartridge case.

it in place in larger calibres, and European cannon primers are often screwed into the case, apparently because this makes it easier to replace the propellant (the first element of ammunition to deteriorate after long storage). The only major departure has been the replacement in some cases of percussion ignition with electric.

Electric ignition is achieved by passing an electric current from the gun through a special primer which is heated to ignition point virtually instantaneously. It was first used in automatic weapons in Germany to facilitate the synchronisation of aircraft guns designed to fire through the propeller disc of a single-engined fighter. Previously, this had involved a complex mechanical or electromechanical linkage between the propeller and the gun-firing mechanism to ensure that the gun fired only between the propeller blades. It was obviously simpler to design a direct electrical link between the propeller and the cartridge. Ironically, it came into service in the Second World War just before the need for it disappeared because of the advent of jet engines.

Electric priming does have other advantages. It simplifies gun design because the firing pin and its associated spring and mechanism for releasing, withdrawing and recocking the pin are replaced by a simple electrical contact. However, it obviously requires a reliable supply of electricity and is therefore most suited to vehicle-mounted applications.

It is usual for cartridges to be designed either for percussion or electric ignition, but there are some cases where a particular cartridge has been available in both versions. They are difficult to tell apart visually, since only the internal design of the primer

percussion cap design have been refined. The push-fit of the primer in the case, typical of small arms, is supplemented by more positive means of holding

is different. However, in electric ignition the primer has to be insulated from the rest of the case and this insulation is sometimes visible. Needless to say, percussion and electric versions of the same cartridge have to be used in the appropriate gun as they are not interchangeable. The best known examples are the $15 \times 96$ and $20 \times 82$ rounds for the MG 151, the $20 \times 128$ Oerlikon and the $30 \times 165$ Russian (which uses electrical priming for naval and aircraft weapons, percussion for the AFV guns). There are others: the percussion-primed $20 \times 110$ widely used in the HS 404 and related guns was produced in an electrically primed version for the post-war American M24.

## THE CARTRIDGE CASE

THE CARTRIDGE CASE HAS TWO MAJOR FUNCTIONS. First, it holds together all the active components of the cartridge – the projectile, propellant and primer – in a waterproof container which is rugged enough to withstand rough handling, especially in automatic weapons. Second, when the gun is fired, the cartridge case is expanded by the pressure against the walls of the firing chamber, forming a gas-tight seal which prevents any propellant gas from seeping back into the gun mechanism – and possibly into the firer's face.

The second function explains why brass is still the most popular material for small-arms cartridge cases, despite its weight and cost. Standard cartridge brass (70% copper, 30% zinc) has exactly the right characteristics in that it expands instantly to form a seal without being split open. Nowadays steel is normally used in larger cannon, particularly linear-action guns with a high rate of fire, because its extra strength is better at coping with the violent treatment the cartridge is given by the loading mechanism. It is also slightly lighter and cheaper. However, it requires more protection against corrosion and, being less resilient, forms a less perfect seal on firing. This is a potential disadvantage in turret-mounted applications as it means that more propellant gas might seep back into the turret.

Light alloy has even more attractions (it saves 25–38% of the total weight of a cartridge) but for a long time it proved very difficult to achieve satisfactory results with this material and it has only recently come into common use. The first and most notable example is the $30 \times 173$ ammunition for the General Electric GAU-8/A fitted to the A-10 aircraft. This has such a large ammunition capacity that a weight saving of over 270kg is achieved compared with the Oerlikon KCA's dimensionally similar steel-cased rounds (the actual difference in empty case weight being 143g instead of 350g). Light-alloy ammunition in this calibre is also used in the Mauser MK30 (the weight of a complete HE/I cartridge being 670g compared with 890g for the steel-cased rounds) and has been developed for the $30 \times 113B$ used in the M230 chain gun.

The earliest cartridge cases were made in more than one piece, typically an iron head to which was fixed a tube made from coiled brass. These were very much an interim measure, soon replaced by the one-piece case which has been universal since the latter part of the nineteenth century. This is formed by discs, punched from a thick sheet of metal, being repeatedly 'drawn' – that is, mechanically pressed into a hollow shape, until the desired case shape has been achieved. At the same time, information such as the cartridge designation, maker and year of manufacture are stamped into the head. The final operation is usually the cutting of the extractor groove close to the head.

*Headstamp for 20mm Madsen, made by Kynoch in 1954 and loaded with an armour-piercing tracer projectile (not all headstamps are so helpful!)*

Cartridge case design is a science in itself. There are certain basic requirements – the case must locate the projectile in precisely the correct position in the firing chamber (with the exception of advanced primer ignition – API – blowback guns which fire as the case is moving forwards); it must be easy to extract once fired; and it must function well in automatic weapons – but there are various methods of achieving these aims.

Before proceeding further it is well to be clear about the nomenclature of cartridge cases. The basic elements – head, rim and neck – are shown in the drawing on page 10 (unfortunately these terms are rather confusing in that the head is as far from the neck as possible!). Cases usually have an identifying headstamp around the primer pocket, which may contain information about the cartridge, the manufacturer and the year of production. Rimless cases need an extractor groove and 'bottleneck' cases also have a shoulder, where the case is reduced in diameter down to the neck in cartridges in which the calibre is significantly smaller than the case diameter. Some cases have a belt – an annular projection – just above the extractor groove.

*Cartridge case types (from left to right): Rimmed, straight (20 × 99R), Semi-rimmed (13 × 92SR), Rimless, bottle-necked (15 × 115 experimental), Rebated (20 × 72RB), Belted (13 × 93B experimental)*

In modern small-arms cartridges the inside neck diameter is made fractionally smaller than the bullet, thereby ensuring that the bullet is gripped firmly until it is fired. In the larger calibres considered here, a more authoritative means of securing the projectile is normally required and this is provided by crimping: the case neck is pressed into recesses in the projectile, either all around the circumference or at several points on it.

Accurate location in the firing chamber is essential to the ignition of the primer; the cartridge needs to enter the chamber, but not too far or the firing pin (or electrical contact) will not touch the primer. It is also important in the internal ballistics of the gun, as the projectile must be in the same place, relative to the conical section leading to the rifling, to achieve consistent pressure characteristics. The distance between the face of the bolt and the part of the chamber which locates the cartridge is known as the 'headspace'.

The earliest method of achieving accurate location was by means of a rim around the head of the case. This remains outside the chamber or in a recess so that it is flush with the breech face. The rim also provides something for the extractor to hook on to in order to pull the fired case from the chamber. Rimmed cases are still satisfactory except that the rim can complicate ammunition-feed arrangements in automatic weapons. In spring-loaded magazines the rims can foul each other if improperly loaded, while in belt-fed guns it is usually necessary for the cartridge to be withdrawn backwards from the belt before being pushed forwards into the chamber. This design has therefore largely been replaced for military purposes, although it is still encountered, for example, in some Russian small arms and in larger cannon from 40mm upwards.

By far the most common military case type is the rimless, in which the rim is reduced to the same diameter as the case so that the cartridges in magazines can be stacked on top of each other or pushed forward from ammunition belts without risk of jamming. To give the extractor something to hook on to, an extractor groove is cut into the case. There have been a few examples of semi-rimmed (or semi-rimless) cases, in which the rim is only fractionally wider than the case and is combined with a small extractor groove, but these have not been a particularly successful compromise.

Rimless cases need a method of accurate location in the chamber and this is normally achieved by using a bottleneck case, in which the headspace is determined by the contact between the shoulder of the case and the matching part of the chamber. With straight or tapered cases this becomes more difficult to achieve, so such cases often have a projecting belt just in front of the extractor groove to provide positive location.

A few cases have seen service with rebated rims, i.e. with a rim of smaller diameter than the case. This is essential in API blowback cannon (described in the next chapter) which fire before the cartridge is fully chambered, as it allows the bolt and its extractor claw to follow the case into an extended or hooded chamber. This ensures that the cartridge is fully supported at the instant of firing.

Blowback weapons do not strictly require case extractors to function, as the fired case is pushed out of the chamber by gas pressure. Some early designs for such weapons accordingly used cartridges without rims or extractor grooves. This was soon proved to be a bad idea, because the only way of unloading an unfired cartridge was to poke a stick down the barrel.

Military cartridge designations are usually given via metric case measurements of the calibre and case length. The .50″ Browning is therefore described as the 12.7 × 99, as the calibre is 12.7mm and the case length is 99mm. Note that this is not the same as the overall cartridge length; in the .50″ Browning, this is usually around 137mm but does vary according to the length of the projectile. Letters may be added after the numbers to denote some variation from the military standard rimless head. The 20mm Becker is known as the 20 × 70RB because it has a rebated rim (sometimes expressed as RR); the 30mm Aden is called the 30 × 113B because the case is belted; the rimmed 20mm ShVAK was known as the 20 × 99R; the semi-rimmed 1.1″ US Naval round as the 28 × 199SR. Note that the calibre measurements are notional; they may refer to the diameter of the projectile, or to the gun bore, or to some convenient figure reasonably close to either. It must therefore not be assumed that a projectile from one 12.7mm cartridge can necessarily be used in another.

## BALLISTICS

BALLISTICS IS A COMPLEX AND HIGHLY TECHNICAL subject. In this book, it will be covered only in sufficient detail to enable the reader to grasp the essentials.

The subject is generally divided into internal and external ballistics. The first deals with the passage of the projectile up the gun barrel, the second with what happens to the projectile between the gun muzzle and the target. There is a third category – terminal ballistics – concerning what happens when the projectile hits the target, but that has largely been dealt with in the section on projectiles.

Some of the issues involved in internal ballistics have already been touched on. The relationship between the calibre and weight of the projectile and the weight, form and chemical composition of the propellant, together with the barrel length, will determine the pressure exerted on the chamber and gun barrel by the expanding propellant gas, the rate of acceleration of the projectile up the barrel, and the velocity achieved at the muzzle.

A high muzzle velocity is almost always regarded as desirable. In ground fighting, it provides a flatter trajectory and therefore makes it easier to hit distant targets. The armour penetration of solid shot is also, other things being equal, directly related to the striking velocity. In aircraft or anti-aircraft applications, high velocity reduces the time of flight and therefore simplifies aiming at moving targets.

The problem is that high muzzle velocity carries penalties. To achieve a significant increase in velocity, far more propellant is needed which requires a larger and heavier cartridge case and a bigger and heavier gun. A longer barrel is required to give the projectile time to accelerate to its higher speed. Recoil, muzzle blast and barrel wear will all be much worse, and in an automatic weapon the rate of fire is likely to be less than in a lower-velocity gun of the same type.

There are also limiting factors. For a given projectile there is a velocity beyond which it is not practically possible to push it in a conventional gun. Adding more propellant will just increase the muzzle blast and barrel wear without achieving any

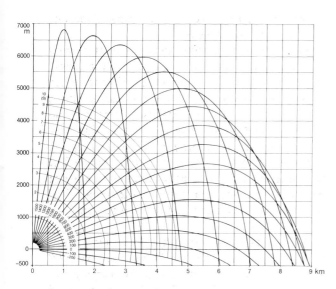
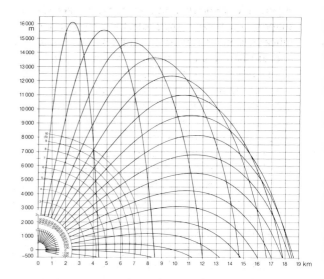

*Trajectory diagrams for two loadings of the 25 × 184 Oerlikon KBB ammunition.*
*LEFT: TP-T and HEI shells. Muzzle velocity $v_0$ at +15°C = 1160 m/s. Shell mass = 230g.*
*RIGHT: APDS-T/AMDS shells. Muzzle velocity $v_0$ at +15°C = 1355 m/s. Shell mass = 156g.*
*(Courtesy: Oerlikon-Contraves)*

worthwhile further improvements. In most cases, a muzzle velocity of around 1,100–1,200 m/s is the practical maximum for conventional full-calibre projectiles. Sub-calibre projectiles such as APDS and APFSDS can achieve more, in the latter case up to 1,700 m/s in tank guns, but only by using projectiles which are very light for the calibre, usually fired from a low-drag smooth-bored barrel.

Internal ballistics provide only the starting point in achieving the desired effects on the target. The design of the projectile is also significant. The two key factors are the shape of the projectile and its weight relative to its calibre.

For a given calibre, a heavy projectile has more momentum and is therefore slowed down less by wind resistance. Heavy AP shot also has better armour penetration, other things being equal, and as it slows down less, this advantage will increase with range. The disadvantage of heavy projectiles is that they require much more work to accelerate to a high muzzle velocity. These conflicting demands explain the great success of sub-calibre ammunition such as APDS (and even more so APFSDS), which is extremely light for its calibre in the barrel (i.e. the calibre of the sabot) but extremely heavy for its very narrow calibre once the sabot has dropped away.

There is a penalty in that the energy used to accelerate the sabot is wasted, so this is made as light as possible.

The advantages of these sub-calibre projectiles are immense. For example, a modern high-velocity 25mm HE shell has a maximum range of 9,000m and will travel about 1,800m in three seconds (a reasonable limit for effective AA fire). The APDS version will reach over 2,300m in the same time, and will travel to a maximum theoretical range of over 18,000m. These figures explain the attraction of the new FAPDS rounds for AA fire, in which time of flight to the target is of crucial importance to the hit probability.

The fin-stabilised APFSDS shot tend to be less accurate in theoretical terms than conventional spin-stabilised projectiles, but in practice this is more than compensated for by their flatter trajectory and shorter time of flight, which combine to increase greatly the hit probability, especially against moving targets.

It appears evident that a pointed projectile will lose less velocity due to wind resistance than a blunt one, and will therefore maintain its performance for a longer range. In fact that is only partly true; the shape of the nose is of paramount importance at supersonic velocities, but at subsonic speeds the shape of the base of the projectile also becomes significant. Long-range projectiles have a tapered base and are described as 'boat-tailed' or 'streamlined'. Those in larger calibres which combine this with a long, gradually tapered nose to achieve the maximum possible range are called 'extended range'. Such projectiles often have a large HE capacity and Bofors ammunition of this type is called HCER, for high-capacity extended range. Early *M-Geschoss* projectiles were round-based to achieve the maximum capacity and strength, but this shape tends to be unstable in flight and is not now generally used.

Wind resistance can also be affected by the burning of tracer elements. The gas released by this reduces the pressure differential between the front and rear of the projectile, reducing aerodynamic drag. Furthermore, the weight and balance of tracer rounds alter as the tracer compound is burned up, all of which causes the ammunition designer great problems in matching the trajectory of tracer rounds with that of other types. It is common for this to be achieved precisely only at a specified range.

The airflow smoothing effect is deliberately utilised in some long-range projectiles in larger calibres. A streamlined unit containing a combustible substance is added to the base of the projectile, adding considerably to the effective range. This is known as 'base bleed' (or 'drag-reducing fumer' in the USA) and it is commonly used with extended-range projectiles, leading to the designation ERF-BBB, the FB referring to full bore, to distinguish this from sub-calibre ammunition.

The muzzle velocity achieved by a cartridge will clearly depend on the projectile weight, and this can vary considerably. It is therefore usual for the power of cartridges to be described in terms of their muzzle energy (normally expressed in joules). This is a calculation which takes into account the projectile's weight and velocity to enable comparisons between cartridges to be made.

## AMMUNITION CHOICES

THE SELECTION OF THE APPROPRIATE AMMUNITION type to load into magazines or belts clearly depends on the expected targets. This might not be a simple choice in circumstances when the nature of the target can change rapidly, for example, from aircraft to armoured vehicles.

There are three possible solutions to this problem. The first is to provide the gun with a quick-change dual-feed system, so it is possible to switch rapidly from HE to AP belts or magazines. This is desirable in vehicle- or ship-based guns but too bulky in aircraft. The second is to use multipurpose ammunition as previously described, accepting some loss in absolute HE or AP performance. The third is to mix different types of ammunition in one belt, acknowledging that some of the rounds fired will always be less than ideally effective against any particular target.

The mixed-belt solution was common in aircraft machine guns in the Second World War, with AP and HE or incendiary rounds mixed in varying proportions as required, usually with a tracer round added in every fifth or sixth position. It was less necessary in aircraft cannon ammunition as the HE/I shells were usually powerful enough to penetrate aircraft armour and large enough to carry a tracer if required. However, it was common to cover the muzzles of cannon with cloth or rubber to prevent the blast of air from freezing the mechanism. In such circumstances, it was prudent to ensure that the first round fired was an AP shot in order to remove the cover without risk of explosion.

## CALIBRES

AS DESCRIBED IN THE NEXT CHAPTER, THE distinction between 'heavy machine guns' (HMG) and 'automatic cannon' is an arbitrary one which has varied in different countries and at different times. As far as projectiles are concerned, the generally accepted convention has been that HMGs are designed to fire ball, incendiary and AP projectiles similar in design to those used in rifle-calibre machine guns (RCMGs), while cannon usually fire HE shells or specialised AP shot. HMG projectiles are therefore usually jacketed with a relatively soft, usually copper-based, alloy which can be formed to fit the rifling grooves. Cannon projectiles are normally of steel with separate, softer driving bands to take the rifling. Two exceptions to this general rule were the 13mm Rheinmetall-Borsig MG 131 and 15mm Mauser MG 151 aircraft gun rounds, which used cannon-type projectiles.

The popularity of different calibres has varied depending on the tactical needs of the time. However, the first true automatic cannon emerged in the nineteenth century in 37mm calibre for legal reasons. In the middle of that century explosive projectiles were introduced in small arms. These were felt to be inhumane when used against soldiers, so an international convention was held which led to the St Petersburg Declaration of 1868, limiting their use to artillery projectiles weighing just under one pound (400g). At the time, this equated to a calibre of 37mm, so this became an international standard which was honoured for the next half century. By the start of the First World War, except for a few obsolete weapons there was a huge calibre gap between RCMGs and 37mm cannon.

The pressure of war eventually led to a demand for intermediate calibres, partly to deal with the new tanks and partly to provide more firepower for aircraft without burdening them with large cannon. Aircraft weapons in 20mm and 25mm were developed which, although initially available only with solid shot, used HE projectiles by the end of the war. Weapons of 12.7–13mm were also being developed when the war ended.

In the inter-war period, several automatic weapons in 12.7–15mm were introduced, but 20mm became established as the smallest calibre whose projectiles were capable of carrying a useful quantity of HE. It therefore became a standard calibre with the great majority of nations and has remained so up to the present time. The 37mm calibre remained popular and was joined by 40mm weapons from Britain and, most notably, Bofors in Sweden. This remained the largest calibre to see significant service in automatic weapons until the middle of the twentieth century (with the exception of the early Hotchkiss manually driven revolver cannon).

*Experimental HMG cartridges (from left to right): .50" Colt-Kynoch (North) (12.7 × 110SR), 13mm TuF (13 × 92SR), .5" Vickers HV (12.7 × 120SR), .60" US T17 (15.2 × 114), .50/60" US (12.7 × 114), .50" HV US (12.7 × 120), 13mm MG215 (13 × 92B), 15mm MG215 (15 × 83B), .50" Browning salvo-squeezebore with projectiles alongside (12.7 × 99), 15mm FN-BRG, (15 × 115), 15.5mm FN-BRG (15.5 × 106)*

Before the Second World War there were few weapons in calibres intermediate between 20mm and 37mm, the most significant being 25mm AA guns used by France, Japan, Sweden and the Soviet Union and the American 1.1″ (28mm) naval gun. More emerged during the war, with 23mm weapons becoming established in the Soviet Union and 30mm guns, initially for aircraft, in Germany. Attempts were made in both Germany and Britain to produce fast-firing automatic weapons in 50–57mm calibre, but these were not particularly successful until after the war.

After the lessons of the war had been absorbed, NATO broadly settled for automatic cannon in 20mm, 30mm and 40mm calibre (with 35mm, 27mm and 25mm being added later) plus a few naval guns in 57mm. NATO cartridges are allocated STANAG (Standardisation Agreement) numbers, which specify characteristics required to ensure inter-operability in different weapons. The Warsaw Pact (and by extension China) has used

weapons in 23mm, 25mm, 30mm, 37mm, 45mm and 57mm calibres. It should be noted that NATO currently produces weapons using three different 20mm cartridges, two 25mm and at least four 30mm (six if variations using different case materials are counted) as well as 27mm, 35mm and 40mm. In contrast, the complete and considerable range of Russian automatic cannon currently in production uses either the $23 \times 115$ or the $30 \times 165$ cartridge (although the latter has percussion and electrically primed versions), with the 30mm dominating.

In the HMG field, NATO adhered to the 12.7mm calibre and the Pact, while retaining and improving their 12.7mm guns, added a 14.5mm weapon. Naval requirements saw the introduction of automatic weapons in larger calibres from 76mm upwards and there was much experimentation with large-calibre army AA guns before the advent of guided missiles. For the most part these lie outside the scope of this book and will only be mentioned briefly.

# Chapter Two

# THE GUNS

This book is concerned with heavy machine guns (HMGs) and automatic cannon. The current usage of these terms has only become generally accepted since the Second World War. Before then, the term 'machine gun' was used to describe a relatively small-calibre weapon normally firing solid projectiles, while larger weapons were called 'automatic guns'. The name 'cannon' was in English usage an obsolete term for artillery, which by that time were known as guns or howitzers depending on their function. The situation changed in British practice with the selection for the RAF of the French Hispano *moteur-canon* in the late 1930s. Anglicised as 'cannon', the name became adopted for the Hispano and subsequently for all other automatic shell-firing guns of 20mm or more calibre.

Different nations had different practices. In Germany, automatic weapons of up to and including 20mm were known as machine guns (*Maschinengewehr*) with larger calibres being known as cannon (*Maschinenkanone*), leading to the MG and MK prefixes. In addition, designations based on function were used for particular applications, whether or not the weapons were automatic. A gun intended for the anti-aircraft role was called *Fliegerabwehrkanone* (sometimes given as *Flugzeugabwehrkanone* or *Flugabwehrkanone*), for the anti-tank role *Panzerabwehrkanone* and for mounting in armoured fighting vehicles *Kampfwagenkanone*; FlaK, PaK and KwK for short. The BK (*Bordkanone*) designation was used in the Second World War for very large calibre (37+mm) airborne cannon intended for ground attack.

Nomenclature also varied between services. In Sweden, the air force called their m/39 12.7mm and 13.2mm guns *automatkanon*, presumably because they were larger than usual for aircraft guns at the time, while their navy called the m/32 25mm a *kulspruta* (which translates as machine gun), presumably because this was a small weapon by naval standards.

Since the war the definition of a cannon as any fast-firing automatic weapon of 20mm or more has become generally accepted, at least in NATO. The term 'heavy machine gun' has also seen some changes. At one time it was literally used to describe a gun which weighed a lot, of the sturdily built sort which might be used to defend fortifications, even if it was of rifle calibre. Such weapons have long gone, however, all current rifle-calibre machine guns (RCMGs) being relatively light by previous standards, so the term HMG has come to be used for a class of weapon which fits in between RCMGs and cannon. By some form of convergent evolution, the calibre of virtually all HMGs to see service has fallen within the range 12.7–15mm.

It has also been only in the last half-century that metric calibre measurements have almost entirely taken over from inch measurements in Britain and the USA. Even within the metric group, practices have varied. In wartime Germany, heavy weapon calibres of 2cm or more were usually described in centimetres rather than millimetres.

## GUN DESCRIPTIONS

A GUN IS IN PRINCIPLE A SIMPLE DEVICE. ITS essential components are a chamber shaped to fit

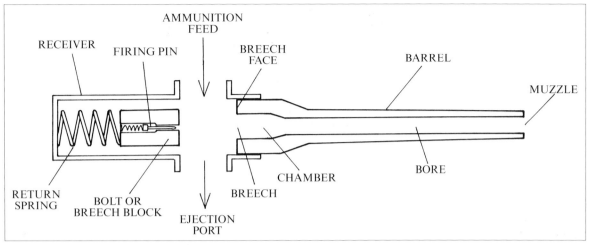

*Basic elements of the gun (schematic)*

the cartridge, and strong enough to resist the firing pressures (which may exceed 400 MPa); a barrel to guide the projectile and contain the propellant gases for long enough to permit the projectile to accelerate to its maximum velocity; a method of firing the cartridge at the required instant; and some means for removing the fired case and inserting a new cartridge.

The last requirement results in the need for a break, or breech, in the rear of the chamber, to enable cartridges to be inserted or withdrawn. The back of the chamber is known as the breech face. The part of the gun which is pressed against the open rear of the chamber during firing, and is moved out of the way to permit reloading, is known as the bolt or breechblock; generally the term 'bolt' is used if it moves to and fro along the same axis as the barrel, and 'breechblock' if it is moved vertically, sideways or tilted away from the breech. This usually contains the mechanism to fire the cartridge. In all except revolver mechanisms, the chamber is contained in the rear section of the barrel. Sometimes the barrel is extended rearwards in order to provide the locking surfaces for the mechanism; this part is unsurprisingly known as the barrel extension. The body of the gun, into which the barrel, bolt and other mechanisms are fitted, is known as the receiver.

Other components are some means of holding an ammunition supply ready for loading, an appropriate method of mounting the gun (which may be fixed or mobile, and in larger calibres may require some mechanism to absorb recoil) and a sighting device to give some expectation that the projectiles will hit their target.

All cannon and HMG barrels are rifled, except for those specifically designed to function with fin-stabilised projectiles. The rifling consists of spiral grooves in the barrel which grip the projectiles (by their driving band in the case of cannon projectiles) and spin them to ensure they are stable in flight. The degree of twist needed depends on the length of the projectile the gun is designed for; the longer and heavier the projectile, the steeper the twist. There is a risk that the impact of hitting the rifling might strip the driving band, so some cannon are designed with progressive rifling – that is, the grooves start out being parallel with the barrel to offer the minimum resistance, then gradually begin to twist until they achieve the desired rate.

Some artillery weapons have had the final section of the barrel smooth-bored at the projectile diameter so that the driving band (which is cut up by the rifling) is squeezed smoothly against the projectile to reduce aerodynamic drag. The USN's peculiar Mk 11 20mm aircraft gun, which had rifling in only the first few centimetres of the barrel, is a very rare example of this being applied to automatic weapons. It was not regarded as successful.

In the case of machine guns and cannon, the

most complex and troublesome areas are those concerned with ammunition handling: the mechanisms for loading, firing, extracting, ejecting, and reloading. All such guns can be divided into four classes according to the motive power used to achieve this: externally powered, blowback-operated, recoil-operated and gas-operated. Each of these major categories has sub-groups, for example recoil-operated weapons may have short- or long-recoil mechanisms, and in some cases elements of two or more classes may be combined in one gun.

Machine guns may also be described by the design of the mechanism for chambering and firing ammunition. This may be linear (i.e. the bolt is thrust back in a straight line, collecting a new round on the return stroke), revolver (in which there is a cylinder containing several chambers rotating around the rear of the barrel, into which cartridges are inserted and removed in stages) or rotary (similar to the revolver except that there is a barrel attached to the front of each chamber and the whole contraption rotates). One variation applying in the case of rotary cannon is the number of barrels used, usually between three and seven. Similarly, the number of chambers in a revolver cannon may vary, but there are usually four or five. Another variation, this time to the linear system, is a tilting or sideways-sliding breechblock instead of a rearwards-moving bolt, in which case another element of the mechanism is required to load a fresh cartridge.

A third form of description is the method of holding the ammunition ready to be loaded into the gun. This may be contained in a belt (pulled into position for reloading by another mechanism driven by the gun, or more rarely separately powered), in a box magazine (with a spring used to ensure that the cartridges are held in position) or in a drum or pan magazine (which may be gun-powered, spring-driven or use some other form of external power). Other methods include gravity feeding (using guides or hoppers, now generally restricted to large AA weapons), in which several rounds are sometimes held together by clips for ease of handling, and (in smaller calibres) rigid strips of ammunition which may be clipped together.

Still further descriptors concern the method of ensuring that barrels are not damaged through overheating. They may be water- or air-cooled, and in the latter case may have fixed or interchangeable barrels.

The above list of possibilities is not comprehensive but does give the major categories, which will be expanded on below.

## GUN MOUNTINGS

ALL HEAVY AUTOMATIC WEAPONS NEED SOME TYPE of mounting. For the simplest infantry use, heavy machine guns will typically use a tripod with a limited range of elevation. If intended for AA work, the tripod needs to be much higher to permit the gunner to sight the elevated gun; some tripods can be adjusted to meet either need. For use from a vehicle, the gun may be mounted on a simple pintle (a post with a head which permits traverse and elevation), or on some kind of horizontal ring mounting which surrounds the gunner, so that he can rotate the gun through 360°. This was common for defensive use in early aircraft and is still used in some light vehicles.

All but the lightest cannon are not only heavier but also recoil much more heavily than HMGs and so need more sophisticated mountings. Almost all such mountings allow for the gun to move backwards in recoil in order to soften the impact by spreading it over a longer period; the only significant exceptions being the long-recoil mechanisms and API blowback guns described later in this chapter, whose mechanisms act as recoil absorbers. The energy generated by the gun's recoil movement is partly absorbed by friction, pneumatic or hydraulic buffers and partly by a recuperator which uses springs or compressed air to return the gun to the firing position. In smaller-calibre guns these two functions may be combined.

The reduction in the recoil impact from a well-designed system can be dramatic; in the case of the British Rarden long-recoil gun, the peak impact force is reduced by 95%. Recoil-absorbing mountings have improved in effectiveness in recent decades to the point at which a 30mm gun, the American MDHC ASP-30, can be fired from a tripod designed for a .50″ HMG.

Some weapons are able to use even lighter mountings by being designed to use the differential recoil principle, which is also known as soft

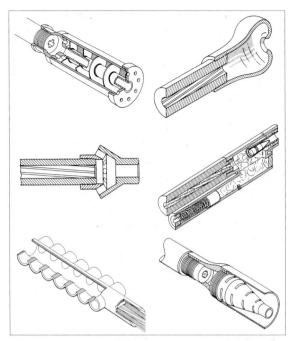

*Flash hiders and muzzle brakes (experimental, except for lower left = Rheinmetall-Borsig MK 103)* (BuOrd, USN)

complicate the use of some ammunition, however, such as APDS and APFSDS, and also may not be wanted in recoil-operated guns which need a certain amount of recoil in order to work.

All but the simplest army and navy AA cannon mountings are powered so that the gunner can quickly swing the gun to follow the target without any muscular effort being required. AFV turrets are also nowadays usually powered, at least in traverse if not in elevation. Naval AA gun mountings, and the more sophisticated SPAAGs (self-propelled AA guns, i.e. mounted on an army vehicle) are often stabilised as well, to keep the gun pointing at the target regardless of the movements of the ship or vehicle.

Naval (and flexible or turreted aircraft) mountings need some restrictions on their freedom of fire, otherwise they could shoot holes in their own vessel or aircraft. Such mountings therefore usually have 'taboo zones' within which the gun is prevented from firing. At its crudest this may be achieved via a simple framework which prevents the gun from pointing in sensitive directions. More sophisticated versions have mechanical restrictors built into the mounting, or electrical firing restraints.

Aircraft mountings are of four basic types: permanently fixed into the aircraft, temporarily fixed in an underwing or under-fuselage pod, free-swinging or in a turret. Turret mountings were initially unpowered when introduced in the 1930s, but power operation (either electric or hydraulic) became usual during the Second World War. Most early turrets were also manned but some later ones used for bomber defence, and all current ones fitted to helicopters, are remotely controlled. Free-swinging guns were the earliest form of aircraft armament and still survive in doorway mountings in some helicopters.

Of the fixed mountings, most of the early ones were in front-engined propeller-driven fighters. Those using vee engines had the potential to mount a gun between the cylinders of the engine so that it could fire through the hollow propeller hub, provided that the axis of the propeller was geared above the crankshaft line and the propeller design permitted it. Guns designed for such mountings usually had long, slim barrels, such as the HS 404 Hispano, MG 151 and NS-37.

recoil, counter-recoil and floating firing or floating mounting. This was invented early in the twentieth century and used in the Krupp 75mm 'motor gun' of 1909, in which application it reduced the recoil blow to 25% of the normal level. It involves the gun being held back in the full recoil position before firing. The firing process starts with the gun being released to run forward under the pressure of the recoil spring. The cartridge is fired just before the gun reaches the full run-out position (a position referred to as 'in battery'). The initial recoil force is therefore absorbed in stopping the forward movement of the gun before beginning to thrust it back again, greatly reducing its impact. The penalties are a delay before the first shot is fired, and some loss of accuracy. Nonetheless, the advantages are such that it is a common system among modern army AA cannon.

Further recoil reductions can be achieved by using muzzle brakes; devices fitted on to the end of the muzzle which allow some of the gun gas to escape to the sides and rear before the projectile leaves the gun. The jet effect of the gas drives the barrel in the opposite direction to the recoil and can effect recoil reductions of up to 30%. They can

Engine mounting was not possible with radial engines and most fighters up to the 1930s fitted guns mounted within the engine cowling, whose firing was synchronised to fire between the propeller blades as they revolved (the correct timing often being determined by trial and error, the propeller being replaced by a plywood disk to provide visual verification of the bullet strikes). As gun reliability improved and large batteries of guns were introduced, wing-mounting became more common. The advent of jet aircraft saw the guns moving back into the fuselage, which provided more room, a more rigid mounting and concentrated fire at all ranges. A common problem with fuselage-mounted installations before pilots had self-contained air supplies was contamination of the cockpit from gun gases on firing.

The mounting of guns some distance from the cockpit required some means of remote firing. Cables were inadequate to ensure the simultaneous firing of multi-gun installations so electric, hydraulic or pneumatic systems were employed. These were also used in some of the more sophisticated multi-gun turrets. Such weapons therefore usually had no visible triggers, in contrast to those intended for flexible mounting which were either fitted with pistol grips or rear spade-type grips. They also usually featured hydraulic or pneumatic cylinders alongside the gun (chargers or cocking units) to cycle the action in order to load the weapon or eject a faulty round. Flash hiders (conical tubes attached to the muzzle) were often used with flexibly mounted or turret guns to avoid the gunner losing his night vision whenever he fired.

Another problem unique to aircraft, and especially fighter, installations was the need to ensure that the ammunition would feed into the gun even at extreme positive or negative gravitational forces during violent manoeuvring. This was not always achieved.

For most aircraft cannon it is necessary to spread the recoil force and thereby reduce vibration by allowing the guns to recoil. This caused significant difficulties in mounting powerful Second World War cannon. By the end of the war, the idea of internalising this recoil movement within the receiver had emerged in the Rheinmetall-Borsig MK 103. It is now common practice as it enables

the guns to be fixed rigidly wherever required, although in modern fast-firing revolver cannon there is no time between shots for any large recoil movement, so the recoil spring is typically replaced by a vibration-absorbing buffer. However, the Aden 25 still recoils 16.5mm and even the fast-firing 20mm M61A1 rotary cannon recoils some 6.35mm in its mounting.

Gun pods attached under the wings were used in the Second World War, particularly by the German *Luftwaffe* for ground attack or in order to boost the firepower against heavy bombers. They are still available in a variety of calibres for fitting to fixed-wing aircraft and helicopters, usually for ground attack. In some Russian equipment, the podded guns can be angled downwards (and even sideways) to facilitate this.

Another complication with aircraft mountings is the need to keep the gun mechanisms from freezing up at high altitude (reported, for example, as a significant problem with the Messerschmitt Bf109s MG-FF cannon in November 1940). This had not been a problem with cowling-mounted guns which were kept warm by the engine, but multi-gun layouts with remote mounting had no such protection. Special anti-freeze lubricants were developed, but as operating altitudes increased during the Second World War, much attention was paid to gun-heating arrangements. These normally used hot air ducted from the engine, but separate electric heaters were often fitted to wing-mounted guns. Another protective measure was to seal the muzzles of the guns by fabric or rubber covers to prevent freezing air from blasting down the muzzle – obviously only effective until the first rounds had been fired. Guns varied in their sensitivity to this problem: the .50″ Browning reportedly could continue functioning at temperatures 10°C colder than the 20mm Hispano. Conversely, engine-mounted guns sometimes suffered from unreliability problems due to overheating.

The advent of the jet engine gave aircraft designers the welcome freedom to locate cannon in the fuselage without worrying about synchronisation or shooting through propeller hubs. A problem soon emerged, however: jet engines did not take kindly to ingesting the large quantities of gun gas which blasted from the muzzles and it was necessary to locate the guns to avoid this problem. Where this was not possible, other solutions were devised, such as varying the fuel flow at the instant of firing.

## SIGHTS

THE SIMPLEST TYPE OF GUNSIGHT IS FITTED TO small arms such as HMGs intended for ground fighting, in which there is time to aim and targets do not usually move quickly. All that is required is an aperture, adjustable to allow for range, at the back of the gun and a reference point such as a bead or blade on the barrel, which is lined up with the target. Tracer ammunition can be used to correct the aim. Telescopic sights are used to improve long-range accuracy, particularly in vehicle mountings, and image-intensifying or infra-red sights are increasingly common to assist night fighting.

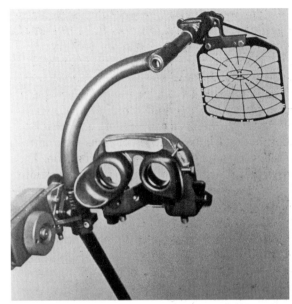

*Sight for Oerlikon GA1-B01 20mm AA gun*
*(Courtesy: Oerlikon-Contraves)*

Sights for AA guns and aircraft are more sophisticated since they have to allow for rapid target movement in three dimensions; in fact, the quality of the sights makes a huge difference to the effectiveness of the weapons. The simplest AA type uses an open metal or clear Perspex grid with radial elements. The sight must be positioned so that the target is pointing into the centre of the sight, with the distance from the centre being determined by the speed and range. This still requires considerable judgement on the part of the gunner, so various attempts were made, particularly in the 1930s, to produce more sophisticated optical sights into which the estimated speed and range of the aircraft could be set.

Similar problems were experienced by defensive gunners in bombers, who also had to bear in mind the question of wind resistance and trajectory curvature. Even if two aircraft were flying side by side at the same speed, simply aiming straight at the enemy would not necessarily ensure success, as wind resistance would tend to cause the projectiles to fall behind the line of sight. In some sights, use was made of the wind to push the foresight off-centre in order to compensate for this problem.

A major advance in the late 1930s was the first

*Range-adjustable rearsight on a .50" Browning. Note the spade grips and central trigger (Courtesy: MoD Pattern Room)*

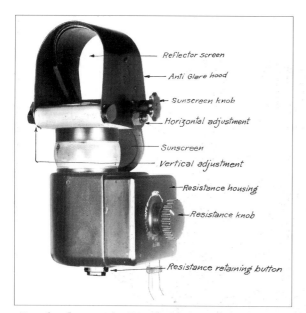

*Aircraft reflector sight, British, WW2 (Courtesy: R.W.Clarke)*

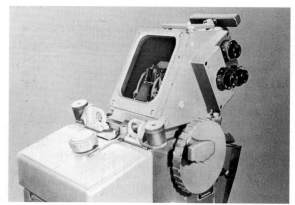

*Optical sight for Oerlikon 20mm GA1-D01 AA gun (Courtesy: Oerlikon-Contraves)*

use of the reflector sight, in which the aiming marks were projected onto an angled glass screen, arranged so that they were in focus at infinity so that the gunner did not have to refocus between the aiming mark and the target. First fitted to fighter aircraft, these were later applied to other uses.

A further advance in aircraft gunsights during the war was the gyro sight, in which an integral gyroscope was used to assist deflection shooting (i.e. aiming in front of a manoeuvring aircraft in order to hit it). This worked by resisting the movement of the aiming mark as the aircraft or turret was swung to keep the target in the sight. The fighter pilot or gunner had to swing the plane or turret to a greater degree in order to get the aiming mark onto the target, thereby automatically allowing for deflection. This was an important advance, especially for fighter aircraft. German analysis in the early 1940s showed that the maximum deflection angle for effective shooting without a gyro sight was 15°, with most successful attacks being at zero degrees deflection. However, German gyro gunsights were not as good as the Allied ones.

Radar-directed fire control systems for naval AA weapons were introduced during the Second World War, although nearly all automatic weapons remained manually aimed. Radar is now an essential component of gun-type naval CIWS (close-in weapon systems) and army AA gun systems as well as larger naval guns. Radar gunsights for aircraft were also under development during the war but these did not reach service until later, and only became dependable much later still.

The more sophisticated modern optical AA gunsights include a laser rangefinder linked to a ballistic computer to create a lead computing sight, able to calculate the distance, direction and speed of the target and adjust the sights accordingly. They can also allow for any tilting of the gun mounting, and in SPAAGs for the movement of the vehicle. Such facilities are also common in main battle tanks and are beginning to appear in MICVs (mechanised infantry combat vehicles). Also becoming common are optronics systems (from 'optical' and 'electronics'; basically, video cameras incorporating night vision capability) which are often used as a back-up to radar-controlled AA mountings in the most modern naval and SPAAG systems.

## AMMUNITION FEEDS

THE EARLIEST MACHINE GUNS RELIED ON GRAVITY to feed ammunition to the weapons. Typically, there would be some form of vertical guide above the gun into which the cartridges would slot, properly aligned with the chamber. The lowest cartridge would be suspended just above the bolt, or pressed against it, so that after recoiling to the rear, the bolt would push the next cartridge into the chamber on its return.

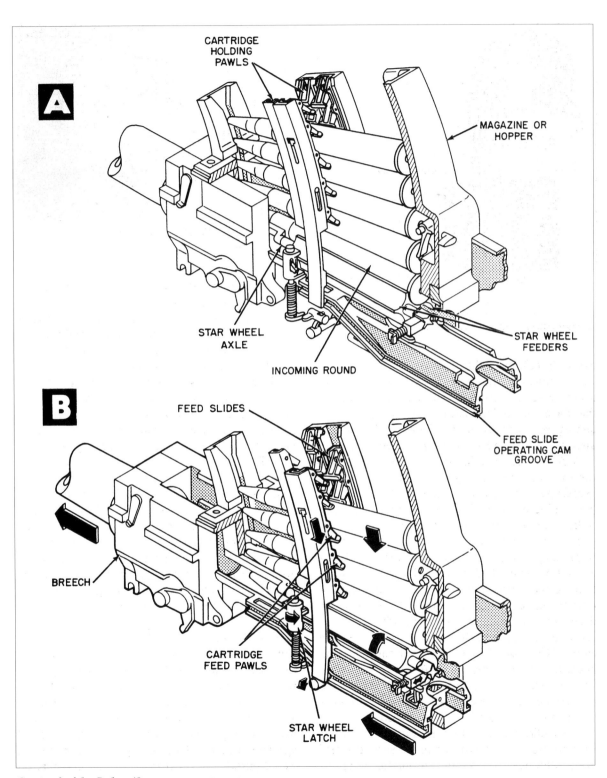

*Gravity feed for Bofors 40mm gun* (*BuOrd, USN*)

*Gravity feed for Molins
6pdr gun ( BuOrd, USN)*

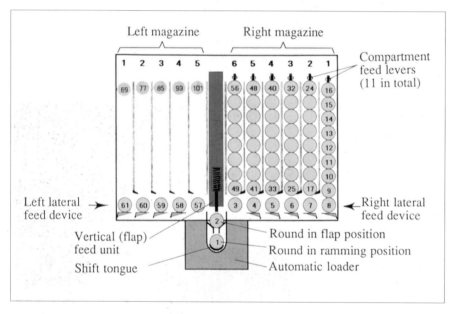

*Rear view of Bofors 40mm
101-round magazine
( Courtesy: Celsius)*

This form of gravity feed remained popular in larger cannon calibres for many decades, as it is simple and reliable. Ammunition for the original Bofors gun, for example, was held in groups of four by a light-alloy clip fitting around the head of the case. Each clip was dropped into the guides above the gun as required. In modern versions, large-capacity magazines are available together with automatic clip handling, but gravity is still utilised.

The main problem with the basic version of this method is that only a small quantity of ammunition is ready to fire at any given moment. Continuous fire requires loaders who are kept very busy scurrying to and fro, feeding the beast. It is therefore only appropriate for circumstances where the gun is stationary and there is plenty of room around it for the gun crew to operate without much fear of being gunned down – in other words, in land- or ship-based anti-aircraft weapons.

The many and various means of providing an

*Lateral feed device
for Bofors 40mm
101-round magazine
(Courtesy: Celsius)*

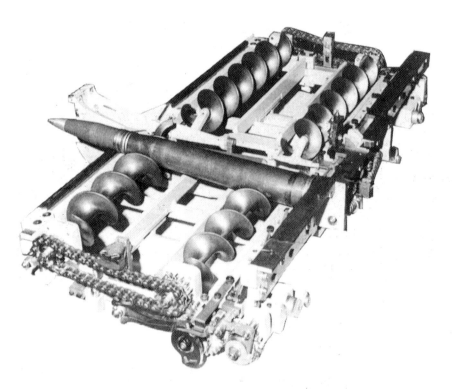

extended period of uninterrupted fire account for the different types of ammunition feed currently in use. In larger calibres, this has been achieved by retaining gravity feed but arranging a device which holds several stacks of cartridges side by side, from which rounds are moved to the breech in turn. This method was used in the 57mm Molins gun carried by Coastal Command's Mosquito XVIII anti-submarine aircraft, in which gravity was assisted by a spring-powered arm on top of each bank, with electrical power being used to shift the banks into position. A modern example is the Bofors SAK 40/70E naval gun, which has a 101-round magazine consisting of ten columns.

In smaller calibres, detachable box, drum or pan magazines have sometimes been used. In a box magazine the cartridges are stacked on top of each other, in one or two rows. A drum is a cylindrical container which holds the rounds parallel to each other. A pan magazine (sometimes also referred to as a drum) is circular but flat, with the cartridges arranged radially, all pointing inwards. All of these types usually have an internal spring which keeps the cartridges pressed against the open end of the

*Drum magazine on Oerlikon S (Courtesy: MoD Pattern Room)*

magazine; they are stopped from falling out by lips which only permit them to slide out lengthways. A less common variation with drum or pan magazines is for them to be rotated by the gun's mechanism, as in the Lewis RCMG, or by some other external power source.

Advantages of magazines are that the ammunition is protected from damage and collecting dirt, and the feed will work at any angle or even in a

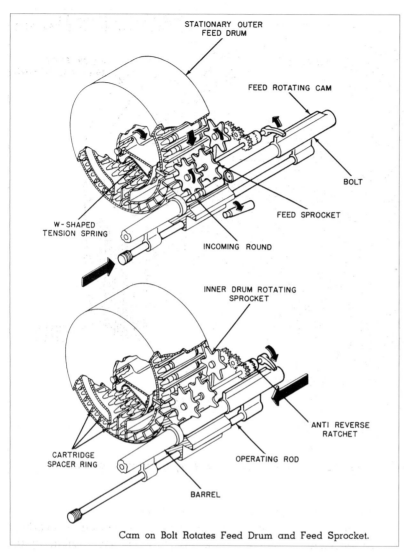

STATIONARY OUTER
FEED DRUM

FEED ROTATING CAM

BOLT

W-SHAPED
TENSION SPRING

FEED SPROCKET

INCOMING ROUND

INNER DRUM ROTATING
SPROCKET

ANTI REVERSE
RATCHET

CARTRIDGE
SPACER RING

OPERATING ROD

BARREL

Cam on Bolt Rotates Feed Drum and Feed Sprocket.

*Drum magazine operation*
*(BuOrd, USN)*

violently manoeuvring aircraft. The main disadvantage is of course that their capacity is necessarily small, both because of their bulk and because there is a limit to the amount of work a spring can reliably be expected to do.

The simplicity and low cost of the box magazine has led to it becoming the standard ammunition feed used by virtually all military rifles, submachine guns and pistols today. However, they rarely hold more than twenty rounds in large calibres, which once again calls for an energetic loading crew and limits the effective rate of fire. One of the best examples is the German 2cm FlaK 30 and FlaK 38 – the standard wartime light AA weapons

– which normally used twenty-round boxes.

The radial pan magazines were at one time popular in RCMGs, but not in larger calibres except in special circumstances, the necessarily large diameter normally being a deterrent. Parallel drum magazines have been far more common. The best known is probably the original Oerlikon S 20mm cannon, used by the Royal Navy from the Second World War until very recently, which used a sixty-round drum. The earliest marks of 20mm Hispano aircraft cannon of the 1930s also used a drum of this capacity, as did most of the *Luftwaffe*'s 2cm MG-FF. However, while the need to change drums at frequent intervals was just about acceptable in a

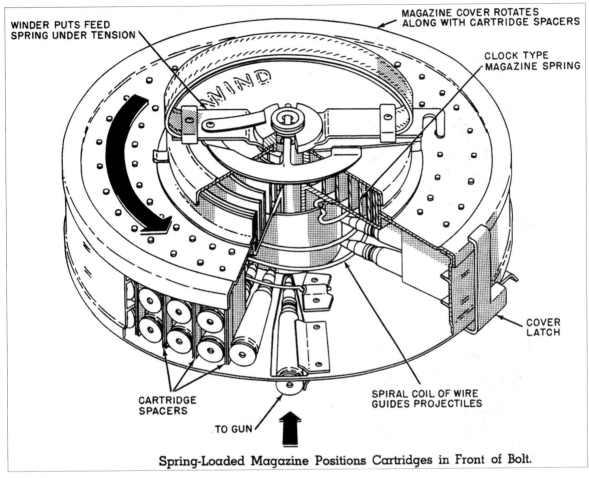

*Pan magazine operation (BuOrd, USN)*

warship, the capacity soon proved inadequate in aircraft use. Larger drums of up to 100 rounds were developed, but their bulk counted against them and

*Pan magazine for experimental .5" BSA*
*(Courtesy: MoD Pattern Room)*

attention turned to belt feeds.

Belt feeds were actually developed very early in the life of machine guns, and were utilised by the original Maxim. In this weapon, as with the early Vickers derived from it, the belt was of canvas with pockets sewn into it for the cartridges. As the early military cartridges were rimmed, this meant that they had to be withdrawn to the rear by the loading mechanism before being pushed forward into the chamber. Canvas also had the problem of being affected by moisture. Finally, the existence of the emptied belt flapping about clearly proved a nuisance in aircraft applications, prompting the introduction of the disintegrating link steel belt.

As its name suggests, the belt is formed of individual steel links which clip the cartridges together. The cartridges form an integral part of the belt, and the links are designed to fall free of each cartridge as it is chambered. Initially devised in Germany, this was quickly introduced into British service in 1916 (the Air Service Mk I) and was rapidly adopted elsewhere. Not all steel belts have been of the disintegrating type, and some (e.g. for the German MG 131 and 151) were designed to be convertible between disintegrating and non-disintegrating depending on the installation requirements. Disintegrating-link belts can be extended by clipping on additional sections, whereas non-disintegrating ones generally cannot.

Belt design has to take into account a number of factors. The clips must be strong enough to maintain their grip on the cartridges while not being so tight that cartridge extraction is hindered (not always achieved, particularly with aircraft belts subjected to high G forces in violent manoeuvring). The belt must obviously be flexible in the vertical plane but also needs to permit curvature in the horizontal plane to allow for the needs of different installations and for some gun movement relative to the ammunition container. This was of particular importance in aircraft turret mountings, in which ammunition was commonly contained within the fuselage, so the belt feed had to allow for

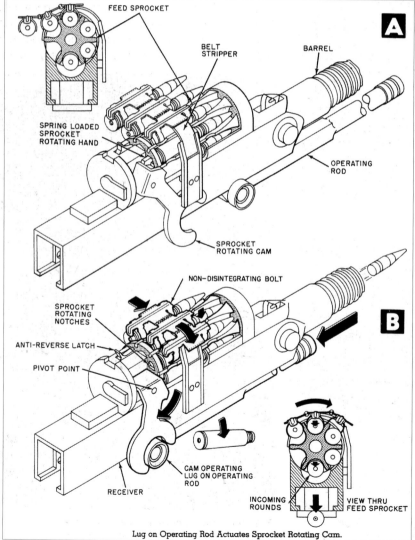

*Belt feed mechanism for DShK-38 (BuOrd, USN)*

*Cloth belt feed for .50" Browning*
*(Courtesy: MoD Pattern Room)*

*Steel non-disintegrating belt for DShK-38*
*(Courtesy: MoD Pattern Room)*

be provided in several ways. In HMGs it is usually provided by the movement of the bolt, which drives a mechanism to pull the cartridges into place; some cannon also utilise this method. Alternatively, in cannon fitted to recoiling mountings the recoil movement is often used. A rare variation, demonstrated by the Rheinmetall-Borsig MK 103, involved the drive being taken from the recoiling barrel. Gas can be tapped from the barrel to drive the belt (as distinct from the gun mechanism), or a separate electric or hydraulic motor can do the work. An interesting hybrid was the Chatellerault-based drive for the 20mm Hispano; this was driven by a pre-wound spring, the tension of which was maintained by the gun recoil movement. The advantage of this complexity was a smooth belt-pull, unaffected by the jerkiness of the gun motion. One unusual method, tried (apparently

*Belt feed sprockets in Oerlikon KCB cannon*
*(Courtesy: MoD Pattern Room)*

both gun elevation and turret traverse. It is common for belt-feed systems to incorporate belt guides to ensure that the belts are fed smoothly into the gun.

The power to move the belt through the gun can

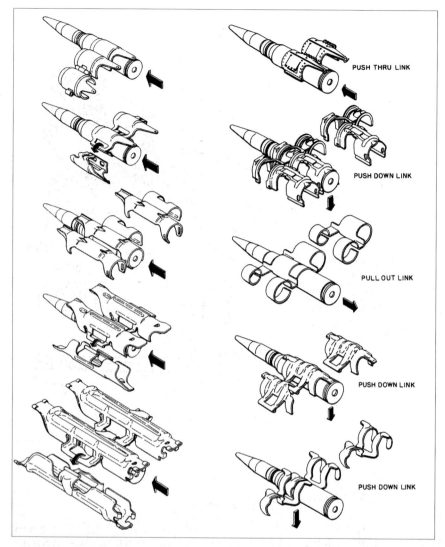

*Ammunition belt link types*
*( BuOrd, USN )*

PUSH THRU LINK

PUSH DOWN LINK

PULL OUT LINK

PUSH DOWN LINK

PUSH DOWN LINK

unsuccessfully) in the Ikaria MG-FF, utilised the force of the gas escaping from the muzzle.

The advantage of belt feeding is that large quantities of ammunition can be held ready to fire, limited only by the space available to store it. In ground guns, it is also unnecessary to pause while reloading, as in most cases the belt links are designed to allow a new length of belt to be clipped onto the end of the old one. These merits have made belt feeding by far the most common method used by the kind of heavy weapons described in this book; but there are also disadvantages which have led to the use of alternatives in certain circumstances.

The main problem in systems which use the gun's action to drive the mechanism is that this places certain limitations on the arrangements for holding the belt. The gun cannot be expected to pull a heavy belt very far, and even in the best of circumstances the rate of fire of a belt-fed gun is likely to be lower than that of an equivalent magazine-fed weapon. There are also the problems in aircraft installations of disposing of the belt links and cartridge cases (the bulges underneath the nose of the Hawker Hunter jet fighter are containers for links), and in some cases of the belts jamming or even pulling apart under G forces. In the largest calibres of automatic weapons a belt would simply be too

*Ammunition feed for aircraft wing mounting* (*BuOrd, USN*)

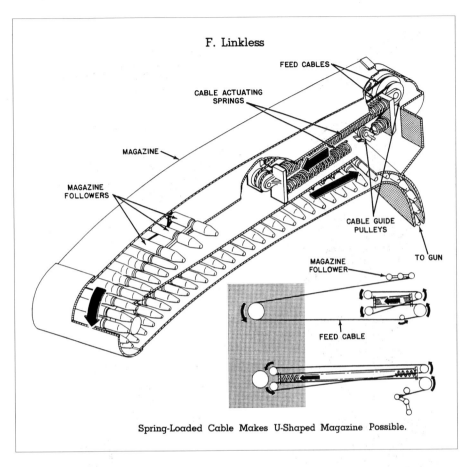

F. Linkless

FEED CABLES

CABLE ACTUATING SPRINGS

MAGAZINE

MAGAZINE FOLLOWERS

CABLE GUIDE PULLEYS

TO GUN

MAGAZINE FOLLOWER

FEED CABLE

Spring-Loaded Cable Makes U-Shaped Magazine Possible.

*Belt guides for M61A1 in gun pod* (*Courtesy: MoD Pattern Room*)

*Oerlikon linkless ammunition feed system for BK27 cannon (Courtesy: Ian Hogg)*

unwieldy although a variation in the form of a continuous-loop belt (i.e. forming an endless chain) was used in some aircraft installations such as the USAAF's 37mm M4.

These difficulties have led to the development of linkless feeds for use with heavy automatic cannon or where very high rates of fire are required. These are often power-driven, the best examples being those for the rotary cannon used by most American aircraft. In most installations, the ammunition is arranged in a large helical drum, with the cartridges pointing inwards. The ammunition feed is driven by the same motor which powers the gun, ensuring that the cartridges are fed into the weapon at the appropriate rate. Because of the difficulty of disposing of empty cartridge cases from a supersonic aircraft, the ammunition feed slots the fired cases tidily back into the drum.

Magazine capacities for the fast-firing rotaries are necessarily high (exceeding 2,000 rounds in one M61 installation) which poses obvious problems in reloading. These have been tackled by the universal ammunition loading system (UALS) which is a mobile unit specifically designed to reload M61 guns (and remove the fired cases). It contains its own pneumatic drive and can reload a 515-round magazine in four minutes.

An alternative approach to reloading has been adopted for the 30mm M230 chain gun in the AH-64D Apache Longbow helicopter. The 'Sideloader' unit is a mechanical system built into the aircraft which enables one man to load 1,075 rounds, in eleven-round strips, in less than fifteen minutes. This contrasts with the AH-64A, which is reloaded by three men, using ground support equipment, in more than half an hour.

Ammunition feeding is complicated by the fact that the majority of heavy automatic weapons are designed to recoil in their mountings in order to spread out the recoil force and minimise vibration. A clip, or a box or small-drum magazine, can recoil with the gun, but it is not feasible to arrange this for belt-drives or other large ammunition capacity systems. It is therefore necessary for designers to find some way of transferring ammunition from a stationary supply to a moving gun.

## BARRELS AND COOLING

THE BURNING OF PROPELLANT, AND THE FRICTION of projectiles accelerating down the barrel and being gripped and rotated by the rifling, combine to generate considerable heat in gun chambers and barrels. The higher the rate of fire per barrel, the more heat is generated and the less time there is available for it to be dissipated. The problem is also exacerbated by high-pressure, high-velocity cartridges.

Heat generation causes two problems. The first is that after firing, the heat of the chamber might be enough to ignite, some time later, the propellant in a cartridge left in the chamber, with potentially disastrous results. This is known as 'cooking off' and is overcome in most heavy weapons by ensuring that the chamber is left empty after use. In linear weapons, this is achieved by designing the gun to fire from an open bolt, i.e. the bolt is held back after each burst (an inherent feature of API blowback weapons anyway). In the case of revolver or rotary cannon, the mechanism is generally arranged to ensure that the multiple chambers are cleared at the end of each burst. In the larger American rotary cannon this is achieved by reversing the mechanism in order to load unfired cartridges back into the feed.

There was a problem with open-bolt firing in the past in the case of aircraft guns which were synchronised to fire through the propeller disc. The accurate timing necessary to avoid shooting off a propeller blade meant that the instant of firing had to be under precise control, which could be achieved by firing from a closed bolt or, where open-bolt firing was retained, by separating the initiation of the firing cycle (by pressing the firing button to chamber a cartridge) from the ignition of the cartridge (controlled by a mechanical or electrical link from the propeller). In the case of the synchronised .50″ Browning M2, pilots were instructed to lock the bolt to the rear for two minutes after a long burst of fire.

The second problem is more difficult to overcome. In extended firing, the barrel and chamber can reach such high temperatures that they glow visibly. Initially, this will result in a much increased rate of wear of the rifling. Again taking the .50″ M2 aircraft gun as an example, about thirty seconds of continuous firing was enough to ruin the barrel. In extreme cases, the mechanism loses its integrity and becomes jammed.

This does not always matter. Aircraft guns are only used in short bursts and have a high-speed airstream to keep them cool. Aircraft also usually return to base between missions, where the gun

barrels can be changed if necessary. Indeed, in the case of the latest revolver cannon, combining a single barrel, high velocity and an extremely high rate of fire, it is reportedly not unknown for the barrel to be changed almost as often as the magazine is reloaded. Even so, restrictions on weapon firing have been applied. For example, Second World War US fighter pilots were told to fire 20mm bursts of no more than twenty rounds and preferably ten, with 37mm figures being fifteen and five respectively.

Ground- and ship-based guns have to find other means of overcoming the heat problem. It has always been common for shipboard automatic guns of all calibres to have water-cooled barrels, as the added weight and complication are less of a problem. Russian armament firms, exercising their usual inventiveness, have even managed to provide water-cooling to rotary cannon. In the past, water-cooled guns have been easily recognisable because of the large-diameter water jackets. Modern weapons use pumped systems which have very slim jackets. At least one of the Russian rotary cannon and their 30mm 2A38M twin-barrel AA gun, use 'transpiration cooling', which relies on the evaporation of a cooling fluid.

Water-cooling has also been common in ground-based guns in the past – the Vickers machine gun range, for example – but has since fallen out of favour as it is more suited to a static battle where arrangements can be made for a reliable supply of water. Instead, heavier barrels with greater capacity to absorb heat are fitted, sometimes finned or fluted to increase the surface area and thereby assist cooling, and the barrels are commonly lined with Stellite or some similar heat-resistant material. In heavy machine guns, it is common to emulate the practice of lighter automatic weapons and provide spare barrels along with a quick-change barrel design.

## THE FIRST EXTERNALLY POWERED GUNS

THE DESIRE TO INCREASE FIREPOWER BY FIRING multiple shots in quick succession is probably as old as the development of firearms. Initially, this was achieved by fitting multiple single-shot barrels to one mounting, which permitted a high rate of burst fire followed by a long delay for reloading. The tactical possibilities were somewhat limited. This system survived into the metallic cartridge era in the form of the French *Mitrailleuse* used in the Franco-Prussian War of 1871, but did not last for much longer in the face of competition from the new machine guns.

The earliest machine guns were externally powered. The external power source was manual labour, in that the guns were made to operate by the gunner cranking a handle. The rate of fire was therefore largely dependent on the energy of the gunner, and tended to slow down as the gunner tired.

The earliest known design of machine gun was a flintlock revolver – the impractical Puckle gun of 1718. It was to be nearly 150 years before the development of the cartridge permitted the first effective

weapons (although the very earliest versions used pre-loaded steel chambers which contained the powder, shot and primer). These were of rotary and linear types; the revolver vanished from the service automatic weapon scene until the mid-1940s.

By far the most famous of the early manually powered guns was a rotary weapon, the Gatling, named after its American inventor Dr Richard John Gatling. The earliest working models appeared in 1862, but it was the adoption of the copper, rimfire cartridge in 1865 which led to its success. Several barrels, each with its own chamber and bolt, were arranged in parallel to rotate around a common axis. Ammunition was fed by gravity, dropping into a trough between the bolt and the chamber associated with each barrel. As the mechanism rotated, the bolt was pushed forward, chambering the cartridge which fired as each barrel reached the bottom (six o'clock) position. Further rotation extracted and ejected the empty case.

Most Gatlings were made in the rifle calibres of the day – .45″ (11.4mm) or larger – but some .65″ (16.5mm), .75″ (19mm) and 1″ (25.4mm) weapons were made, primarily for naval use. The number of barrels varied between six and ten, with ammunition usually being loaded into hoppers or vertical guides.

The French firm Hotchkiss (named after the designer, an American who worked in France) also produced manually powered rotary cannon in the latter part of the nineteenth century, although the mechanism differed in detail from the Gatling

*.65″ Gatling Gun (Courtesy: MoD Pattern Room)*

*Hotchkiss 47mm revolver cannon (Courtesy: Royal Armouries)*

(barrel rotation was stopped for each shot, and there was only one bolt shared by all the barrels) and the calibres were much larger. The first weapons were developed in the 1860s in 40mm calibre, with six barrels and mounted on a wheeled carriage, although it was the late 1870s before any were officially adopted. Some 47mm and 53mm versions were also produced, but by far the most popular were the 37mm guns, primarily for naval use.

The linear guns, mainly produced by Gardner and Nordenfelt, were also successful but achieved less publicity. The Gardner was developed by an American, William Gardner, in the 1870s but initially adopted by the United Kingdom. It again used a rotary crank handle to move the bolts backwards and forwards, only in this case the chambers and barrels were fixed in place. The original version had two barrels which fired alternately, each having its own gravity-fed ammunition supply, but versions with one, three and five barrels were also developed. It was only ever available in rifle (.45") calibres.

The Swedish Nordenfelt (named after the banker who backed it rather than the inventor, Palmcrantz) was one of the last of the manually powered machine guns to be successful. Of similar appearance to the Gardner, the mechanism differed in detail and involved a lever being cranked to and fro, each stroke loading and firing a round in each barrel. The number of barrels varied, but was commonly four. A version in 1" (25.4mm) calibre was adopted by the Royal Navy in 1880 to replace their .65" Gatlings.

Although the British used Gatlings in various calibres, they preferred the linear weapons, the Gardner in particular being considered the best of them. With one or two barrels, it was appreciably more portable than the Gatling and was accordingly used by the Royal Marines in various colonial battles. By the end of the nineteenth century, all externally powered weapons had been reduced to obsolescence by the new self-powered weapons, commencing with the recoil-operated Maxim.

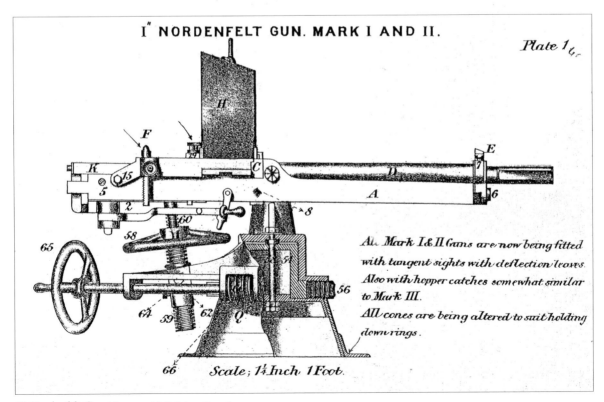

*1" Nordenfelt Gun* (Courtesy: MoD Pattern Room)

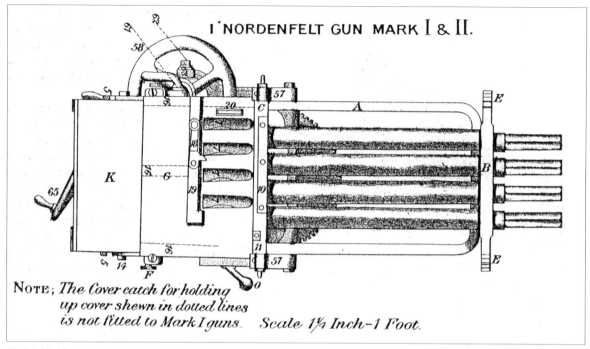

1" NORDENFELT GUN MARK I & II.

NOTE; *The Cover catch for holding up cover shewn in dotted lines is not fitted to Mark I guns.* Scale 1¼ Inch–1 Foot.

*1" Nordenfelt Gun viewed from above* (Courtesy: MoD Pattern Room)

*1" Nordenfelt 4-barrel gun* (Courtesy: MoD Pattern Room)

*Nineteenth Century Cartridges (left to right): .303" (7.7 × 56R), 11mm Gras (11 × 59R), .577/450 Martini-Henry (11.7 × 59R), 1" Gatling (25 × 88R), 1" Nordenfelt (25 × 94R), 37mm Hotchkiss (37 × 94R), 47mm Hotchkiss (47 × 131R)*

## RECOIL-OPERATED GUNS

IN RECOIL-OPERATED SYSTEMS, WHICH MAY BE OF short-recoil or long-recoil types, the energy to drive the reloading cycle comes from the recoil force generated by firing the gun. Part of the gun is designed to recoil against the remainder, compressing a spring, as the breech is opened and the fired case extracted and ejected; the energy stored in the spring is used to drive the bolt back into battery, thrusting a fresh cartridge into the breech as it does so. A key point is that the bolt is mechanically locked to the breech at the instant of firing and remains so until the projectile has left the barrel, thereby ensuring that the breech cannot open until the gas pressure in the barrel has dropped to a safe level.

The difference between long and short recoil is that in the former, the barrel travels all the way back with the bolt before being unlocked. The barrel is then pushed forward by a spring, extracting and ejecting the spent case. The bolt is pushed forward by a second spring once the barrel has returned to battery, collecting and chambering a new cartridge as it does so, and is locked to the breech again before the next shot is fired. In the short-recoil mechanism, the barrel travels only a few millimetres (or centimetres in large cannon) before the bolt is

unlocked; the barrel is then stopped and the bolt continues its rearward movement alone, extracting and ejecting the fired case before reaching the rearward limit of its travel. The return movement of the bolt chambers a fresh cartridge and relocks the bolt, as in the long-recoil system.

The drawback of recoil-operated guns is that the barrel has to be free to slide to and fro while its support is engineered closely enough to maintain acceptable accuracy. Some mechanical means of locking and unlocking the bolt and breech at the appropriate moments are required, and variations in how this is achieved are the main distinguishing features of the different designs to have seen service. This type of mechanism has proved to be very suitable for heavy automatic weapons and is still in common use today. Despite this, it was the first self-powered mechanism to appear, in the Maxim machine gun family.

*37mm Vickers-Maxim Mk 1 'Pom-pom'*
*(Courtesy: MoD Pattern Room)*

The Maxim is significant because it was the first automatic machine gun, i.e. not manually powered, and because it saw such widespread use. It was first invented by Hiram Maxim, an American living in England, in 1884. The gun was immediately successful and by 1891 had become the standard machine gun of the British Army. A 37mm cannon version, popularly known as the 'Pom-pom' because of its distinctive sound on firing, was also produced and saw extensive international service.

The mechanism utilises a toggle joint, which is similar in principle to an elbow joint. The bolt is hinged in the middle so that it can bend like an

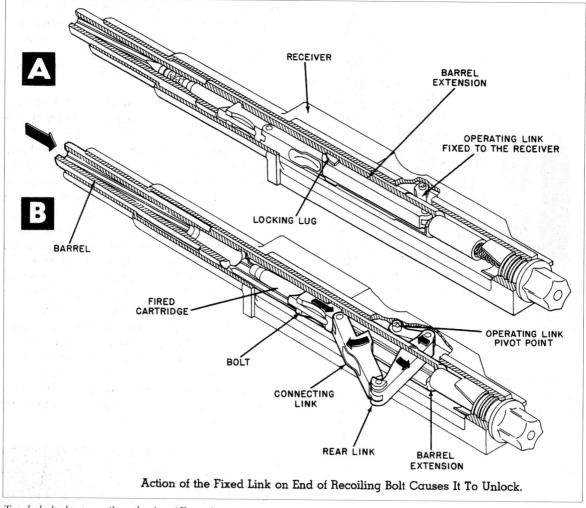

**A**

**B**

RECEIVER

BARREL
EXTENSION

OPERATING LINK
FIXED TO THE RECEIVER

LOCKING LUG

BARREL

FIRED
CARTRIDGE

OPERATING LINK
PIVOT POINT

BOLT

CONNECTING
LINK

REAR LINK

BARREL
EXTENSION

**Action of the Fixed Link on End of Recoiling Bolt Causes It To Unlock.**

*Toggle-bolt short-recoil mechanism (Furrer) (BuOrd, USN)*

elbow, but when the gun is ready to fire the bolt is straight, like an outstretched arm. On firing, the bolt and barrel recoil backwards together for a few millimetres until a part of the mechanism forces the joint to bend. At the same time, the rearward movement of the barrel is stopped. As the bolt bends, the head is pulled back away from the breech, extracting the fired case. A spring then straightens the bolt, which chambers a fresh cartridge on the way back. It was therefore the first member of the short-recoil family. The Luger pistol uses the same toggle bolt principle, as did several Swiss cannon of the 1930s and 1940s in 20mm, 24mm and 34mm calibre. These were designed by Colonel Adolf Furrer and

manufactured by *Eidgenössische Waffenfabrik* of Berne.

Early in the twentieth century, the design was refined by Vickers to create the Vickers-Maxim, later known simply as the Vickers machine gun. This remained the standard medium machine gun of the British Army until 1956. Apart from special applications, such as air-cooled aircraft variants, it was generally water-cooled, belt-fed and mounted on a sturdy tripod for accurate long-range fire.

Although best known in its rifle-calibre version, it was also made in larger calibres. The 37mm Pom-pom was used by all sides in the First World War and Vickers .5″ machine guns saw service in the

*The 'Pom-pom' family of cartridges (from left to right): 37mm Maxim (37 × 94R), 3.7cm Sockelflak (37 × 101SR), 1pdr Vickers Mk III (37 × 69R), USN Heavy One-Pounder (37 × 137R), 1½pdr Vickers (37 × 123R), 2pdr Vickers (40 × 158R)*

Second World War, but these were eclipsed in importance by the naval 2pdr (two-pounder, after the projectile weight) gun of 40mm calibre, which inherited the Pom-pom nickname. Other nations also adopted the Maxim or the Vickers and there are undoubtedly many Maxim-type machine guns still giving good service all around the world today, even though their heyday was over by the end of the Second World War.

## OTHER SHORT-RECOIL MECHANISMS

THERE ARE MANY DIFFERENT WAYS OF LOCKING THE bolt to the barrel extension. The strongest is probably the rotating bolt, held by locking lugs on the bolt which fit into recesses in the barrel extension, just as in a bolt-action rifle. During the initial rearward movement of the barrel/bolt assembly, the bolt (or more commonly just the head of the bolt) is forced to rotate by cams until it is unlocked. This system was used by the Rheinmetall-Borsig 3.7cm FlaK 18, 36 and 37, the Mauser MG 151 and the Soviet 14.5mm KPV (*Krupnokalibernyi Pulemet Vladimirova*; heavy-calibre machine gun designed by Vladimirov) NS-23, NS-37 and NS-45 (designed

by Nudelman and Suranov). During the 1960s, a range of rotary-locked short-recoil cannon was developed by Hispano-Suiza. These consisted of the HS 827-B (20 × 139), the HS 827-C (23 × 133), the HS 836 (30 × 136) and the HS 837 (30 × 170), but none was adopted.

Another rotating mechanism is the Solothurn lock (invented by Louis Stange early in the twentieth century), which consists of a rotating collar fitting around the barrel extension and locking this to the bolt by means of an interrupted thread. As the barrel/bolt assembly moves rearwards, the collar is rotated by cams in the receiver, thereby disengaging the lock and enabling the bolt to be separated. The Solothurn lock was used in various infantry weapons developed between the wars and in the S12-100 2cm cannon. Rheinmetall reclaimed the design in the 1930s and produced an improved version, the MG 204 (initially known as the Lb 204) aircraft gun. This fired the 20 × 105B short Solothurn cartridge which resembled a slightly shortened, belted Hispano (later replaced by a version firing modified beltless 20 × 105 ammunition). The Solothurn lock was also used in the 13mm MG 131, the 2cm Solothurn S18-100 and S18-1000 anti-tank rifles and the 2cm S18-350 and 3cm MK 101 aircraft guns.

*Sectioned MG 131 mechanism showing curved cam-track for unlocking the bolt (Courtesy: MoD Pattern Room)*

The firm *Waffenfabrik Solothurn* was established in Switzerland in 1929 as a subsidiary of the German firm *Rheinische Metallwaaren-und-Maschinenfabrik*, better known by its trade name Rheinmetall, as a way of evading the limitations on weapon development imposed by the Treaty

*Short-recoil mechanism* (*Courtesy: D.F. Allsop*)

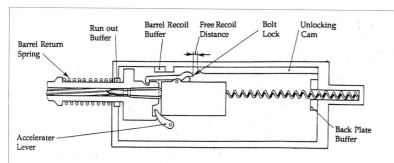

The barrel and breech block move into the forward position and a round is fed into the chamber

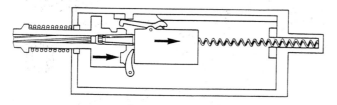

The round is fired and the barrel and breech block are pushed to the rear by the recoil forces. After a short distance they are unlocked and the barrel is halted. Additional momentum is given to the breech block by an accelerator lever before the barrel stops moving

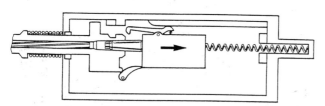

The breech block moves to the rear of the body of the weapon under its own momentum

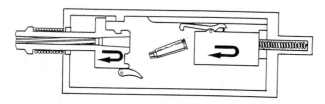

The spent case is extracted and ejected, the breech block is halted by the buffer and the barrel is held to the rear

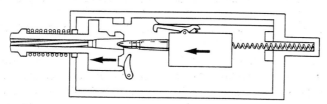

The breech bolt moves forward and chambers a fresh round

*Recoil-operated rotary locking sleeve mechanism*
*(BuOrd, USN)*

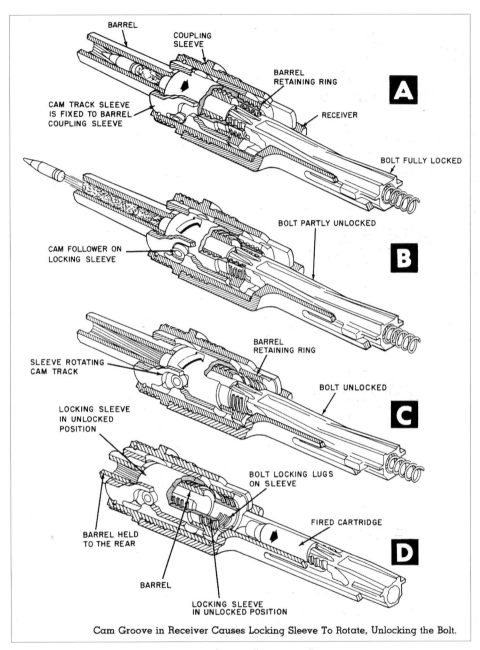

BARREL

COUPLING SLEEVE

BARREL RETAINING RING

CAM TRACK SLEEVE IS FIXED TO BARREL COUPLING SLEEVE

RECEIVER

**A**

BOLT FULLY LOCKED

BOLT PARTLY UNLOCKED

CAM FOLLOWER ON LOCKING SLEEVE

**B**

BARREL RETAINING RING

SLEEVE ROTATING CAM TRACK

BOLT UNLOCKED

LOCKING SLEEVE IN UNLOCKED POSITION

**C**

BOLT LOCKING LUGS ON SLEEVE

FIRED CARTRIDGE

BARREL HELD TO THE REAR

**D**

BARREL

LOCKING SLEEVE IN UNLOCKED POSITION

Cam Groove in Receiver Causes Locking Sleeve To Rotate, Unlocking the Bolt.

of Versailles. These nominally Swiss weapons therefore featured significantly in German rearmament plans. Two years after the acquisition of August Borsig GmbH in 1933 the firm became Rheinmetall-Borsig, a designation which lasted until 1956, after which it re-formed as Rheinmetall.

An alternative system uses a pivoting lever or plate, fixed to the barrel extension and incorporating lugs which fit into recesses in the bolt to hold them together. The initial movement of the barrel pivots the lever, lifting the lugs and releasing the bolt. An early example of this was invented by Louis Schmeisser in the early 1900s and used in the Dreyse machine gun and, in enlarged form, the 20mm Erhardt cannon under development in 1918. Erhardt was one of the key figures in Rheinmetall,

*2cm Erhardt FlzK aircraft cannon*
*(Courtesy: MoD Pattern Room)*

so this mechanism was incorporated in various Rheinmetall weapons thereafter. Strenuous efforts at the end of the war to keep the Erhardt secret from the Allies were largely successful and few examples survived.

The Erhardt was too late to see service in World War One (although at least fifty-one were made) but the design was eventually passed by Rheinmetall to their Swiss subsidiary, Solothurn, who developed it into the S5-100, in which the design was enlarged to take the long Solothurn 20 × 138B cartridge. This was further developed into the important FlaK 30, KwK 30 and MG C/30L family. The design was subsequently modified by Mauser to improve the rate of fire, leading to the FlaK 38 and KwK 38.

Another variation is the rising block lock, with that invented by the prolific American John M.

Browning being the most successful. In this case the barrel and bolt are connected by a locking piece which is vertically cammed out of engagement. The Browning short-recoil machine gun emerged during the First World War in rifle calibre as the M1917, later refined into the M1919, in which form it remained in service until well after the Second World War. The same basic design was scaled-up to a new .50″ (12.7 × 99) calibre towards the end of the First World War, eventually emerging as the M1921. Subsequently refined to the M2, this was extensively used by all three services in various versions during the Second World War and has remained in service ever since. The M3 was a post-war aircraft version with a very high rate of fire, achieved in part with the aid of a recoil booster attached to the muzzle.

During the Second World War, the Japanese were great enthusiasts of the American Browning-type aircraft guns and fielded a variety of weapons using this design. The smallest was the army's Ho-103 aircraft gun, scaled down to use the export version of Vickers' .5″ cartridge, which for some obscure reason was slightly different from the British service round, being semi-rimmed (12.7 × 81SR). The cartridge was apparently obtained via Italy, which had acquired manufacturing rights for use in the Breda-SAFAT aircraft machine gun. The compact round enabled the gun to weigh only 22kg while firing at 900 rpm from its disintegrating-link belt. This was an impressive combination of small size and power which would have been most useful to the RAF (particularly for bomber defence) if they had thought of developing such a Vickers/Browning hybrid.

Short-recoil guns designed for water-cooling frequently had the barrel supported at the muzzle end via a sliding fit at the front end of the cooling jacket. In air-cooled versions of such guns, a perforated barrel casing often performed the same function, particularly in Browning-pattern weapons.

The later Japanese Navy Type 3 aircraft gun was a direct copy of the .50″ Browning except that the calibre was amended to the 13.2 × 99 Hotchkiss already in service as an AA weapon, an easy task as the cartridges were almost identical. Probably the most successful of the Browning copies was the army's Ho-5, scaled up to take a 20 × 94 cartridge,

*Sectioned Browning .50" M2 showing chamber (Courtesy: MoD Pattern Room)*

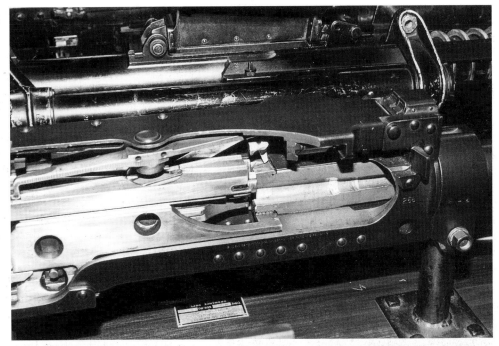

*Sectioned Browning .50" M2 showing rear of action (Courtesy: MoD Pattern Room)*

and this was followed into service by the Ho-155 in 30 × 114 and the massive Ho-204 in 37 × 144. All of these were aircraft guns, but the last two saw little use.

Short-recoil mechanisms do not generate much energy for the reloading cycle, which can result in a low rate of fire. It is therefore common for them to incorporate a bolt accelerator, a pivoting lever which kicks the bolt rearwards as soon as it is unlocked. A further problem in belt-fed guns is the need for the recoil to lift the ammunition belt from its container and pull it through the gun. As the available power is rather marginal to achieve this, recoil-operated guns (particularly in rifle-calibre versions) are sometimes seen with a bulbous device on the muzzle which uses the power of the escaping propellant gas to boost the recoil – the exact opposite of a muzzle brake. It is popularly known as a muzzle booster, more formally as a recoil intensifier. Strictly speaking, this turns it into a gas-assisted recoil-operated gun.

Recoil was the force driving a famous twin-barrel gun. As already noted, the first twin-barrel machine guns were manually powered: the nineteenth century Gardners. During the First World War, the German firm Gast devised a different form of mechanism for an aircraft RCMG, in which the recoil of each barrel operated the loading and firing mechanism of the other, leading to a high rate of fire of around 1,600 rpm. This principle was adopted in revised form much later, in the Russian GSh-23 (Gryazev-Shipunov after the designers) and GSh-30 aircraft guns and the 2A38 AA gun, all of which display the usual national characteristics of compactness, light weight and a high rate of fire, and the American 25mm GE 225. These all use gun

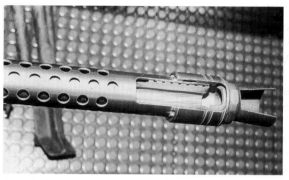

*Muzzle booster on MG 131 (sectioned)*
*(Courtesy: MoD Pattern Room)*

gas to operate the mechanism and are therefore properly hybrid guns. The GE 225, which has not so far been adopted for service, was also offered in an externally powered version.

New short-recoil designs are now very uncommon, having been largely replaced by gas-operated or externally powered designs. One surprising exception is the current Russian aircraft cannon which arms the MiG-29 and Su-27 families, the GSh-301. Despite many Western sources assuming that this is a revolver cannon, it does in fact utilise a short-recoil mechanism with a sliding-wedge breech. Performance is comparable with Western revolver cannon, while weight is reduced by half and the action is much slimmer.

## LONG-RECOIL MECHANISMS

THE NEED FOR THE ENTIRE BARREL/BOLT UNIT TO recoil a considerable distance, followed by a delay in commencing reloading while the barrel returns into the firing position, gives long-recoil mechanisms a relatively low rate of fire. As a result, weapons using this system are much less common than the short-recoil type. However, the long and relatively soft recoil push puts less strain on the mechanism and makes accuracy easier to achieve while avoiding the need for the whole gun to recoil in its mounting. It has therefore been more popular in large-calibre cannon of 37mm and upwards, one of the earlier examples being the British 1½ pdr (one-and-a-half pounder) COW (Coventry Ordnance Works) gun of the First World War. This weapon was not particularly successful but did lead to the Vickers 40mm Class 'S' aircraft gun of the Second World War.

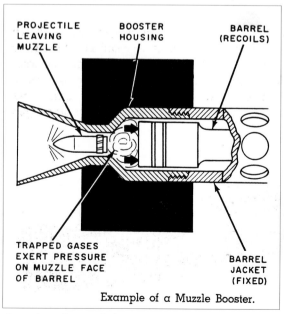

*Operation of a muzzle booster (BuOrd, USN)*

The ubiquitous John Browning also produced long-recoil designs, most notably used for the 37mm M4 and M10 aircraft guns, the 37mm M1 AA gun (and its M9 aircraft gun derivative) and the USN's 1.1″ AA gun. The Japanese 37mm Ho-203 and the scaled-up 57mm Ho-401 aircraft guns also used long-recoil mechanisms.

The British Rarden 30mm AFV gun is a current example of this system, adopted partly because the main priority was for single-shot accuracy rather than rate of fire, and partly because the much longer period before the breech opens after firing allows more of the propellant gas to escape from the barrel, minimising gas pollution within the enclosed turret. The same reasoning led to the development of the Oerlikon KDE, a member of the 35mm gun family and the only one not to use gas operation. The combination of a low rate of fire and the relatively long recoil movement (which has a recoil distance of 170mm, rather than the usual 55–60mm of the gun mounting) makes the KDE much easier to control than its faster-firing cousins.

The Russians learned the same lesson following unsatisfactory experiences with the gas-operated 30mm 2A42 cannon in the BMP-2 AIFV (armoured infantry fighting vehicle), which suffered considerable problems (especially at its higher rate of fire) with fumes and smoke entering the turret. While the 2A42 has remained in use for external mounting in helicopters, the long-recoil 2A72, with a 330mm recoil movement, has been developed for the BMP-3. Both were designed by Gryazev.

The most famous users of a version of the 'long-recoil' system are the Bofors family of weapons. In this case a vertically sliding breechblock opens

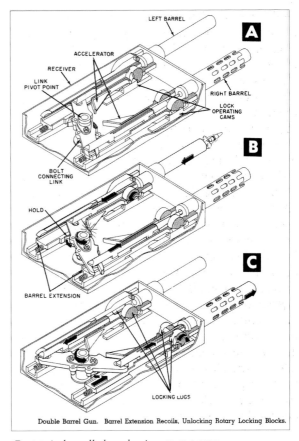

*Gast twin-barrelled mechanism (BuOrd, USN)*

during the recoil phase and the spent case is ejected rearwards by a separate mechanism. During the 1930s automatic weapons from this firm were available in 20mm and 25mm (with a 37mm version adopted by Russia and subsequently China) but these were eclipsed by the success of the 40mm gun

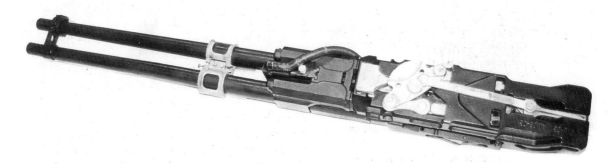

*GSh-23 twin-barrelled gun (Courtesy: MoD Pattern Room)*

*Long-recoil mechanism* (*Courtesy: D.F. Allsop*)

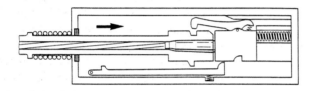

**Barrel Spring** · **Bolt Lock** · **Bolt** · **Return Spring**

**Back-Plate Buffer**

**Run-Out Buffer**

**Bolt Latch**

With the round chambered, the breech block is locked to the barrel. Upon firing the breech block and barrel are driven backwards

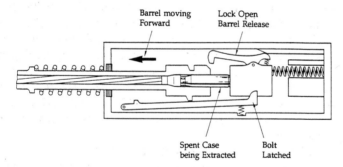

The breech block and barrel are slowed by the barrel spring and the breech block return spring. Towards the end of the stroke the breech is unlocked from the barrel

**Barrel moving Forward** · **Lock Open Barrel Release**

**Spent Case being Extracted** · **Bolt Latched**

The bolt is held to the rear and the barrel moves forward under the influence of the barrel spring. As the barrel moves forward the empty cartridge case is extracted and ejected

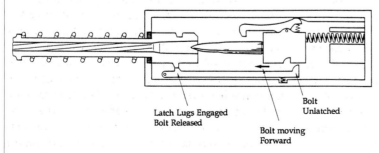

**Latch Lugs Engaged Bolt Released**

**Bolt Unlatched**

**Bolt moving Forward**

The breech block is released, a fresh round is chambered and the breech block is locked to the barrel

*30mm Rarden long-recoil gun (Courtesy: Ian Hogg)*

which achieved fame as an AA weapon in the Second World War and has been continually updated ever since.

The original 40mm gun, the L56 (now commonly known as the L60), was developed in the early 1930s and fired a powerful 40 × 311R cartridge. The quality of the design and manufacture were such that the rate of fire was a competitive and reliable 140 rpm, and the combination of virtues which this gun represented was enough to make it the supreme weapon of its class. The gun was available in both air-cooled and water-cooled versions (for army and navy use respectively) but with the exception of some USN versions was always fed by a four-round clip held in guide rails above the breech.

After the war an improved L70 version was developed which used an even more powerful cartridge, the 40 × 364R. The rate of fire was increased, initially to 240, subsequently to 300 and, in the latest Trinity version, 330 rpm. Improved mechanisms for feeding ammunition to the breech also improved the sustained rate of fire, and with powered mountings, advanced fire-control systems and the latest ammunition technology, the gun system remains highly competitive today. The 40mm guns were also joined by 57mm versions post-war. These were produced in an army version but have achieved more success as naval weapons. A Bofors 57mm gun designed for aircraft, the m/47, used a much smaller and less powerful cartridge.

Incidentally, the term L70 (or L/70) means that the barrel length is seventy times the calibre; in this

case, the barrel is therefore 2.8m long. Generally speaking, the higher the L number or calibre length, the higher the muzzle velocity.

The particular type of recoil mechanism used in the Bofors has the advantage that the length of the recoil stroke is not determined by the cartridge length. In fact this, like the Oerlikon KDE, is not a 'pure' long-recoil design as the breechblock is unlocked and extraction commences before the barrel has recoiled the full distance required to chamber a fresh cartridge. It is therefore possible to shorten the recoil stroke, and this has been done (from 250 to 100–110mm) by OtoBreda in its Fast Forty gun, as part of a package of measures which have increased the rate of fire to 450 rpm. The speed of the Chinese NORINCO 37mm Type 76A, based indirectly on the Bofors mechanism, has been increased in a similar way.

The long-recoil mechanism has also been adopted for some of the new generation of automatic grenade launchers (AGLs), although most use API blowback.

Finally, it is worth mentioning one interesting American experimental gun of the 1950s, the 20mm T220, which had two rates of fire: 1,500 rpm for AA use (operating in short-recoil mode) and 500 rpm for ground fire (operating as a long-recoil gun). The idea was unsuccessful and was not pursued, although the concept of variable rates of fire survived in the service 12.7mm M85 AFV gun and is easily achieved in modern power-driven weapons.

## BLOWBACK MECHANISMS

THE SIMPLEST FORM OF AUTOMATIC OPERATION IS the blowback. In this, the cartridge is held in the chamber by a heavy bolt, which is in turn kept pressed forward by a strong spring. When the cartridge fires, the expanding gases push the projectile up the barrel and the cartridge case back against the bolt. The inertia of the bolt holds it in place for the fraction of a second necessary to allow the projectile to reach the end of the barrel, by which time the bolt is being pushed back, ejecting the fired case and compressing the return spring as it goes. This leaves the rear of the chamber open so that the bolt, now being pushed forward again by the return spring, can pick up another cartridge from the ammunition feed and chamber it in the gun. During this cycle the bolt also recocks the firing mechanism.

The problem with the simple blowback is that it only works well with low-powered ammunition such as small pistol cartridges. Military cartridges are so powerful that the bolt would need to be prohibitively heavy to hold the cartridge case in place until the projectile had cleared the barrel. The penalty for premature opening of the breech is likely to be a burst case, with high-pressure gas escaping from the breech. Various methods of modifying the simple blowback have therefore been developed and many of these are in service today.

Some of the modifications involve engineering a delay to the movement of the bolt. This may be arranged by locking the bolt to the barrel at the instant of firing, then unlocking it as soon as pressures have dropped to safe levels and allowing the blowback cycle to proceed (delayed blowback) or arranging for the bolt to push some mechanism out of the way, engineered to provide maximum resistance for the first few millimetres of travel (retarded blowback). Delayed blowback has been frequently used in heavy automatic weapons (see 'The hybrids') but retarded blowback has been restricted to small arms. Even less common is the gas-retarded blowback, in which gas tapped from the barrel is used to hold the bolt against the breech face until the gas pressure in the barrel has dropped enough for the breech to open safely.

The simplest variation in heavy weapons, however, uses advanced primer ignition. API blowback is mechanically almost identical to the pure blowback, with two principal differences: first, it fires as the bolt is moving forwards and just before the cartridge is fully chambered; and secondly, an extended or hooded chamber is used, within which the cartridge can slide while remaining supported. The effect of these differences is that the recoiling cartridge case has to arrest the forward movement of the bolt before it can begin to push it back again. The result is that a much lighter bolt is required; it is commonly stated that for a powerful API cannon, the bolt is only one-tenth the weight it would need to be if the gun used a pure blowback system. The reduced inertia of the light bolt permits a much higher rate of fire than would be possible with a pure blowback.

All simple and API blowbacks have in common a bolt which is unlocked (i.e. not mechanically locked to the chamber) at the instant of firing, and all the blowback family suffer from a common problem: a weakness in the positive extraction of the fired case. This is blown out of the chamber by gas pressure in the barrel rather than positively pulled as with most other mechanisms, and there is a risk that the pressure will instead stick the case to the walls of the chamber. At best this stops the gun from firing until the case has been cleared by the charger mechanism; at worst, the case may be pulled apart by the tension, leaving a section of case in the chamber and putting the gun out of action for some time.

The most effective solution to this problem is to wax or oil the cases before they are fired, but this carries its own problems such as collecting grit and carrying it into the mechanism. A later approach which works in some circumstances (actually developed in the 1930s) is to engrave shallow grooves or flutes into the chamber, leading from the case neck back to the body of the cartridge case. This provides a route for a thin film of propellant gas to seep back around the case, thereby preventing it from sticking.

Another characteristic of blowback weapons is that some cartridge shapes work better than others. Straight cases work well because they remain fully supported by the chamber walls as they slide backwards through the chamber after firing. Tapered or bottlenecked cases are far less effective, as the first rearward movement leaves a part of the case unsupported by the chamber. The gas pressure will instantly expand that part of the case to fill the gap, and may split the case or pull it apart. The only successful API blowback cannon with a (slightly) bottlenecked case is the 20 × 110RB Oerlikon S. Even so, the neck and shoulder of the fired case are considerably expanded from the unfired shape.

API case designs also need to take account of the fact that the cartridge is deep within the extended chamber when it is fired. All the cases in cannon calibres therefore have a rebated (reduced diameter) rim to enable the bolt, with extractor claw hooked over the rim, to follow the cartridge into the chamber. The cases also often feature a considerable thickness of metal near the head, to reduce the risk

*Advanced Primer Ignition
Blowback (schematic)*

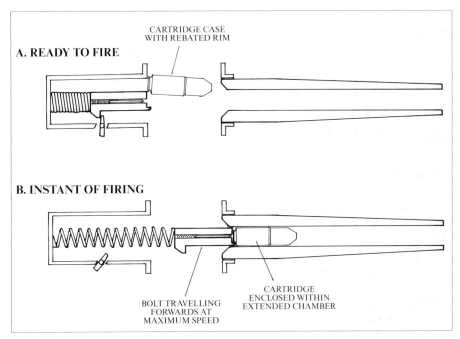

A. READY TO FIRE

CARTRIDGE CASE
WITH REBATED RIM

B. INSTANT OF FIRING

BOLT TRAVELLING
FORWARDS AT
MAXIMUM SPEED

CARTRIDGE
ENCLOSED WITHIN
EXTENDED CHAMBER

of the unsupported head of the case splitting open as it is extracted.

A related characteristic is an unusual sensitivity to different types of ammunition. It is particularly difficult to balance the pressure characteristics of different cartridge loadings with the mechanism, and in extreme cases the need to fire new loadings required the gun mechanism to be rebalanced with different bolt weights and spring strengths, as in the change from the German MG-FF to the MG-FFM (described in more detail in Chapter 5).

A requirement of the API system is that the gun can only fire from an open bolt, i.e. with the bolt held fully back. In some respects this is desirable because it means that the chamber is left open between bursts of fire and therefore has a chance to cool down, so there is no risk of a cartridge 'cooking-off' in a hot chamber. However, it also means that there is a significant delay between pressing the trigger or firing button and the first round being fired. This system was therefore never suitable for synchronised mountings in piston-engined fighter aircraft, which required each shot to be precisely timed to avoid shooting off the propeller.

A result of the API principle is that the recoil forces generated are relatively low, because much of the recoil energy is absorbed stopping the forward movement of the bolt before it can be thrust to the rear. As a result there is little surplus energy to drive a belt feed without slowing down the rate of fire, so most examples have been drum-fed. The main exceptions have been those such as the MK 108 whose design permitted the use of a very light bolt, the energy required to drive the belt feed being balanced by a reduction in bolt weight. The light recoil push also means that the complication of recoiling mountings can be avoided in all but the largest calibres.

The API blowback principle is used in virtually all sub-machine guns (although the relatively low pressures and velocities mean that extended chambers and rebated-rim cartridges are not required) but its use in heavy automatic weapons has mainly been restricted to a chain of development originating in a German gun, named after Reinhold Becker, which was developed during the First World War. This simple weapon of modest performance, which used a 20 × 70RB cartridge, saw limited service in both aircraft and anti-aircraft roles towards the end of the war, but its significance lies in its post-war descendants. After the First World War, severe restrictions were placed on German armaments and few new developments were possible, but some German firms avoided the restrictions by working

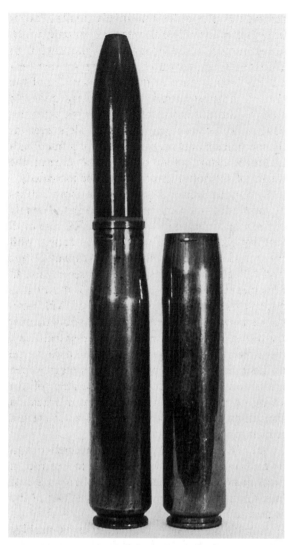

*Oerlikon S 20 × 110RB: fired case next to unfired cartridge, showing expansion of case neck on firing*

through subsidiaries abroad, especially in Switzerland.

The Becker Works sold the design of their cannon to SEMAG (the *Seebach Maschinenbau Aktien Gesellschaft,* an engineering firm near Zurich) who introduced more powerful models, but after that firm's liquidation the patents were bought by another Swiss company, Oerlikon (named after the Zurich suburb in which the company was located). Although the design was developed in various forms and in a wide variety of specifications

(including anti-tank weapons) it did not achieve great success until the rearmament boom of the late 1930s. By this time it was available in three main forms, all of which retained the API blowback mechanism.

The first form was the Swiss Oerlikon FF aircraft gun, a development of the Becker, which originally retained the Becker's 70mm case length, but was later extended to 72mm. This is sometimes referred to as the FFF, to distinguish it from the FFL and FFS. The term FF, applied to all Oerlikon's aircraft guns of the period, stood for *flügelfest,* or wing-mounted, as that was their intended use. The FF was adopted by the Japanese Navy as the Type 99-1. Manufacturing rights were also obtained by Ikaria Werke of Berlin who considerably modified the design, lengthening the case to 80mm (although the cartridge remained approximately the same overall length). The gun was used in various forms by the *Luftwaffe* as the MG-FF. While it was percussion-primed, the bolt was released electrically by means of a solenoid.

The next size up produced by Oerlikon was the mechanically similar FFL aircraft gun, using a still longer and more powerful version of the straight-cased, rebated-rim cartridge (20 × 100RB) introduced by SEMAG, which was adopted and further developed, with a case length slightly extended to 101mm, by the Japanese Navy as the Type 99-2. The original Swiss version (the SEMAG Type L) weighed 43kg and achieved 670–700 m/s and 350 rpm. This was later improved in the FFL to 30kg, 750 m/s and 500 rpm.

The considerably larger and more powerful S series, developed by Oerlikon themselves, fired a much larger, bottle-necked cartridge (20 × 110RB). It was offered as an aircraft gun (the Type S) in which form it weighed a hefty 62kg and could fire at only 280 rpm. Constant development saw these figures significantly improved in the Type FFS of the late 1930s, with the weight reduced to 39kg and the rate of fire increased to 470 rpm. The Type S did see far more use as an anti-aircraft weapon (technically known as the Type SS series), in which form it has survived to the present day.

The five other API blowback weapons of note were the 20mm Polsten (a much simplified Oerlikon S AA gun developed by Polish engineers and manufactured in the UK during the war) and four air-craft guns; the Japanese Navy's 30mm Type 2, the Japanese Army's 40mm Ho-301 and two German guns: the 3cm MK 108 and the experimental 5.5cm MK 112. Of these, only the Polsten and the MK 108 saw significant service. There were other designs of blowback cannon developed in both America and Germany, but they were not successful.

Despite the apparent simplicity of the API blow-back mechanism, the relationship between cartridge power, bolt weight and rate of fire is both subtle and critical. It is essential for the case to remain within the extended chamber until the projectile has left the barrel, thereby allowing the chamber pressure to fall to a safe level. This requires a certain minimum bolt weight (the inertia of the bolt being far more important at this point than the strength of the recoil spring). A powerful, high-velocity cartridge requires a long barrel to achieve the velocity. This inevitably entails a longer delay before the projectile clears the muzzle, which in turn requires a heavier and slower-moving bolt to keep the fired case within the chamber for that period. The consequence of this is a lower rate of fire than with short-barrelled low-velocity guns (to some extent, this is true of all automatic weapons, but in locked-breech types the effect is less severe as the mechanism only needs to allow for a fractionally longer delay before opening the breech; the weight of the bolt does not have to be increased).

During the Second World War the shortcomings of the Oerlikon system became apparent. The rate of fire was limited to little more than 500 rpm in all versions because of the nature of the design, with the exception of the heavily modified Japanese Type 99-2 Model 5, which was too late to see service. In principle (within the limits indicated above) it is possible to accelerate the firing rate of API blow-back guns by lightening the bolt and strengthening the spring. However, the Oerlikon design featured a recoil spring which was wrapped around the barrel in the interests of compactness. This required the use of a strong yoke connecting the front of the spring to the bolt, and this effectively added to the weight of the bolt, preventing much weight reduction.

The MK 108 and MK 112 used a different design in the interests of achieving a higher rate of fire. In experiments towards the end of the Second World War, German technicians increased the rate of fire of the admittedly low-powered MK 108 from an already respectable 600–650 rpm to an astonishing 900 rpm in the MK 108A, not far short of the rate achieved by the far more sophisticated MK 213C revolver gun. This was only made possible by the gun's very short barrel, which reduced the length of time the fired case had to be held in the chamber and therefore permitted a relatively light, low-inertia bolt to be used. Such a bolt could only be designed by departing from the barrel-mounted spring and associated heavy yoke of the Oerlikon, so a change was made to a spring mounted behind the bolt, ironically similar to the original Becker patent. A consequence of the short barrel was a vivid muzzle flash, so the barrel usually came fitted with a long tubular flash hider, which varied in length according to installation requirements.

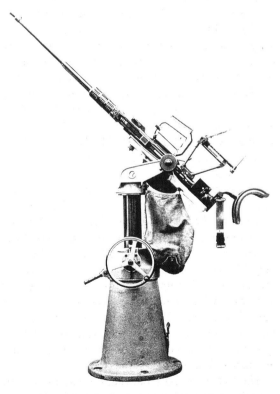

*Oerlikon S on Sockellafette*
*(Courtesy: Verlag Stocker-Schmid, Dietikon-Zurich)*

*Rear of 40mm Ho-301 round with baseplate removed: note small propellant chamber and gas exhaust holes in rear plate (Courtesy: MoD Pattern Room)*

*40mm caseless projectile for Ho-301 (next to 12.7 × 108 for scale) (Courtesy: MoD Pattern Room)*

It is sometimes claimed that the Imperial Japanese Navy's 30mm Type 2 was a copy of the MK 108, but despite some similarities in the ammunition shape they have little in common. The Type 2, which seems to have been developed some time before the MK 108, is simply a scaled-up 20mm Oerlikon with the usual front-mounted recoil spring. It has a much longer barrel than the MK 108, which accounts for both its higher muzzle velocity and its necessarily lower rate of fire. If there is any relationship between the two weapons, it seems more likely that the Germans took the Japanese gun as a starting point for the development of the MK 108, altering the design to sacrifice muzzle velocity in order to achieve a higher rate of fire.

The 40mm Ho-301 was unique, in that the propelling charge was contained within the base of the projectile rather than in a separate cartridge case. This was not a new idea, having been tried in the American Volcanic repeating rifle of the mid-nineteenth century, but it was (as far as this author is aware) the only modern military application to see service.

In appearance the Ho-301's cartridge resembled a small finless rocket, but it differed in principle in that the charge (expelled through twelve 3.8mm diameter holes in the base of the projectile, surrounding the primer) burned out within the barrel, generating a recoil thrust to drive the blowback mechanism. The projectile was 13.5cm long, of which the rear 3cm was devoted to propellant. However, the gun was not successful and saw little use.

Despite the continuing use of Oerlikon S guns for decades afterwards, the API blowback line of development was not continued for very long after the war, the last member of the family being the Oerlikon 5ILA/IISS of 1948. As we have seen, the design has a limited rate of fire and the muzzle velocity has to be kept relatively low because the unlocked breech restricts the maximum chamber pressure. The API principle's sensitivity to ammunition type also limits its flexibility. All other postwar heavy automatic weapons to see service have therefore reverted to some form of locked-breech design. However, the simplicity of the system has its attractions for less demanding applications and it is a common method of operation for the various light automatic grenade launchers which have emerged in recent decades.

## GAS-OPERATED GUNS: LINEAR MECHANISMS

A FEW YEARS AFTER MAXIM INTRODUCED THE short-recoil gun, John Browning invented a different principle of operation for his first machine gun. After observing that the propellant gases escaping from the muzzle still had considerable force, he devised a simple mechanism to trap some of the gas and use it to drive the loading cycle. In his first practical machine gun, the gas was tapped from the barrel before the projectile left the muzzle. A prototype was sold to Colt by 1890 and the gun was adopted by the US Navy in 1895. The inventor cannot have been entirely satisfied for, as we have seen, most later Browning machine guns and cannon used recoil mechanisms.

In principle, gas-operated linear-action machine guns have worked in the same way ever since. There are variations in how far up the barrel the gas port is sited, and in whether the gas drives a piston which is connected to the action or drives the action directly, but these are detailed refinements. The only significant variation is the nature of the mechanism the gas is driving: linear, revolver or rotary. Gas-operated weapons were exclusively linear until the invention of the revolver cannon, which did not see service until after the Second World War. Gas-operated rotary cannon are even more recent.

Gas-operated linear-actions have proved particularly popular in small arms, three of the most famous examples from the first half of the century being the Lewis gun, the Browning automatic rifle (BAR) and the Bren gun. The vast majority of the current generation of assault rifles are gas-operated, as are most light machine guns. Gas operation has two advantages over recoil: as the barrel remains fixed to the weapon, it is more likely to be accurate; and it is easy to regulate the amount of gas operating the mechanism in order to ensure that the weapon functions properly regardless of climatic or ammunition variations. The exact means of locking the bolt to the barrel has as many variations as recoil-operated guns, with rotary bolts, lifting locking pieces and tilting or sliding breechblocks all being employed.

In heavy automatic weapons gas operation has constantly rivalled the recoil type. During the inter-war period, the French Hotchkiss in 13.2mm and 25mm, and Italian Breda M31 in 13.2mm and M35 in 20mm, were among the earliest examples. The Soviet 12.7mm DShK (*Degtyarev-Shpagin Krupnokalibernyi*; heavy-calibre gun designed by Degtyarev and Shpagin) and 20mm ShVAK (*Shpitalnyi-Vladimirova Aviatsionnaya Krupnokalibernaya*; heavy-calibre aircraft gun designed by Shpitalnyi and Vladimirov) followed in the late 1930s. The 12.7mm UB (*Universalnyi Berezina*; general-purpose gun designed by Beresin) also incorporated gas operation in a mechanism reportedly inspired by the 20mm Lahti cannon, captured during the Winter War with Finland, and the later 23mm VYa (*Volkov-Yartsev*, named after the designers) uses the same system.

The two Soviet 12.7mm guns were direct equivalents of the .50″ Browning, the DShK being intended for army use while the UB was an aircraft gun. Both fired a 12.7 × 108 cartridge. Ballistic performance was virtually identical to the Browning, but the UB in particular was both lighter and faster-firing than comparable weapons of other nations. The UB replaced the earlier and little-used ShVAK, designed around a quite different 12.7 × 108R cartridge, which later achieved success when enlarged to 20mm calibre. The UB was available in three versions: the UBK wing gun, the UBS for synchronisation and the UBT for fitting into turrets.

The Soviet ShVAK was a light, reasonably short and fast-firing gas-operated gun firing a rather old-fashioned, straight-cased, rimmed and percussion-primed 20 × 99R cartridge of modest power. In 1944 the ShVAK was replaced in production by the B-20 (designed by Beresin), which used the same ammunition and had the same performance but weighed only 25kg.

The Czech Brno firm used gas operation in their 15mm ZB vz 60 (produced in Britain as the Besa). Wartime Germany saw the development of the Rheinmetall-Borsig 3.7cm FlaK 43, as well as the unsuccessful 5cm FlaK 41 and the experimental 5.5cm FlaK 58 by the same firm.

Post-war, gas operation has featured in several linear guns in which a high rate of fire combined with light weight is required. These include two

*Gas operation* *(Courtesy: D.F. Allsop)*

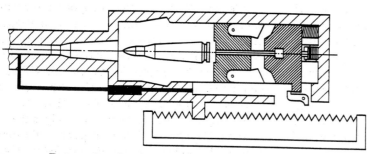

The cannon is ready to fire, the bolt is retained by the sear and the return spring is compressed. A cartridge is ready to be fed into the chamber

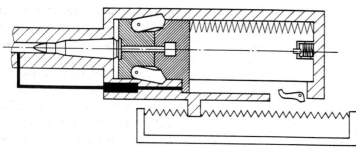

The trigger is released and the bolt feeds a cartridge into the chamber. The breech bolt locks to the barrel, the firing pin strikes the primer and the cartridge is fired

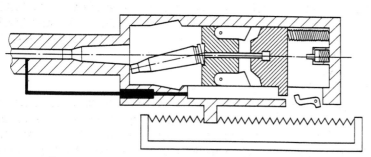

After the projectile passes the gas port, the gas piston unlocks the breech block from the barrel. Residual gas pressure accelerates the breech block after the bolt has unlocked. The empty cartridge case is extracted and ejected

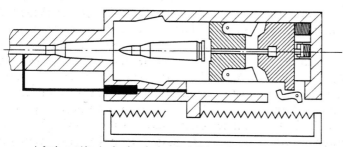

A fresh cartridge is chambered when the bolt is pushed forward by the breech block return spring

HMGs – the Soviet 12.7mm NSV (*Nikitin-Sokolov-Volkov*, named after the designers) and the CIS 50MG (Chartered Industries of Singapore) – Soviet aircraft cannon such as the NR-23 (*Nudelman-Rikhter*, the designers), NR-30 and N-37, and several light AA guns: the Soviet 23mm ZU, French 20mm GIAT M621 and M693, and various Oerlikon and Mauser models. However, for reasons explained later it is arguable whether many of the modern guns should be described as gas-operated or gas/blowback hybrids.

The ZU-23 (*Zenitnaya Ustanovka*, or AA system) uses a vertically sliding breechblock combined with a separate cartridge rammer and extractor, all powered by gun gas. It uses a version of the 23 × 152B cartridge which first emerged in the wartime VYa aircraft cannon, but with steel rather than brass cases, a belt of a slightly different shape and a different primer.

The French firm GIAT (*Groupement Industriel des Armements Terrestres*) has produced the 20mm 20M693 using the percussion-primed 20 × 139 cartridge. It is available with dual belt feed and, like many modern AA cannon, has a floating firing mounting to reduce recoil.

The Oerlikon KAA, KBA, KBB and most of the big 35mm KD series are all gas-operated, albeit with a variety of approaches to locking the bolt and with blowback assistance to aid extraction. Incidentally, the Oerlikon designation system has been quite logical: the first letter – K – stands for *Kanone*; the second stands for the calibre – A = 20mm, B = 25mm, C = 30mm and D = 35mm; and the third indicates the model of gun. The 35/1000 revolver cannon, described later, has broken away from this pattern.

The KAA of the 1950s, initially known as the 204GK (for *Gurt-Kanone*, or belt-fed cannon) introduced a new 20 × 128 percussion-primed cartridge and uses pivoting bolt locks. It is most commonly used in the AA role. The KBA emerged from American developments in the 1960s by TRW (Thomson, Ramo-Wooldridge), which resulted in the experimental TRW 6425, using a rotating bolt-head lock. Oerlikon took over and modified the design into the KBA, using a powerful new 25 × 137 cartridge in a compact, dual-feed gun. This cartridge has become a NATO standard and is

effectively regarded as a higher-powered replacement for the 20mm, although weapons in the latter calibre remain in production and widespread use. The 25 × 137 has become available in a wide variety of weapons with every conceivable use in all three services. More recently, the powerful KBB has been developed, based on a 25 × 184 cartridge which is a lengthened version of the 25 × 137.

The largest of the gas-operated family is the big Oerlikon KD series (with the exception of the long-recoil KDE), which is effectively a scaled-up KAA based around the very powerful 35 × 228 cartridge. It combines the usual features of the modern series including floating firing and selective ammunition supply, which in this case can be via belts or a linkless feed system.

It should be noted that the full range of Oerlikon cannon is more complex than is indicated here, with many sub-types developed for specific applications.

Mauser has produced a range of guns based on a mechanism which uses gun gas not just to power the firing cycle but also to drive the ammunition feed, which may be linkless or via a disintegrating belt. Three calibres have been offered – the MK20 (20 × 139), MK25 Mod E (25 × 137) and MK30 Mod F (30 × 173) – of which the largest has so far been the most successful.

## THE HYBRIDS

MANY AUTOMATIC CANNON COMBINE ELEMENTS OF more than one operating system in their design. Probably the most common of these are the gas/blowback hybrids, typified by the famous Hispano-Suiza HS 404 aircraft gun.

It should be explained at this point that Hispano-Suiza was a rather complex organisation, with (at least) semi-independent branches in France, Switzerland, Spain and (later) the UK: the British Manufacturing and Research Company (BMARCO) was established in the late 1930s to manufacture the HS 404. Post-war, the Swiss and French branches were sometimes in competition with each other, offering separate products.

The 20mm HS 404 was developed by the French branch during the 1930s by a Swiss, Marc Birkigt, in order to improve upon the unsatisfactory rate of fire of the Oerlikon FFS guns which Hispano-Suiza was then making under licence. It is a linear-action

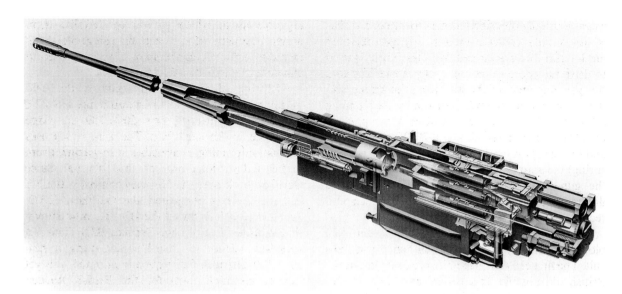

*25mm Oerlikon KBB sectioned* (*Courtesy: Ian Hogg*)

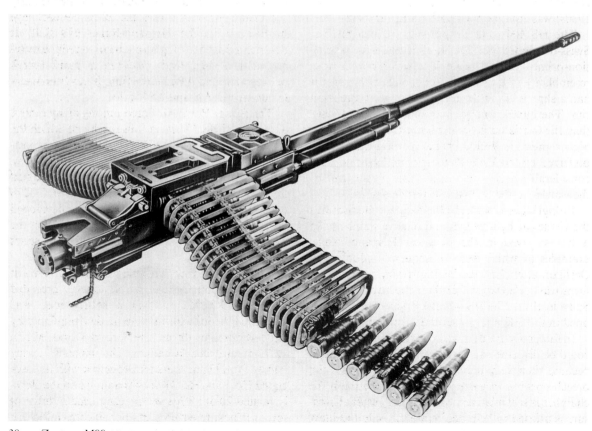

*30mm Zastava M89* (*Courtesy: Ian Hogg*)

weapon usually described as gas-operated, but that is not strictly correct. In a purely gas-operated mechanism, the gas tapped from the barrel is used to drive the entire reloading cycle; in the Hispano, this gas only unlocks the bolt from the breech and the remainder of the cycle is driven by the recoiling cartridge case, just as in a blowback weapon. In fact, the entire gun recoils about 20–25mm on firing and this energy is used to drive (via an intermediary spring) the ammunition feed in belt-fed versions, so the gun system incorporates elements of three different operating principles: gas, blowback and recoil.

One consequence of the similarity to the API blowbacks is that case extraction can prove difficult. The first HS 404s used oiled cartridges, but the British did not like this system and were able to design a cartridge case which did not need oiling. Most guns of this type now have fluted chambers, so it is surprising that the USN's Mk 16 (a modified HS 404 on a naval mounting, still in service in the 1980s) was equipped with a built-in cartridge oiler.

The HS 404 (and its post-war refinement, the Swiss-developed HS 804) fired a powerful percussion-primed $20 \times 110$ cartridge which bore a close resemblance to that of the Oerlikon S except that it had a sharper shoulder and did not have a rebated rim. The muzzle energy was some 15–20% higher than the Oerlikon, probably because it could accept higher pressure limits. Initially, ball rounds were preferred by the RAF as these were found to have considerable destructive effect, but by the end of the war HE/I and AP/I shells were standard.

Birkigt's gas-unlocked blowback mechanism has the virtues of light weight and relative simplicity so it has survived in the post-war Hispano range, examples of which were subsequently adopted by Oerlikon after the long-lasting rivalry between the firms was ended when Oerlikon absorbed Hispano-Suiza in 1971. The HS 404 itself was further developed in the UK and, in several forms, in the USA.

In fact, most modern gas-operated linear cannon could be described as gas/blowback hybrids. This is because their very high firing rates necessitate the breech opening very early, while gas pressure in the chamber is still relatively high, so this residual pressure is utilised to help accelerate the bolt and blow the fired case out of the chamber. It is therefore arguable as to which section to describe them under. As with other weapons using blowback extraction, fluted chambers are commonly used to ensure that the fired cases do not stick.

The first of the post-war guns in the field in 20mm calibre was the Hispano-Suiza HS 820, based on a powerful new $20 \times 139$ cartridge developed in the late 1940s. The gun, which uses percussion priming, is available in magazine, drum or belt-fed versions, but belt feed is usual. Since Oerlikon took over the Hispano company, the HS 820 has been redesignated the Oerlikon KAD. Hispano next introduced the HS 831, now known (in a modified form) as the Oerlikon KCB. This is a scaled-up version of the HS 820 using a new $30 \times 170$ cartridge (subsequently adopted in a yet further modified form for the British Rarden cannon).

The Hispano/Oerlikon family has not been the only one to use a gas-unlocked blowback mechanism. The Rheinmetall Rh202 is a particularly successful gun which uses the $20 \times 139$ cartridge introduced in the Hispano-Suiza HS 820. It features a floating firing mechanism to reduce recoil and a dual belt feed, enabling a rapid switch between HE and AP ammunition. It has been widely adopted in AA and AFV roles.

The British Royal Air Force, among many others, adopted the HS 404 in various marks, of which the most common were the Mk II and the (mainly post-war) Mk V. The HS 404 was also made in the USA, initially as the 20mm AN-M1/M2 and in modified form post-war as the M3 (percussion) and M24 (electric ignition). The design was further developed into the Mk 12 naval cannon, chambered for the more powerful $20 \times 110$ USN or Mk 100 series round.

The gas/blowback principle was also featured in the Italian Scotti system (which actually preceded the HS 404), except that a rotary lock was employed. Scotti designs were made (frequently by Isotta-Fraschini) during the Second World War in 12.7mm and 20mm calibre. The Japanese Army 20mm Type 97 anti-tank gun, together with its associated Ho-1 and Ho-3 aircraft cannon and the closely related 20mm Type 98 AA gun, used a different form of lock, in which a gas piston cams a locking piece down, leaving the breechblock to recoil.

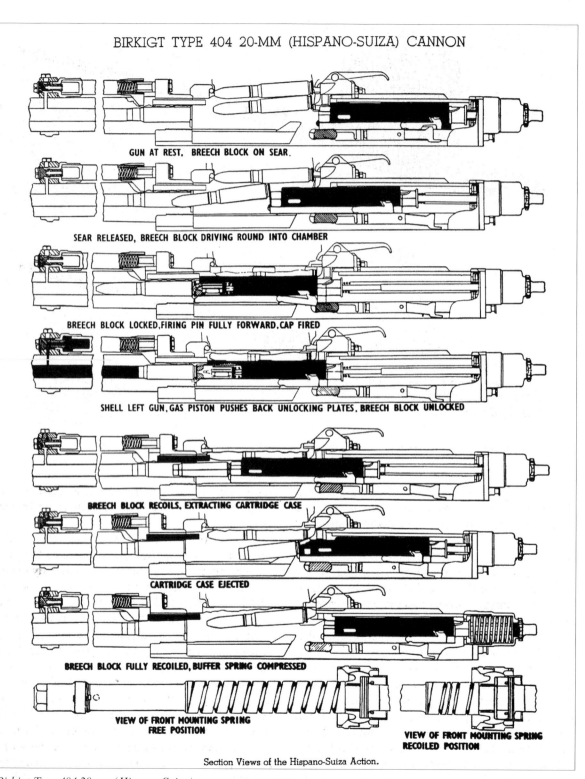

## BIRKIGT TYPE 404 20-MM (HISPANO-SUIZA) CANNON

GUN AT REST, BREECH BLOCK ON SEAR.

SEAR RELEASED, BREECH BLOCK DRIVING ROUND INTO CHAMBER

BREECH BLOCK LOCKED, FIRING PIN FULLY FORWARD, CAP FIRED

SHELL LEFT GUN, GAS PISTON PUSHES BACK UNLOCKING PLATES, BREECH BLOCK UNLOCKED

BREECH BLOCK RECOILS, EXTRACTING CARTRIDGE CASE

CARTRIDGE CASE EJECTED

BREECH BLOCK FULLY RECOILED, BUFFER SPRING COMPRESSED

VIEW OF FRONT MOUNTING SPRING
FREE POSITION

VIEW OF FRONT MOUNTING SPRING
RECOILED POSITION

Section Views of the Hispano-Suiza Action.

*Birkigt Type 404 20mm (Hispano-Suiza) cannon* (BuOrd, USN)

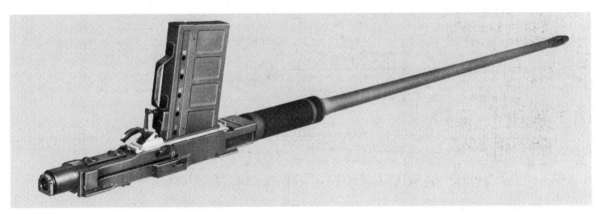

*20mm HS 820/Oerlikon KAD: top = 50-round drum, bottom = 10-round box (Courtesy: Oerlikon/Ian Hogg)*

The French GIAT 20M621 is a modern lightweight gas/blowback gun based on the American electrically primed 20 × 102 round.

Not all hybrids have used gas pressure to unlock the bolt; it is equally possible for a delayed blowback weapon to use recoil unlocking. These are much more difficult to distinguish from short-recoil mechanisms, however, as the initial rearward movement of the barrel gives some impulse to the bolt before unlocking occurs and blowback takes over. The distinction is that in a short-recoil gun, the principal driving force is the momentum of the bolt assembly, which therefore needs to be reasonably heavy. In a recoil/blowback hybrid, the principal driving force is blowback, so the bolt can – and, indeed, needs to be – as light as possible. In practice, the difference between short-recoil and recoil-unlocked blowback is one of degree rather than kind and is related to the rate of fire.

As the bolt is lightened in order to increase the firing rate, blowback becomes steadily more important.

These hybrids can achieve higher rates of fire than other linear mechanisms, due to the fact that the maximum potential rate of fire is directly linked to bolt speed, which in turn depends on bolt weight, and delayed blowbacks can utilise the smallest and lightest bolts. This is because they neither need much momentum nor carry the additional weight of a gas piston assembly. Of the types of hybrid, the short-recoil/blowback has the potential for the fastest rate of all, partly because the initial barrel movement gives the bolt a 'flying start', partly because the design lends itself to the use of a bolt accelerator to give a further impulse to the bolt. There is another incidental advantage of the short-recoil type: it is easier to engineer the design so that the bolt is pulled slightly away from the breech face during the initial barrel movement, providing some positive initial extraction and reducing the risk of sticking cases.

These advantages may well explain why the Russians adopted recoil-operation for the remarkable GSh-301 aircraft cannon, which has such a high rate of fire for a single-chamber gun (1,500–1,800 rpm) that blowback forms an important element of its operating cycle. Gas pressure remaining in the barrel when the breech is opened is so high that the fired cartridge case is ejected at a 'breech velocity' of 100 m/s. A 'return accelerator' is also used to return the breechblock as quickly as possible. The barrel is somewhat shorter than that of most of the Russian 30mm guns, in order to permit the quickest possible breech-opening time.

Not all hybrids have relied on blowback. One of the notable exceptions was the Rheinmetall-Borsig MK 103 aircraft gun, in which barrel recoil operated the belt feed and initiated bolt motion, while a conventional gas system unlocked and accelerated the bolt. A primary concern of the designers appeared to be to ensure that the bolt did not unlock too early, so unlocking was delayed until the chamber pressure had dropped to the point at which blowback was not a dominant feature. It seems that the main reason for the barrel recoil was to absorb the recoil pulses without the necessity of allowing the whole gun to recoil in its mounting. The designers then presumably reasoned that the recoil movement might as well be put to good use. This is an interesting example of the difficulties that can exist when trying to place gun mechanisms into neat categories.

More recently, the Russians developed the 2A42 AFV/helicopter cannon which first emerged in the early 1980s in 30 × 165 calibre. It is perhaps surprising that it is not externally powered, given the modest rate of fire requirements, but it is quoted as using a mixture of gas operation and barrel recoil in the design.

Hybrid power sources can relate to the ammunition feed as well as the gun action. Externally powered ammunition feeds are normally associated with externally powered guns, but there have been rare exceptions, e.g. the GZ 1–FF electrically driven belt feed for the MG-FF API blowback cannon.

## REVOLVER CANNON

GAS OPERATION IS USUALLY THE MOTIVE FORCE for revolver cannon. The first practical example of these was invented in Germany towards the end of the Second World War by Anton Politzer of Mauser, who were seeking to improve the rate of fire of aircraft cannon. The main limiting factor was the length of time it took for the fired case to be removed and a fresh cartridge inserted into the chamber.

Politzer conceived the idea of achieving this movement in several stages rather than all at once, thereby effectively slowing down the process without slowing the rate of fire. He did this by designing a rotating cylinder, with its axis parallel to the barrel, which contains several chambers, just like a giant revolver handgun. With each shot, the cylinder is rotated to move the next chamber in line with the barrel. As it rotates, so the fired case is extracted and a live round loaded, in gradual stages – how gradual depending on the number of chambers, originally five but varying between four and seven in current weapons. The original design provided for blowback extraction, but this was soon replaced by mechanical means.

An obvious problem is the loss of propellant gas through the gap between the cylinder and the barrel. This is usually overcome by fitting each chamber with a sliding sleeve which bridges the gap at the instant of firing, forming a gas-tight seal, or by pressing the cylinder against the rear of the barrel. A further alternative is to make the cylinder shorter than the cartridge, so that the cartridge case extends into the barrel, sealing the gap. Another difficulty is that unless the mechanism is externally driven (normally gun gas is used) there has to be some means of starting the process. Special pyrotechnic cartridges are often used to generate the gas to initiate the cycle.

The Mauser guns, the MG 213C in 20mm and the MK 213/30 in 30mm, were at an advanced stage of development by the end of the war and inspired the subsequent development of the principle. Politzer and other members of the Mauser team went to various western firms to continue their work; it took the Soviet Union years to catch up. The best known of the revolver cannon are the five-chamber British Aden and French DEFA

*Mauser MG 213/C
revolver mechanism
(BuOrd, USN)*

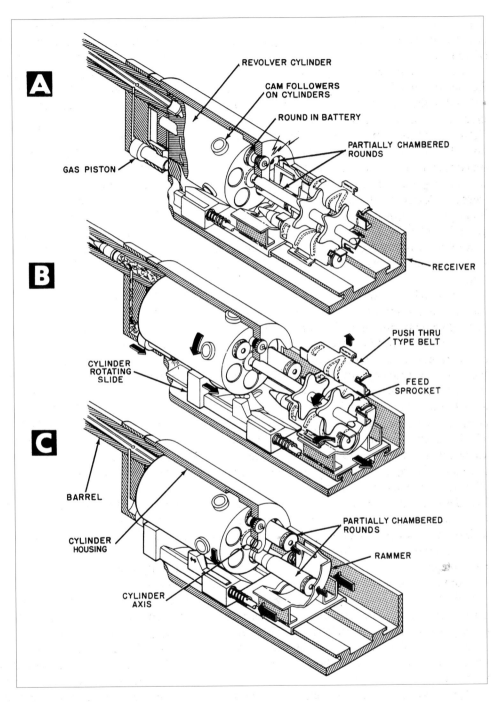

(*Direction des Etudes et Fabrication d'Armement*), now GIAT, most of which have used the same-shape 30mm ammunition. The only obvious changes have been to cartridge case length, which has grown from 85mm to around 113mm in service weapons in order to increase the muzzle velocity, although the weapon development programmes have been rather more complex than this suggests. The most recent of the GIAT series is the 30M791 which fires a much more powerful 30 × 150B

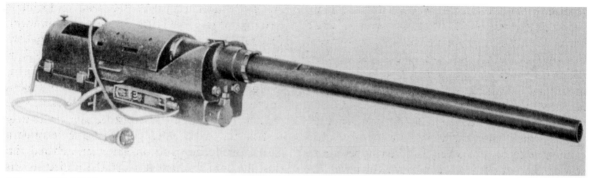

*Mauser MG 213/C (BuOrd, USN)*

cartridge, resembling a stretched 30 × 113B but different in detail. The gun achieves a very high (2,500 rpm) rate of fire by using seven chambers.

The Americans adopted the revolver principle soon after the war (in fact the idea was patented in 1905 by Charles Clarke of Philadelphia, but then forgotten), but unlike the British and French chose a 20 × 102 cartridge, later also used in their M61 rotary cannon. This led to the Pontiac M39, introduced in the early 1950s, which over thirty years later was improved to create the lightweight, faster-firing Ford Tigerclaws intended for the abortive Northrop F-20 Tigershark. Other calibres of revolver ranging up to 37mm were built but not adopted.

The Swiss Oerlikon firm, another recipient of a Mauser engineer, developed a range of revolvers commencing with the 20mm 206 RK (*Revolver Kanone*), which used an electrically primed version of their new 20 × 128 cartridge, and the 30mm 302 RK. Other variants followed, perhaps the most unusual being the abortive 42mm 421 RK AA gun developed for the UK, which featured two barrels loaded from a single seven-chamber cylinder to achieve 450 rpm. This led to the 'Red Queen' weapon which was tested secretly in the early 1950s before being abandoned.

Later versions of the Oerlikon aircraft guns differed from the original Mauser design in using four rather than five chambers. However, none was adopted for service until the massive KCA (initially developed as the 304 RK), firing the powerful 30 × 173 cartridge, was selected by Sweden in the 1970s. The 304 RK was also chosen by the USA as

a back-up in case of the failure of the GAU-8/A rotary cannon for the A-10 aircraft, slightly modified and dubbed GAU-9. In the mid-1990s Oerlikon-Contraves announced a scaled-up version of this gun: the 35mm 35/1,000.

Mauser have appropriately reclaimed their invention in the five-chamber BK 27 aircraft gun, which fires their unique 27 × 145B cartridge. Incidentally, *Mauser-Werke Oberndorf* was acquired by Rheinmetall in 1995 but continues to exist within the larger group. Rheinmetall also took over Oerlikon-Contraves in 1999.

An unusual revolver cannon was the American Mk 11 designed by Frank Marquardt, chambered for the 20 × 110 USN (Mk 100) cartridge. Like the Oerlikon 421 RK this featured two barrels, in this case fed by one eight-chamber revolver cylinder from two separate belts, with firing from both barrels simultaneously. The gun used both gas and recoil to power its operation. Prototype versions were even more peculiar as they used a unique ammunition feed system which enclosed the cartridges within linked 'projectors' (like large cartridge cases) from which the cartridges were fired into the chambers. Production versions used a more conventional belt feed. The Mk 11 was only ever used in the Mk 4 gun pod carried by various naval aircraft.

At the time of its introduction, the revolver cannon offered almost double the rate of fire of comparable linear-action weapons, i.e. around 1,200–1,400 rpm. Since then it has been doubled again, up to 2,500 rpm. This extremely high rate of fire has mainly limited the applications of the revolver cannon to aircraft, which only need to fire very short bursts. At this rate of fire, the single barrel would clearly overheat and be worn out very quickly. In recent years, however, Mauser have adapted their BK 27 to naval AA and anti-missile mountings, as in these applications there is a similar need for short bursts of intense fire, and Oerlikon now offer the 35/1,000 for the same role.

The Soviet Union has made little use of revolver cannon, with only two very different types seeing service. The best-known is a powerful naval AA weapon, the four-chamber NN-30, introduced in 1959 and firing a 30 × 210B cartridge. This has been adopted in China as the NORINCO Type 69 and was adapted by the Romanian Army as a towed AA gun, the A436. In addition there is the little-known Rikhter R-23, a 23mm aircraft gun developed in the 1950s which is unlike all other service revolvers in being front-loaded – that is, the ammunition feed arrangements are underneath the barrel and the cartridges are fed backwards into the chambers. It is a four-chamber design with fluted chambers and utilises gun gas not only for the gun action and ammunition feed but also to blow out the fired cases.

The advantage of the R-23's layout is a much shorter gun with an ammunition feed close to the centre of gravity of the weapon. This is particularly valuable in defensive turret mountings in which the gun pivots on its centre of gravity, for which the R-23 was specifically designed. This method of loading would not work with conventional ammunition, which is wider at the head than the neck, so special tubular cartridge cases about 260mm long are used, tapered towards the head to facilitate feeding and with the projectile buried within them. The need for this special ammunition may have been its downfall as the R-23 saw little use. Versions in other calibres up to 30mm are reported, but it appears that these did not see service. The experimental American T168, developed at the same time and for the same purpose, used a similar loading system; the 30 × 136RB cartridge also featured a case tapering down to an extremely rebated rim (just 17.3mm in diameter) but the projectile was exposed in the usual way. The front-loading concept has been revived and combined with recoilless operation in the new Mauser RMK 30, described in Chapter 6.

## GAS-OPERATED ROTARY CANNON

THE ROTARY CANNON IS USUALLY EXTERNALLY driven. However, Russian armament firms have developed this type of gun with gas operation, despite the problems of achieving this when the barrels are spinning round at about 1,000 rpm. The advantage, apart from not needing an external power source, is quicker acceleration to the maximum rate of fire, an important consideration in aircraft weapons. The six-barrel GSh-6-23 in 23 × 115 and the GSh-6-30 in 30 × 165 have achieved extremely high rates of fire for their calibres. The YakB-12.7 (*Yakushev-Borzov*, the designers) four-barrel rotary 12.7mm HMG for helicopter mounting also uses this system.

A self-powered version of the American M61A1 described below, the GAU-4/A, was developed in the 1960s for installations with limited available

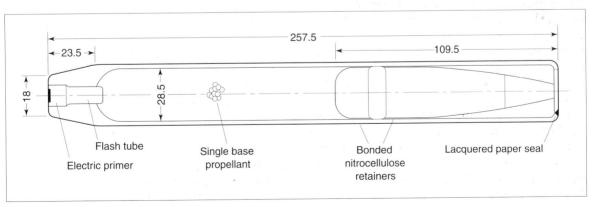

*Sectioned cartridge for Rikhter R-23* (*Courtesy: Dr J.R. Crittenden Schmitt*)

power. This version still needs an electric motor to start firing (although a powerful spring was developed as an alternative), after which gun gas takes over. It was fitted to the SUU-23/A gun pod, which also carried 1,200 rounds of ammunition.

## THE REVIVAL OF EXTERNALLY POWERED GUNS

FOR HALF A CENTURY AFTER THE DEMISE OF THE Gatlings, Gardners and Nordenfelts, the externally powered weapon disappeared from service, although some thought was given in Germany during the First World War to a gun driven by an aero-engine. The reason for this was that the most successful formula for fighter aircraft was found to be a front engine with fuselage-mounted machine guns. In order to avoid shooting the propeller away, complex engine-driven mechanisms to synchronise the firing of the guns with the rotation of the propeller were adopted. It would have been a logical progression, and in principle much simpler, to achieve this by using the engine to drive the gun. Several firms worked on prototypes, but the war ended before any saw service.

It was the demands of air fighting which led to the revival of the externally powered gun, this time driven by electricity. The first trials with coupling an electric motor to a Gatling gun actually took place much earlier than this, in experiments beginning in 1890 which eventually achieved 3,000 rpm. In the early 1930s the British considered fitting a Gatling-type gun to the Westland F.7/30 experimental fighter (which also presaged the Bell P-39 in having the cockpit between the engine and the propeller). None of this led to anything until close to the end of the Second World War, when the American 'Project Vulcan' was established.

This led to the famous M61 Vulcan rotary cannon, essentially similar to the Gatling. In 20 × 102 calibre, with six barrels and a rate of fire between 4,000 and 7,200 rpm (normally set at 6,000 rpm), this has been the USAF's standard air combat gun since the early 1960s. Guns of this type have been produced in all calibres from 5.56mm to 30mm, with between three and seven barrels. The external power source can be electric, hydraulic, pneumatic or even (in aircraft pods) from a turbine driven by the slipstream.

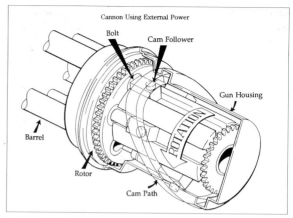

*Powered Gatling cannon rotor assembly*
(*Courtesy: D.F. Allsop*)

Current large-calibre models are the three-barrel GAU-19A in 12.7 × 99, the six-barrel M61A1 in 20 × 102 (known as the M168 in army AA service), the three-barrel M197 version in the same calibre, the five-barrel GAU-12/U in 25 × 137, seven-barrel GAU-8/A in 30 × 173 and the four-barrel GAU-13/A version also in 30 × 173. All of these normally use external power, and the demands are considerable. The M61A1 has an engine of 26 kW, the GAU-8/A requires 52 kW – enough to drive a small car at 160 km/h. In the SUU-16/A gun pod, a ram-air turbine is used to power the M61A1, a neat solution with the disadvantages of a slower spin-up time (around one second) and a rate of fire which reduces below 6,000 rpm if the airspeed drops below 650 km/h. Guns can also be powered by gas bled from the engine, a solution adopted for the GAU-12/U fitted to the AV-8B.

At least one externally powered version of the Russian rotary cannon is also available (the AO18L lightweight naval gun), but most of them are gas-operated and are described in the previous section.

Finally, Oerlikon have joined the group of rotary cannon manufacturers with the KBD, a seven-barrel gun in 25 × 184 calibre, which is intended initially for the naval CIWS (close-in weapons system) role.

There are two major advantages of the modern rotary cannon. The first (shared with the revolver mechanism) is that the cartridges are moved into and out of the chambers in gradual stages, which permits a much higher rate of fire as well as

*Gatling rotary
mechanism
(BuOrd, USN)*

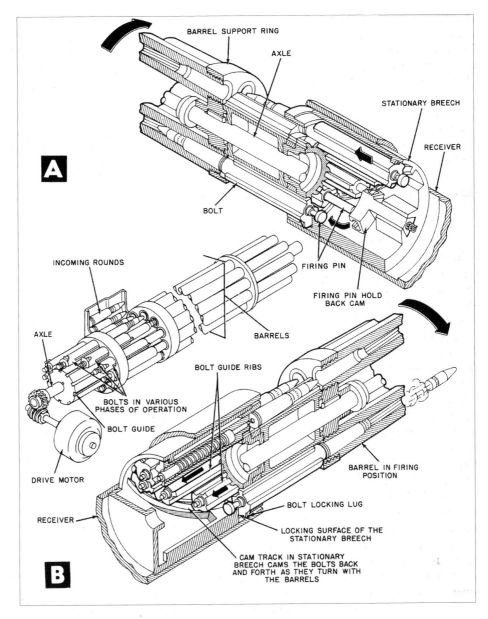

treating the ammunition to relatively gentle handling. The second is that with several barrels in use, a high rate of fire can be achieved without overstressing the barrel. As a result, rotary guns tend to be remarkably reliable for the high performance they achieve.

Another advantage shared with other externally powered mechanisms is that they operate independently of ammunition quality, pressure or recoil characteristics; if a cartridge fails to fire, the gun simply ejects it and loads the next one. Such a failure in a recoil- or gas-operated gun will normally stop the mechanism until the dud cartridge has been manually ejected, although some modern self-powered weapons have complex pyrotechnic devices to eject dud cartridges automatically. The Oerlikon KCA revolver cannon has four such charges; the Russian GSH-301 uses a small explosive charge, directed through a small hole in the chamber wall, to penetrate the cartridge case and ignite the propellant directly – a brutal but apparently effective solution.

The main disadvantage, apart from its bulk and the need for an external source of power, is that the gun takes a significant fraction of a second to speed up to its maximum rate, whereas gas-operated weapons reach peak firing rate almost instantaneously. This is important in circumstances such as air combat in which firing opportunities may be extremely brief. The latest version of the M61, the A2 selected for the F-22, has been redesigned to achieve quicker acceleration (mainly by reducing the weight of the barrels) but still takes a quarter of a second to reach maximum speed.

There is also a problem in achieving high levels of accuracy with a rotary gun, not just because of the need to align several barrels to the same point of impact (the alignment of the barrels can be adjusted), but also because the projectiles are thrown sideways by the rotary motion of the gun, to a degree which varies as the gun accelerates to its maximum rate of fire. This delays the firing of the first effective shot. Having said that, the M61 has a reputation for high accuracy once it is spinning at peak rate. Rotary cannon also make great demands upon the ammunition feed system, both in terms of the quantity required and rate at which the cartridges have to be supplied to the gun. Finally, along with other externally powered automatic cannon they are vulnerable to 'hang fires', or delayed ignition. It could clearly be disastrous if a cartridge fired after its barrel had moved from the normal firing position.

More recently still, external powering has been introduced in a range of single-barrel machine guns and cannon. Many of them are known collectively as chain guns. These are simple linear weapons, named after the chain which drives the reciprocating bolt mechanism. Unlike the Vulcan, the purpose of this design is not rate of fire but reliability, combined with the ability to vary the rate of fire depending on the tactical needs of the moment. This is particularly important in AFVs and helicopters, which might need to switch between slow, deliberate fire and a high-rate burst at short notice. Chain guns also have a very compact mechanism, a major advantage in AFVs in which turret space is always at a premium. Power demands are much lower than with rotaries: the 30mm M230 requires a motor of only 5 kW.

The chain gun concept originated in the USA and has been applied to weapons in a variety of calibres from 7.62mm upwards. The two most important large-calibre versions are the MDHC (now Boeing) M242 'Bushmaster' in 25 × 137 calibre and the MDHC M230 in 30 × 113B; the former for general AFV/naval use, the latter for helicopters. More powerful versions have been developed: the Bushmaster II, chambered for the 30 × 173 cartridge, and the Bushmaster III in 35 × 228 (with an option to upgrade to the 50 × 330 'Supershot' calibre). An interesting side-effect of external powering is its insensitivity to ammunition type. The Bushmaster II can quickly be adapted, by exchanging a few parts, to fire 30 × 170 Oerlikon (KCB) or Rarden ammunition.

Externally powered weapons have also been developed in France. GIAT offers two such weapons: the 25M811 gun in 25 × 137 and the 30M781 in 30 × 113B. In Germany, Rheinmetall developed the Rh 503 in both 35 × 228 and 50 × 330 'Supershot' calibres; development of these weapons has been taken over by Boeing as the Bushmaster III. Yet another weapon in 35 × 228 is the South African EMAK 35. As will be seen, externally powered guns are beginning to dominate the AFV and helicopter weapon fields, with the main exception of Russian equipment.

A unique application of external powering is used by the Spanish Meroka CIWS. This mounting contains twelve externally powered guns, using

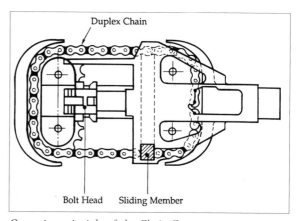

*Operating principle of the Chain Gun* (Courtesy: D.F. Allsop)

electrically primed $20 \times 128$ ammunition, which are closely packed together in two rows of six, each row with its own belt feed. Reloading utilises a combination of compressed air and the recoil of the breechblock. Each belt is moved on six places to reload. The guns fire in salvos of twelve shots, the slightly staggered firing giving a burst rate of fire of 9,000 rpm, with a pause of one-fifth of a second before the next volley. It is a modern revival of the 'volley gun' concept, made obsolete in the 1870s by the first manually driven machine guns, now using modern technology to provide an impressive performance. Its only real drawback is that its weight limits the system to naval applications.

# Chapter Three

## ARMY WEAPONS

HEAVY AUTOMATIC WEAPONS FOR GROUND FORCES have been developed to meet a varied range of threats. The first automatic cannon, introduced towards the end of the nineteenth century, were intended for anti-personnel use. By the end of the First World War, these weapons were being adapted, and new ones developed, to counter two quite different threats: aircraft and armoured fighting vehicles. In both cases, this led to an emphasis on high-velocity cartridges. Against aircraft, the main reason for this was to reduce aiming errors by minimising the time of flight. Against AFVs, the need was to increase armour penetration.

These concerns have remained dominant until quite recently, when they have been joined by a renewed interest in large-calibre, low-velocity automatic weapons for use against troops and unarmoured or lightly armoured vehicles.

In a form of parallel evolution, automatic cannon proper have occasionally been supplemented by shoulder-fired weapons, often firing the same ammunition and sometimes capable of fully automatic fire, which are described in Appendix 1.

### THE 'POM-POM'

THE EARLY HISTORY OF THE HEAVY AUTOMATIC weapon has already been related. To recap, the first of these weapons intended for army use was the Hotchkiss rotary cannon, but this was far more successful as a naval gun. The 37mm Maxim, which effectively superseded the Hotchkiss two decades later, was much more compact and saw land service (most notably in the Boer War), mounted on a typical large-wheeled carriage. Despite this, by the

*Vickers-Maxim 1-Pounder 'Pom-pom'* (Courtesy: R.W. Clarke)

First World War the 'Pom-pom', as it became known because of the rhythmical firing rate, had largely fallen out of fashion.

The reason for the automatic cannon's decline was the dramatic improvement made in light artillery at the turn of the century. Field guns became much faster-firing and more effective. The most famous of these was the French '75', named after its 75mm calibre, but other nations had their equivalents. The British introduced the thirteen-pounder and eighteen-pounder guns, the former still used ceremonially by the King's Troop, Royal Horse Artillery, for firing salutes in St James's Park on royal occasions.

These new field guns combined a fixed cartridge for rapid handling with breech mechanisms designed for quick reloading, and recoil control systems which kept the gun pointing at the target without the need for re-laying after each shot. The result was a dramatic increase in the rate of accurate fire, up to 25 rpm. Combined with the shrapnel shell,

*37mm Maxim 'Pom-pom' on improvised AA mounting*
*(Courtesy: Verlag Stocker-Schmid, Dietikon-Zurich)*

which contained a time fuze which could be set to burst the shell just before reaching the target, showering the area with lethal balls, the new guns were devastatingly effective against troops caught in the open. The guns were also just as easy to manoeuvre as the Pom-poms and had a much longer range, so they could engage and destroy a Maxim battery with impunity.

What saved the Pom-pom from obscurity was a sudden and urgent need to fire at aircraft from the ground. All manner of light artillery were adapted to high-angle mountings but the Pom-pom (known in British service as the one-pounder or 1pdr, after its projectile weight) had the huge advantage of a high rate of fire which made it feasible to engage low-flying aircraft crossing at relatively high speed. The first installation of a Pom-pom into a high-angle mounting for AA fire was actually approved for the British Army before the First World War, in February 1914.

These advantages also prompted the development of a larger version, the 40mm 2pdr for the Royal Navy. As is usual in any extended war, good ideas spread and the 'naval' 2pdr found itself pressed into land service, including mounting on railway trucks.

As well as pressing their Pom-poms into AA service, the Germans developed a version using a unique 37 × 101SR cartridge, the *Sockelflak*, which was intended as a Zeppelin defensive weapon but saw more use in the AA role.

## LESSONS OF THE FIRST WORLD WAR

THE GREAT WAR, AMONG MANY OTHER LESSONS, emphasised the need to provide various kinds of anti-aircraft fire. These ranged from high-velocity large-calibre cannon for engaging high-flying bombers, to light machine guns on mountings which permitted high-angle fire in order to provide a last-ditch defence against low-flying strafing fighters. To these problems was added a new threat: the tank.

It was soon realised that the design of weapons to deal with aircraft and tanks had certain similarities. Above all, they both needed a high muzzle velocity, although for different reasons. The four-dimensional problem of engaging aircraft (estimating altitude and speed as well as range and direction) was greatly simplified by the shortest possible time of flight of the projectiles. In dealing with tanks, a high impact velocity was needed to ensure penetration of the armour, with the added benefit of providing a flatter trajectory to minimise aiming errors. In both cases, a projectile weighing significantly more than that of the standard infantry cartridge was desirable to achieve the necessary destructive effect. These priorities combined to produce both the heavy machine gun (HMG) and the anti-tank rifle (ATR).

First in the field were the Germans, with a weapon which set a trend which continues to this day: the 13mm MG TuF, for *Tank und Flieger*, the intended targets. (There is an alternative view that this designation referred to the TuF being fitted to tanks and aircraft and there is one report of a Fokker D.VII being experimentally equipped with this gun. However, the only published photograph shows one on a wheeled carriage, and the water-cooled barrel does not indicate aircraft use.) This was a Maxim-type gun, essentially a scaled-up version of the infantry's 7.92mm MG08. While there had been various pre-war experiments with large-calibre machine guns such as the .50″ Colt-Kynoch (or North), the TuF was the original heavy machine gun in the modern idiom, and although it was developed too late to see service in the war (about fifty were built) all current HMGs owe something to this gun. Also under development at the end of the First World War was the Browning HMG, a gun which survives in service with many nations to this day.

A separate line of development came from the need to produce a hard-hitting, but still compact and lightweight, weapon for aircraft. Once again it was German firms who led the way with the development of the first 20mm cannon, the Becker. It was mainly used, as intended, as a defensive weapon in aircraft, but some of the small number of Beckers which saw service in 1918 were issued to the army for anti-aircraft and possibly anti-tank purposes, although their low muzzle velocity must have made them of dubious value. They were also considered for arming the A7V tank, but rejected as unreliable.

## THE INTER-WAR AND WARTIME HEAVY MACHINE GUNS

AFTER THE GREAT WAR, VARIOUS NATIONS examined the MG TuF with interest and started to develop their own ideas about this type of weapon. The first tanks were proof only against rifle-calibre ammunition (and barely so at that). While armour was later improved, it was in most cases to counter steel-cored armour-piercing ammunition, still in the standard rifle calibres. Most early armoured fighting vehicles were therefore vulnerable to the new breed of HMGs in 12.7mm (0.5″) calibre, which typically fired projectiles weighing three to four times as much as rifle-calibre weapons at a similar muzzle velocity.

Despite this, few of the HMGs were introduced with a specifically anti-tank role. The reason is not too difficult to discover. While shooting at aircraft requires a high-angle mounting and weapons with a high rate of fire and large magazine capacity, these are unnecessary to deal with tanks. They are much easier targets, and tank crews will often be disabled (or at least discouraged) by only one penetrating shot as it bounces round inside the vehicle.

While some HMGs and light automatic cannon had a secondary anti-tank role, they were therefore generally designed for anti-aircraft use. Inter-war emphasis on anti-tank developments followed two main routes: conventional small artillery pieces, usually in 37–47mm calibre, and AT rifles for the use of infantry. Some of the latter not only used the same ammunition as HMGs or automatic cannon, but also used the same mechanisms together with

*Swiss 12.7mm MG 64 (.50″ Browning M2HB) on AFV mounting (Courtesy: Verlag Stocker-Schmid, Dietikon-Zurich)*

their capacity for automatic fire. These are strictly outside the scope of this narrative but are described in Appendix 1.

One of the first of the post-war HMGs was the classic .50″ Browning. The final design of the cartridge was influenced by the 13 × 92SR TuF round, although it was different in appearance, being longer, fully rimless and with a slightly smaller calibre, as indicated by its metric designation of 12.7 × 99. It is a simple and reliable weapon firing an effective cartridge which, coupled with its wide distribution to American allies, accounts for its longevity. Initial M1921 versions were water-cooled, but the air-cooled M2HB version (introduced in 1933) rapidly became more popular in army service. These were usually tripod-mounted (or pintle- or ring-mounted on vehicles) but the power-operated quadruple M45 mounting was also fielded on the M51 four-wheeled carriage, the M55 two-wheeled trailer designed for air transportation and on the M16 half-track.

The British also produced HMGs of various types, although only one saw British service. This was the Vickers .5″, designed round a smaller cartridge than that of the Browning and accordingly lighter and more compact. Initial experiments during the First World War with a .600/.500 round, originally based rather bizarrely on the rimmed .600 elephant gun cartridge, led to a version with a belted case used in the experimental Godsal AT rifle, and ultimately to the rimless 12.7 × 81 which was adopted for service. The cartridge was significantly less powerful than the .50″ Browning but still had three times the hitting power of the .303″ round used in other Vickers machine guns.

Although the .5″ Vickers was rejected by the RAF, it was used as a close-range AA gun by the Royal Navy. The army only appear to have used it as the armament of some small AFVs, among them the original A11 Matilda 1 infantry tank, the Mk VI light tank and some armoured cars. It was replaced in this role by the 15mm Besa.

Vickers also produced a semi-rimmed version of the 12.7 × 81 for export purposes. This was adopted by several countries including Italy and Japan for air service weapons, so will be dealt with in the

*Soviet 12.7mm DShk-38 on wheeled carriage with gun shield (Courtesy: MoD Pattern Room)*

*Soviet 12.7mm DShK-38 on tripod mounting (Courtesy: MoD Pattern Room)*

*Czech 15mm ZBvz/60 on ground mounting*

appropriate chapter. Much more impressive was the .5" Class D High Velocity, using a powerful 12.7 × 120SR cartridge, which appears only to have been acquired by Japan and possibly China, to whom ammunition was supplied by Kynoch. All of these Vickers guns had the characteristic large-diameter water-cooling jacket, except for the experimental air service versions.

After experimenting with a 12.7 × 108R rimmed cartridge, the Soviets settled on a rimless 12.7 × 108 round for their standard wartime HMG, the DShK-38. Although the cartridge is slightly larger than the Browning's, the performance is very similar. The DShK is a direct equivalent for the Browning M2HB, the main difference being its gas-operated mechanism, based on that of the Degtyarev rifle calibre machine gun. It has only ever been air-cooled, with a distinctive finned barrel to assist cooling. The gun is a little lighter and more compact than the Browning, but that advantage was wasted by the heavy wheeled carriage, usually seen with an armoured shield. It was belt-fed, but with fifty-round belts which could not be linked together.

As well as its use as an infantry weapon, the DShK (in its post-war DShK-38/46 version) was until recently commonly fitted to the turret tops of tanks in order to give the commander some local defence against air attack. Post-war, its widespread distribution around the world to allies and sympathisers of the Soviet regime have made it the only rival to the .50" Browning as the world's most popular HMG.

Other nations also produced HMGs. In the late 1930s the Czech armament industry developed the ZB vz/60 (*Zbrojovka Brno vzor 60*, the name of the factory in Brno and the model number), which used a powerful 15 × 104 cartridge. The big ZB was used as an AA weapon by Czechoslovakia and Yugoslavia and taken over in quantity by Germany, who shortened the case to 101mm in order to accept the longer projectiles from the MG151 aircraft gun ammunition. It was also adopted by the UK, as the 15mm Besa, to replace the .5" Vickers, but was never popular as its size made it difficult to handle in the cramped and unpowered turrets of the light tanks and armoured cars which used it. Some thought was given to converting it to use 20mm Hispano ammunition (the diameter of the cartridge case was the same), but this did not succeed.

The French conducted a wide range of experiments between the wars in order to develop an HMG. Unlike other nations, a variety of different calibres was tried, leading to such cartridges as the 9 × 66, 10 × 71 and 13.5 × 97. The only outcome

*Italian 13.2mm Breda Model 1931 (BuOrd, USN)*

in terms of service was the 13.2 × 99 Hotchkiss of 1930, which was identical to the 12.7 × 99 Browning except for the slightly larger calibre (versions with slightly shorter case necks to accommodate different projectiles were also produced). As one might expect, bullet weight was slightly higher at around 52g, muzzle velocity a little lower at 790 m/s.

The Hotchkiss HMG was, however, a completely different design from the Browning, being gas-operated. Like the DShK-38 it utilised a finned, air-cooled barrel, but most unusually for an HMG it normally fired from a thirty-round box magazine mounted above the gun. The Hotchkiss was available on various mountings including a wheeled carriage and a complex AA mounting for one or two guns. Apart from France, it was used by Japan, Poland, Romania, Yugoslavia and Greece.

The Italians also used the 13.2mm Hotchkiss cartridge but in a gun of their own design, the Breda Model 31. This was intended for mounting in AFVs, which makes even more surprising the fact that it was designed for a twenty-round vertical box magazine, which might have been expected to foul the roof of a turret. It does not appear to have been very popular. Another 13.2mm AFV weapon was

the Finnish Lahti L-35, about which little information appears to have survived, other than it saw service in the Winter War.

Japan adopted and adapted a wide variety of HMGs, mostly for aircraft purposes, with only the navy using HMGs (the 13.2mm Hotchkiss) in the AA role. Germany made use of various captured HMGs for AA purposes and towards the end of the war mounted the MG 151 aircraft gun in a triple mounting on a half-track carrier. However, there were no HMGs designed specifically for the army, the Germans reckoning quite correctly that the 20mm cannon was a much better weapon for AA use and as a light AFV weapon.

## AUTOMATIC CANNON: THE 20MM GUNS

THE EVOLUTION OF AUTOMATIC CANNON (THAT IS, of calibres between 20mm and 40mm) between the wars can generally be characterised as a long period of casual development until the late 1930s, followed by a frantic rush to re-equip for the impending conflict.

As with HMGs, automatic cannon did not find much favour in the anti-armour role, being reserved almost entirely for aircraft or anti-aircraft purposes. There were some exceptions, however. Some of them were intended as anti-tank weapons but carried by aircraft, so they will be dealt with elsewhere. Others were given a dual role, which basically meant developing armour-piercing ammunition so that AA cannon could defend themselves. Only Germany made extensive use of automatic cannon as the main armament of light armoured fighting vehicles, although the Russians did fit the 20mm ShVAK aircraft cannon to the T-60 light tank. The Germans used the KwK 30 and 38, closely related to the FlaK 30 and 38 AA guns and using the same ammunition. Armour penetration was quoted as 31mm/100m/60° and 25mm/300m/60° for AP-T ammunition, increased to 49mm and 37mm respectively with PzGr40 *Hartkernmunition*.

The use of Becker 20mm cannon for AA purposes has already been mentioned. However, the only really successful API blowback AA gun was the Oerlikon S. It was used by the British Army in a variety of mountings, some with several guns. The Oerlikon was supplemented in British service during the Second World War by the Polsten, a simplified version developed by Polish engineers. This was only 20% of the cost to manufacture and also lighter, weighing 55kg instead of 67kg, and typically used a thirty-round vertical box magazine instead of the Oerlikon's sixty-round drum. A large number of multiple Oerlikon and Polsten mountings of various types, some fitted to tanks or armoured cars, saw action as a part of the 'Diver Belt' – the AA

*20mm Becker-Semag*
*( Courtesy: Verlag Stocker-Schmid, Dietikon-Zurich)*

*Quad 20mm Oerlikon S on British 4 × 4 mounting*
*(Courtesy: MoD Pattern Room)*

*Various methods were used to move guns No.1 (Swiss 20mm Flab. Kan. 38) (Courtesy: Verlag Stocker-Schmid, Dietikon-Zurich)*

*Various methods were used to move guns No.2 (Swiss 20mm Flab. Kan. 38) (Courtesy: Verlag Stocker-Schmid, Dietikon-Zurich)*

zone established off the south-east coast of England in 1944 to defend against the V-1 flying bomb attacks. Somewhat surprisingly, the Polsten also appeared as the secondary armament of the prototype Centurion tank, but this was not successful.

Several other 20mm AA guns and cartridges were introduced before and during World War Two. Bofors of Sweden produced the m/40 using their own 20 × 145R cartridge, which was totally eclipsed by the commercial success of its 40mm design. The Swiss Furrer-designed Flab Kan 38 (*Fliegerabwehrkanone 1938*) AA gun remained in service until 1947. It was designed around a

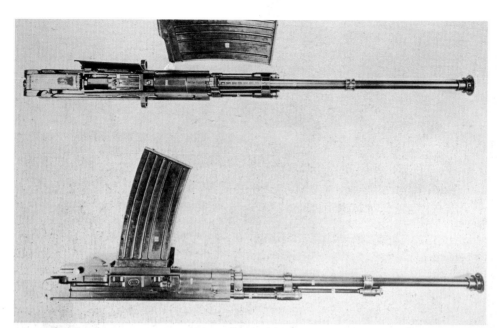

*Japanese 20mm Type 98 AA gun (Courtesy: MoD Pattern Room)*

powerful 20 × 139 cartridge, very similar to the post-war HS 820 round but with a thin-rimmed case which may be brass or steel.

The Danish firm Madsen produced the Model 1935, designed round a large, thick-rimmed 20 × 120 cartridge (also available, although apparently not sold, in a 23 × 106 version). The guns were initially intended for use in aircraft, but saw most service use in the AA role. The Madsen Model 1935 was fitted to a turntable rotating on a cruciform mounting, the whole package weighing 260kg in action (307kg in travelling form). It normally used ten- or fifteen-round magazines, but a sixty-round magazine and belt-fed versions were also available. The equipment was successful, being licence-built in France and Belgium and used by about twenty different nations throughout the world. It is presumably still in use, as 20mm ammunition is still in production.

The Finnish designer Lahti also worked on a number of experimental 20mm cannon between the wars, leading to the L-40 (properly the 20ItK/L-40), a twin AA gun using the 20 × 138B Solothurn cartridge and closely related to the L-39 anti-tank rifle, of which some 200 systems were manufactured up to 1945. The total weight was 652kg, and the rate of fire is variously given as 2 × 700 rpm or 2 × 250 rpm, the latter being rather more likely.

The Japanese produced the largest cartridges of all in this calibre, the 20 × 158 Type 94 and the 20 × 142 Type 98, the latter apparently superseding the earlier weapon, of which few were made. The Type 98, introduced in 1938, used a vertical twenty-round box magazine. It could be fired from its travelling position, on a carriage with large, wooden wheels, but was normally supported on a flat tripod. It weighed 269kg in action. As well as the usual HE shells, the gunners were provided with AP ammunition for its secondary AT role.

One of the most widely used 20mm cannon cartridges was the 20 × 138B round (the 'long Solothurn', to distinguish it from the 20 × 105B 'short Solothurn') fired by the *Wehrmacht*'s standard light AA guns. The first weapon to introduce this cartridge was the Solothurn S5-100, a direct descendant of the Erhardt introduced in the First World War. This in turn was developed by the parent company of Rheinmetall-Borsig into the FlaK 30, which entered service in 1935 and remained in use throughout the war. The gun was fed by a twenty-round box magazine, which must have provided a lot of work for the reloading crew in an extended engagement.

The FlaK 30 had a rather low rate of fire (280 rpm) and was somewhat prone to jamming so it was supplemented and later supplanted in production

*Flakpanzer IV (2cm): 2cm Vierlingsflak 38 on chassis of Pz IV (Imperial War Museum)*

by a Mauser-modified version which used the same ammunition and magazines, the FlaK 38. This equalled the Oerlikon S's rate of fire at around 450 rpm but the cartridge was more powerful with a higher muzzle velocity. The FlaK 38 weighed 406kg in action, compared with 483kg for the FlaK 30.

The FlaK 38 also saw service in a four-barrelled version, the *Flakvierling*, which weighed 1,520kg and was probably the most formidable short-range AA weapon anywhere in the world until the introduction of the post-war Soviet quad 23mm ZSU-23-4. Both single and quad mountings were fitted to a variety of tracked armoured vehicles, usually redundant tank chassis, to form *Flakpanzers*. These were desperately needed on the Eastern Front from 1943 onwards to try to protected armoured columns from the marauding Il-2 *Shturmovik*

*Italian 20mm Scotti (BuOrd, USN)*

ground-attack aircraft.

The long Solothurn cartridge saw use in a variety of other weapons including two Italian AA guns: the Breda Model 35 and the Scotti. The gas-operated Breda was more common, but had a modest performance with a 200–220 rpm rate of fire, made worse by the feed method which involved a twelve-round strip. The Scotti used a gas-unlocked blowback system similar to the Hispano, but could still achieve only 250 rpm. It was, however, somewhat lighter than the Breda at 227kg in action (including mounting) instead of 307kg, and was available with a twelve-round strip feed, a sixty-round drum magazine or belt feed.

## WARTIME 24–30MM WEAPONS

THE 24MM CALIBRE WAS ONLY USED BY THE SWISS, in the automatic-loading Pzw Kan 38 (*Panzerwagenkanone 38*) light AFV weapon, which used a powerful 24 × 138 cartridge. This was another of the Furrer designs, utilising a short-recoil toggle-bolt mechanism.

Neither France nor the Soviet Union developed 20mm AA guns, both preferring to use larger-calibre weapons of 25mm, while Germany went to the 30mm calibre late in the war in the search for more power. The attraction of these larger calibres was their greater range, with a practical ceiling (depending on the speed of the aircraft being engaged) in the region of 3,000m instead of the 2,000m achieved by 20mm equipment.

Despite the similarity in calibre, the French and Soviet 25mm guns used quite different cartridges and gun designs. During the 1920s and 1930s Hotchkiss conceived the need for lightweight anti-aircraft and anti-tank weapons with appreciably more hitting power than the 20mm calibre could achieve but with more mobility than the 37mm guns. The 25mm calibre was selected and, rather surprisingly, two different cartridges were introduced.

The larger of these was the 25 × 194R for the manually loaded Mle 1934 anti-tank gun (a shortened cavalry weapon – the Mle 1935 – and the lightweight Mle 1937 were also designed to fire this round). This was a powerful cartridge firing a 320g projectile at up to 960 m/s, producing more than double the muzzle energy of the most

powerful contemporary 20mm cannon, the 20 × 138B Solothurn. There was no doubt that the Hotchkiss, which was also fitted to light armoured vehicles, was effective against most mid-1930s tanks, although it was of course soon outclassed by the growth in tank armour thickness. The British Army did acquire some in 1939 and although they were used mainly for training some saw active service in France and Norway. They were not popular, however, because of their marginal effectiveness (by then) and fragility when being towed.

For the anti-aircraft weapon Hotchkiss developed a different cartridge, the rimless 25 × 163, used in the fully automatic *Mitrailleuse de 25mm sur affut universel Hotchkiss*. By the start of hostilities this was available in two versions with different mountings, the Mle 1938 and Mle 1939, weighing 950kg and 1,150kg respectively. As described in Chapter 4, this gun was also adopted by the Japanese Navy in various mountings.

The Soviet 25mm AA guns were based on a Bofors design and used the 25 × 218R M1940 cartridge (slightly different in shape from the Bofors m/32 round). Their entry into service was delayed by the higher priority given to the development of the 37mm Model 1939, which used a similar mechanism. The 25mm gun was carried on a four-wheel platform, the combination weighing 1,073 kg. There was also a twin-barrel version carried on trucks.

The German 30mm equipment was the 3cm FlaK 38, which was simply the MK 103 aircraft cannon fitted to the 20mm FlaK 38 mounting. This was a powerful weapon, using a big 30 × 184B cartridge, and the belt-fed gun had an impressive rate of fire. The problem was that the 2cm mounting was not really sturdy enough for the job, giving rise to vibration and unreliability. The 3cm FlaK 38 was introduced in 1944 and only saw service in small numbers. The gun also featured in a remarkable prototype SPAAG (self-propelled anti-aircraft gun), the *Leichter Flakpanzer IV 'Kügelblitz'* (Ball lightning), in which two MK 103s were contained within a ball mounting, shared with the commander and two gunlayers, and mounted on a PzIV tank chassis. Only five were made.

*Swiss 34mm Flab. Kan. 38: note water-cooled barrel (Courtesy: Verlag Stocker-Schmid, Dietikon-Zurich)*

## THE 34–40MM GUNS

ONCE AGAIN, THE SWISS CHOSE AN ODD CALIBRE for the largest of the Furrer designs, the water-cooled 34mm Flab Kan 38 AA gun, which used a powerful 34 × 239 cartridge. This remained in service until 1968.

In contrast, the 37mm calibre was extremely popular, with a wide range of ammunition being developed for aircraft, anti-aircraft, tank and anti-tank weapons. The Japanese used six different 37mm cartridges during the Second World War, and the French, Germans and Americans at least three each (all different). At the bottom end of the power scale, the original 37 × 94R ammunition from the nineteenth century Pom-pom was still in service, mainly in French light tanks. At the other end of the spectrum came the immense 37 × 380R SK C/30 German naval weapon. Both of these guns were manually loaded, however. The range of automatic weapons was much more restricted.

In army use, 37mm automatic weapons were intended solely for AA purposes. Guns in this

calibre were developed in and employed by the USSR, the USA, Germany, France and Italy. Of all the major powers, only Japan and the UK did not develop automatic 37mm AA weapons. The calibre was popular because it was almost the largest for which fully automatic weapons could be designed at the time, and the shells were big enough to stand a reasonable chance of knocking down an aircraft with one hit. The 37mm guns therefore provided an important layer in AA defence with an effective ceiling of up to 3,500m, in between the light cannon and the larger, manually loaded guns of 75mm and more.

The German Army was among the most prolific users of 37mm AA guns, developing no fewer than four different models, although these encompassed only two different guns, and all used the same 37 × 263B ammunition. The first three variants, the 3.7cm FlaK 18, FlaK 36 and FlaK 37, all used the same gun, a Rheinmetall-Borsig design which was basically a scaled-up 2cm FlaK 30. The difference between the FlaKs 18, 36 and 37 was confined to the mountings and sights. The FlaK 18, which

*World War 2 AFV gun cartridges (left to right): 7.92 × 57 (for scale), .5" Vickers (12.7 × 81), .50" Browning (12.7 × 99), 15mm Besa (15 × 104), KwK 30/38 (20 × 138B), Swiss Pzw. Kan. 38 (24 × 138)*

emerged in 1935, was considered too cumbersome at over 3,600kg (1,750kg in action) and it was soon replaced in production by the FlaK 36, with the weight reduced to 2,400kg/1,550 kg. The FlaK 37 was a modification of the 36 to take a new mechanical computing sight.

The FlaK 43 was a very different weapon, a gas-operated Rheinmetall-Borsig design based on a scaled-up version of the MK 103 aircraft cannon mechanism. The rate of fire increased and this could be sustained more easily because the side-loading tray ran through the trunnion axis so its position did not alter as the gun changed its elevation. A two-barrel version, the *Flakzwilling 43*, was also produced. This had the barrels vertically stacked and weighed 2,800kg in action, compared with 1,250kg for the single-barrel model.

As with the 2cm weapons, German 3.7cm guns found themselves fitted to a variety of armoured vehicles in order to provide air defence to armoured columns. Some were open in action, providing little protection for the crew, but the best known was the turreted vehicle with the impressive title *Flakpanzer IV 3.7cm FlaK 43 auf PzIV/3 'Ostwind'*, based on the ubiquitous Panzer IV chassis. Few were built before the end of the war.

Despite developing the intermediate 25mm Hotchkiss, the French had earlier produced a 37mm AA gun, the Schneider M1930. Little information is now available about either the gun or the ammunition, but they can be presumed to have been unsuccessful as only about twenty were in service by the start of the Second World War, participating in the defence of Paris. The equipment is quoted as weighing 1,800kg in travelling order, 1,340kg in action. The Italians also produced a weapon of this calibre, the *Cannone-Mitragliera da 37/54 modello 39*, a Breda design firing a 37 × 230SR cartridge. It was unusual in being designed for fixed defences, presumably accounting for its substantial weight of 2,975kg, but the exigencies of war forced the adaptation of some of the guns to mobile mountings.

The Soviet 37mm M1939, as already indicated, bore a strong resemblance to the 40mm Bofors and differed principally in using a smaller and less powerful 37 × 250R cartridge. The travelling weight on its four-wheeled mounting was 2,100kg. The American 37mm Gun M1, chambered for a 37 × 223SR cartridge, was generally similar, but on paper at least somewhat inferior in rate of fire and in the equipment weight of 2,780kg. Two minor variations of the M1 were produced; the M1A1 (with a charging handle) and the definitive M1A2, with different rifling. The gun was sometimes combined with two .50" Brownings in the Combination Mount M54 (normally mounted on the M15 half-track), the intention being to use one of the .50"s for spotting, opening fire with the other guns when the range was found. Although the M1 remained in service throughout the war, the 40mm Bofors was clearly superior and was adopted by the US Army as its main light AA weapon. Incidentally, the standard US (manually loaded) tank and anti-tank gun at the start of the war used a 37 × 223R cartridge which was almost identical to the AA round except for the rimmed case.

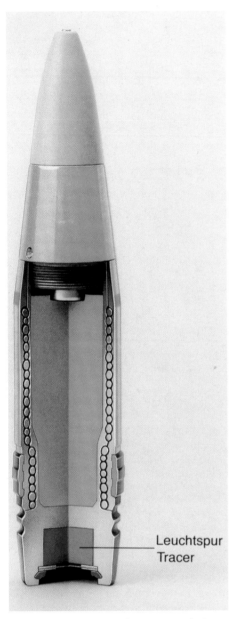

Leuchtspur
Tracer

*Sectioned prefragmented HE projectile for*
*Bofors 40 × 364R* (Courtesy: Diehl)

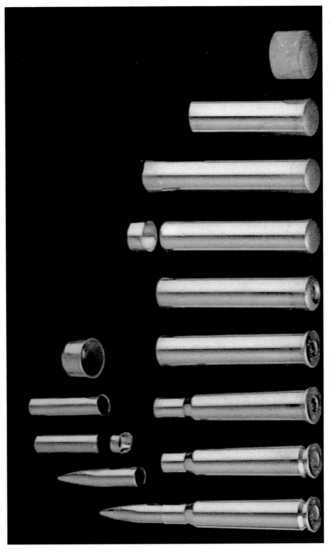

*Stages in the formation of a .50" Browning cartridge case and*
*bullet jacket* (Courtesy: Eurometaal)

*Sectioned Bofors 40 × 364R HEI-T round* (Courtesy: Diehl)

*Sectioned base-fuzed HE-SD projectile for Bofors 40 × 364R*
*(Courtesy: Diehl)*

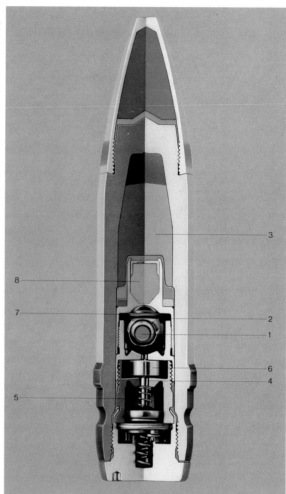

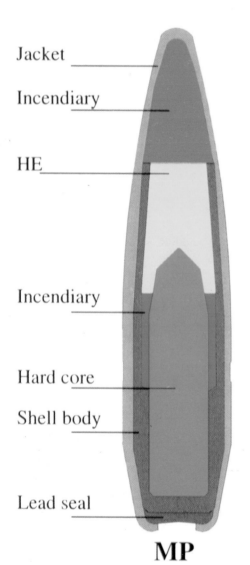

Jacket

Incendiary

HE

Incendiary

Hard core

Shell body

Lead seal

**MP**

*Sectioned Raufoss 12.7mm Multipurpose projectile*
*(Courtesy: Raufoss)*

The detonator (1) is mounted in rotor (2) which is in out-of-line-position. Thus the main charge (3) cannot be ignited in case of an accidental initiation of the detonator. The firing pin (4) resp. the hammer is held by a pressure spring (5) and a slotted sleeve which is secured by a coil tape (6). This coil provides the arming safe distance of the fuze since it prevents the firing pin (4) from hitting the detonator (1) within a certain flight path of the projectile.

Due to the centrifugal forces depending on the projectile spin a safety circlip (7) in the rotor (2) is bent open in a defined place. The rotor (2) with detonator (1) aligns its axis with that of the firing pin, simultaneously the coil tape (6) unrolls and opens the slotted sleeve which releases the firing pin (4). Now the fuze is sensitive to impact on specific targets over its tactical range. If the projectile hits a target of sufficient thickness within this range, the firing pin (4) with its hammer moves forward thus piercing the detonator (1). The detonator (1) is initiated and ignites the booster (8) which explodes the main charge. If the projectile does not hit a target within tactical range, the SD-unit detonates the projectile.

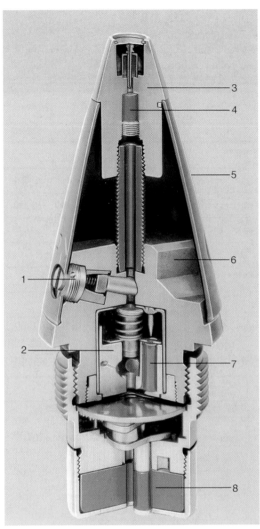

1 Setting sleeve (SQ-delay)
2 Delay plunger assembly
3 Head
4 Detonator
5 Ogive
6 Body
7 Delay element
8 Booster M 125 A1

*Sectioned impact fuze with settable delay* (Courtesy: Diehl)

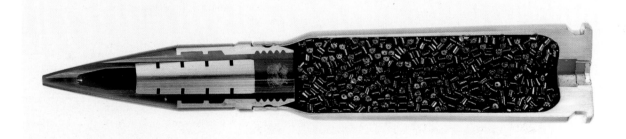

*Sectioned M50 series (20 × 102) Frangible Armour Piercing round* (Courtesy: Oerlikon-Contraves)

*Sectioned family of Oerlikon 35 × 228 ammunition: APFSDS, two APDS, base-fuzed HE and AHEAD*
*(Courtesy: Oerlikon-Contraves)*

*Family of projectiles for Bofors 40 × 364R ammunition: APFSDS-T, PFHE, HET and TPT*
*(Courtesy: Celsius)*

*Dual belt feed, for the experimental FN-BRG 15* (Courtesy: Ian Hogg)

*Dual belt feed with belt guides, for the Mauser MK30F* (Courtesy: Mauser)

*Multiple-barrelled percussion gun: a Russian 31-barrel .75" model (Courtesy: MoD Pattern Room)*

*Early manually-driven rotaries: .65" Gatling (foreground) and 37mm Hotchkiss*
*(Courtesy: MoD Pattern Room)*

*GE-225 25mm twin-barrel gun* (Courtesy: GE/Ian Hogg)

*Oerlikon KBA 25mm cannon* (Courtesy: Oerlikon-Contraves)

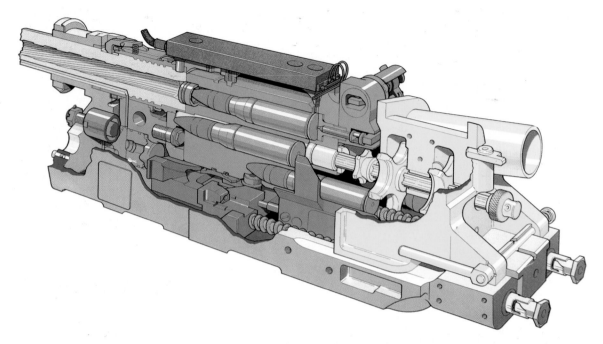

*Aden 25mm revolver cannon*
*(Courtesy: Royal Ordnance/R. W. Clarke)*

*Phalanx CIWS* *(Courtesy: Raytheon)*

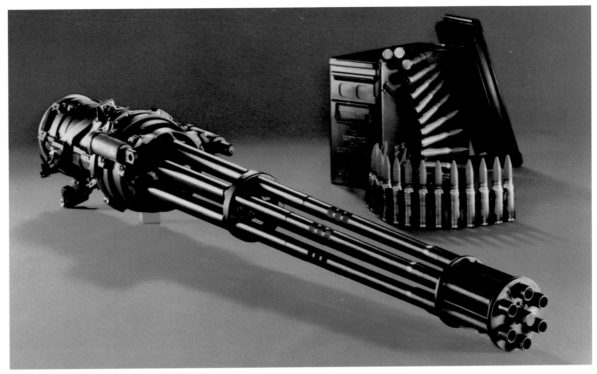

*GE 20mm M61A1 rotary cannon* (Courtesy: GE/Ian Hogg)

*GE 30mm GAU-8/A rotary cannon* (Courtesy: GE/Ian Hogg)

*Boeing 30mm M230 Chain Gun*
*(Courtesy: MDHC/Ian Hogg)*

*GIAT 25M811 25mm externally-powered dual-feed gun*
*(Courtesy: Ian Hogg)*

*Bofors 40mm L/60* (*Courtesy: Celsius*)

*GIAT 53 T4 AA mount with two 20mm 20M693 belt-fed cannon* (*Courtesy: GIAT*)

*SIDAM 25 SPAAG (four 25mm Oerlikon KBA)*
*(Courtesy: Oerlikon-Contraves)*

*Arrow AA system (two 30mm Mauser MK30F)* *(Courtesy: Mauser)*

*Oerlikon-Contraves 35mm Twin Field*
*Air Defence Gun Type GDF-005*
*(Courtesy: Oerlikon-Contraves)*

*Skyshield 35 with Oerlikon-Contraves 35/1000 Revolver Gun*
*(Courtesy: Oerlikon-Contraves)*

*Bofors 40mm TriAD SPAAG* (Courtesy: Celsius)

*Bofors 40mm Tridon* (Courtesy: Celsius)

*Dutch FMC AIFV with 25mm Oerlikon-Contraves KBA (Courtesy: Oerlikon-Contraves)*

*Korean IFV with Mauser MK30 cannon (Courtesy: Mauser)*

*Oerlikon KCB 30mm gun in twin naval mounting GCM-A03-3*
*(Courtesy: Oerlikon/Ian Hogg)*

*Bofors 40mm L/70 naval gun with 101-round elevating magazine (Courtesy: Celsius)*

*1½pdr COW gun on AA mounting* ( *RAF Museum* )

The Japanese Army never developed an automatic AA weapon larger than the 20mm Type 98, although they did make use of some 200 Bofors guns captured from British forces in Malaya. The British ignored the 37mm calibre almost completely, with the exception of some old COW (Coventry Ordnance Works) 1½pdr cannon of essentially First World War origin, which were used for airfield defence.

Indeed, the British General Staff and War Ministry took some convincing that anything larger than LMGs was needed to equip the new Light AA Batteries established from 1935. However, experiments had revealed that nothing smaller than a two-pound shell was likely to inflict serious damage on aircraft structures.

Britain therefore selected weapons of 40mm calibre, using three different cartridges. The two-pounder Pom-pom was adopted as a naval weapon and originally selected by the British Army as well, but dropped in favour of the Bofors after only sixty guns had been built. The army's manually loaded 2pdr tank and anti-tank gun used a more powerful cartridge (40 × 304R instead of 40 × 158R for the naval 2pdr) but the Bofors used a different round again, the 40 × 311R, which was slightly more powerful than the tank gun cartridge and much more so than the naval 2pdr. Bofors HE shells were

*Flakpanzer IV (3.7 cm)*
( *Imperial War Musuem* )

initially fitted only with contact + self-destruction fuzes.

The combination of high performance, mobility and reliability were sufficient to make the Bofors the outstanding heavy automatic weapon of the war in army as well as naval use. It was probably employed by virtually every combatant nation, officially or otherwise. The towed version weighed 2,460kg in travelling form, 1,980kg in action. British Bofors were originally produced with a simple 'cartwheel' (open framework) AA sight, but by 1939 Colonel A. V. Kerrison's No.3 Predictor (popularly known as the Kerrison Predictor) was being introduced. This provided direct power control of the gun via hydraulic motors, using information about the angular rate of change of the target from a telescopic sight, once slant range had been set manually. It proved very accurate, given a well-trained crew.

Many self-propelled variants of the Bofors were also fielded, some on wheeled trucks, others in mountings on tank chassis. The best known of the latter was the American Gun Motor Carriage M19, which carried two guns on an M24 light tank chassis. The British fielded the Crusader AA Mark 1, using a single Bofors in a hydraulically operated mounting behind an armoured gunshield. Despite their AA purpose, these vehicles proved handy in the ground role, their firepower obliterating lightly protected defensive positions.

## LESSONS OF THE
## SECOND WORLD WAR

AS USUAL AT THE CONCLUSION OF A MAJOR conflict, the end of the Second World War saw a pause in arms production and a dramatic scaling-down of military forces. At the same time, intensive reviews of future requirements were conducted in the light of war experience and some technical experiments were followed up at a more leisurely pace.

The evaluation of heavy machine guns was rather confused. They had proved largely ineffective in the AA role. An American analysis based on the last year of the war showed that over 50,000 .50" rounds were fired for every aircraft brought down, compared with 500 Bofors rounds – that is, almost two hours of continuous firing per gun, compared

with four minutes. However, they never quite died out and the faithful M2 remained in service, mainly fitted to single mountings, either on a tripod for infantry use or on vehicles. One M2 was commonly provided on a pintle mounting by the commander's hatch on tanks.

The use of multiple M2 mountings was also continued for a while, the power-operated quadruple M45 lasting in service until 1955. They were designed to put up an immense volume of fire against low-flying aircraft, but actually proved very effective against 'human wave' attacks in the Korean War. The Soviets showed faith in HMGs, producing not only an improved 12.7mm gun but a brand-new and much more powerful weapon, the 14.5mm KPV, specifically intended for the light AA role.

Most other nations abandoned HMG development to concentrate on weapons of 20mm or more. It was clear that short-range AA defence required the shortest possible time of flight and the highest possible rate of fire, stimulating the development of new weapons and high-velocity cartridges. Some effort was also devoted to producing properly designed SPAAGs, with cannon in fully enclosed turrets on tracked chassis, able to provide immediate cover for armoured columns.

Curiously, the British Army showed little interest in light cannon, rapidly abandoning the various 20mm guns for improved models of 40mm Bofors. This view was probably influenced by operational research into the relative effectiveness of the 20mm Oerlikon and 40mm Bofors in dealing with low-flying coastal raiders. It was noted that these were not usually spotted until only 1,400 metres away, so the Bofors could not use its range advantage. Engagement times were only about thirteen seconds (from first sighting the target to the last shot) and the Bofors fired an average of seven or eight rounds to the Oerlikon's fifty. Even so, in most circumstances the Bofors was more effective.

Calculations were made about the probability of success (immediate break-off, or eventual crash) against a Junkers 88. Using simple sights only, the Oerlikon's chances were estimated at 3% against a crossing target, 12% against one approaching head-on; the Bofors' 18% and 20% respectively. With more advanced sights, performance was much

*5cm FlaK 41*
*(Courtesy: MoD
Pattern Room)*

better. Using predictor control, the Bofors' success rate rose to 35% and 39%. The addition of a Triple Gyro sight had an even more dramatic effect on the Oerlikon's performance – to 17% and an astonishing 76% respectively. More surprisingly, the British Army only fielded towed weapons; for several decades, the only instant-response air defence for armoured columns consisted of the rifle-calibre machine guns mounted on the top of tank turrets. This glaring oversight can presumably be attributed to the fact that by the end of the war, the British Army had become accustomed to fighting in conditions of total air superiority and found little use for their AA equipment. In the early 1970s the Bofors guns were retired in favour of the Rapier missile system, but even this was for some time available only on towed mountings. It remains in service, supplemented by smaller AA missiles. There was a minor revival in British use of AA guns following the Falklands War, when some Oerlikon 35mm systems were 'liberated' from Argentinian forces and donated to the RAF Regiment.

The use of light cannon for ground fighting also fell out of favour for some time. The light armoured vehicles which constituted their obvious targets were relatively uncommon on the battlefield after the first post-war phase of re-equipment, as the

Warsaw Pact had largely abandoned light tanks, using main battle tanks for most reconnaissance purposes. The first generation of armoured personnel carriers, such as the American M113, were intended as 'battle taxis', designed to carry troops to where they were needed rather than engage in the fighting themselves.

Much effort was expended in producing automatic AA guns of larger calibre, to cope with aircraft of ever higher performance. Even during the war, there had been experiments in many countries with weapons in the 50–57mm class. The Germans developed the 5cm FlaK 41 which saw limited service, but was judged a technical failure. The more promising 5.5cm FlaK *Gerät 58* was still under development at the war's end, but it appears that the Soviets studied it before producing their own S-60 gun. The British experimented with the six-pounder 6 cwt AA gun of 57mm calibre in both single- and twin-barrel versions without producing a viable weapon. Bofors completed the development of their 57mm, started before the war. Better known as a naval gun, this was also adopted by the Swedish and Belgian armies as the m/54.

The USA and the UK also developed rapid-firing AA cannon in even larger calibres, coupled with advanced radar-directed fire control systems and

*75mm Skysweeper M51 (Leo Marriott)*

the new proximity fuzes. Starting in 1944, the Americans concentrated on 75mm weapons, culminating in the Gun M51 'Skysweeper', which entered service in the early 1950s and remained alongside the 40mm Bofors until both were replaced by the HAWK missile in the early 1960s. The British commenced 'Project Ratefixer' in 1946, aimed at automating the successful 3.7″ (94mm) Mk 6 AA gun, which was eventually pushed to a cyclic rate of 75 rpm. Much experimentation, including a dalliance with 4.26–3.2″ taper-bore design, ultimately resulted in 'Longhand', a version of the 3.7″ Mk 6 fitted with a twelve-round rapid-loading conveyor, which was approved for service introduction in 1957. However, development had taken too long and the weapon never saw service, being superseded by guided missiles.

## POST-WAR HEAVY MACHINE GUNS

AS ALREADY INDICATED, THERE WAS ON THE FACE of it little post-war development of HMGs. However, the USSR produced a revised version of the 12.7mm gun, the DShK-38/46, with an improved ammunition feed, using belts which could be linked together, and a quick-change barrel (something the Browning M2 still lacks). They also produced a brand-new weapon, the formidable 14.5mm KPV, the king of the HMGs. This is based around the powerful 14.5 × 114 AT rifle cartridge and uses recoil operation with gas assistance provided by a muzzle booster.

The KPV has had two major applications: as an AA weapon on towed mountings known as ZPU-1, -2 or -4 depending on the number of guns fitted and as an armoured vehicle gun, typically mounted in turrets in various light AFVs. ZPU stands for *Zenitnaya Pulemet Ustanovka*, or AA machine gun system. ZPU-2 mountings were also fitted to light SPAAGs such as the BTR40B 4 × 4 and the BTR152A 6 × 6. The high muzzle velocity of up to 1,000 m/s coupled with a heavy projectile gives a performance in a different league from that of other HMGs. It has an effective ceiling of 1,400m, a horizontal range of 8,000m and the AP shot can penetrate 32mm of armour at 500m. Poland has developed a ground-support version, the KPWT *Pirat*, on a recoil-absorbing tripod of considerable weight.

The Russians did not abandon the trusty 12.7 × 108 cartridge, however, and have developed a new weapon around it, the NSV. This is gas-operated, using a version of the Kalashnikov rotary-bolt design. The gun, which only weighs 25kg, is available for infantry use on a tripod but is most often seen fitted on a pintle mounting on battle tanks. In this guise, known as the NSV-T, it can be operated from within the turret.

The Chinese have produced their own versions of many of the Soviet guns, including the 12.7mm DShK-38/46 (known as the Type 54) and the 14.5mm ZPU-1, -2 and -4 (Types 75 and 80, 58 and 56 respectively). They have also designed their own HMGs around the 12.7 × 108 round. The first, the Type 77, is claimed to weigh only 56kg including its tripod. An even lighter weapon at 39kg all-in (18.5kg gun only) is the Type W-85 in the same calibre. These guns are available with tripods and sights to facilitate AA use if required.

Despite the continuation of the .50″ Browning M2 in American and other service, many attempts have been made to produce a more modern weapon using the same ammunition. Some, by firms such as FN, RAMO and SACO, have mainly consisted of updating the basic M2 by improving the somewhat convoluted method of barrel changing and, in later SACO/RAMO versions, by reducing the barrel length and weight. Another weapon which saw service in AFVs was the M85, which had the advantage of a much shorter receiver and two rates of fire but was regarded as less than successful. Still others have been more radical, such as the prolonged American attempt to produce a brand-new GPHMG (general-purpose heavy machine gun).

The American GPHMG project resulted in a viable weapon, nicknamed 'Dover Devil'. It was a gas-operated, modular design with a quick-change barrel and dual feed, and weighed considerably less than an M2. The project was cancelled due to lack of funds, but a very similar weapon has been put into production by Chartered Industries of Singapore as the 50MG.

This does not mean that American HMGs begin and end with the M2 and M85. Another quite different weapon using the 12.7 × 99 cartridge is the General Dynamics GAU-19/A, an externally powered three-barrel rotary gun capable of up to 2,000 rpm. It is primarily designed for helicopter mounting, in order to provide a high volume of suppressive fire against enemy troops, but can also be fitted to land vehicles.

The Madsen company, in the form of Madsen-Saetter, produced a final flurry of new offerings in the late 1950s, including an HMG chambered for the 12.7 × 99 cartridge, but this saw little or no use.

A different attempt to produce a new Western HMG was the Belgian FN BRG-15, intended for AFV use. This was originally developed in the 1980s around a 15 × 115 cartridge based on the 20mm HS 404/804 case (which was therefore almost identical to the old 15mm Besa cartridge except for its extra length), but later versions used a 15.5 × 106 case which was essentially a 'necked-out' 14.5mm KPV round. The gun delivered a formidable AP performance, even better than the KPV's, but did not achieve commercial success.

While the emphasis has so far been on new guns and cartridges, the usefulness of HMGs has also been extended by less obvious developments in ammunition and mountings. In the latter case, new recoil-absorbing mountings have enabled far more accurate long-range fire as the gun is no longer shaken off aim by recoil. Ammunition developments have proceeded in two different directions: more effective shells, and APDS rounds.

HMG ammunition has generally been considered too small for an effective HE shell, but modern developments have altered this. In particular, the Norwegian firm Raufoss has developed a range of multi-purpose ammunition which combines a chemical impact fuze with HE and incendiary elements as well as a useful armour-piercing performance. In .50″ calibre this round is known as the NM140, and this APHEI projectile is claimed to be as effective as earlier generations of 20mm ammunition.

Even more spectacular is the improvement in AP performance achieved by the latest APDS rounds. The American version is known as the .50″ SLAP (saboted light armour penetrator), and consists of a .50″ Browning case loaded with a 7.7mm 27g tungsten carbide projectile in a plastic sleeve. It is fired at a muzzle velocity of 1,215 m/s and will penetrate around 25mm of armour at 1,000m, compared with 10mm for a conventional .50 AP round. Similar ammunition has been developed for the 12.7 × 108 round.

The .50″ Browning continues to be offered in

*Oerlikon 20mm KAD on GA1-C01 mounting (Courtesy: Ian Hogg)*

turret mountings for APCs, no doubt prompted by the current emphasis on low-intensity peacekeeping. The Denel LCT-12.7, introduced in 1999, is the latest example.

## POST-WAR 20–25MM ANTI-AIRCRAFT CANNON

THE SEARCH FOR HIGH-VELOCITY 20MM CANNON with a high rate of fire led both Hispano-Suiza and their rivals Oerlikon to develop new cartridges and guns, as described in detail in Chapter 2. The new cartridges, $20 \times 139$ and $20 \times 128$ respectively, offer muzzle velocities of around 1,000 m/s, while the guns fire at 1,000 rpm, both very significant improvements on the equivalent Second World War equipment. GIAT, Rheinmetall and Mauser have built rival weapons around these cartridges.

The army mountings in which the new guns are fitted are also a huge improvement on earlier models. The high speed of modern aircraft means that the guns must be capable of extremely rapid but controlled movement to follow their targets, so powered mountings have become common. The guns are typically set very low in their mountings in order to preserve stability, and may be operated by only one gunner.

Typical examples are: the lightweight Oerlikon

HS 669A, featuring a single KAD cannon in a manual mounting weighing 512kg (370kg in action); the French Tarasque Type 53, with a single GIAT M693 cannon in a powered mounting weighing 660kg in action; and the Rheinmetall twin Rh202 in a powered mounting which weighs 1,640kg in action. All three guns use the $20 \times 139$ cartridge.

The 20mm calibre is too small to be favoured for the sophisticated, tracked SPAAGs but AA mountings have been fitted to smaller vehicles, particularly light armoured cars of French origin. Many versions have been produced, but a typical example is the SAMM TAB 220 turret, designed around two M693 cannon, which can be fitted to vehicles as small as the Panhard AML $4 \times 4$ armoured car, for a total weight of only 5.5 tonnes.

The USA also stayed with the 20mm cannon, but in the mid-1960s selected the M168 rotary cannon based on the M61 Vulcan aircraft gun and its $20 \times 102$ electrically primed ammunition. The two-wheeled M167 mounting weighs 1,500kg and the gun is capable of firing at up to 3,000 rpm. The most common SPAAG variant is the M163, based on the tracked M113 armoured personnel carrier and including an on-mount radar, which weighs 12.3 tonnes. This proved most effective in Vietnam at breaking up enemy infantry attacks.

*ZSU-23-4 Shilka (four 23mm ZU guns)*
*(Courtesy: MoD Pattern Room)*

The old Hispano 20 × 110 cartridge and its HS 804 gun have retained some popularity, being produced by both Israel and Yugoslavia. The Israeli TCM-20 is a simple towed mount carrying two of the guns and weighing 1,350kg; it is fitted to various wheeled and half-track vehicles. The Yugoslavian application is a triple mounting weighing about 1,200kg. This mounting is also fitted to the BOV-3 SPAAG, which uses a 4 × 4 chassis weighing 9.4 tonnes.

The USSR ignored the 20mm calibre, selecting instead a much more hard-hitting 23mm gun using a variant of the wartime aircraft cannon. The 23 × 152B cartridge was retained, but modified to a steel case with a different primer. The resulting ZU-23 cannon delivers a 50% increase in power over the new 20mm rounds. The gun was available in a twin towed manual mounting weighing 950kg, but is much better known in the SPAAG version.

Unquestionably the most famous of the post-war SPAAGs, the Soviet ZSU-23-4 or *Shilka*, entered service in the early 1960s. ZSU stands for *Zenitnaya Samokhodnaya Ustanovka*, or self-propelled gun. As the designation indicates, four of the

23mm cannon, specially fitted with water-cooled barrels, are mounted in a turret fitted to a tracked chassis. A powerful target acquisition and tracking radar is fitted to the mount, and the total assemblage weighs 20.5 tonnes. It is credited with 50% more accuracy and 66% more range than the 20mm Vulcan system, and apparently performed extremely well against Israeli warplanes in 1973. Thousands were built, and they have seen service in around thirty countries. As so often with SPAAGs, the Shilka's high rate of fire also made them very useful in ground fighting and they saw much use in this role in Afghanistan.

The next cartridge size up, the Oerlikon 25 × 137, is a relatively recent Western revival of the 25mm calibre after a long period of post-war absence. Despite its late start, it has become very popular as a replacement for the 20mm weapons as it is not much larger but, like the Soviet 23mm, offers a 50% increase in power. This improvement in performance has become increasingly important as both aircraft and ground targets have become tougher and acquired longer-range weapons, extending the desirable engagement distance.

The Oerlikon 25 × 137 cartridge is available in a wide range of guns and mountings. The simplest is the Oerlikon-Bührle GBI, a single KBA in a manual mounting which weighs 660kg in travelling order and 500kg in firing position. At the other extreme, four of the KBA cannon are fitted, two each side, to the SIDAM 25 turret designed by OTO Melara of Italy. Mounted on the ubiquitous M113 tracked chassis, this has become the Italian Army's standard SPAAG.

The 25 × 137 is also used in the GAU-12/U five-barrel rotary cannon which is fitted to the General Electric Blazer air defence turret, along with four Stinger light AA missiles and a pod of high-velocity HYDRA-70 unguided rockets. Rate of fire of the GAU-12/U is limited to 1,800 rpm. Mounted on the 8 × 8 LAV (light armoured vehicle), this has been adopted by the USMC.

The Blazer represents an extreme example of the current trend towards combining guns and missiles on one AA mounting, the theory being that one radar and fire control system can look after both, with the weapon selected depending on the circumstances. The gun is most effective at up to 2,500m,

*Oerlikon ILTIS mounting (25mm KBB gun)* (Courtesy: Oerlikon-Contraves/Ian Hogg)

*Oerlikon-Contraves Diana (two 25mm KBB)* (Courtesy: Oerlikon-Contraves/Ian Hogg)

while the Stinger has a range of up to 5,000m. The HYDRA-70 missiles are intended for use against hovering helicopters which may be shielded against the heat-seeking Stinger; they have a range of up to 7,000m.

In the ever-increasing escalation of military equipment, the $25 \times 137$ has more recently been joined by a lengthened version, the $25 \times 184$ KBB. This fires a heavier projectile at a higher velocity, including an APDS shot which can penetrate 30mm of armour at a striking angle of 60° at 2,000m. The lightest mounting for the KBB is the unusual Oerlikon-Bührle ILTIS, a single manual mounting weighing only 240kg in travelling trim. This is intended as an infantry weapon against low-flying aircraft and light AFVs, and features a low mounting with a prone operator's position. In contrast, the Oerlikon-Bührle Diana twin powered mounting includes its own optical fire control system incorporating a laser rangefinder and digital computer and weighs around 3,000kg. Perhaps the most remarkable military acquisition of the KBB cannon is the reported purchase of a land-based version of the Oerlikon-Contraves Sea Zenith quadruple naval CIWS by the PLA, the Chinese Army!

## MODERN 30–76MM AA GUNS

ANY WEAPON SYSTEM REPRESENTS A TRADE-OFF between conflicting requirements and AA gun calibre is no exception. Larger cannon need more substantial mountings and usually suffer a lower rate of fire. On the other hand, they gain in range and hitting power, so fewer strikes are necessary to destroy the target. Given effective sighting arrangements, the maximum effective AA range of a typical heavy machine gun is around 1,000–1,500m, of a 20mm cannon about 1,500–2,000m, a 25mm some 2,500m, and a 30mm about 3,000m.

The longer the range, the more difficult it is to score hits, regardless of the power of the cannon. It takes about three seconds for a modern 20mm projectile to reach 2,000m, during which time the target might easily have altered its course away from the predicted path; in that time, an aircraft travelling at 800 km/h will have covered nearly 700m. Larger-calibre weapons therefore need sophisticated fire control systems, usually with integral radar sets, to make effective use of their greater reach.

Such systems are equally compatible with many AA missiles, so towed (and some self-propelled) AA guns are often coupled with missile systems to deal with long-range targets.

Among the first of the post-war 30mm cannon was the big Hispano-Suiza HS 831 (later to be known as the Oerlikon KCB). This was used in the HS 661, a simple, manual single mount which weighed 1,540kg in travelling order and 1,150kg in action. Few other land AA mountings appear to have used this cannon, although two were fitted to the French AMX-13DCA and AMX-30 SPAAGs, based on the light and medium tank chassis respectively. Apparent similarities in equipment can conceal important differences in quality; the AMX-13 model used visual sighting and was therefore limited to clear-weather action while the AMX-30 version has an integrated acquisition and fire control radar.

The rival Oerlikon $30 \times 173$ round has been rather more successful, but in a German gun, the Mauser MK30 Model F, which has been incorporated into several towed and self-propelled mountings. In the former category are the Breda Sentinel Twin 30mm (a version of their naval AA weapon), with two barrels mounted close together, and the German Arrow and the Greek Artemis, both with two more widely separated guns. These equipments weigh between five and seven tonnes and are power-operated. While the Breda is autonomous, with its own fire control system and gunner, the others are usually linked to a central radar and fire-control system which operates the weapons remotely.

The MK30 has also featured in the Krauss Maffei Wildcat, a $6 \times 6$ armoured vehicle with one gun on each side of a turret which can also mount an integrated radar set. It is worth commenting on the modern tendency to mount AA cannon on the side of turrets, rather than close together. Apart from the fact that gun barrels too close together can disrupt accuracy (the muzzle blast from one barrel affecting the trajectory of a shell fired from the other), external mounting leaves the turret space free for crew and ammunition and also keeps it clear of fumes, as the fired cases are ejected outwards.

The largest of the army 30mm weapons were developed in Eastern Europe. The Romanian A436

*Czech M53/70 (two 30mm M53)* *(Courtesy: Ian Hogg)*

towed AA gun incorporates two of the Soviet naval NN-30 revolver cannon, firing the powerful $30 \times 210B$ cartridge. The same cartridge is used in the Yugoslavian Zastava M86, although this is a gas-operated linear-action gun with a lower rate of fire. The M89 is a version adapted for dual belt feed. In both guns, gun recoil is used to drive the belt feed. Two of these guns are used in the BOV-30 wheeled SPAAG, externally mounted in a cradle at the front of the turret. This is a simple, manually aimed system suitable only for clear-weather use.

Most powerful of all is the Czech M53. This fires a huge cartridge, the $30 \times 210$, which is even bigger than the NN-30 round due to its larger diameter. The twin mounting, which weighs 1,750kg in action, is also fitted to two six-wheeled vehicles, the M53/59 and M53/70, in which applications it is hydraulically or electrically powered respectively. Ammunition supply, initially by a short belt, is achieved in these SPAAGs by huge fifty-round boxes on top of the guns. Because of their weight (84.5kg when full) they are able to be reloaded while in place, from the top. The mounting was one

of the first applications of floating firing to an automatic cannon, but the fire control arrangements are primitive and the system is effectively obsolete. At the end of the 1990s it achieved international notoriety in Yugoslav hands, providing fire support for ground operations in Kosovo.

It appears surprising that the Soviet Union, so keen on equipment standardisation within the Warsaw Pact, permitted the Czechs to develop the M53 instead of using the 23mm ZU. The reason is that the weapon had already been developed at the *Waffenwerke Brunn*, the Czechoslovakian arms works at Brno, by the end of the Second World War. Known to the Germans as the Krieghoff MK 303, it was intended to provide the AA armament of the *Kriegsmarine*'s revolutionary Type XXI U-boats, but never entered service.

More recently, the Russians have developed their own 30mm AA equipment, but only in SP form. Most impressive is the formidable 2S6M *Tunguska* (named after the place in Siberia which was devastated by a comet or meteorite in 1908). This combines two twin-barrel, water-cooled, 2A38M

*Russian Tunguska SPAAG (two twin-barrelled 30mm 2A38M, plus AA missiles)* (Courtesy: Scorpion/KBP)

cannon together with eight AA missiles (SA-19 *Treugolnik*, or Triangle) and a multi-sensor target detection and fire control system on a tracked chassis. The cartridge is the current all-purpose $30 \times 165$ and the guns are capable of 2,500 rpm – each! The *Tunguska* has replaced the *Shilka* in Russian service and is undoubtedly the most effective short-range SPAA system in existence. A more modest effort is the *Pantsyr-S1*, a truck-based SPAA system combining two slower-firing 2A72 cannon (also $30 \times 165$) with twelve AA missiles.

Following in logical sequence, the next calibre of automatic cannon in service is the 35mm, this time represented by only one cartridge: the $35 \times 228$ Oerlikon. This is available in the widely sold Oerlikon KD series (in several versions for different purposes), and more recently the American ARES Talon, the South African GA-35 and the Oerlikon-Contraves 35/1000 revolver cannon. The cartridge is impressively powerful and provides effective

competition for the classic 40mm Bofors while most of the guns manage appreciably higher rates of fire.

The biggest of the Oerlikons, the KD appeared in the 1960s in two forms: the KDB in the GDF twin mounting, and the KDA in the *Gepard* SPAAG, with two guns fitted one on either side of a turret mounted on a Leopard tank chassis. The *Gepard* has been in effect the German equivalent of the *Shilka*, trading rate of fire (550 rpm per gun) for effective range (up to 4,000m). The GDF is intended for use with central fire control systems such as the Contraves Skyguard, which may also incorporate Sparrow AA missile launchers.

The *Gepard* has attracted various competitors, all using the KD series cannon in a similar arrangement. Japan has developed the closely comparable AW-X system. The Marconi Marksman is the British equivalent, a twin 35mm turret which can be fitted to a range of tank chassis and has achieved some foreign sales successes. South Africa has

*Flakpanzer Gepard (two 35mm Oerlikon KDA)* (Courtesy: Ian Hogg)

developed a twin 35mm system on a modified 8 × 8 armoured car chassis (the ZA-35, using the GA-35 cannon which has a similar performance to the KDA) and Oerlikon themselves have developed the GDF-DO3 Escorter 35 system, which mounts twin KDF cannon on a large 4 × 4 chassis. One variation is the American Eagle system, which differs in using two ARES Talon automatic cannon of a similar performance to the Oerlikons. European production of this gun has been licensed to Mauser as the Model G.

The traditional ammunition for the 35 × 228 consists of a 550g projectile fired at a very high 1,175 m/s. However, APDS loadings have also been developed for dealing with light AFVs and these are capable of penetrating 40mm/1,000m/60°, compared with 15mm for the SAPHEI round. The 35/1000, intended for integration into the Skyshield 35 Air Defence System, has been designed to utilise the Oerlikon AHEAD ammunition, but earlier guns can also be adapted to use it.

The 37mm calibre, so common up to and during the Second World War, has now virtually disappeared. The sole survivors are the Chinese Type 55 (single barrel), Types 65 and 74 (twin) and P793

*Damage inflicted by 35mm Oerlikon HEI shell*
(Courtesy: Oerlikon-Contraves)

(more advanced twin) weapons made by NORINCO. They are directly developed from the wartime Soviet M1939. Modern fire control systems give them an effective range of about 3,000m. SPGs using a twin turret on a tank chassis are also in service.

The 40mm cannon calibre is synonymous with Bofors, who have indefatigably continued to develop what is fundamentally a seventy-year-old design, with such success that it can still stand comparison with the newest equipment. Since the introduction of the L70 version, most efforts have concentrated on improving ancillary aspects such as the ready supply of ammunition, powered mountings and a range of fire control systems to suit all requirements and budgets. An established system is the BOFI-R, which incorporates an on-mount radar. The most recent innovation is the Trinity system, a package of improvements to the fire control, gun and ammunition which results in a controlled dispersion burst of fire, intended to bracket the position of the target with 3P proximity-fuzed HE shells.

SPAAG mountings for the big Bofors have not been common, the best known being the American M42 of the 1950s, achieved by fitting the wartime M19 turret (with two of the older L56 guns) on the hull of the M41 light tank. It lacks a modern fire control system but nonetheless proved most effective in the Vietnam War – in ground fighting.

Almost as well known, or rather notorious, is the US Army's attempt to produce a modern equivalent, the Sergeant York DIVAD (Divisional Air Defence) of the 1980s. Despite assembling well-proven chassis, gun (two L70s) and radar components, it was a technical failure and was cancelled before entering production, after a huge sum had been spent trying to make it work properly. The Bofors SPAAG flag is currently kept flying by TriAD, the air defence version of the Swedish CV 90 light AFV which mounts one gun in a modified turret with an appropriate fire control system, and by the Tridon, on a 6 × 6 wheeled vehicle.

Calibres larger than 40mm are now uncommon for AA purposes, as their long-range performance has mainly become the realm of missile systems. The few exceptions are worth mentioning, however. It is also worth pointing out that just as with warship armament, guns have the advantage of versatility as they can engage light AFVs and other lightly protected ground targets to great effect. To be fair, however, some SPAA missile systems (notably the Oerlikon ADATs) are also capable of engaging AFVs, although it would clearly be far too expensive to use such missiles to provide general supporting fire.

The Soviet 57mm guns, both towed and SP (self-propelled), are essentially of the same vintage as the 1940s Bofors 57mm and were apparently developed from the wartime German 5.5cm gun, but designed around a 57 × 347SR cartridge. Despite lacking modern radar-guided fire control systems, Chinese versions of the SPAAG remain in service. The towed guns can be linked to modern fire controls and are still used by many countries associated with the former USSR; they saw action in Iraqi hands during the Gulf War. The towed version (Russian S-60, Chinese Type 59) has a single barrel and weighs around 5,000kg. The SPAAG (Soviet ZSU-57-2, Chinese Type 80) has two barrels in a turret mounted on a tank chassis. The gun has a claimed effective range of up to 6,000m (rather less for the SP version).

The last and largest of the SPAAGs is the Italian 76mm OTOMATIC, which in effect mounts the famous OtoBreda naval gun in a tank turret! The massive turret weighs 15 tonnes and can therefore only be carried by main battle tank or heavy SP artillery chassis. The gun has a 120 rpm rate of fire and an effective AA range of 6,000m. It is primarily intended for engaging combat helicopters before they can come within missile range, but the APFS-DS rounds also have an impressive anti-armour performance. Despite (or perhaps because of) its unique blend of abilities, it does not so far appear to have achieved any sales.

## MODERN CANNON FOR GROUND FIGHTING

THE USE OF automatic CANNON FOR GROUND fighting in recent decades has almost entirely been restricted to mountings (usually in turrets) in light AFVs, with the main purposes of engaging other light AFVs and of providing general fire support for infantry attacks. The cannon have two origins: adapted versions of the automatic cannon also used in air defence weapon systems, and specially developed weapons optimised for the ground-fighting role.

After the Second World War, there was some debate about the most appropriate armament for armoured cars (ACs) and other light armoured fighting vehicles (LAFVs). The British Saladin 6 × 6 AC epitomised the conflict. First designed with a modified manually loaded 40mm gun (called 'Pipsqueak') firing APDS shot, it was eventually produced with a low-velocity (also manually loaded) 76mm gun which relied on HE shells for effect. Clearly, fire support had been given a higher priority than the anti-armour role.

Most other nations followed the same route. Low-velocity manually loaded guns of 76–90mm, firing HEAT (shaped charge) shells against armour, became the common armament of ACs. An early exception to this was the French range of high-velocity automatic cannon, commencing in 75mm calibre, which were fitted in oscillating turrets in light tanks and heavy ACs.

The starting point for this weapon was reputed to be the excellent gun from the German Panther tank, which was given an automatic-loading mechanism and modified ammunition. To solve the problem of how to reload the gun at different elevations, two six-round revolver magazines were mounted, one on each side of the gun breech, which moved with the gun. The whole mechanism was rigidly fixed into the upper half of the turret, which oscillated (elevated) in relation to the lower half of the turret. This was a clever idea which dispensed with the loader and permitted the rapid firing of twelve shots (at 12 rpm). The downside was the need to withdraw to a place of safety in order to reload the magazines, which could only be done from outside the vehicle.

A different approach to the same problem was taken by the Swedish Strv-103 S-Tank, which dispensed with a turret altogether. Instead, finely controlled hydraulic systems were used to achieve gun aiming by adjusting the bearing and tilt of the whole vehicle. This enabled the 105mm gun and fifty-round autoloader to be rigidly mounted into the hull, leading to a very low and compact AFV capable of rapid fire. The disadvantages were the impossibility of firing on the move, or without the engine running, which effectively limited it to a tank-destroyer role.

More recently, large-calibre (up to 125mm) self-loading cannon have become more popular in MBTs (main battle tanks), starting with Soviet designs. It is likely that all future MBTs will feature mechanisms to achieve this, despite the complexity they add to the design.

To return to fully automatic cannon in light AFVs, the German Army was unsurprisingly among the first to reintroduce the concept, with the adoption of the *Schützenpanzer* SPz 12-3 APC in the late 1950s. In modern parlance, this was really an AIFV or MICV, as it was intended for fighting as well as carrying troops. It was low, with well-sloped armour, and carried a 20mm HS 820 cannon in a turret. The SPz 12-3 was supplemented by the *Spähpanzer Luchs* 8 × 8 AC and eventually replaced from the late 1960s by the much heavier *Marder* MICV. Both of these feature an Rh202 cannon (firing the same 20 × 139 ammunition as the HS 820) in a turret mounting.

During the 1960s Hispano-Suiza offered a range of cannon in 20 × 139, 23 × 133, 30 × 138 and 30 × 170 calibres. These all used a short-recoil mechanism and were intended for AFV use. However, they might have been ahead of their time as they failed to achieve any sales.

Despite this failure, many other nations have since adopted high-velocity, small-calibre cannon for arming their light AFVs, a typical example being the South African Vektor G1-2 in 20 × 139 which is fitted to light armoured cars. The initial exception was the Warsaw Pact, whose BMP-1 tracked MICV of the late 1960s featured a 73mm low-velocity smooth-bore cannon with an autoloader, in a turret which also featured an externally mounted rail for an anti-tank guided missile. Incidentally, the reason for the smooth-bore barrel in the 73mm gun is that it achieves better armour-piercing performance from HEAT shells, whose effect is lessened if the shell is spinning. There is a quite different reason for most modern MBTs having smooth-bored barrels, which is that rifling disturbs the stability of APFSDS shot.

The subsequent BMP-2 of the early 1980s switched to the 2A42 30mm cannon, which uses a percussion-primed version of the universal

*Bulgarian BMP-23 AIFV with 23mm cannon (Courtesy: MoD Pattern Room)*

30 × 165 cartridge. The gun was specifically designed for the AFV role and features a variable rate of fire (either 200–300 or 600–800 rpm) although the higher rate is not used due to problems with excessive fumes in the turret. APDS (*Kerner*) ammunition is available with a claimed penetration of 25mm/1,500m/60°. In the recent BMP-3, the Russians have covered all the options, providing the turret with 7.62mm, 30mm (a 2A72, lighter than the 2A42 and with long-recoil instead of gas operation) and 100mm cannon; the latter is manually loaded but capable of firing a laser-beam-riding ATGW. One hopes that the vehicle won't be knocked out in combat while the crew is still trying to decide which weapon to shoot back with!

The Yugoslav Army went their own way with their locally designed 30mm M86 or M89 cannon (also used in the AA role) in the BVP M80AK MICV. Armour penetration is claimed to be 60mm at 1,000m (striking angle not specified).

During the 1980s the Bulgarians introduced the BMP-23 AIFV armed with a new 23mm cannon, the 2A14. It is believed to use the same 23 × 152B

ammunition as the ZU AA gun; the 2A14 reportedly uses a different mechanism although no details had emerged at the time of writing. Armour penetration is a modest 25mm/500m/90°. The BMP-30 version uses the Russian BMP-2's turret and 30mm 2A42 gun.

The British Army also moved to automatic cannon in the series of LAFVs introduced in the early 1970s, with the Fox 4 × 4 AC and the Scimitar tracked reconnaissance vehicle, which were both equipped with the ROF L21 Rarden cannon. This was a ground-breaking weapon in two ways: it introduced the 30mm calibre to AFVs, in a gun which was specifically designed for AFV use. The Rarden's cartridge was not new, being an adaptation of the HSS831 (Oerlikon KCB) 30 × 170 round, redesigned for a brass rather than steel case (as with the earlier HSS830) in order to improve the gas sealing on firing and thus reduce the amount of gun gas seeping into the turret. The low rate of fire means that the extra strength of steel cases is not required. The gun is very different from the KCB, being optimised for maximum single-shot accuracy

*Scimitar LAFV with 30mm Rarden cannon (Courtesy: MoD Pattern Room)*

rather than a high rate of fire, and despite the similar cartridge shapes, they cannot use each other's ammunition. The main anti-armour APDS round has a sharply pointed tungsten-alloy projectile which will penetrate 40mm/1,500m/45°.

Interestingly, the British backed both horses with the 1970s LAFVs, as the original version of the Scimitar, the Scorpion, was introduced with a modified version of the Saladin's 76mm manually loaded gun. This battle has evidently been won by the Rarden, since the 30mm gun has not only been fitted to the MCV-80 Warrior but is now being retrofitted to the Scorpion, using turrets from scrapped Fox ACs to create a new model called the Sabre. Incidentally, this change also indicates that the tracked reconnaissance vehicle has triumphed over the wheeled armoured car, at least in current British thinking.

The US Army was surprisingly slow to adopt the MICV concept. In fact their only modern light combat vehicle throughout the 1960s and 1970s was the M551 Sheridan, which featured a very

*M2 Bradley MICV with 25mm Bushmaster cannon (Courtesy MDHC/Ian Hogg)*

low-velocity 155m gun, capable of firing the Shillelagh beam-riding ATGW. It was not regarded as successful. Some use was also made of the 20mm M139, which was the US Army's term for the HS 820, but this was not found to be satisfactory as it

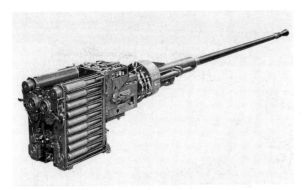

*35mm Oerlikon KDE AFV gun with two 17-round magazines (Courtesy: Oerlikon/Ian Hogg)*

needed to be kept clean and well-lubricated to function properly. The 1980s saw the introduction into US service of the M2 Bradley MICV, equipped with a turret-mounted 25mm McDonnell Douglas M242 Bushmaster, popularly known as the chain gun. This weapon has become a standard fitting in a wide range of light AFV turrets (including the USMC 8 × 8 LAV), with some competition from both the Oerlikon KBA and Mauser E, conventional fast-firing cannon using the same ammunition, and from the externally powered GIAT 25 M 811.

There is clear evidence of a classic gun-armour race taking place in MICVs. As their armour becomes tougher under the threat of attack from enemy MICVs, so the gun calibre goes up in order to defeat the thicker armour. The high-velocity 25mm Oerlikon KBB is attracting some attention as a LAFV weapon. Norway has recently selected the 30mm Bushmaster II for its new CV-90/30 AIFV. The Bushmaster II has reportedly also been selected for the US Marines' AAAV and the Swiss Army's SPZ2000 programmes, while Korea has selected the Mauser MK 30F for the KIFV (Korean infantry fighting vehicle), as have Austria for the ULAN AIFV and Spain for the almost identical Pizarro. Japan has chosen the 35mm Oerlikon KDE for its M80 MICV and other 35mm weapons are now offered, as described in Chapter 6. Sweden has already introduced a version of the classic Bofors 40mm L70 in its CV-90/40 – to date, the most powerful automatic cannon selected for service in a MICV.

The reasons for this increase in calibre can clearly be appreciated by looking at comparative armour

*Postwar AFV cartridges (left to right): 20 × 139 APDS (HS820, Oerlikon KAD, Rh202); 25 × 137 AP (Oerlikon KBA); 30 × 165 APHE (2A38/42/72); 30 × 170 APDS (Rarden); 35 × 228 APDS (Oerlikon KD series); 40 × 364R with experimental APDS (Bofors)*

penetration figures. Depending on the striking angle, a good 12.7mm API-HC will penetrate 12–15mm at 1,000m, a 20mm APCR shot about 25mm, a 25 × 137 APHE 20–27mm and APDS about 30–40mm, a 25 × 184 APDS 55mm, a 30mm APDS 40–60mm, 35 × 228 APDS 85mm and a 40mm APFSDS over 100mm at the same range.

A less expensive approach is to upgrade the ammunition rather than the gun. The 25 × 137 NATO cartridge is also available with an APFSDS projectile, which extends the APDS performance (30mm/1,000m/60°) to 1,400m. Attempts to produce similar ammunition for the 30mm Rarden have so far been unsuccessful.

Even larger calibres have been proposed, and in the 1980s both IMI of Israel and OTO Melara of Italy developed conventional 60mm high-velocity

*Russian 30mm AGS-17 with cartridges* (*Courtesy: MoD Pattern Room*)

automatic cannon (this was originally a co-operative effort). The Israeli gun is known as the hyper-velocity medium support weapon (HVMS 60) and is understood to have been sold to Chile to re-equip old light tanks. The gun weighs 700kg and fires at 100 rpm. The Italian version is heavier, at 1,000kg, and fires at 30 rpm. In both cases, the 870g APFS-DS penetrator, which has a diameter of 17mm, is fired at 1,620 m/s and is claimed to penetrate 120mm/2,000m/60°.

The conventional turret mounting of such weapons is also under threat in favour of external mounting. This in effect reduces the 'turret' to the gun mounting, leaving the crew sitting down inside the vehicle. The advantage is that only the gun need be exposed when firing from cover. This has only become feasible because of modern sighting arrangements, using low-light or thermal imaging electro-optical sights on the mounting, providing a day/night, all-weather image which can be viewed on screens inside the vehicle.

So far, all the weapons described have been for turret mounting. Some lighter weapons, however, have been developed for pintle and even tripod mountings, to replace the traditional .50″ calibre HMGs. An entirely new class of automatic weapons has also been introduced for infantry use in recent years: the grenade launchers.

Among the light automatic cannon, which use older-generation, less powerful cartridges in order to minimise weight and recoil, are the South African 20mm GA-1 Cobra, which uses 20 × 82 MG 151 ammunition and weighs just 39kg, the Israeli G360, firing the 20 × 110 Hispano cartridge, which weighs 48kg, and most remarkably the 52kg McDonnell Douglas ASP-30, designed around the 30 × 113B Aden and DEFA aircraft cannon round. Despite the 450 rpm rate of fire, recoil reduction techniques applied to the gun and mounting are so good that the ASP-30 can be fitted to a standard .50″ M2 tripod (admittedly at a significant price in terms of full-auto accuracy), while offering vastly greater destructive power than any HMG.

Last but far from least are the grenade launchers. First introduced by the USA as single-shot shoulder-fired weapons, using a $40 \times 46SR$ cartridge with a 76 m/s muzzle velocity, these have now developed into sophisticated tripod- or vehicle-mounted automatic weapons (known as AGLs: automatic grenade launchers) firing a slightly longer 'high-velocity' (240 m/s) $40 \times 53SR$ round. This was developed for the American Mk 19 introduced in the Vietnam War, which can fire at 325–385 rpm and has a range of up to 2,000m. The gun weighs 33kg but with cradle and tripod added the overall weight is 62kg. Many similar weapons, using the same ammunition, have since been developed: Spain has produced the Santa Barbera SB40LAG, Singapore the CIS 40 AGL, Germany is developing the HK 40 GMG (grenade machine gun) and South Africa the Vektor AGL. The versatility of these weapons has been increased by the introduction of the Primex High Velocity Canister Cartridge, which fires a cluster of flechettes for use in short-range perimeter defence roles.

The Russians have produced various calibres of grenade launcher, but the one used in their automatic weapon is the 30mm VOG-17M ($30 \times 29B$). The original AGS-17 weapon weighed 18kg (31kg with tripod) but the latest AGS-30 version weighs only 16kg on its tripod, and 30kg with a loaded ninety-round belt, contained in a magazine. It fires at up to 425 rpm and has a range of up to 1,700m.

The Chinese firm NORINCO has produced the 35mm W-87, which weighs only 12kg with a bipod and uses six- or nine-round top-mounted box magazines or a twelve-round drum. When mounted on a tripod, the effective range is increased from 600m to 1,500m. Romania has developed the 40mm RATMIL AGL, which rather curiously uses its own $40 \times 74.5$ ammunition, despite this having no significant ballistic advantage over the usual $40 \times 53SR$ round.

It is interesting that this most recent type of military automatic weapon is, in its intended use of firing a stream of small explosive shells against enemy troops, identical in purpose to the original 37mm Hotchkiss revolver cannon of more than a century earlier. The principal difference is that the Hotchkiss was a massive piece of artillery while the grenade launchers, as well as benefiting from modern rangefinders which dramatically improve first-shot accuracy, are light enough to be carried and manned by a couple of soldiers, transforming their tactical potential.

# *Chapter Four*

## NAVAL GUNS

*Nordenfelt two-barrelled 1" (25mm) gun on naval mounting (Courtesy: Royal Armouries)*

## EARLY BEGINNINGS

THE FIRST HEAVY MACHINE GUNS WERE DESIGNED for naval use. The main tactical problem at that time (the late nineteenth century) was the introduction of the self-propelled torpedo, which had led to the development of small, fast craft to carry them. These vessels were too large to be damaged by rifle-calibre machine gun fire and too agile to be hit by slow-firing, manually-loaded naval cannon, so an intermediate weapon was sought.

The first response was simply to scale up the existing rifle-calibre, manually driven machine guns such as the Gatling and the Nordenfelt to larger calibres of between .65" and 1" (16.5mm to

25.4mm). These fired steel bullets rather than explosive projectiles, but their weight gave them sufficient range and penetrative power to damage light craft. The 10-barrel .65″ Gatling adopted by the British Royal Navy weighed 370kg and could fire at up to 400 rpm from its 50-round drum. The four-barrel 1″ Nordenfelt mounting which later replaced it weighed 200kg and was capable of firing at a maximum rate of 200 rpm (120 rpm in aimed fire) and of penetrating about 20mm of steel at 100m.

An alternative approach was adopted by the French firm Hotchkiss, which developed a range of shell-firing rotary cannon. These were still manually driven but were capable of a much higher rate of fire than conventional manually loaded artillery and became very popular, particularly in European navies. The French Navy tested the gun in 1873 and adopted a 37mm five-barrel version as the *Modèle 1877*. A maximum of sixty of the 37 × 94R rounds could be fired each minute (although the accurate rate of fire was more like 20 rpm), the crew keeping the machine fed by means of ten-round clips. The weight was similar to that of the rival 1″ Nordenfelt four-barrel mounting; armour penetration was less but destructive effect against unarmoured targets much greater.

The 47mm was a scaled-up version, the 47 × 131R round having a more effective 1.1kg shell which reached a range of 3,600m, while the largest of the rotaries was in 53mm calibre. In all,

the French Navy alone ordered 10,000 of the Hotchkiss cannon, and at least thirty other countries acquired them. The weapons were effective enough to remain in service well into the automatic weapon era, still being in use at the beginning of the twentieth century. By then, however, they were being displaced by automatic weapons of the Maxim type.

The first 37mm Maxim gun, which used the same ammunition as the Hotchkiss, was introduced in the 1890s, and with its rate of fire of 200–300 rpm completely outclassed the older gun. It first came to fame as an army weapon, when used against the British in the Boer War, but was soon fitted to warships. During the First World War, many were fitted to high-angle mountings for anti-aircraft purposes.

More powerful 37mm guns firing longer cartridges, such as the USN heavy 1pdr (37 × 137R), developed from the Maxim 1¼pdr, saw limited service. Another US design which used the same 37 × 137R cartridge was the McClean cannon. This was a gas-operated weapon which, despite failing US tests, was purchased by Russia and Spain. In Britain the RN 1½pdr (37 × 123R) was introduced in 1915 but saw little service as it was soon eclipsed by a larger version, the Vickers 2pdr of 40mm calibre, named for the nominal two-pound (0.9kg) weight of the shell. By then, torpedo boats were evolving into destroyers and were far too large to be damaged by such a weapon, so it was introduced from the outset as an anti-aircraft gun.

## THE ANTI-AIRCRAFT PROBLEM BETWEEN THE WARS

THE EXPERIENCE OF THE FIRST WORLD WAR MADE it clear that in any future conflict naval vessels not only had to fear enemy surface ships, submarines and mines but also torpedoes and bombs dropped by aircraft. As with any radically new problem this took some time to become accepted, but the steady improvement in aircraft speed, range and load-carrying performance in the inter-war period eventually prompted navies around the world to devise and fit various forms of specialised anti-aircraft guns.

For long-range fire the preferred approach was manually loaded guns, of between 3″ and 5.25″ calibre, on high-elevation mountings. In addition, the

*37mm Hotchkiss on naval mounting (BuOrd, USN)*

need to provide a second and even a third layer of defence against aircraft pressing home their attacks was realised. This invariably took the form of rapid-firing machine guns for the short-range role and automatic guns of calibres up to 40mm for medium ranges.

In deciding the appropriate weapons to be fitted, there were, and still are, various considerations apart from the obvious ones of cost and availability. The range, hitting power and rate of fire of the guns, the weight of the mountings and the problem of locating them to provide the maximum field of fire ('sky arcs') without blowing holes in the superstructure were basic concerns.

Perhaps less evident were questions of power requirements. Powered mountings offered much faster training and elevation rates but were more expensive and vulnerable to loss of power through

*.5″ Vickers quad naval mounting*
*(Courtesy: MoD Pattern Room)*

action damage. Also of concern was the crew required to man them (as warships were commonly overcrowded in wartime) and the maintainability of the equipment; wartime experience led to simplicity and reliability becoming highly valued.

The method of aiming was also a factor; machine guns and light cannon used open sights so their accuracy was greatly dependent on the gunner's skill. The larger automatic cannon mountings commonly featured director control, which added to the mounting and manning demands.

## BRITISH WEAPONS

DURING THE EARLY 1930S THE ROYAL NAVY selected two weapons to fulfil the short-range AA roles: the .5″ Vickers Mk III heavy machine gun and the 2pdr which has already been mentioned. Both guns were belt-fed and water-cooled.

The .5″ was originally intended for all three services, but only the RN made extensive use of it. The gun used Vickers's own 12.7 × 81 cartridge and fired at a rate of about 700 rpm. The first naval application appeared in the early 1930s in a four-barrel mounting (most unusually, with the barrels vertically stacked) which weighed between 1,000kg and 1,300kg and was intended mainly for destroyers. Subsequently, twin- and single-barrelled versions were produced for smaller craft. All of these were unpowered except for the hydraulic Mk V twin, which had respectable training and elevation rates of 72 and 50 degrees per second respectively. This weighed about 500kg and was typically fitted to fast patrol boats.

The 2pdr gun weighed between 356kg and 416kg. Ammunition was in disintegrating steel-link belts which could be joined to provide up to 140 rounds per gun. Initially, muzzle velocity achieved by the 40 × 158R cartridge was only 620 m/s and the rate of fire some 90 rpm. The 2pdr was designed to be fitted in two mountings: an eight-barrel mounting weighing around 16,000kg which was intended to arm battleships and aircraft carriers (first fitted to HM ships *Warspite*, *Rodney* and *Nelson* in the late 1930s), and a four-barrel version which first emerged on County class cruisers and Tribal class destroyers. In contrast to the .5″, the barrels were arranged in two side-by-side pairs, one above the other. Initial marks of this were manual

*2pdr Vickers quad naval mounting (Leo Marriott)*

and weighed 8,700kg; later, powered marks weighed between 10,000kg and 11,000kg. Single barrel mountings weighing 1,400–1,800kg appeared later and were used in a wide variety of vessels including fast patrol boats.

The size and weight of the four- and eight-barrel mountings is emphasised by comparison with typical medium-calibre equipment. A single 4″ Mk XX weighed 10,000kg, a twin 4″ Mk XIX 15,000kg, and a single 4.7″ destroyer (low-angle) mounting some 9,000kg.

## THE NAVAL ANTI-AIRCRAFT GUNNERY COMMITTEE

EVEN AT THE BEGINNING OF THE 1930S THERE WAS some concern about the adequacy of the British weapons. The problem was considered by the Naval Anti-aircraft Gunnery Committee, which produced a report in April 1932.

The committee went into great technical detail in calculating the effectiveness of different guns. They took into consideration such matters as the nature of the threats, the time during which aircraft could be brought under effective fire by different weapons, the range and rate of fire of the guns, the effectiveness of shells and fuzes, and appropriate methods of fire control. Their conclusions make interesting reading.

Three types of attack were considered: precision (i.e. level) bombing, torpedo bombing and close-range attack with bombs or machine guns. With remarkable prescience, the committee also identified a further potential risk:

> The possibility of explosive aircraft being manoeuvred by human pilots to hit ship targets cannot however be ruled out. It is reported that, sooner than accept defeat, ramming other aircraft is a recognised principle among Japanese pilots.

Note: The Air Ministry regard this idea as exceptionally secret and would prefer that it be not generally promulgated.

It was clear that the committee considered such attacks to be potentially extremely difficult to deal with, a concern fully justified by the experience of a dozen years later.

In considering short-range defence, the committee was most concerned about torpedo bombers, calculating that any weapon system able to cope with them would be able to deal with other forms of short-range attack easily enough. Exercises between 1928 and 1931 had shown that the probability of a torpedo bomber hitting a ship was only 10% at 1,250 yards (1,140m) but rose to 30% at 1,000 yards (910m), 50% at 750 yards (690m) then increased very sharply to 85% at 600 yards (550m).

This led to a demand for a range of 2,500 yards (2,300m) from automatic AA guns, in order to achieve the aim of certain destruction of an aircraft with ten seconds of firing at a mean range of 2,000 yards (1,820m). It was estimated that an aircraft dropping a torpedo from 1,200 yards (1,100m) would already have been under fire from such weapons for seventeen seconds, which was assumed to be more than enough time to shoot it down.

The two existing weapons – the .5″ machine gun and 2pdr – were considered in detail. There were strong indications that the committee was not much impressed with either, suspecting that the .5″ was ineffective and that the 2pdr Pom-pom (yes, that was the title they gave it!) had too low a muzzle velocity. They were also concerned about the 2pdr's rate of fire. This was felt to be just about adequate in its eight-barrel form but the committee recommended that no further steps should be taken to develop the four-barrel version, which was all that smaller vessels could carry. They expressed a hope that both guns would be replaced by an intermediate calibre with a 760 m/s muzzle velocity and a total output of at least 1,250 rpm, and recommended a series of trials to determine the ideal calibre.

In fact, two experimental weapons emerged. One was the very powerful Vickers .661″ heavy machine gun developed between 1935 and 1938, which was intended to be fitted in a six-barrel mounting. Development was cancelled in 1938 in favour of the 20mm Oerlikon S, which had the advantage of firing the explosive shells which were by then regarded as essential. The other, somewhat closer to the committee's views, was the 35mm 1½pdr Mk V, which fired a 0.68kg shell at 790 m/s. However, the eight-barrel mounting ended up weighing more than the 2pdr's, and the weapon was cancelled in 1937.

Later, a more powerful 'high-velocity' loading of the 2pdr was introduced which raised the muzzle velocity to 730 m/s, partly achieved by reducing the shell weight from 0.9kg to 0.76kg. This could only be fired in modified guns and the 'hot' high-pressure loading cannot have done much for the reliability. The rate of fire was also increased to 115 rpm.

## AMERICAN WEAPONS

THE UNITED STATES NAVY HAD A GENERAL BOARD whose task it was to consider ship armament. In 1929 they also went through a process of determining future AA needs. The conclusions they came to were generally similar to those of the British equivalent, although they differed in certain important respects.

The main short-range automatic weapon in USN service at the time was the .50″ Browning M1921 machine gun, introduced in 1925. In principle, this was similar to the Vickers weapon, being belt-fed and water-cooled and with a similar rate of fire, although it used a more powerful 12.7 × 99 cartridge. Unlike the Vickers, the Browning was initially only available in a single, manually operated mounting, although a twin mounting later emerged and during the war the standard army quadruple, air-cooled mounting saw some use.

Although the improved .50″ M2 was adopted in 1933, the General Board felt that the Browning was inadequate against dive bombers so a larger weapon was sought. Attention soon focused on an automatic cannon firing a shell weighing 0.9 pound (400g). The St Petersburg Declaration banning smaller shells was still officially in force, and although this had been widely flouted in the Great War there was still uneasiness about ignoring it in peacetime planning – a concern also referred to by the British committee.

In the past, this weight of shell had been

associated with the 37mm gun and the USN was at one time interested in the Browning-designed cannon in this calibre which was later adopted by the army. By the 1930s, more advanced weapons technology now meant that this projectile weight was appropriate for a smaller calibre; so the 1.1″ (28mm) gun was conceived, using a mechanism very similar to the army 37mm weapon. The shell, which actually weighed 416g, was fitted with a super-sensitive contact fuze with a short delay, and ammunition was loaded in eight-round clips. The cartridge was powerful, but the gun only fired at 150 rpm.

Development was very slow but eventually resulted in a complex, four-barrel, powered mounting weighing in its different versions from 4,800kg to 6,350kg. Maximum elevating and training speeds were 24° and 30°/sec respectively, but the guns (which were arranged side by side) could also be slewed up to 30° either side without needing to rotate the mounting. The reason for this curious measure was to aid aiming when the guns were pointing vertically for use against dive bombers;

*.5″ Browning on pedestal mounting (Courtesy: V. Forgett)*

*1.1″ USN quad mounting, ready for action on board USS* Ranger, *North Africa, December 1942; note additional ammunition being brought up (Courtesy: US Naval Archives)*

traversing the mounting has little effect in these circumstances. The 1.1″ gun was adopted and rushed into service in the late 1930s before the system had been debugged, leading to a reputation for unreliability.

## EUROPEAN AND JAPANESE EQUIPMENT

EUROPE AND JAPAN are CONSIDERED TOGETHER because at that time the Imperial Japanese Navy was heavily influenced by European practices and bought much of their equipment from European firms, particularly the smaller automatic weapons.

For the most part, plans followed a similar pattern to those of the RN and USN, in that two different classes of automatic weapon were generally adopted: automatic cannon of 25–40mm and heavy machine guns of 12.7–13.2mm. There were, however, some exceptions.

The principal French automatic weapon was the 13.2mm Hotchkiss HMG which fired a 13.2 × 99 cartridge almost identical to the Browning's except for the slightly larger calibre. The 13.2mm had a relatively low rate of fire of 450 rpm, and its effective rate of fire was far lower still than that of the belt-fed, water-cooled guns because of the need to change magazines and allow time for barrel cooling. It was widely used in single, twin and quadruple mountings.

The French Navy's standard AA cannon was the 37mm M1925 (single mounting) and M1933 (twin), firing a 37 × 277R cartridge. It compared very poorly with most other weapons in this calibre as it was manually loaded, which limited its rate of fire to 30–42 rpm. This is surprising, considering that the French Army adopted a fully automatic Schneider 37mm gun during the same period. Some limited naval use was also made of the army's 25mm Hotchkiss, which will be described in more detail below.

The Japanese automatic weapons were mainly of French origin: the 25mm and 13.2mm Hotchkiss. The 25mm was fitted in single (free-swinging), twin and triple mountings which weighed 785kg, 1,100kg and 1,800kg respectively. The cartridge was a rimless 25 × 163 and the rate of fire was around 220 rpm, but limited to far less than this in practice by the air-cooled barrel and the use of fifteen-round

*13mm Type 93 (13.2mm Hotchkiss) aboard Japanese ship during surrender to USN, September 1945*
*(Courtesy: US Naval Historical Centre)*

vertical box magazines. The maximum effective range was claimed to be between 1,500m and 3,000m. Some older Vickers 2pdrs, acquired prewar, also remained in service.

The German Navy differed from most others at the start of the war in that their standard automatic weapon was in 20mm calibre – the Mauser 2cm FlaK 38 in single, twin and quadruple mountings. The weight of the mountings was around 400kg, 1,000kg and 2,200kg respectively, manually operated in all cases. The rate of fire was around 450 rpm per barrel, but again this was limited by air-cooling and the use of horizontal box magazines with twenty or (rarely) forty rounds. There were also examples of the earlier Rheinmetall-Borsig FlaK 30 in use; this used the same ammunition and magazines but had a lower rate of fire of 280–300 rpm. The 20 × 138B cartridge was appreciably more powerful and effective than the equivalent HMGs of most other nations. In particular, the four-barrel *Flakvierling* (adapted from the army weapon) was devastatingly effective at short range.

As with the French, the German 37mm gun in use early in the war was not automatic. The 3.7cm SKC/30 fired an exceptionally powerful 37 × 380R cartridge (750g at 1,000 m/s) but at only 30 rpm.

The Italians also used 37mm and 20mm cannon, the former using a 37 × 230SR cartridge and the latter firing the same (20 × 138B) ammunition as the German guns. There was also a 13.2mm Breda M1931 machine gun, using Hotchkiss ammunition and with a similar specification, fitted to submarines in both single and twin mountings. Some earlier 40mm Vickers-Terni in single mountings, licence-produced versions of the British 2pdr, remained in service.

The 37mm Breda was available in a variety of single and twin mountings, one of which was

*Effect of 25mm Type 96 fire; damage to P-47 wing*
*(Courtesy: US Naval Historical Centre)*

*25mm Type 96 (25mm Hotchkiss) triple mounting installed on Guadalcanal beach, October 1942*
*(Courtesy: US Naval Historical Centre)*

*20mm Flakvierling installed on* Prinz Eugen *in preparation for the Channel Dash, February 1942*
*(Courtesy: US Naval Historical Centre)*

stabilised – an unusual degree of sophistication for any weapon at that time. Most were air-cooled (although the stabilised M1932 twin was water-cooled), but all were fed by six-round magazines. Mounting weights varied between 1,500kg and 5,000kg and the rate of fire was 120 rpm per barrel.

The gas-operated air-cooled 20mm Breda was also available in a stabilised twin mounting, the RM1935, in which the guns were arranged in a diagonally staggered mounting weighing 2,200kg. There was a free-swinging single M1940 mounting weighing a more realistic 312kg. The rate of fire was 240 rpm, but the magazine held only twelve rounds. The *Regia Navale* also made use of the Isotta-Fraschini-built Scotti 20mm which used the same ammunition. It was available in twin (RM1935) and single (M1939) mountings.

The prolific Aimo Lahti also achieved some success in Finland with the L-34 boat gun, a 20mm cannon which used his own 20 × 113 cartridge. Not much information about this has survived, but it is known to have been recoil-operated and fired at 350 rpm from either a fifteen-round box or forty-five-round drum. In Sweden, the Vickers-Terni 25mm, firing a 25 × 87R cartridge, was produced as the *'25mm kulspruta M/1922'* and fitted to some submarines. The Bofors 25mm was also used.

The Soviet Union developed weapons in 12.7mm, 25mm and 37mm calibres. The two larger

weapons were derived from the Bofors 25mm of 1932, the Soviets concentrating first on adapting the gun to 37 × 250R calibre to produce the M39. This was initially an air-cooled weapon available in a single manually operated mount weighing 2,800kg and fed by five-round clips, although a water-cooled version, the W-11-M, in a single mounting or a twin weighing 3,800kg, appeared after the war. The 25mm version, the M1940, fired a 25 × 218R cartridge based on the Bofors' (but slightly different in dimensions), and did not enter service until 1941. The 12.7mm gun was a version of the army's Degtyarev (DShK) heavy machine gun, available in single, twin and quadruple mountings.

## THE SECOND WORLD WAR

WAR EXPERIENCE SOON JUSTIFIED THE CONCERNS of both the British and the Americans about the .5″ machine gun's lack of range and hitting power. Their high rate of fire meant that they had some effect against strafing aircraft which came too close, but they were of little use against torpedo and dive bombers.

The smallest calibre to prove its worth was the 20mm. In Allied navies, this calibre became virtually synonymous with the Oerlikon S, the most powerful of a family of API blowback 20mm weapons developed by the Swiss firm between the wars. It was introduced by the RN in 1939 and by the USN in 1941.

Performance was only average, the $20 \times 110RB$ cartridge being fired at a rate of about 450 rpm – no better than the significantly more powerful German 2cm FlaK 38. The cartridges normally had to be greased to ensure reliable extraction of the fired cases, although during the war a fluted chamber was introduced in the American Mk 4/4. This worked with brass cartridge cases, but the alternative steel cases still required greasing.

The sixty-round ammunition drum allowed only 7.5 seconds' firing before reloading, but the air-cooled barrel limited the continuous rate of fire in any case. While the gun had a theoretical maximum range of 4.4km, the practical maximum was only about 1.5km. However, its advantages were great simplicity, ruggedness and reliability. Most mountings had no power requirements and could be sited wherever there was space.

The most common mounting in British service was the Mk II single, which weighed between 500kg and 750kg. The hydraulically powered Mk V twin weighed 1,200kg, but later manual twin mountings weighed less than 600kg. A complex, four-barrelled, belt-fed mount was developed but not adopted. The Oerlikon was always best suited to the simple manual mount, as was emphasised by the later conversion of Mk V mounting to take a single Bofors gun instead.

American mountings were generally similar to the British but they did introduce a powered quadruple mount, albeit still with drum-fed guns. Although it lost favour towards the end of the war, as the small shell was inadequate in dealing with kamikaze attacks, the Oerlikon was still immensely popular. At the end of the war the British and Commonwealth navies alone had about 55,000 in service, the USN 12,500, with some of their capital ships being fitted with as many as 100 of the guns. The USN rated the Oerlikon as between eight and ten times more effective in the AA role than the .5″, and estimated that it accounted for 32% of Japanese aircraft destroyed by naval AA fire between Pearl Harbor and 1944, after which the figure dropped to 25%.

Many other machine guns and light cannon were pressed into British service, particularly in

*Twin 20mm Oerlikons on RN Mark V mounting (early type). (John Lambert)*

defensively equipped merchant ships (DEMS). The RAF's 20mm Hispano cannon (HS 404) saw limited use. Its superior performance in terms of muzzle velocity, rate of fire and lighter weight did not compensate for its relative fragility. Incidentally, the US Navy and Coastguard adopted a version of the HS 404 in the 1970s as the Mk 16, fitted to a simple manual mounting and complete with a recoil-operated chamber lubricator to avoid the need to pre-lubricate the ammunition. It should be noted that although the $20 \times 110$ Hispano cartridges were about the same size as those used in the Oerlikon, they were not interchangeable. The *Kriegsmarine* also fitted non-standard weapons alongside their FlaK 30 and FlaK 38, such as the Danish 20mm Madsen, firing a unique $20 \times 120$ round, and the *Luftwaffe*'s Mauser MG 151, as well as various Oerlikons.

The intermediate calibres – the 25mm Hotchkiss and the 1.1″ USN – were not a great success. Their mountings were generally much heavier and more complex than most of those for the simple Oerlikon, but the shells lacked range and destructive power in comparison with the 37mm and

40mm cannon. The 25mm mountings were criticised by the Japanese for their slow rates of elevation and training, inadequate sights, excessive vibration and limited magazine capacity. The 1.1″ took a long time to overcome its reputation for unreliability (not helped by the reduced training for wartime personnel) and the rate of fire was too low. It proved incapable of dealing with kamikaze attacks and was replaced in US service by the 40mm Bofors, the remaining 1.1″ guns being scrapped in 1945.

The automatic 37mm weapons appeared to be effective but, not surprisingly, the French and German manually loaded single-shot guns were unsatisfactory and work commenced on automatic guns. The French did not have time to put their Hotchkiss M1935 into service (it used a unique 37 × 218R round) and it was still on trial at the start of the war. A further development, the M1936, had some minor alterations to the ammunition feed. Mounted on the aviso *Amiens* it reportedly shot down several German aircraft during the defence of Le Havre in early June 1940.

The Germans adopted a Rheinmetall-Borsig weapon, the FlaK M 42. This was surprisingly designed around the 37 × 249R cartridge (loaded using five-round clips) used in the army's tank and anti-tank guns instead of the 37 × 263B used in the other AA weapons. Single and twin manual mountings weighed 1,350kg and 1,750kg respectively. Not satisfied with this, the *Kriegsmarine* later adopted the FlaK M 43, which was also a Rheinmetall-Borsig design. This used the same 37 × 263B ammunition as the land-based FlaK 36 (this time loaded by a tray) and was also air-cooled, but had gas instead of recoil operation. It had an impressive cyclic firing rate of 250 rpm instead of around 170 for the M 42, but the practical rate of fire was about 150 rpm. The single unpowered mounting weighed 1,350kg.

Towards the end of the war, two advanced 30mm mountings were being developed for the *Kriegsmarine*, one using the MK 103 aircraft cannon and the other, intended for the *S-boote* and the revolutionary Type XXI U-boats, the even more powerful MK 303 weapon, which featured a differential recoil or floating firing mounting. These were intended to replace the 20mm which was beginning

to be regarded as inadequate in range and hitting power, but neither had time to see service. The 5.5cm FlaK *Gerät 58* referred to in Chapter 3 weapons was also being developed for the *Kriegsmarine*, but was again too late to see service.

The British 2pdr had a rather controversial history. It proved prone to stoppages for a variety of reasons but a good gun crew could keep it going and it gave sterling service. However, it was clearly outclassed in performance by the Swedish 40mm Bofors which had already been selected by the British Army in preference to the 2pdr.

The 2pdr was ultimately replaced by the 40mm L56 Bofors, but it remained in British service throughout the war and for some years after. In particular, it experienced a minor revival in the Far East in 1945 in single-barrel form, to replace twin Oerlikon mountings, because the heavy shell was more effective against kamikaze attacks.

This brings us to the 40mm Bofors which is probably the most famous light anti-aircraft gun in the world. In comparison with the 2pdr, the Bofors fired a much larger and more powerful 40 × 311R cartridge (loaded in four-round clips) with a significantly longer effective range of around 3km instead of 2km, although the maximum range of both guns was about three times further. Most important of all, the Bofors was light, simple and reliable.

The first weapon adopted by the RN was the army's air-cooled, single-barrel version, which when first fitted to ships in 1941 was all that was available. The single unpowered mountings weighed between 1,200kg and 1,400kg and fired at a rate of 120–150 rpm. This proved an immediate success but supply did not catch up with demand until 1943.

Following the loss to Japanese air attack of the battleship HMS *Prince of Wales* and the battle-cruiser HMS *Repulse* off the coast of Malaya in December 1941, an analysis of the anti-aircraft fire by the gunnery officer of the *Prince of Wales* revealed that the 2pdrs suffered frequent stoppages due to the separation of the shell from the cartridge case. Furthermore, they were not firing tracer ammunition and thus had no deterrent effect. By contrast, the single 40mm Bofors gun was very reliable and the tracer ammunition from this (and even

*Twin 40mm Bofors on Hazemeyer stabilised mounting (Courtesy: MoD Pattern Room)*

the Oerlikons) was seen to disturb the approach of the Japanese aircraft. The recommendation was strongly in favour of fitting Bofors guns in the future.

The air cooling obviously limited the continuous rate of fire. The navy therefore adopted the twin-barrel, water-cooled Hazemeyer mounting of Dutch origin, the first RN vessel being equipped in November 1942. This was a complex powered mounting, triaxially stabilised so that the guns would (at least in theory) be held on target regardless of ship movement, but it weighed over 7,000kg and was not noted for reliability. Towards the end

of the war the simpler and slightly lighter (6,500kg) Mk V twin mounting was developed instead and this became the basis of the standard post-war twin mounting.

The increase in automatic AA firepower fitted to British ships was considerable. At the start of the war, destroyers were typically fitted with a pair of quadruple .5″ mountings (and their main gun armament was incapable of AA fire). The late-war Battle class destroyers were equipped with up to eight Bofors and six Oerlikon guns, as well as having dual-purpose main guns.

Both air- and water-cooled Bofors guns were

also adopted by the USN from 1942 to replace the 1.1″. They were fitted in single, twin and quadruple mountings, weighing about 1,100kg (unpowered air-cooled single), 1,900kg (powered air-cooled single), 6,000kg (powered water-cooled twin) and 11,000kg (powered water-cooled quad). The larger mountings were generally aimed by director fire and considered effective at 2,500m range. Even the 40mm calibre was found by the Americans to be marginal against kamikaze attacks, so they developed a very fast-firing 3″ gun, although it did not see service until after the war. This also helped to bridge the range gap to the 5″ DP gun, which had a *minimum* effective AA range of 5,000m. Despite these reservations, the Bofors was credited with 50% of Japanese aircraft shot down by USN AA fire between October 1944 and March 1945.

Not all of the wartime naval automatic cannon were intended for the anti-aircraft role. Small patrol craft such as motor torpedo and motor gun boats (MTBs and MGBs and German *S-boote*) fought a vicious little war with their opposite numbers, particularly in the North Sea and English Channel, and apart from the usual machine guns and 20mm

and 40mm cannon they were sometimes equipped with unique weapons, the best known example being the British gun popularly known as the 6pdr, or 57mm Molins gun.

The Molins had a chequered history, being designed in 1942 as an automatic version of the army's anti-tank gun for mounting on a fast, wheeled tank-destroyer, the autoloader being designed by the Molins company. The arrival of the German Tiger tank switched the army's interest to bigger things, so Molins offered the gun to the navy instead (and subsequently to the RAF as well, as will be described later). The gun was recoil-operated and air-cooled, its gravity loading system fed by four-round clips of the bottle-necked 57 × 441R cartridges. Strictly speaking it was semi-automatic as the gunner had to pull the trigger for each shot, but it was capable of 40 rpm. In naval use the weapon was known by the snappy title of the '6pdr 7 cwt Mk 11A on 6pdr Mk VII power-operated mounting', the total equipment weighing 1,747kg.

Other small-calibre cannon used on British craft were manually loaded or semi-automatic, such as the 40mm Rolls-Royce BD gun (using

*20mm Oerlikon (furthest from camera) and 37mm M4 on US PT Boat in 1944. Note the continuous-belt feed forming a hoop over the M4 (Courtesy: US Naval Historical Centre)*

*OtoBreda 40mm Fast Forty (Courtesy: Alenia)*

*Spanish Meroka 20mm CIWS (Courtesy: Ian Hogg)*

*Mauser Drakon 27mm CIWS* (*Courtesy: Mauser*)

*Mauser naval 27/30mm gun system during firing trials at sea* (*Courtesy: Mauser*)

*Sea Cobra CIWS with twin Mauser MK30* (Leo Marriott)

*Russian Kashtan CIWS with twin 30mm 6K30-GSh rotary cannon* (Courtesy: Scorpion/KBP)

*Millennium 35/1000 naval gun system* (Courtesy: Oerlikon-Contraves)

*Bofors 57mm Mk 2 onboard Gothenburg class corvette* (Courtesy: Celsius)

*Bofors 57mm Mk 2 without cupola* (*Courtesy: Celsius*)

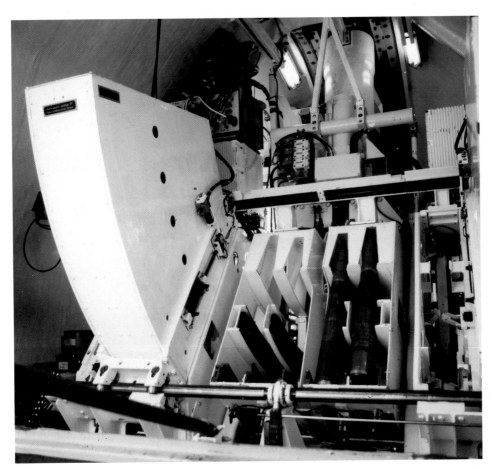

*Ammunition feed for Bofors 57mm Mk 2* (*Courtesy: Celsius*)

*Ammunition for the 57mm Bofors: foreground = HCER, in clip = proximity-fuzed HE, centre = TP, right = HE point detonating (Courtesy: Celsius)*

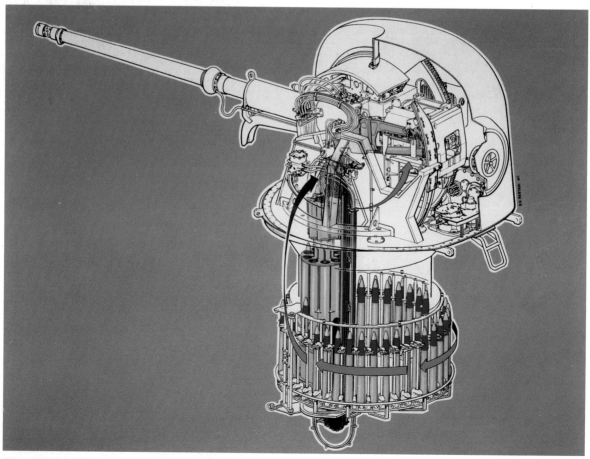

*76mm OTO Melara (Courtesy: Alenia)*

*Soviet aircraft guns at the Monino museum: Left: Rikhter R-23, YakB-12·7, centre: NR-30, NS-23, right: NS-23, N-37*
*(Courtesy: Russian Aviation Research Trust)*

*Twin .50" Browning M2 in Lancaster tail turret*

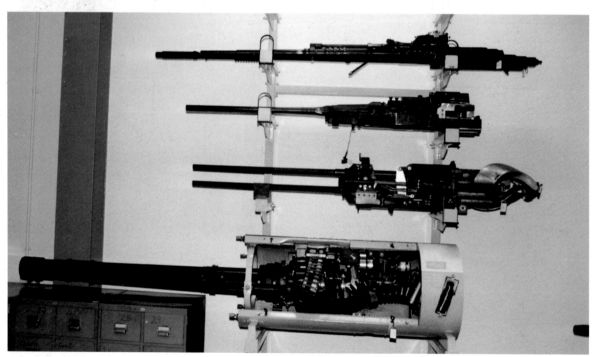

*US 20mm aircraft guns at the MoD Pattern Room (from top to bottom): AN-M2, M39, Mk 11, M61A1*
*(Courtesy: MoD Pattern Room)*

*World War 2 anti-aircraft gun cartridges (from left to right): .303" for scale (7.7 × 56R), .5" Vickers (12.7 × 81), 13.2mm Hotchkiss/13mm Type 93 (13.2 × 99), 20mm Oerlikon S (20 × 110RB), 20mm Madsen (20 × 120), 20mm Long Solothurn/FlaK 30/38/Breda (20 × 138B), 20mm IJA Type 98 (20 × 142), 25mm Hotchkiss/Type 96 (25 × 163), 1.1" USN (28 × 199SR), 37mm US Army M1 (37 × 223SR), 37mm Kriegsmarine FlaK M42 (with non-standard AP projectile) (37 × 249R), 37mm Soviet M1939 (37 × 250R), 37mm FlaK 18/36/43 (37 × 263B), 2pdr Vickers (40 × 158R), 40mm Bofors L/56 (40 × 311R)*

similar ammunition to the 2pdr), 3pdr Hotchkiss (firing a 47 × 376R cartridge) and the 6pdr 8 cwt and 10 cwt, each of which used its own unique ammunition (57 × 306R and 57 × 464R respectively). The 6-pdr 8 cwt was a nineteenth-century Hotchkiss design (also used to arm the first British tanks in the First World War); the 10 cwt was an army coast defence gun, known as the Twin Six as it was only fitted in a twin mounting, which saw limited RN service as an anti-*S-boote* weapon.

The British were not alone in 'borrowing' useful weapons from other services for their smaller warships. The USN made some use of the 37mm M4 aircraft cannon for arming PT boats for surface

action and was the only user of the more powerful 37mm M9, fitted to a few PT boats by the end of the war. Also designed for aircraft, this featured a hoop-type ammunition feed over the gun similar in appearance to the M4's continuous-loop belt (which was shaped to fit inside an aircraft's nose) but in this case acting as a guide for the disintegrating-link belt. A 'wet' version of the M9 was reportedly developed for submarines, but not used.

## POST-WAR ANTI-AIRCRAFT GUNS

THE POST-WAR DEVELOPMENT OF HEAVY AUTOMATIC naval weapons can be divided into three strands. First is the continued development of manually aimed light cannon of up to 40mm calibre, with improved weapons, ammunition and mountings. These are normally intended for low-intensity 'police' work, when the use of major cannon or missiles might be inappropriate, although they may also have a backup AA role in an emergency, depending on the sophistication of their mountings and sighting arrangements.

The second strand is the introduction of remotely controlled and usually radar-directed light cannon specifically intended for anti-aircraft use, with the more sophisticated versions also being intended to destroy anti-ship missiles in flight. Missiles are much more difficult targets than aircraft due to their small size, high speed and low-level approach path.

The third strand is the extension of automatic loading to all naval guns, whatever their calibre. New guns of up to 3" (76mm) have been primarily intended for the AA role with a secondary capability against small craft, with 4–5" guns being all-purpose weapons and 6–8" guns intended for surface action, including shore bombardment. These larger calibres do not strictly concern us here but mention will be made of them for comparative purposes.

Describing the development of these weapons in a coherent way is difficult because of the modern tendency for several different guns, often of different nationalities, being developed to use each cartridge, and of many different mountings, also of various nationalities, being designed for any given gun. To make matters even more complicated, mountings are often offered with different types of gun. The emphasis in this section will therefore be placed on the major strands described above, with comments on the choices made by different navies.

## MANUALLY-AIMED LIGHT CANNON

HEAVY MACHINE GUNS ARE STILL FITTED TO SOME light naval vessels, but only on the simplest of mountings with virtually no technical changes since the Second World War. In contrast, several new 20mm, 25mm, 30mm and 40mm cartridges and weapons have been introduced and are used in mountings under local control – that is, with the gunner standing behind or sitting on the mounting in order to aim the gun.

One of the few points they share in common is

that they are all air-cooled. The main points of difference, apart from calibre, concern the mountings. Small-calibre cannon are usually on free-swinging mountings with the gunner standing behind them (in which case they may be entirely unpowered or have power assistance to help the gunner aim them). Larger weapons normally have the gunner sitting on the mount, which may again be unpowered, have power assistance or even be fully stabilised.

The sighting system is also important. This may range from a simple open sight to a highly sophisticated device combining a laser rangefinder with a ballistic computer so that all the gunner has to do is keep the sight pointing straight at the target; the sighting system will calculate where the gun has to point in order to hit the target.

The combination of mounting and sighting system does far more to determine the usefulness of a light cannon than the calibre. An unpowered mounting and open sights limit the weapon to engaging nearby stationary or slow-moving targets in reasonably calm seas (especially when fitted to small craft). In contrast, a stabilised mounting and a computer sight will convert almost any cannon into a highly effective surface-fire weapon with a credible back-up anti-aircraft performance. Broadly speaking, unpowered free-swinging mountings tend to be of 20mm calibre, with 25mm calibres seeing some powered assistance and 30+mm are fully powered and often stabilised.

Very few of the light cannon used in naval mountings have been developed solely for naval purposes. Most are also found in ground mountings, armoured fighting vehicles, helicopters and even fighter aircraft, and they will therefore be mentioned more than once in this book. Description of the weapons can be found in Chapter 2, with data summarised in Appendix 2 (Table 3). It should be noted that naval cannon have a long life and some pre-Second World War designs are still in front-line service alongside the modern versions.

Most of the modern 20mm guns, whether gas/blowback or gas-operated as described in Chapter 2, have a comparable performance, with projectile weights of 120–130g, muzzle velocities in the region of 1,000–1,100 m/s, rates of fire of about 1,000 rpm and gun weights of 80–100kg. The

$20 \times 102$ cartridge in the GIAT M621 is less powerful, firing projectiles of around 100g, but the gun weighs only 45kg.

Modern 20mm guns are usually belt-fed, although the drum-fed Oerlikon Type A41A (previously known as the Hispano HS 804 which uses the same $20 \times 110$ ammunition as the wartime HS 404 aircraft gun) was reintroduced in the 1980s to meet a demand for less sophisticated weapons.

In naval use 20mm guns are usually found in single, unpowered, free-swinging mountings weighing around 400–500kg. A typical example is the Oerlikon GAM-BO1 which carries a KAA cannon and has been fitted to several RN ships as a consequence of the suddenly renewed interest in light cannon after the 1982 Falklands conflict. The maximum range is 6.8km, although the effective range is about 1.5km against aircraft and 2km against surface targets.

The Soviet Army's 23mm ZU gun was not used by the Soviet Navy but was sold abroad in both twin (ZU-23-2) and quad (ZU-23-4) mountings, fitted to ships of the Finnish and several other navies. The twin mounting weighed 980kg with ammunition. The Polish Navy have adopted an indigenous version of the twin mounting, the ZSU-23-2MR 'Wrobel' (sparrow). It is also available fitted with

*Twin 23mm ZU naval mounting*
*(Courtesy: MoD Pattern Room)*

twin *Strela-2M* missiles as well as the guns.

The 25mm calibre has progressed in two completely different ways. First, the Soviets reworked the wartime 25mm M1940 in two versions (known as the M-110 and 110-PM) to take a new $25 \times 218$ cartridge. These were available in hydraulically powered twin mountings (the 2M3, 2M3M and 2M8) weighing around 1,400kg with a 450 rpm rate of fire. These weapons, also produced by the Chinese as the Type 61, were claimed to have an effective range of 2,300m. However, they were replaced by a radar-directed 30mm mounting and are now obsolete in Russian service.

Two cannon using the NATO standard $25 \times 137$ cartridge are in service: the Oerlikon KBA, with a 600 rpm rate of fire, and the electrically powered Hughes M242 'Bushmaster' chain gun, which has a rate of fire variable between 100 and 500 rpm. Either can be fitted to single mountings, but entirely unpowered operation is becoming marginal at these calibres.

The American Mk 88 mounting, using the Bushmaster cannon, is entirely unpowered and weighs 560kg. It is only suitable for 'police work' and will be difficult to aim unless the sea is calm. In contrast, the 930kg Italian OtoBreda mounting, using the KBA gun, provides hydraulic assistance to the gunner and has some potential as a back-up AA gun.

The 30mm calibre is represented by two different weapons using different cartridges: the Oerlikon KCB ($30 \times 170$) and the slightly faster-firing Mauser MK30 ($30 \times 173$). Both are very powerful,

*Oerlikon 20mm naval gun Type GAM-B01*
*(Courtesy: Oerlikon/Ian Hogg)*

giving an effective AA range of about 2.5km and a maximum of 8km.

The KCB cannon has been ordered in two mountings for the Royal Navy: twin- and single-barrelled. The twin (GCM-AO3) is fully stabilised with a self-contained power supply and weighs just over 2,500kg. It has been sold to fourteen countries. The single-barrelled mounting (DS30B, which is also offered for export with the MK30) has a simplified form of stabilisation, weighs 1,200kg and has been ordered in quantity to replace the remaining 40mm Bofors in various classes of frigates and minehunters.

The 30mm KCB has also been fitted to the American Emerlec twin stabilised mounting, which weighs in at 3,450kg and features an enclosed, environmentally controlled cabin for the gunner. It has been acquired by several navies, usually for fitting to smaller warships.

The latest contender is the 30mm Boeing Bushmaster II chain gun, which uses the same $30 \times 173$ ammunition as the GAU-8/A and Mauser MK30. This has been selected for fitting to new USN amphibious ships, together with an electro-optical fire control, for close-in defence against small boats and helicopters.

This section cannot end without mention of the immortal Bofors 40mm. This is available in a variety of mountings, most of which fall into the next section, but is still widely used in locally controlled mountings. Nowadays, most weapons have automatic ammunition supply systems and are fitted to stabilised mountings which are capable of being remotely controlled.

## RADAR-DIRECTED ANTI-AIRCRAFT AND ANTI-MISSILE GUNS

THE PROBLEM OF HITTING FAST-MOVING AERIAL TARGETS is so difficult for manually aimed weapons that this task is now given to missile systems or remotely controlled guns which are automatically directed by radar. All the gunner has to do is specify the target and command the system to open fire. These are generally known as close-in weapon systems (CIWS). Many of these mountings also carry electro-optical back-up sights to provide an alternative control mode.

Sea-skimming anti-ship missiles are even harder targets than aircraft and there is usually very little warning of attack. Systems to combat them are therefore normally fitted with fire controls which automatically detect and engage incoming missiles without the intervention of a gunner, who merely has to make sure that the system is switched on.

There are two different philosophies in the design of anti-missile gun systems. One relies on large-calibre cannon (35mm and upwards) firing explosive projectiles which are detonated close to the target by a proximity fuze (or in the case of the 35mm Oerlikon AHEAD system, by a time fuze). The other fires intense bursts of small-calibre solid projectiles from fast-firing cannon of 20–30mm which are intended to score direct hits on the target, penetrating and detonating the warhead.

There is much debate about the merits of each approach. Large-calibre cannon systems permit engagement at a longer range and are inherently more versatile, being well suited to anti-aircraft and possibly anti-surface vessel applications. On the other hand the most advanced small-calibre systems, such as Phalanx and Goalkeeper, are very accurate because they have a 'closed loop' fire control system which monitors via the on-mount radar the trajectory of the gun's projectiles as they speed towards the target, calculates the probability of hitting and adjusts the aim accordingly.

There is considerable overlap between anti-aircraft and anti-missile gun systems. Many of the former, even at gun calibres as large as 100mm, are claimed to be effective in the anti-missile role when used with an appropriate fire control system, and the latter are all capable of acting in the anti-aircraft role, although in some cases only at short range.

Large-calibre weapons usually have their radar directors sited many metres away from the gun mountings, which can cause accuracy problems if there is the slightest flexing of the ship's hull in rough seas. A further problem with very large-calibre AA guns in the anti-missile role is that their proximity fuzes are usually set to detonate the shell some distance from the target because of the large lethal radius of the shell. However, many modern anti-ship missiles fly so low that large shells might be detonated by the proximity of the sea before they reach the target. Advanced fuzing systems have been developed to circumvent this problem.

Some of the guns used in radar-directed systems are also available in locally controlled mountings and have therefore already been described. The main exceptions are at the extremes: larger-calibre guns which are always radar-directed, and very fast-firing cannon used in the specialised CIWS anti-missile mountings.

Dealing with the weapons in calibre order means starting with the CIWS. The American Phalanx was the first in the field in the late 1970s and is now in service with many navies including the RN. The gun used is the six-barrel 20mm M-61 Vulcan cannon firing $20 \times 102$ ammunition and originally designed for equipping fighter aircraft. In that form, it is capable of firing at 6,000 rpm, although it is derated to between 3,000 and 4,500 rpm (depending on the version) for the Phalanx application.

In common with most other CIWS, Phalanx does not fire the usual full-calibre explosive shells but APDS rounds instead: solid, high-velocity, depleted-uranium projectiles of 12.5mm calibre contained in a light sleeve which falls away as it leaves the muzzle.

The reason for this choice of projectile, which is actually less effective than HE shells against aircraft, is that while larger guns and AA missiles can knock down anti-ship missiles at a distance by blowing away their wings and controls with proximity-fuzed explosive warheads, once the missiles get within 600–700m of a ship, their ballistic momentum is likely to carry them to the target even if they are damaged. Phalanx bullets are therefore intended to penetrate and explode the missile's warhead. Even so, a typical 200kg RDX warhead has to be exploded at least 150m from the ship to avoid blast damage.

The Phalanx mounting weighs about 6,000kg and contains ammunition for nearly twenty seconds' firing; this is enough for several engagements as the gun fires in short bursts. The maximum range is about 1.5km. A significant advantage of the mount is that it requires no deck penetration and thus can be bolted in any convenient location, top-weight considerations permitting.

Another mounting which uses a 20mm rotary cannon is the Sea Vulcan 20. This is very different from Phalanx as it is intended for small craft and does not use closed-loop guidance technology. The gun is a three-barrel M197 version (using the same $20 \times 102$ ammunition) capable of up to 1,500 rpm and the mounting is very small, weighing only 318kg when empty.

An alternative approach to obtaining a high rate of fire is used by the Spanish Meroka. This

*Oerlikon Sea Zenith CIWS with four 25mm KBB cannon* (Courtesy: Oerlikon/Ian Hogg)

mounting contains twelve externally powered guns, using electrically-primed $20 \times 128$ ammunition, which are closely packed together in two rows of six. The 4,500kg mounting includes a guidance radar, but without a closed-loop system.

Another CIWS which has achieved service status (with the Turkish Navy) is the Contraves Seaguard. The 3,500kg gun module, called Sea Zenith, uses four Oerlikon KBB cannon, which fire a lengthened, large-capacity $25 \times 184$ cartridge to improve the performance over the KBA. The speed of reaction required of an anti-missile system is apparent in the expected time of four seconds to destroy the target following the receipt of data from the ship's radar.

The $25 \times 184$ cartridge is also used in the new Oerlikon KBD seven-barrel rotary cannon, which manages an impressive 5,000 rpm. Two of these guns are fitted to the 9,000kg Barrage mounting,

part of the Myriad CIWS which has so far not seen service. The extremely high combined rate of fire is intended to cope with the next generation of anti-ship missiles, which are expected to be both supersonic and highly manoeuvrable, giving defence systems only the briefest of opportunities to engage them. The KBD is also offered to upgun the Phalanx system; it will fit in the same mounting.

A rival weapon is the GAU-12/U rotary chambered for the standard NATO $25 \times 137$ round. This has featured in several CIWS proposals, including the stabilised Sea Vulcan 25, a scaled-up version of the Sea Vulcan 20 weighing 1,270kg fully loaded and similarly intended for arming small craft. The maximum rate of fire in this application is limited to 2,000 rpm, apparently by ammunition feed arrangements.

Yet another variation on the European CIWS theme is the Mauser *Drakon* (originally developed

*Goalkeeper CIWS with 30mm GAU-8/A* (Courtesy: MoD Pattern Room)

as the Mauser-Signaal MIDAS), which uses four of Mauser's BK27 aircraft revolver cannon, giving a maximum rate of fire of some 6,800 rpm. A special FAPDS loading of the 27 × 145B ammunition has been developed for this purpose. The total weight of the mounting, with ammunition, is 4,600kg. At the time of writing, this had been developed for service but not adopted. A simpler system is also offered, using a single BK27, which is also remotely controlled.

A more powerful anti-missile CIWS operating on similar principles to Phalanx is the Dutch Goalkeeper system which the RN ordered in 1984 to supplement and partially replace Phalanx. This is based on the much more potent 30mm GAU-8/A rotary cannon, also developed for aircraft use, which fires 30 × 173 ammunition at 4,200 rpm. The maximum range is 3km, although fire is normally opened at a closer range to avoid wasting ammunition, of which some fifteen seconds' worth is held on the mounting. It has considerably more 'ship impact' than Phalanx, as the mounting penetrates two decks, and thus cannot easily be retrofitted to smaller vessels. The mounting weight is 6,350kg, with a further 3,500kg off-mount.

Other 30mm radar-directed mountings have been produced by both the Soviet Union and Italy. The first of the Soviet weapons, the NN-30 revolver cannon, fires a massive 30 × 210B cartridge and is available in the AK-230, a twin, helmet-shaped, remotely controlled mounting weighing 1,800kg. It was also built in China as the Type 69. In current Russian systems this has been replaced by six-barrel revolver cannon. There appear to be three different versions, all firing the current standard 30 × 165 round.

One version is the GSh-6-30K, a version of the aircraft cannon but with longer, water-cooled barrels, fitted to the AK630 mounting (two of these guns are mounted one above the other in the AK-630M1-2 mounting). An apparent variation of this (sources are inconsistent on this point) is the 6K30-GSh, a lightened version adapted for transpiration cooling. The third gun is the AO18L, a lightweight model which is the only one to be externally powered (the others being gas-operated). It also has a lower rate of fire of 1,000–3,000 rpm instead of 4,000–6,000. It is found in the AK306 mounting, which is optically sighted instead of radar-controlled. Both the AK306 and AK630 are available fitted with four *Vikhr* missiles for long-range engagements.

The latest Russian CIWS is a formidable device called *Kashtan*. This mounting carries two 6K30-GSh, eight ready-to-fire SA-N-11 AA missiles, on-mount radar and a sensitive electro-optical system which incorporates automatic target tracking claimed to be capable of guiding a missile to within one metre of the target. It is fitted to the nuclear-powered missile cruiser *Petr Veliki* (Peter the Great), which has experienced protracted construction and commissioning problems, and to other major warships.

The theory behind the combined gun-missile mount, also seen in a different form in land service, is that while missiles have advantages at long range and guns are better at short range, they both require similar detection and fire control systems. It therefore makes sense for them to share the expensive radar, electro-optical and guidance computer systems. *Kashtan* is expected to engage with its missiles from 8km (12km with later, more advanced missiles) and with guns from 4km (although the effective anti-missile range will be much less) and is claimed to be capable of dealing with four simultaneous missile attacks.

After *Kashtan*, anything else seems something of an anti-climax. However, the Italian firm OtoBreda has produced some popular equipment using other people's guns in their own mountings. Their 30mm naval weapon (which does not have an on-mount radar) is available with single or twin barrels and can be fitted with a wide range of 30mm or 25mm cannon, although the standard is the Mauser MK30. The twin mounting weighs 2,800kg without ammunition, 4,400kg with. The weathershield has a characteristic spherical form also shared by their larger mountings.

Just as in the Second World War, while Bofors dominated the larger automatic cannon, Oerlikon has mainly concentrated on the smaller calibres, but Oerlikon also pushed closer to Bofors territory with the 35mm KD series developed in the 1960s as an army and naval AA gun. It has only been offered in twin mountings; for naval purposes, there is a choice between Oerlikon's own Type GDM-A and

*OE/OTO mounting with twin 35mm Oerlikon guns* (*Courtesy: Oerlikon/Ian Hogg*)

the Italian OE/OTO mounting, both introduced in the early 1970s.

The latest Oerlikon development is the Millennium system, being developed in conjunction with Royal Ordnance, who are supplying the gun mounting. It is designed around Oerlikon's new 35/1,000 gas-operated revolver cannon which fires at 1,000 rpm via a linkless feed. The associated AHEAD ammunition system previously referred to has a greater effective range than most CIWS and is claimed to be highly effective against both missiles and aircraft. The current mounting, weighing 2,660kg loaded, has only one barrel with a distinctive bracing to steady it against the rapid traversing rate of 120°/sec (the elevation rate is 60°/sec).

A typical Millennium engagement would consist of a burst of eighteen rounds at an engagement range of 1.65km, taking 1.5 seconds and firing a hail of 2,736 high-velocity sub-projectiles at a cone angle of 15° into the path of the aircraft or missile. At the maximum engagement range of 2.1km, a thirty-six-round burst is calculated to be necessary

to ensure target destruction. This system is still being developed but appears to offer significant advantages in the anti-missile role, which will become more difficult in the future with the advent of supersonic anti-ship missiles. The AHEAD system has already been selected for use in the South African Navy's GA-35 twin mounting, to be fitted to four new corvettes.

It has recently emerged that China has breathed new life into the old 37mm calibre by introducing a rimless 37 × 240 cartridge for the NORINCO Type 76A twin mounting. This has a larger capacity than the usual 37x250R case to achieve a higher muzzle velocity, and an effective range of 3.5km is claimed. The new mounting (also referred to as the NG15-2) is described as a locally produced version of the Italian 40mm *Dardo*, with the characteristic domed gunshield and using the same Fast Forty design concept to increase the rate of fire to around 380 rpm per gun. It is fitted to the *Luda III* and *Luhu* class destroyers.

Finally, we arrive at the 40mm Bofors. Before

looking at later developments, mention should be made of two post-war British mountings for the old L60 guns. The six-barrel Mk VI fitted to the RN's last battleship, HMS *Vanguard*, was the only British Bofors mounting with an automatic ammunition feed (each gun having a thirty-six-round tray) and weighed nearly 22,000kg. The impressive 15,000kg twin STAAG (stabilised tachymetric AA gun), a sort of 'super Hazemeyer' fitted to some classes of frigates and destroyers, had its own on-mount radar. The theoretical performance of this mounting did not compensate for its weight and complexity and the simpler twin Mk V lasted longer, with the original concept of an air-cooled gun on a single mounting lasting longest of all – but not for AA use.

To replace the Bofors L60 in the 1950s the RN favoured obtaining large quantities of the new, high-performance L70 Bofors gun, which had been adopted by the British Army. However, these plans did not come to fruition, presumably because of budget restrictions, the availability of vast numbers of war-surplus older versions of the Bofors, and the development of the Seacat AA missile which was regarded as the replacement for the Bofors. There was no further development of light automatic cannon for the RN until after the Falklands War, the essentially wartime Oerlikon and Bofors guns remaining in service for second-line duties into the 1990s.

Other nations thought differently, and the 40mm Bofors has seen continuous development, including upgrade packages for the older models. The rate of fire of the 40mm L70 is, at 300–330 rpm, more than double that of the original L60

version and the effective range is greater. Current efforts are focused on the Trinity system, a combination of improvements to the ammunition, gun, mounting and fire control system, which results in a burst of proximity-fuzed HE shells fired in a controlled pattern to saturate the target area with lethal fragments.

OtoBreda have produced mountings using their own versions of the Bofors guns. The Twin Compact mounting has the firm's typical spherical gunshield. For the Dardo AA system, which has anti-missile capability, the OtoBreda Fast Forty guns have been substantially redesigned to achieve 450 rpm per barrel. The weight of a mounting without ammunition is about 5,500kg.

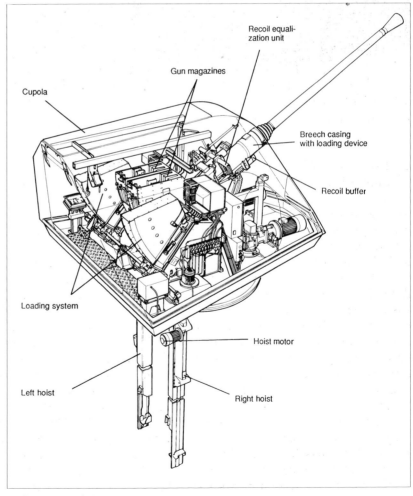

*Bofors SAK 57/70 (Courtesy: Celsius)*

## LARGER AUTOMATIC CANNON

AS WELL AS ACHIEVING GREAT SUCCESS WITH THEIR 40mm L70, Bofors produce a 57mm gun. This is simply a scaled-up version of the 40mm and was developed during the Second World War. Introduced in the late 1940s as the SAK 57 L/60, it was adopted in single or twin mountings by several nations, including the French. The gun fired its 57 × 438R cartridge at 130 rpm and had a maximum range of 15km. The twin mounting weighed 24,000kg. This was replaced by the SAK 57 L/70, which achieved 200 rpm and was offered in a single mounting weighing 6,400kg. It entered service with the Swedish Navy in the 1970s.

The current version of the gun, the SAK 57 L/70 Mk 2, entered service in the mid-1980s. This has the rate of fire increased to 220 rpm and comes in a single mounting weighing 6,800kg. Despite the high rate of fire, improved steels allow an air-cooled barrel instead of the earlier weapon's water cooling. The combination of gun and fire control system is claimed to be effective against anti-ship missiles and a high-capacity, extended-range (HCER) shell intended for anti-ship use has a maximum range increased to 17km. As well as being fitted to the usual fast patrol boats, it was selected as the main gun for the large Canadian 'City' class frigates. The Mk 3 version is compatible with the new 3P

ammunition and is available with a gunhouse designed for low radar reflectivity, which conceals the barrel when not required. This version has been selected for the *Visby* class of 'stealth' corvettes which will enter service early in the new century.

The first post-war Soviet weapon was the 45mm gun, which fired a unique 45 × 386SR cartridge, and was available in single or quadruple mountings, the latter weighing about 11,000kg. The gun had an effective range of 4,000m. This was replaced by a 57mm derived from the army's AA weapon, which was available in single, twin and quad mountings. Early ZIF-31 versions were air-cooled, but the later ZIF-72 version is a water-cooled twin weighing around 25,000kg. The ZIF-31 was produced by China as the Type 66; a water-cooled version of this was designated Type 77.

Until the development of the Phalanx, the US Navy showed very little interest in light radar-guided cannon. However, during the 1950s much time

*Postwar AA gun cartridges 1 (from left to right): 14.5mm KPV (14.5 × 114), 20mm M61 Vulcan (20 × 102), Oerlikon KAA (20 × 128), HS 820/Oerlikon KAD (20 × 139), 23mm ZU (23 × 152B), Oerlikon KBA/NATO (25 × 137), Oerlikon KBB (25 × 184), Soviet 2-M3/8 (25 × 218), Soviet AO-18 (30 × 165), HS 831/Oerlikon KCB (30 × 170), GAU-8/A/Mauser MK30F (30 × 173)*

*Postwar AA gun cartridges 2 (from left to right): Soviet AO-18 (30 × 165), Soviet NN-30 (30 × 210B), Czech M53 (30 × 210), Oerlikon KD/35/1000 series (35 × 228), Bofors 40mm L/70 (40 × 364R), Soviet S60/ZIF 31/72 (57 × 347SR), Bofors 57mm L/70 (57 × 438R)*

and money was spent in developing fast-firing, high-velocity automatic cannon in larger calibres, intended to make the best use of the new VT or proximity fuze, which was at that time too large to be used with 40mm shells.

The most successful of these was the twin 3″ L70 mounting which was produced in two versions – American and British – using the same high-velocity 76 × 669R ammunition. This should not be confused with the earlier 3″ L50, a less sophisticated weapon firing a less powerful 76 × 585R cartridge. The L70 only saw RN service in the three Tiger class cruisers, although the British mounting was also fitted as the main gun armament in some Canadian frigates. The American version, which fired at 90 rpm per barrel instead of the 60 rpm of the British mounting, proved unreliable and was little used, eventually being replaced in almost all of the ships which carried it. The Canadians persevered with their guns, which were apparently capable of being uprated to 120 rpm per barrel if required.

The Russians have also developed various 76mm naval guns, the most capable of them being a single-barrel L60 weapon which fires its 76 × 545R ammunition at 120 rpm and is usually fitted to smaller warships.

Unquestionably the most successful of the 3″/76mm calibre automatic guns is the OtoBreda 76mm L62, which fires a 76 × 636R cartridge. Originating in the early 1960s, this became immensely popular when a compact version weighing only 7,500kg was introduced in 1969. The rate of fire, initially 60 rpm, was increased to 85 rpm in the Compact and has since been boosted to 120 rpm. For anti-missile purposes a lightweight (5.25kg instead of 6.3kg), high-velocity (1,250 m/s instead of 915 m/s) AMARTOF proximity-fuzed shell is being developed, able to reach a target 3km away in less than three seconds.

Mention should also be made of an unusual weapon, the Bofors 76mm, which used the same ammunition as the USN's 3″ L50. This was intended for surface fire only and therefore featured a low (30°) maximum angle of elevation and a modest (30 rpm) rate of fire. The benefits were an extremely compact, low-profile mounting which weighed only 6,500kg despite having a 6mm-thick steel gunhouse. It was fitted to small patrol craft.

For the sake of completeness, significant larger naval fully automatic guns are listed below. The rates of fire given are per barrel; mountings are single-barrel unless otherwise stated.

---

French Creusot-Loire Mle 53/64/68 and Compact (100 × 700R); 60–90 rpm (current)
British Vickers 4.5″ Mk 8 (114mm); 25 rpm (current)
Swedish Bofors 4.7″ (120 × 615R); 80 rpm (limited post-war use)
US 5″ Mk 42 (127 × 835R); 34 rpm (major post-war use)
US 5″ Mark 45 (127 × 835R); 20 rpm (current)
Italian OTO Melara 127mm (127 × 835R); 40 rpm (current)

Russian 130mm; 30 rpm (current – twin mounting)
US 6″ L/47 (152 × 972R); 12 rpm (*Worcester* class post-war cruisers – twin mounting)
British 6″ Mk 26 (152mm); 20 rpm (*Tiger* class post-war cruisers – twin mounting)
US 8″ (203 × 1280R); 10 rpm (*Des Moines* class post-war heavy cruisers – triple mounting)

---

# *Chapter Five*

# WEAPONS FOR AIR FIGHTING

THE POSSIBILITY OF USING AIRCRAFT AS WEAPONS of war was not lost on even the earliest aviation pioneers, although the nature of their ultimate use was not at first generally understood. Initial plans saw the new aeroplanes as much more versatile replacements for the balloons used by artillery observers, which were used to direct the fire of the gunners onto targets which could not be seen from the ground. It was obvious that aeroplanes could also perform more general reconnaissance duties, providing valuable information to army commanders about the disposition of enemy troops.

The first military aircraft were therefore intended for the observation role, with the observer being in command (the pilot merely being a chauffeur). This affected aircraft design, as stability was much more important than speed or manoeuvrability. It also drove certain technical developments, particularly airborne wireless telegraphy. Until this was available, observers had to resort to dropping written messages in containers with colourful streamers attached and hope that these would reach their intended destination in time to be effective.

Not surprisingly, it soon occurred to some fliers that if the information being relayed back to the enemy base was valuable, it was worth expending some effort to stop it arriving. Aircrew therefore took to carrying a variety of weapons aloft, including pistols, rifles and shotguns, to take pot-shots at any enemy aeroplanes they might see (a development predicted by Colonel Capper of the Royal Engineers as early as 1911). Inevitably, methods of fitting more effective weapons were soon devised and the classic fighter plane emerged.

The rifle calibre machine gun was the pre-eminent air weapon from the First World War to early in the Second. Initial attempts to achieve a clear field of forward fire by designing 'pusher' aircraft, with the engine and propeller behind the pilot, showed serious performance disadvantages, so single-seat fighters soon adopted the front-engined layout. The need to keep the guns within the pilot's reach in order to reload or clear jams, combined with the desirability of firing directly forwards through the propeller disk, caused some headaches until synchronisation gear was perfected. After that, the classic twin machine gun biplane fighter ruled the skies for nearly twenty years.

## EARLY EXPERIMENTS

IT WAS NOT UNTIL LATE IN THE WAR THAT THE performance of aircraft improved sufficiently for them to carry enough of a bomb load to pose any sort of threat to ground or naval targets. Before then, large airborne cannon were thought to have major potential in the offensive role and various types were tried, initially with disappointing results, although as we shall see this is a concept which has refused to go away.

Large cannon featured among the first experiments in aircraft armament, with the Frenchman Gabriel Voisin showing an aircraft with a 37mm cannon as early as 1910 (the same year in which a rifle was first fired from an aircraft, in the USA). Airborne firing experiments took place with a 37mm cannon fitted to a Voisin machine in 1913, only a year after the first firing of a machine gun (a Lewis) from an aircraft (a Wright B) in the USA.

The first British experiments took place in 1912 and involved the firing of a standard Vickers .303″ infantry machine gun from an FE2. This was followed up by the Admiralty, eventually leading in May 1914 to tests of specially designed pusher seaplanes from Shorts (S81 Gun-carrier) and Sopwith (No.127), equipped with a 1½pdr (37mm) Vickers Type B gun.

This was not the naval automatic Pom-pom, although it seems that it used the same 37 × 123R ammunition, firing a 680g projectile at 365 m/s. It had a semi-automatic breech which would eject the fired cartridge case but required the next round to be loaded by hand. While both the planes and the crew survived the firing tests, it was clear that the 50kg weight and the low rate of fire were too limiting for practical purposes, and the similarly armed Vickers No.14B project never materialised.

## THE FIRST WORLD WAR:
### MANUALLY LOADED CANNON

THE USE OF LARGE-CALIBRE CANNON CONTINUED into the First World War, although mainly on a small scale or experimental basis, with two principal uses in mind: downward firing, against ground or naval targets, and upward firing, against airships. In either case, this meant that the guns were rarely fixed to fire forward, being either flexibly mounted and fired by a gunner, or fixed to fire upwards or downwards. These planned uses also meant that rate of fire was not particularly important, so the development of automatic weapons had a low priority and almost all of the guns which saw service were manually loaded.

Throughout the war, the lighter-than-air dirigibles of the Zeppelin and Schütte-Lanz types, in which Germany had a massive technical lead, had a vastly greater range and load-carrying ability than aeroplanes and were perceived as the major threat in long-range reconnaissance and bombing missions. Initially, they also had a better climb and altitude performance and could often climb away from attacking aircraft despite their low maximum speed.

This led to the development of specialist anti-airship armament, designed to exploit their Achilles' heel: the huge volume of highly inflammable hydrogen which kept them aloft. While some use was made of rockets, large-calibre cannon firing incendiary shells were the preferred weapons. These could not only carry far more incendiary material than rifle-calibre projectiles but were more effective at tearing open the airships' envelope to enable the gas to escape – a necessary precursor to setting the craft alight as the gas would only burn in air. The British devised a highly sensitive nose fuze, the No.131, designed to be detonated by passing through airship fabric. Some of the weapons were mounted so that they could fire upwards, a precursor of Second World War night-fighter tactics.

Most of the large-calibre cannon developed during the First World War are of peripheral concern here because they were not fully automatic. At best they were semi-automatic (which in artillery terms means that the fired cartridge case is automatically ejected after firing, but the new round has to be loaded by hand) but some required manual opening of the breech as well, and were thus painfully slow and awkward to use under combat conditions.

The most common calibre in the manually loaded cannon was the ubiquitous 37mm, usually firing the standard 37 × 94R Pom-pom cartridge, although in some instances more powerful rounds were used; e.g. the early French experiments with an adapted version of the naval *Modèle 1902* 'Tube-Canon', designed for fitting in large-calibre guns for sub-calibre training purposes, and chambered for a unique 37 × 201R cartridge. Larger calibres were also tried, particularly by the French, who were quite enthusiastic about large-calibre cannon. They made some use of 47mm guns (created by dismantling surplus Hotchkiss rotary cannon) and the Germans experimented with guns of up to 130mm, but the heaviest conventional cannon fired in action appears to have been a 66mm flying-boat weapon used briefly by the Austro-Hungarians against light naval vessels. In 1917 the French specified a 75mm cannon in a flying boat, which was tested post-war.

The British made operational use of at least one manually loaded weapon, the 1.59″ Crayford, which was popularly but misleadingly known as the 'rocket gun'. This was a lightweight (21kg) gun produced at Vickers' Crayford works, firing a cartridge using a much shortened version of the case from the naval Vickers 2pdr Pom-pom (40 × 79R instead of 40 × 158R). It appeared to be used for only a short

*Davis recoilless gun being loaded (BuOrd, USN)*

period in 1917, primarily in the anti-Zeppelin role. The nickname apparently resulted from a particularly vivid tracer or incendiary projectile.

The problem of coping with the weight and recoil of heavy weapons in early aircraft led to the development of recoilless cannon: the American Davis guns. These were first tested in a 6pdr (57mm) version by the Admiralty in 1915 or 1916, but 2pdr (40mm) and 12pdr (76mm) versions were also tried, for both anti-ship and anti-Zeppelin purposes. As they relied on the rearwards propulsion of lead shot to counteract the recoil impulse of the shell, the mounting of these guns required some care. In practice, the tail blast was so severe that it was difficult to avoid damage to the fragile structure of the aircraft. They were also very slow and awkward to reload.

Much more significant to the future applications of cannon were the French 37mm installations developed late in the war. Unlike the earlier weapons, these were not flexibly mounted for use by an air gunner, but fixed between the cylinder banks of a vee-engine to fire forwards through the hollow propeller hub. There is some confusion about identification of the gun and ammunition; most sources list the gun as a Puteaux but there were in fact two guns; the first was developed from the *Modèle 1885* naval gun and was a single-shot weapon fitted with a smooth-bore barrel to fire shotshells (canister). The other was the SAMC which featured a five-round vertical feed ammunition hopper and had a conventional rifled barrel for firing HE shells. Both weapons were chambered for the usual 37 × 94R cartridge and were manually loaded.

The SPAD S.XII fighter planes armed with these weapons first emerged in July 1917 and were employed with some success by the French aces Guynemer and Fonck. However, they were not generally popular because of the cumbersome manual loading. Automatic 37mm guns, featuring a long-recoil mechanism and a five-round hopper feed, were being tested at the end of the war but did not see service.

## THE FIRST HEAVY AUTOMATICS

ALL THE SERVICE WEAPONS DESCRIBED SO FAR WERE manually loaded. Only four fully automatic cannon appear to have seen service during the First World War. Two were British (the 37mm Vickers 1pdr Mk III and 1½pdr COW gun), one was Italian (the 25mm FIAT) and the fourth was German (the 20mm Becker).

In addition, some use was made of heavy machine guns firing large-calibre rifle ammunition, such as the 11mm Gras. This was the French 11 × 59R cartridge for the obsolete Gras rifle (albeit with a far more powerful loading) for the Vickers machine gun, which was adapted to fire it. The reason for this apparently retrograde step was that the large projectile was able to contain a much greater volume of incendiary material than the usual .303″ ammunition, which made it particularly useful against artillery observation balloons. British experiments with 11mm Desvignes incendiary ammunition showed a higher success rate than was achieved with the .303″ Buckingham ammunition, but the gun recoiled heavily and was not popular. However, over 1,200 were built in the second half of 1918. The British also experimented in 1916 with modified .45″ calibre Maxim machine guns and some may have seen unofficial service.

The 1pdr Vickers Mk III automatic belt-fed gun was first accepted into service in 1915 but did not see action until the spring of 1917, fitted in small numbers to some FE2b (and possibly other) RAF aeroplanes for both home defence against Zeppelins and ground attack on the Western Front. Contrary to most accounts this was not the same gun as the 1pdr Pom-pom used by the other services; at 62 kg (127 kg including cone mounting and ammunition) it was much lighter and fired less powerful ammunition, using a shortened (37 × 69R) cartridge case. There were various projectile types, including a high-explosive shell fitted with the No.131 fuze. The Vickers was flexibly mounted and fired by a gunner, which meant that its light weight was largely negated by the weight and space required for the gunner and mounting. A few examples of a revised version, the Mk V, were built in 1917 and tested post-war on the R31 airship.

In 1915 work on the more powerful 1½pdr began, still in 37mm calibre but with a larger cartridge case (37 × 190), and this was the basis for future development. The gun was relatively light for a fully automatic cannon at 64kg (91kg including mounting). The mechanism used a long-recoil system which limited the rate of fire, reportedly to between 60 and 100 rpm, and the use of five-round clips which had to be replaced by hand reduced the effective rate of fire even further. Progress was slow, and although the FE4 of 1916 was designed to use two COW guns, it was not until 1918 that two DH4s were accepted for anti-Zeppelin service, with a single COW gun mounted in the rear cockpit and firing upwards at a steep angle. These aircraft (or possibly two others) were sent to France as bomber destroyers, but there are no reports of any combat use.

Automatic cannon of 25mm calibre were produced by both Vickers and FIAT, but only the

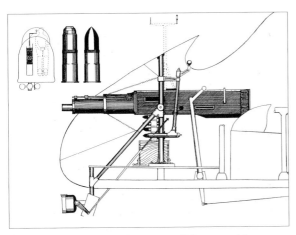

*Vickers 1pdr Mk III with its 37 × 69R ammunition*
(*Courtesy: R.W. Clarke*)

The most promising British large-calibre weapon by the end of the First World War was the Coventry Ordnance Works 37mm 1½pdr. The Coventry Ordnance Works actually started to develop their automatic cannon before the First World War. It was initially tested (but not flown) in one-pounder form in an FE3 in the summer of 1913. A version of the FE6 was also fitted for this gun. The cartridge case was a unique rimless type measuring 37 × 93mm.

*1½pdr COW gun in Backburn Perth flying boat*
(*BuOrd, USN*)

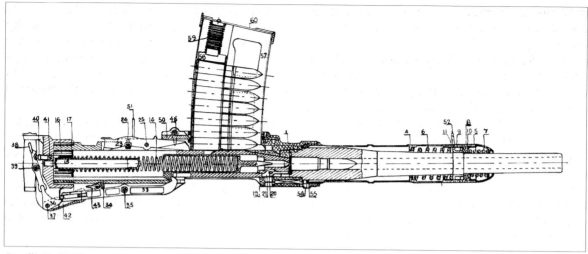

*Revelli-FIAT 25.4mm* *(Courtesy: MoD Pattern Room)*

latter saw service. The FIAT *(Fabbrica Italiana di Automobili Torino) modello 1917* gun, generally called the Revelli after its designer, used an eight-round magazine which was a major limitation on the practical rate of fire. The gun was light but not popular, partly because of the low muzzle velocity but mainly because of the very sensitive fuze which was inclined to explode prematurely. Despite this, it did see service, mounted on the Caproni Ca 5. FIAT stopped production after about 200 had been made, mainly because Vickers claimed that it infringed their patents.

The Vickers gun actually preceded the FIAT. It used a 25 × 87R cartridge and a twenty-five-round belt feed. It seems that Revelli modified the cartridge case to a rimless 25 × 87 with a sharper shoulder and used the Vickers gun as a starting point for his design. The Vickers was made in Italy as the Vickers-Terni but it appears that the only service use of this gun was, rather curiously, as an AA weapon in some Swedish submarines.

By far the most significant of the wartime automatic guns was the first 20mm automatic cannon in the modern sequence of development, the German Becker. Development started even before the war but significant use was not made until 1917, when it was primarily used for the defence of heavy bombers and airships. Its potential as a fighter weapon was never realised as it was, as usual,

flexibly mounted and fired by a gunner and its mechanism was unsuitable for synchronisation. It also saw relatively little service before the end of the war, with just 362 examples being discovered post-war by the Allied Aeronautical Control Commission, of which 131 were used in the anti-aircraft role. Two other German cannon, the 19mm Szakats and the 20mm Erhardt, were at an advanced stage of development by the end of the war.

## THE PATH TO THE SECOND WORLD WAR

FROM 1918 TO THE MID-1930S, FIGHTERS BECAME heavier, more powerful and faster but for the most part still retained the classic biplane formula together with its twin rifle-calibre machine gun armament. The advent of fast, strongly constructed monoplane bombers and, subsequently, fighters, more difficult both to hit and to destroy, prompted a reappraisal of armament requirements which in turn led to a remarkably wide range of solutions.

Three separate but simultaneous lines of the development of heavy weapons can be discerned: the introduction of the heavy machine gun as an air-fighting (as opposed to anti-balloon) weapon, the development of medium calibre (mainly 20mm) guns, and the continuation of the large-calibre (37+mm) cannon, with various largely fruitless attempts to produce an effective air-fighting gun, followed by more successful use as airborne anti-tank guns.

In the lead-up to the Second World War, aircraft designers had a wide choice of rifle-calibre (7.5–8mm) and heavy machine guns and large-calibre cannon from which to choose. Trying to decide which combination of weapons would be best was not easy, even with war experience, because the circumstances kept changing. The basic characteristics which had to be taken into account when drawing up armament specifications were:

1. The weight of the gun and of the ammunition (typically for up to twenty seconds' firing although some early drum-fed cannon were limited to much less by the magazine capacity). This determined the number of weapons which could be carried within a given weight limit.
2. The rate of fire of the gun, or more significantly of the total number of guns carried. This was increasingly important given the improving performance of aircraft, which limited the time available for firing.
3. The muzzle velocity of the projectiles, which determines the time of flight to the target; the shorter this is, the greater the hit probability, especially where rapidly manoeuvring targets requiring deflection shooting are concerned (US wartime calculations indicated that a 50% increase in muzzle velocity tripled the chance of a hit).
4. The destructive effect of the projectiles, in terms of armour-piercing ability and (for cannon shells) explosive power – particularly important in dealing with bombers.
5. The range of the armament, a function of calibre and muzzle velocity, which became important to both sides in the battles between bombers and fighters.

The rifle-calibre machine guns were light, compact and fast-firing. They normally weighed 10–15kg and fired bullets weighing 9–12g at 730–850 m/s at a rate of about 1,200 rpm (typically reduced to about 1,000 rpm in synchronised installations). There wasn't much variation in performance between the guns of the warring nations, although the Soviet 7.62mm ShKAS achieved 1,800 rpm and

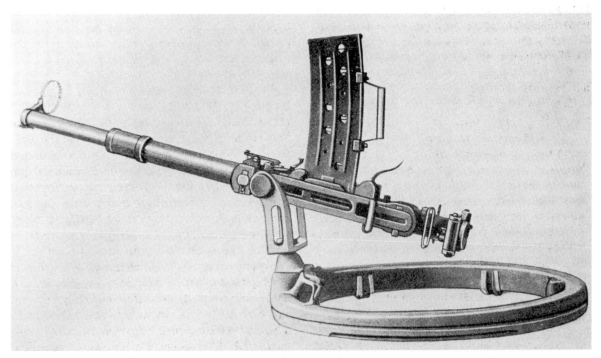

*2cm Becker-Semag on ring mounting* (*BuOrd, USN*)

the Mauser MG 81Z twin no less than 3,200 rpm with a weight of only 9.5kg. Their effectiveness diminished during the Second World War as aircraft adopted armour plating and self-sealing fuel tanks. There was some use of incendiary (and even HE) projectiles of which the RAF's 'De Wilde' incendiary was particularly well known.

HMGs were typically about two or three times as heavy as RCMGs and fired more slowly at about 750–900 rpm. Muzzle velocities were similar to the lighter weapons but the bullets were appreciably heavier at 35–55g; they were accordingly much more effective against armoured targets, could carry more incendiary material and had a longer range.

As might be expected, cannon were heavier and slower-firing still, although the range of specifications was much wider. The Becker's line of development continued via SEMAG and then Oerlikon, the Erhardt's via Solothurn and then directly by Rheinmetall. By the late 1930s there were several different 20mm guns available offering a wide range of performance, from the Oerlikon FF at the low end of the muzzle energy spectrum to the Swiss HS 404 and FMK, Danish Madsen and Japanese Ho-1 and Ho-3 at the other. Few larger guns existed at that time, although there was some interest in 23mm guns and also in new weapons in 37mm calibre.

As with all weapon systems, it was necessary to reach a compromise between conflicting requirements. The balance of the characteristics chosen for fighter aircraft depended on the nature of the likely opponents. Bombers were relatively large, easy targets but their size made them difficult to shoot down and they usually carried defensive machine guns. The most important characteristics were therefore destructive effect and range.

Fighters on the other hand were easier to damage but much more difficult to hit. The rate of fire and muzzle velocity were most important, although during the course of the Second World War destructive effect became more significant as fighters acquired armour plate and protected fuel tanks. The heavier the armament carried, the more the performance and handling of the aircraft were degraded, particularly important when facing opposing fighters.

The skill and training of pilots also affected this issue. By and large, expert fighter pilots who were confident of their shooting preferred few guns, whereas a larger number of guns gave novices more chance of scoring hits.

Bomber aircraft logically needed defensive armament capable of defeating fighters, and therefore should have possessed weapons at least equal in range and hitting power. In fact, a British inter-war study concluded that bombers needed *more* powerful weapons in order to destroy the engines of fighters as they attacked head-on. In practice, the size of weapons fitted was more limited than in fighter aircraft. Bomber armament was either free-swinging, in which case a heavy machine gun or low-powered 20mm cannon was usually as much as could be handled, or turreted, which again placed limits on size and weight.

An issue in single-engined fighters was the location of the armament. The ideal armament layout was to have the guns mounted near the centre-line of the aircraft; this concentrated the fire, kept the weights close to the centre to assist manoeuvrability and provided the most solid and substantial mounting in the interests of accuracy and of absorbing the recoil of heavy weapons. This was easily achieved with twin-engined aircraft, but the problem with single-engined fighters was that the ideal aircraft layout for optimum performance and handling – front-engined, with a tractor propeller – was the worst for mounting guns because the engine and propeller got in the way.

There were therefore three alternatives: to mount a gun to fire through the hollow propeller hub (only possible with vee-engined aircraft designed to accept this, and only room for one gun anyway); to mount the guns in the engine cowling or wing roots and synchronise them to fire only when the propeller blades weren't in the way (which added complication and reduced the guns' rate of fire – typically by 10–20%); or to mount them in the wings and accept the disadvantages. These included dispersed weights (affecting manoeuvrability), dispersed fire (the guns had to be adjusted to concentrate their fire at particular distances), reduced accuracy due to wing flexing during gun firing and manoeuvring, problems in absorbing the recoil of powerful cannon, and special gun-heating arrangements because of the distance from the engine.

The traditional inter-war twin-RCMG equipment was almost invariably mounted in the engine cowling and synchronised to fire through the propeller disc. As the number and size of guns increased, differences in national preferences began to emerge. Soviet, German and Japanese practice generally continued to favour cowling-mounted synchronised guns and Soviet, German and French air forces also used aircraft with engine-mounted cannon. In contrast, British and (slightly later) American practice favoured fitting a relatively large number of guns, which made wing-mounting unavoidable.

A particular problem was caused by the tendency in most air forces to fit mixed armament, i.e. RCMGs, HMGs and cannon, especially where the ballistics of the weapons varied. The differing trajectories of the projectiles meant that they could only be adjusted to strike a single aiming mark at a particular range; at shorter distances the lower-velocity guns would strike above the higher-velocity ones, at longer distances the reverse would apply. Different times of flight could also cause significant problems in deflection shooting. Finally, the aiming problems with mixed armament were exacerbated (except at short range) whenever aircraft fired while banking; the lower-velocity projectiles fell off more to one side (from the pilot's point of view) as gravity had more time to affect them.

The consequences are illustrated by wartime tests of the British Hurricane IID ground-attack aircraft, equipped with two 40mm guns and two RCMGs for sighting. Shooting the 40mm guns with HE ammunition proved to be twice as accurate as with AP; the muzzle velocity of the HE rounds matched that of the RCMG, while the heavier AP shot had a significantly lower velocity.

## BRITISH DEVELOPMENTS

THE FIRST BRITISH EXPERIMENTS WITH A different armament from the usual two RCMGs were with large cannon. Between the wars a variety of installations for the 37mm COW gun appeared, mainly in the form of flexible nose mountings in multi-engined aircraft, either for self-defence or for anti-shipping use. Two were apparently proposed for the huge Handley Page V/1500 bomber and among many other fruitless schemes were those in 1927 for heavy three-seat fighters, carrying two flexible COW guns, and a projected development of the 1931 Vickers C.16/28 bomber-transport to produce a 'Battleplane' armed with three COW guns as well as machine guns. The gun did see service, however, in the Blackburn Perth.

An intriguing application was in the two single-engined, single-seat fighters built to Specification F29/27, which appeared in 1931: the Westland and Vickers COW Gun Fighters. These revived the First World War concept of upward-firing fixed cannon. In both cases, the gun was fitted alongside the cockpit to fire upwards at 55° for use against bombers (an idea to re-emerge to great effect in the Second World War in both Japanese and German night-fighters). The Vickers was a pusher biplane, the Westland a more modern-looking low-wing monoplane, but the Vickers had fifty rounds in special oversize clips while the Westland had a thirty-nine-round rotary dispenser mechanism from which the pilot had to push each round by hand. The RAF lost interest and neither went into production.

Schemes to use the COW gun continued into the late 1930s, the last on record being anti-submarine applications in the Blenheim 1 and the Sunderland, one of the projects for the latter involving two guns firing vertically downwards through the hull via watertight doors. The only practical use they saw in the Second World War was as airfield defence weapons.

During the 1920s and 1930s the British approached the question of armament systematically, analysing the effects of different weapons. Towards the end of the First World War the advent of armoured aircraft had prompted the development of a .5″ HMG. The war ended before much work had been done and development of what became the .5″ Vickers (which fired Vickers' own $12.7 \times 81$ cartridge) proceeded very slowly. In 1924 three early models of the .50″ Browning were purchased and over the next three years comparative tests were conducted between the Vickers and Browning weapons. Neither had a clear advantage over the other; the Browning fired a more powerful cartridge but was longer and heavier. There was also an experimental pan-fed BSA (Birmingham

Small Arms) .5″ observer's gun intended for flexible mounting, which initially used similar but slightly different ammunition, although it was later adapted to fire the standard Vickers round. However its size, low rate of fire and the small magazine capacity of 37 rounds deterred the RAF from adopting it. Tests against aircraft structures and engines in comparison with .303″ guns favoured the smaller calibre and work on the HMGs stopped in 1928, although versions of the .5″ Vickers were selected for both the Army and the Royal Navy.

Even larger calibres were considered. After experiments with 20mm test guns in the early 1920s, Oerlikon 20mm cannon were acquired and tried in the late 1920s and mid-1930s, but again the added destructive effect was not considered worth the extra weight. The RAF was particularly concerned about the increasing speed of aircraft and the short time available for firing, so put rate of fire at the top of the priority list. This meant that the new generation of monoplane fighters were equipped with an impressive battery of eight Browning .303″ RCMGs, with a combined rate of fire of over 9,000 rpm, or 150 rounds per second. This was a logical decision at the time, as aircraft were not equipped with armour or self-sealing fuel tanks and were therefore vulnerable to RCMG fire. It was not, however, very far-sighted, as the British aircraft were at an immediate disadvantage as soon as enemy aircraft adopted protective measures.

This danger was realised before the war, leading to an urgent search for a more powerful weapon. The British planners decided to leapfrog the HMG category and go straight for a 20mm cannon, and following a demonstration to British officials in the autumn of 1936 of the newly developed French Hispano-Suiza HS 404, test examples were ordered immediately and delivered in early 1937 along with a Dewoitine 510 fitted with the gun. The Hispano (as the British called it) offered the power of the Oerlikon FFS combined with a rate of fire which was 50% higher, and despite some reports that

*Replacing the ammunition drums for the four 20mm Hispano guns in a Westland Whirlwind* (Courtesy: R.W. Clarke)

interest in Oerlikons continued, the RAF never considered buying anything but Hispanos.

Initial British thoughts centred on fitting the big cannon to twin-engined fighters (the Westland Whirlwind was designed around four of them) and there was some controversy about whether single-engined aircraft should be equipped with cannon. Trial two-gun installations in both the Hurricane and Spitfire were tested in 1939, but delays involved in securing production rights and solving various technical problems (coupled with the late arrival of the Whirlwind) meant that the Hispano was not available for any significant use in the Battle of Britain. It began to be fitted to various aircraft from late 1940, starting with the Hawker Hurricane Mk IIC, the Bristol Beaufighter and the Westland Whirlwind.

It took a little time for the Hispano to be completely accepted as a replacement for the .303″ – the massive weight of the cannons had a significant effect on aircraft performance – so the Hurricane Mk IIB and even the new Typhoon IA were fitted with twelve .303″ Brownings instead. The .303″ remained in service throughout the war, supplementing the cannon armament of Beaufighters, some versions of the DH Mosquito and most marks of Spitfire, which did not carry an all-cannon armament until very late in the war.

The Hispano was originally introduced with a sixty-round drum magazine (permitting only six seconds of fire) and with a very long barrel to suit its intended French application as a *moteur-canon*, mounted within the nose of fighter aircraft and firing through the hollow propeller hub. The British never attempted to use this layout, as it was decided from the outset to fit several cannon to each aircraft for which fuselage (in twin-engined fighters) or wing mounting were more suitable.

Great difficulties with wing mounting were initially experienced in the first Spitfire installations. To minimise the aerodynamic drag of the big magazine, the guns were mounted on their sides so that the drums were largely buried in the wings. However, the guns had not been designed to fire in this way and proved very unreliable. After various confusions (including an attempt by Bristol to promote the use of their own mechanism) a belt feed, driven indirectly by the recoil movement, was

developed from the French Chatellerault design. Starting in 1941, this was retrofitted to British guns in service. The slotted 'recoil reducer' (muzzle brake) fitted to drum-fed Hispanos was deleted from the belt-fed guns as they needed the recoil impulse to drive the belt feed.

Difficulties were also caused by the need to allow the gun to recoil about 20–25mm in its mounting. There were two mounting points. One was near the muzzle and was connected to the gun by the characteristic recoil return spring wrapped around the barrel. The other was by the breech and carried the stationary ammunition feed. In the gun's originally-intended application this worked well as both mountings were attached to the rigid engine block. In wing-mounted guns, the wing sections connecting the two mountings had to be particularly rigid for the gun to work properly. This was not easy to achieve and development problems were common. The Hawker Tempest mountings were found to suffer from an unacceptable lack of rigidity when tested in 1943. In the same year, the Fairey Firefly also had major problems with flexibility and resonance when firing the cannon, and even the big Blackburn Firebrand showed flexing of the main wing spar on gun firing. Fuselage-mounted Hispanos exhibited far fewer problems.

By the end of the war the earlier versions were being replaced in British service by the shorter, lighter and faster-firing Mk V. Weight was saved partly by deleting the recocking device (never used in flight) and partly by lopping 30cm from the barrel, which sacrificed some of its high muzzle velocity in the interests of compactness. Incidentally, the firm Molins demonstrated that the gun could be redesigned to achieve 1,000 rpm, but the changes to the design were substantial and not considered worth the trouble of adopting.

The lack of a British HMG was not significant as far as fighters were concerned as the Hispano proved to be a better all-round weapon, but it had serious consequences for bomber defensive armament. The Hispano was a long and heavy gun not well suited to fitting in a turret and the need for a front mounting point caused problems, although a single gun was tested in the turret of a Boulton Paul Defiant as early as December 1939. Plans to introduce 20mm turrets were slowly progressed leading to tests in Lancasters from 1942, but problems were experienced with gun operation, belt feed and the structural strength of the mountings, and effective turrets emerged too late for the war. The RAF tried to secure Browning .50″ HMGs for defensive use but these proved very difficult to obtain, although a few were fitted to bombers, some marks of Spitfire and various American aircraft operated by the RAF. The result was that the increasingly useless .303″ remained in service as a bomber defensive weapon throughout the war.

Before the war an attempt to transform bomber defensive armament had been made. An RAF study into air-to-air fighting concluded that a single hit from a 2lb (0.9kg) shell would be sufficient to destroy most aircraft and in 1938 a specification was issued which led to the production of the Vickers Class S 40mm gun. This was a long-recoil weapon (the 43cm recoil movement absorbing most of the impact) based on the experience gained with the COW gun, but it fired a 40 × 158R cartridge developed from the naval 2pdr AA gun. It should be emphasised that this was not the same as the army's 2pdr tank/anti-tank cartridge or that of the 40mm Bofors, which were both much larger and more powerful.

The first example of the Class S was produced in 1939. Initial plans were to fit the gun into a large turret, complete with a rangefinder and predictor gear, to enable bombers to engage attacking fighters at long range. A turret was duly produced and fitted to a much-modified Wellington bomber for air tests, which proved to be quite successful except for a tendency for the muzzle blast to strip the fabric from the structure. However, by the time it appeared, operational requirements had changed and the idea was taken no further.

After the fall of France the importance of being able to destroy tanks from the air became obvious. Bombs were not sufficiently accurate (the RAF having rejected dive-bombing as a concept too subordinate to army requirements) so thoughts turned to large-calibre guns. The Vickers was the obvious choice, although there was initially some competition from the Rolls-Royce BH using the same ammunition. (The BH did not see service although the simpler, semi-automatic BD was used in naval aircraft.) The relatively low muzzle velocity of 615

m/s was considered acceptable as the aircraft would be firing at very short range. Furthermore, the impact velocity would be increased by the speed of the aircraft, the expected 240 mph attack speed being equivalent to another 107 m/s. Special loadings were developed for the case, the standard 1.13kg AP shot being capable of defeating armour plate about 50mm thick at a range of 400m, although a more typical attack range was 150m. A 1.36kg shot, developed in 1942, improved armour penetration by 9%.

After initial air trials in summer 1941 with a Beaufighter and an RAF Mustang two of these cannon, each with a fifteen-round drum magazine, were fitted to the Hawker Hurricane IID together with two .303″ Brownings used for sighting. This type saw most of its use with No.6 Squadron in the Western Desert between May 1942 and May 1943, with some use in the Far East from December 1943. In 1944 a Class S gun was also flying in a B-17E of Coastal Command, fitted in a Bristol nose turret and intended as an anti-U-Boat weapon. Tests were successful, but this application was not developed further. Despite the power of the gun, coping with the recoil did not cause any structural problems as

*Vickers 40mm Class S gun with 15-round drum magazine* (*RAF Museum*)

the long-recoil design reduced the peak loads to no more than those of the 20mm Hispano.

The Hurricane IID system proved highly accurate, much more so than the rocket-firing Typhoon fighters which replaced it, which despite their reputation were not precision weapons. Under trial conditions, the IIDs could achieve a hit-rate of 25% on tank-sized targets in comparison with less than 5% for airborne RPs (rocket projectiles); Operational Research calculated that in action in Normandy, the strike rate of RPs against tanks dropped to only 0.5%. The main reason was that guns were much easier to aim than the RPs which required complex mental calculations concerning trajectory and wind drift, not easy to perform in the heat of battle, although these problems were reduced with the introduction of a more advanced gyro gunsight in late 1944. To be fair, RPs were devastatingly effective when they did hit and had a severe effect on the morale of German tank crews, the first sighting of the Typhoons frequently causing tanks to be abandoned.

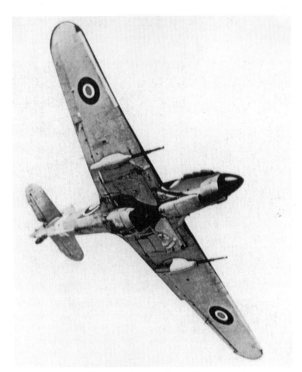

*Hurricane IID fitted with two 40mm Class S guns*
(*Courtesy: R.W. Clarke*)

However, the Hurricanes were withdrawn because the aircraft were too vulnerable to ground fire (thirty-nine were lost to flak), the heavy guns affected the aircraft's performance, the IID was effectively defenceless against enemy fighter aircraft and the gun was incapable of dealing with the Tiger tank. Even so, the Squadron's Mediterranean theatre operations saw claims of 144 tanks hit, of which 47 were destroyed, plus 177 other vehicles. In the Far East the IIDs were mainly used for attacking road and river transport, for which HE shells were used.

Somewhat surprisingly there appears to have been no attempt to develop APCR projectiles like the German *Hartkernmunition*, despite the fact that the technology was known and applied in other fields. On the other hand, a Hurricane-mounted Class S gun was fitted with a Littlejohn squeezebore adapter for tests in May 1944. The Littlejohn system, which saw service in the army's 2pdr AFV gun, used special lightweight, flanged, tungsten-cored projectiles which were squeezed by the cone-shaped adapter from 40mm to about 30mm calibre. Applied to the S gun, this should have delivered a dramatic increase in muzzle velocity and armour penetration (probably to around 80mm), but the system was not adopted and few details appear to have survived. Plans to increase the ammunition capacity by introducing a belt-fed version were also not proceeded with. Despite the introduction of RPs, the War Office never quite gave up the idea of an airborne anti-tank gun and at the end of the war were still playing with a scaled-up version, the 47mm Vickers P gun.

The last of the big guns used operationally by the RAF had a convoluted development history. As already described in Chapter 4, the Molins 6pdr was designed as an automatic anti-tank gun for the army and was later adopted by the RN for coastal craft. Molins then developed their weapon for aircraft use, offering it to the RAF in 1943 as a replacement anti-tank weapon. The RAF duly ordered thirty-six, the first being fitted to a Mosquito in July 1943, with a total of twenty-seven of what became the Mark XVIIIs being constructed. Before they saw action, requirements changed yet again and the 'Tsetses', as they were dubbed, were handed over to Coastal Command for

*6pdr Molins gun with partly-loaded magazine* (Courtesy: R.W. Clarke)

*6pdr Molins gun in DH Mosquito Mk XVIII* (BuOrd, USN)

anti-submarine and anti-shipping duties, which they performed with distinction. The massive recoil load was absorbed by an 80cm recoil movement, which as with the Class S kept the peak loads very low.

## AMERICAN WEAPONS

WHILE THE USAAF AND USN AIRCRAFT STARTED the Second World War with the .30″ Browning as their primary weapon, the story of American air armament is dominated by the .50″ Browning M2 HMG. The big Browning has already been described so it is unnecessary to say more than that it was a belt-fed gun weighing (in light-barrelled aircraft form) 29kg. Although prototypes were tested in the 1920s the gun saw little use until the introduction of the M2 in the mid-1930s. In pre-war form the rate of fire was officially 600 rpm

(although only 500 rpm in actual installations due to belt drag). During 1940 the design was amended with changes to the barrel and recoil springs which improved the rate to 750–800 rpm. Its specification and performance were not particularly remarkable and some early installations suffered from ammunition feed interruptions in high-G manoeuvres, but it is unquestionably one of the classic air-fighting weapons.

It became the standard American aircraft armament, both in fighters (which carried between four and eight, but typically six) and as the defensive weapons in bombers, both in turrets and free-swinging. In the latter form it was fitted with the characteristic spade grips: two handles at the rear of the gun, with a thumb-operated trigger. At the start of the war only a few of the big Brownings were carried, and in fighters such as the Curtiss P-36

*Eight .50″ Brownings in the nose of a B-25 attack aircraft. Note the belt guides from the ammunition boxes* (BuOrd, USN)

Hawk, Bell P-39 Airacobra and early Curtiss P-40 Tomahawks these were fuselage-mounted. These synchronised installations were criticised by British testers as they reduced the rate of fire to 400–500 rpm. As the number increased, guns were moved to the wings and synchronised weapons were abandoned, except in the specialised P-39 and Bell P-63 Kingcobra which were specifically designed for a heavy nose-mounted armament. While the Browning's projectiles lacked the destructive effect of cannon shells, their fairly high velocity and combined rate of fire made a six-gun installation a formidable armament, with the added advantage over mixed-gun installations of a greater ease of aiming.

Contrary to the general impression, the Browning M2 was not the only aircraft gun tried or adopted by the USA. The USAAF, not concerned with shooting down bombers, were not at first particularly interested in adopting 20mm cannon but they did expend much effort in achieving higher muzzle velocities in HMG calibres, partly by using lighter bullets and partly by developing weapons to fire larger-capacity cartridges. One of the best known of these is the T17 series, essentially a re-engineered MG 151 designed around the very powerful .60″ cartridge originally intended for an abortive anti-tank rifle. This was also necked down to .50″ in search of higher velocity (up to 1,340 m/s being achieved with a 32.4g projectile), as was the 20mm Hispano case, but none of these saw service, although over 300 T17s were built and more than six million rounds of .60″ ammunition produced.

The 20mm HS 404 was standardised by the USA in 1940 and manufactured under contract by Bendix, and subsequently other companies, mainly in the AN-M2 version (the designation indicating adoption for both the army and navy), but saw relatively little use. Only the Lockheed P-38 Lightning (which in most versions carried one), the Northrop P-61 Black Widow night-fighter (four) and the Boeing B-29 Superfortress bomber (one in a tail installation, alongside two .50″s) were regular users, although some versions of attack aircraft, and a few American aircraft originally intended for RAF service, were equipped with Hispanos.

An interesting aspect of the P-38 installation was that the gun was mounted in a tightly fitting housing which rigidly connected the front and rear mounting points and to which the ammunition feed was fixed. This produced a self-contained gun/recoil mounting/ammunition feed unit which could be bolted in place without the complexities experienced by the British, at the cost of the extra weight of the housing. This development may have inspired the M3 version which was standardised in July 1944. It was approximately equivalent to the British Mark V, with a shorter barrel, reduced weight and a higher rate of fire, but in addition featured an integral cradle within which the gun recoiled. The Americans also introduced the effective Edgewater mounting (first used on the .50″ M2), a friction-type recoil buffer using a series of ring springs arranged to slide partially over each other.

The USN showed rather more interest in the AN-M2 than the USAAF, presumably because they were concerned with preventing enemy bombers from reaching their ships. Following tests of the HS 404 against the .50″ Browning, the USN's BuAer Armament Branch concluded that one 20mm was equivalent to three .50″s in destructive power. The AN-M2 was fitted to some of the final piston-engined aircraft such as the F4U-5 Corsair and some F6F night-fighters, but was not regarded as very reliable and saw most use post-war. In general, wartime USN pilots seemed to prefer the HMG, possibly because the combined rate of fire of six .50″s (up to eighty rounds per second) was considered more useful in fighter-versus-fighter combat. The extra destructive power of the AN-M2s was not really needed to deal with the relatively vulnerable Japanese aircraft.

The Americans did spend some effort pre-war in developing their own cannon, and much experimental work was carried out in 23mm calibre, resulting in the .90″, which fired a $23 \times 139SR$ cartridge. Four different versions were designed (T1–4), T2 and T3 being of the API blowback type while T1 and T4 used a long-recoil mechanism. All versions were heavy, slow-firing and unsuccessful, and by 1941 the T4 was being considered as an anti-tank gun. The 23mm Madsen cannon attracted interest at one time (this fired a different, $23 \times 106$ round) but this also failed to see service after performing poorly in tests in 1937, as did a 25mm Hotchkiss gun which the French refused to sell because it was still on their secret list.

Much more productive was the work on 37mm cannon, which produced several different types amid some confusion. The American Armament Corporation (AAC) marketed several weapons in this calibre. None of these was successful and suggestions by some sources that they were involved with the development of the Oldsmobile T9 (adopted into service in December 1939 as the 37mm M4) are unfounded.

The M4 was a Browning-type long-recoil gun (the barrel recoiled some 240mm with each shot) firing a $37 \times 145R$ cartridge which was in effect an enlarged version of the old Pom-pom round. The muzzle velocity was much lower than that of the .50" Brownings which were usually fitted alongside it, which could cause significant aiming problems. At a range of 365m, the M4's projectiles dropped 137cm from a straight-line trajectory in comparison with 81cm for the .50"; at 730m the drops were 1,440cm and 867cm respectively. In addition, the times of flight varied. This was presumably one reason why most P-38s used the 20mm, which had ballistics much closer to those of the .50". Initial

unreliability, caused mainly by ejection problems, did not help the M4's reputation, although this was eventually overcome.

The M4 was fitted to various experimental aircraft and to the few Lockheed P-38D Lightnings built, but saw most service in the Bell P-39 Airacobra and early versions of the P-63 Kingcobra. Initially, the ammunition capacity was only fifteen rounds but this was soon replaced by a thirty-round continuous-loop belt which forms a characteristic hoop around the breech, designed to fit the contour of the aircraft nose. The M10 was a version of the M4 adapted to use a disintegrating-link ammunition belt, together with some minor alterations to raise the rate of fire, and was fitted to later versions of the P-63 (A-9 onwards), in which the ammunition capacity was increased to fifty-eight rounds. Many P-39s and most P-63s saw action in Soviet hands. A combination of .50" HMGs and 37mm cannon (presumably M10s) was initially proposed as defensive armament for the giant B-36 bomber, but this was changed to a uniform 20mm battery at the design stage.

Some mystery surrounds the use of the third of

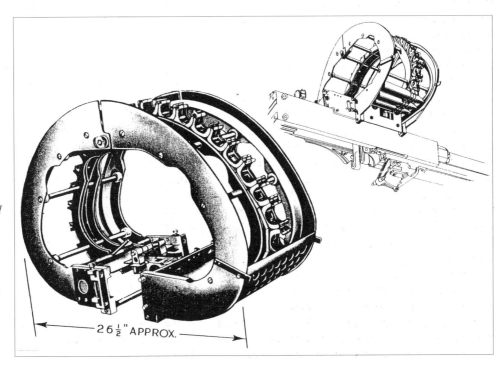

*Magazine (M6) for the 37mm M4 gun. The 30-round endless belt magazine was shaped to fit the nose contours of the P-39 Airacobra. It measured 67 × 46 × 26cm and weighed 16kg (unloaded) (Courtesy: MoD Pattern Room)*

26½" APPROX.

the US 37mm aircraft cannon, the M9, which was a version of the army's M1 AA gun modified to use a disintegrating-link belt. Despite being officially adopted, it only appears to have been fitted in test installations, in aircraft such as the single example of the experimental P-63D (in which forty-eight rounds were carried). Data concerning the M4 and M9 are sometimes confused in aircraft publications, perhaps because the M4 started out life being known as the T9. Some sources suggest that the M9 did see Soviet service in versions of the P-39 and/or P-63 but it has not proved possible to establish this and there is no reference to it in Soviet sources, which do give details of their use of the M4. The only confirmed service use was its installation, towards the end of the war, in some USN PT boats. Some aircraft which failed to reach production namely the XP-58, XP-67 and XP-72, were reportedly intended to be fitted with 37mm guns, but it is not clear which type. Some effort was put into developing slimmer and faster-firing guns such as the T37, but these remained prototypes.

The M9 would undoubtedly have made a formidable 'tank buster', as some high-velocity AP loadings of the $37 \times 223SR$ cartridge were developed with about 50% more muzzle energy than the equivalent standard BK 3.7 ammunition used by Germany. The M80 shot had a claimed penetration of homogeneous plate of 79mm/450m/70°.

The Americans did field some 75mm ground-attack cannon. The M4 was a modified medium-velocity army gun (the later AN-M5 being a light-weight version) and these were carried by some versions of the North American B-25 Mitchell bomber. They were manually loaded, but proved effective against shipping. A version with an automatic feed mechanism to achieve 30 rpm, the M10, was developed by the end of the war but did not see action, the priority having switched to airborne rockets.

## SOVIET EQUIPMENT

BY THE START OF THE WAR ON THE EASTERN FRONT the Soviet Air Force had a choice of three main air-fighting guns: the 7.62mm ShKAS, 12.7mm UB and 20mm ShVAK. During the war these were supplemented by weapons with more of a ground-attack emphasis, such as the 23mm VYa and the NS-37. As might be expected, the armament fit of aircraft became heavier as the war progressed, but not by as much as in the case of most other combatants.

The Soviet Union did not field any large-calibre cannon for air-to-air fighting during the war, except for the 37mm M4 and M10 in the American Lend-Lease P-39 and P-63, although the NS-37 and even the NS-45 were in practice used in this way. However, during the 1930s they had conducted some remarkable experiments with recoilless cannon, some of which saw service. The guns were collectively known as DRP (*Dynamo Reaktivnaya Pushka*, or dynamic reaction cannon) and experiments began in 1931 with guns of 76mm calibre, which were successfully fired from aircraft. The TsKB No.7 single-engined fighter (also known as the Grigorovich I-Z) was fitted with two of these DRP-76, and some seventy-one production machines were built between 1932 and 1935 and taken into service. These guns could only fire one shot, so much work was done to produce an autoloading mechanism resulting in the 76mm APK-4 (*Avtomaticheskaya Pushka Kurchevskogo*, designed by Kurchevski) and the APK-11 of 45mm calibre. In 1934 the IP-1 (*Istrebitel Pushnechnii*, or cannon fighter, also designed by Grigorovich) was initially designed for two APK-4s, but testing of the prototypes showed that the rate of fire was too slow for air fighting, and the DRPs were dropped in favour of the 20mm ShVAK.

The Soviet Union had a record of producing light and fast-firing aircraft guns. The 12.7mm UB

*Grigorovich I-Z with recoilless cannon underwing*
(*Courtesy: Russian Aviation Research Trust*)

offered a better combination of weight and performance than the equivalent .50″ Browning and was one of the best guns in its class. The 20mm ShVAK was also an impressive weapon which first became famous in the Polikarpov I-16 fighter which saw action in the Spanish Civil War, outclassing other aircraft until the arrival of the Bf 109. It was fitted to a wide range of aircraft including Lend-Lease Hurricanes. In late 1944 the ShVAK was replaced in production by the B-20, which used the same ammunition and had the same performance but weighed a remarkably low 25kg.

Soviet fighters did not adopt a uniform armament pattern except for the general avoidance of wing-mounted guns (apart from the obsolete I-16). Vee-engined aircraft such as the Lavochkin LaGG-3 and most Yakovlevs (which used a derivative of the Hispano 12Y engine designed to accept an engine-mounted gun) typically had an engine-mounted 20mm ShVAK supplemented by a pair of synchronised MGs, initially 7.62mm but later 12.7mm. The similar MiG-3, however, used different engines which had been intended for bombers

and were not therefore designed to accept engine-mounted guns. In any event, they were initially equipped with only one 12.7mm and two 7.62mm guns, cowling-mounted and synchronised, although some were later fitted with UBs in underwing gun pods. The La-5 and La-7 radial-engined fighters were fitted with two or three 20mm, all synchronised.

One reason for avoiding wing mounting was apparently the inaccuracy caused by wing flexing during flight. However, this emphasis on a relatively light and centrally mounted armament also indicates a strong concern with performance and handling. This suggests that the main priority was dealing with German fighters, which had outclassed their Soviet opponents in the initial stages of the fighting, mainly because Soviet engines were at that time relatively low-powered.

As the war developed, attention was also paid to ground attack. Designs for large-calibre guns were prepared by two competing design bureaux (*Osoboe Konstruktorskoe Buro*) known as OKB-15 (under Shpitalny) and OKB-16 (originally under Taubin

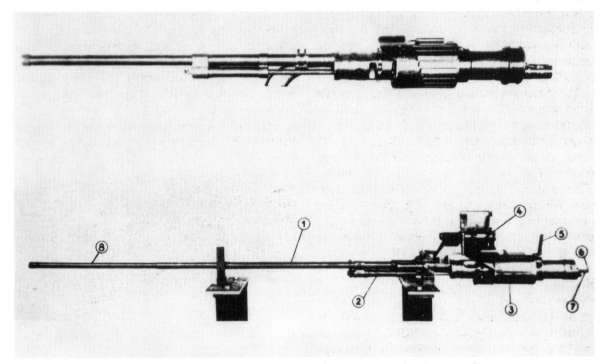

*20mm ShVAK: standard model above, engine-mounted model, with longer barrel, below*
*(Courtesy: Russian Aviation Research Trust)*

*Armourers fitting a 23mm VYa into an aircraft*
*(Courtesy: Russian Aviation Research Trust)*

*NS-37 gun and ammunition by its Ilyushin Il-2 3M Shturmovik aircraft*
*(Courtesy: Russian Aviation Research Trust)*

but later featuring Nudelman, Suranov and Rikhter – famous names in Soviet weapon design).

The Soviets had experimented with armoured ground-attack aircraft mounting up to four 37mm cannon as early as the late 1930s, such as the twin-engined Polikarpov VIT-1 and VIT-2 (*Vosdushnii Istrebitel Tankov*, or aerial tank fighter). This thinking resulted in a heavily armed and armoured aircraft designed specifically for the purpose: the Ilyushin Il-2 *Shturmovik*. Entering service just before the start of the war, the Il-2 saw extensive service with over 36,000 being built. After unsuccessful use of 20mm cannon, the Il-2 was re-equipped with the high-velocity 23mm VYa (*Volkov-Yartsev*) firing a far more powerful 23 × 152B cartridge, capable of penetrating 25mm of armour at 400m. Two of these were carried, with two RCMGs for sighting.

In 1942 the VYa was supplemented in service by the 37mm NS-37 (*Nudelman-Suranov*), which had replaced an earlier design, the Sh-37 (*Shpitalny*), following comparative testing in LaGG-3 fighters, after only a small number of the latter gun had been made. The army was not very happy about this, as the ammunition for the Sh-37 was already in production, so the NS-37 was adapted to fire the Sh-37 cartridge (37 × 195). Two of the NS-37 (also known as the 11 P-37) equipped at least a proportion of the Il-2 type 3M, and the Yak-9T of 1943 mounted one within the engine compartment, firing through the propeller hub. Initial attempts to absorb the big gun's recoil by bolting it to the Yak's engine resulted in damage to the cylinder heads so the mounting had to be redesigned to allow the gun to recoil, resulting in the cockpit being moved further back. Despite its ground-attack orientation, the Yak-9T proved a remarkably successful air fighter. It reportedly achieved a strike rate of one enemy aircraft shot down for every thirty-one of the 37mm rounds fired, which is to say one plane per magazine load. Nearly 4,800 NS-37s were built, almost all in 1943.

Not satisfied with this, the Soviets introduced the NS-45, which was the same gun as the NS-37 except that the barrel and cartridge case were altered to take 45mm projectiles already in service with other weapons (the army used 45mm calibre tank/anti-tank guns). This resulted in the cartridge case being shortened to around 185mm to keep the overall round length the same. The NS-45 retained the same weight and rate of fire as the smaller weapon (with a slight reduction in ammunition capacity from thirty-two to twenty-nine) while increasing the projectile weight and maintaining a respectable muzzle velocity. A substantial muzzle brake was fitted in order to compensate for the increased recoil.

The result was an increase in the claimed

short-range armour penetration from 50mm at 200m to 58mm (as with the VYa, striking angle unspecified). The NS-45 was fitted to the Yak-9K of 1944 but only fifty-three aircraft were delivered for evaluation at the front line. The gun proved unreliable and was not adopted for service despite featuring in various proposals (e.g. the Tupolev Tu-2Sh) as late as 1946. Even so, twelve German aircraft were claimed for the Yak-9K with

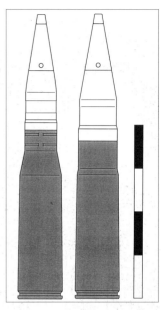

*37 × 195 cartridge for NS-37 (left) next to 45 × 185 cartridge for NS-45 (Courtesy: J-F Legendre)*

an average expenditure of ten rounds, an indication that the evaluation unit consisted of hand-picked pilots.

It is worth observing that mounting a gun to fire through a hollow propeller hub was the optimum solution to the problem of fitting heavy cannon to single-engined aircraft, as it minimised the weight and aerodynamic drag penalties. The Hurricane IID was unable to utilise this as the Merlin engine installation was not designed to accept this type of mounting.

By the end of the war, the development of Soviet airborne anti-tank cannon had reached a climax with the OKB-15-57. This high-performance 57mm gun weighed 290kg, which appears considerable until compared with that of the 6pdr Molins, a gun of similar calibre but lower performance. The post-war Yak-9P was designed to take engine-mounted guns of up to 57mm, but this option was abandoned after initial tests. The Tu-2RShR was also equipped with a RShR-57 gun (probably the OKB-15-57, although the Soviet habit of using different designations to describe basically the same gun lends a degree of uncertainty to identification) but this also failed to see service.

*Muzzle brake of an NS-45 protruding from the propeller hub of a Yak-9K (Courtesy: Russian Aviation Research Trust)*

*NS gun under Ilyushin Il-2 wing, with fairing removed. This appears to be the NS-45 version, as indicated by the muzzle brake. There was only one experimental installation of this gun in the Il-2 (Courtesy: Russian Aviation Research Trust)*

Soviet bombers were generally defended by RCMGs at the start of the war, with the notable exception of the four-engined Petlyakov Pe-8 which featured 20mm cannon in two turrets. The ShVAK could be fitted with either a pistol grip or spade grips when used defensively. The 12.7mm UB soon replaced the RCMGs, and by the end of the war the new lightweight 20mm Beresin B-20 was also being used as a defensive weapon.

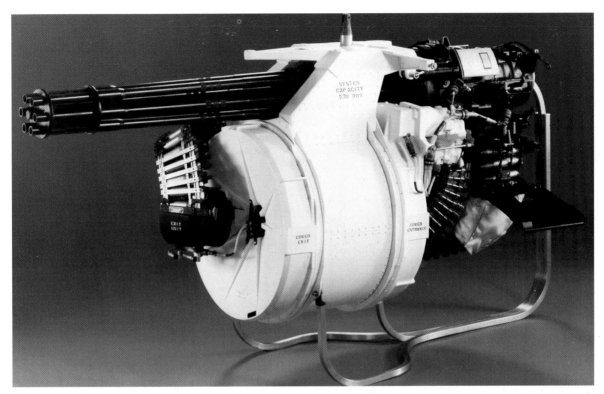

*GE 20mm M61A1 installation for F/A-18, including 570-round magazine (Courtesy: General Electric)*

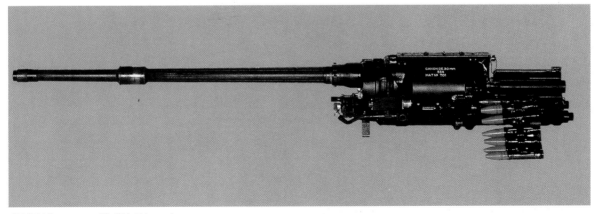

*GIAT 30mm type 30-550 F4 revolver cannon (Courtesy: GIAT)*

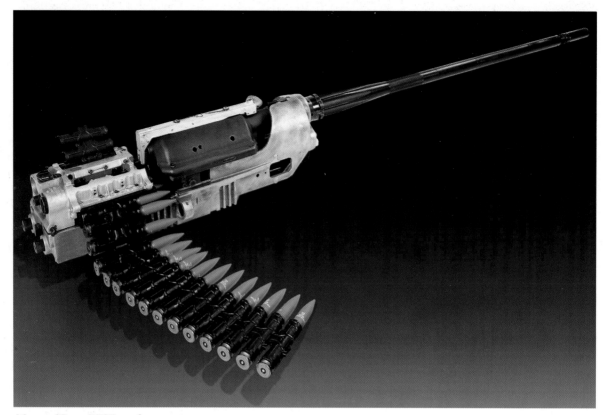

*Mauser 27mm BK27 revolver cannon* (*Courtesy: Mauser*)

*Panavia Tornado firing its BK27 cannon* (*Courtesy: Mauser*)

GIAT 30mm type 30M791 revolver cannon *(Courtesy: GIAT)*

*French 30mm aircraft cannon rounds (from left to right): 30 × 97B for 30-540 DEFA, 30 × 113B for 30-550 DEFA, 30 × 150B for 30-790 DEFA (Courtesy: J-F Legendre)*

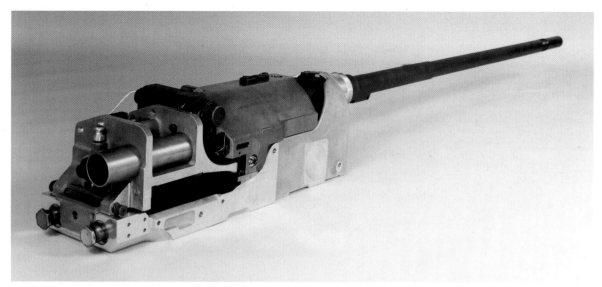

*Aden 25 revolver cannon* (Courtesy: R.W. Clarke)

*GIAT 20mm 20M621 gun in 19A helicopter mounting* (Courtesy: GIAT)

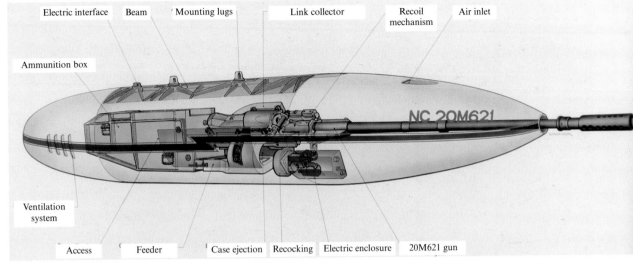

Electric interface   Beam   Mounting lugs   Link collector   Recoil mechanism   Air inlet

Ammunition box

NC 20M621

Ventilation system

Access   Feeder   Case ejection   Recocking   Electric enclosure   20M621 gun

*GIAT 20mm gunpod 20/621 (Courtesy: GIAT/Ian Hogg)*

F-WXFI

*GIAT 20mm 20M621 gun in fixed 22A helicopter mounting (Courtesy: GIAT)*

*30mm M230 Chain Gun on Apache helicopter (MDHC/Ian Hogg)*

*30mm 2A42 on Mi-28 Havoc (Courtesy: Russian Aviation Research Trust)*

*27mm Mauser BK27*
*installation for Eurofighter*
*Typhoon, with linkless feed*
*(Courtesy: Mauser)*

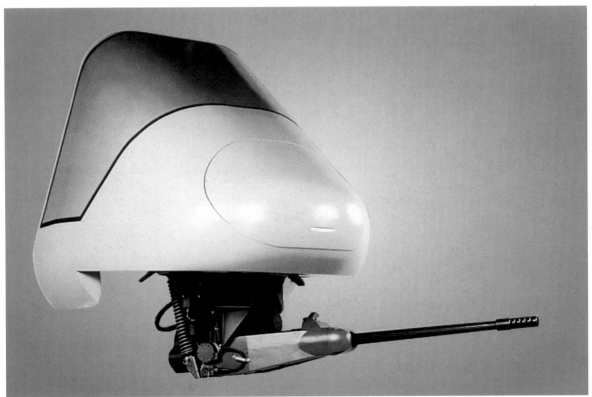

*30mm GIAT 30M781 in THL 30 turret (Courtesy: GIAT)*

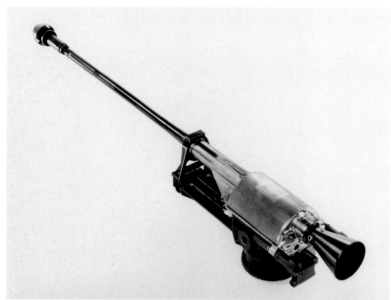

*30mm Mauser RMK 30 recoilless
revolver cannon (Courtesy: Mauser)*

*35/50mm Bushmaster III Chain Gun on M2 Bradley MICV (Courtesy: MDHC)*

*Pe-3 with
12.7mm Beresin
UBT
(Courtesy: Russian
Aviation Research
Trust)*

## THE GERMAN ARSENAL

GERMAN PLANS FOR AIR-FIGHTING AND AIRCRAFT armament went through a dramatic series of changes from the mid-1930s to the end of the Second World War, and resulted in a far greater variety of weapon projects than in any other nation, although many of the most technically interesting were still under development at the end of the war.

While Germany was among the first to introduce one of the new breed of monoplane fighters with retractable undercarriage and enclosed cockpits (the Messerschmitt Bf 109), they were not as far-sighted as the British in specifying the armament. At first, the fledgling *Luftwaffe* was strongly influenced by French thinking about aircraft armament. This included the concept of long-range fire using a single, powerful automatic cannon mounted between the cylinder blocks of a vee-configuration engine, firing through the hollow propeller hub and thereby avoiding all the complications of synchronisation. This layout kept the weight of the weapon and ammunition close to the centre of gravity, to the benefit of aircraft agility.

The French had selected the most powerful of the Oerlikon designs, the FFS, but when the *Luftwaffe* tested it they found a problem: the

maximum diameter of gun which could pass between the cylinder blocks of the German engines was only about 70mm. The FFS was wider than this because all Oerlikon aircraft guns had the main recoil spring wrapped around the barrel and connected to the bolt by a substantial yoke. It simply would not fit. There were other concerns to do with reliability, which was very dependent on the quality of the recoil spring.

Faced with these problems, the *Luftwaffe* took three decisions. In the short term, RCMGs would be used (the 7.9mm MG 17). The Messerschmitt Bf 109 originally carried just two, cowling-mounted and synchronised. The Bf 109B added a third engine-mounted one. In the long term, Mauser was given the contract to develop a new high-powered and fast-firing gun which *would* fit; this became the MG 151. For the medium term, Rheinmetall-Borsig produced the formidable MG C/30L, related to their 2cm FlaK 30 anti-aircraft cannon.

The MG C/30L fired the massive $20 \times 138B$ 'long Solothurn' cartridge, one of the most powerful ever used in a 20mm aircraft gun. The already high muzzle velocity of the FlaK 30 was further improved by the fitting of a longer barrel, intended to extend beyond the propeller hub. The usual twenty-round box magazines were replaced by a

100-round drum, mounted rather unusually underneath the gun. Plans were made in 1936 to equip a prototype Bf 109 and its rival He 112 with this gun in place of the usual twin machine guns. At least one of the He 112 prototypes, known as the *Kanonenvogel* (cannon bird), was so equipped and sent for evaluation to the Spanish Civil War, where it saw action before being destroyed in a crash-landing in July 1937.

Although the MG C/30L was officially adopted for service (and was renamed the MG 102 in 1942), the *Luftwaffe* had a change of heart after only 180 of the big Rheinmetall guns had been made. The main reason for this appears to have been the massive weight of the installation (reported to be around 180kg including ammunition), but there were also concerns about the strain on the weapon caused by the weight of the barrel and the ammunition transport, and in the insufficient reserve of recoil power to operate the weapon reliably. The big guns saw limited service on the ground in the AA role, but fitted with shorter barrels.

This left the *Luftwaffe* with a problem. They had learned that the new British fighters were to be equipped with an impressive eight-gun wing-mounted armament, which the little Bf 109 had never been designed to carry. In the short term two additional RCMGs were fitted to the wings, but more powerful weapons were clearly needed. At this time, the MG 151 was years away from production, so the Germans sought an interim solution in the smallest of the Oerlikon guns, the FF, which was able to fit the engine mounting.

Trials of the gun were satisfactory, except for some magazine feeding problems. It seems that the engine mounting was not considered successful at that time as the much higher operating temperatures caused reliability problems. At the urging of Udet, the head of the LC Air Technical Office of the RLM (*Reichsluftfahrtministerium*, or German Air Ministry) and an outspoken advocate of close-range fighter tactics, the FF was selected for wing mounting. After considerable modification and production by Ikaria Werke-Berlin, the resulting MG-FF, along with RCMGs, equipped almost all German fighters in 1940.

Most Bf 109Es in service in the Battle of Britain carried two MG-FFs in the wings plus two synchronised RCMGs. Later models reverted to the original plan of one engine-mounted cannon and two RCMGs, a very light armament which typified most Bf 109 variants in the early years of the war. The engine-mounted version of the MG-FF, briefly used in an early model of the Bf 109F before being replaced by the MG 151, was a standard gun with the minor addition of a mounting ring clamped to the barrel to enable it to be fixed in place relative to the blast tube. The Bf 110 at this time carried two MG-FFs and four RCMGs in the nose, and most radial-engined Focke-Wulf Fw 190s carried two MG-FFs in the wings as well as two MG 151s, and two RCMGs in the cowling.

The Ikaria cannon was a successful weapon limited by a low rate of fire, low muzzle velocity and (in most applications) a small magazine capacity. Like most of the other Oerlikon-pattern guns, it could not be speeded up to achieve more than 520–540 rpm because of the weight of the yoke connecting the spring to the bolt, which could not be reduced for fear of weakening the mechanism. In fixed mountings, the yoke and spring were exposed. Flexibly mounted guns had a quite different appearance, with a bulbous barrel casing, extending almost to the muzzle, covering the reciprocating parts in order to avoid the gunners' fingers or other loose items becoming entangled with the mechanism. They were also equipped with side-mounted grips and a distinctively curved shoulder stock.

The low muzzle velocity limited effective range, as it magnified any errors in estimating distance or deflection angle. This was not helped by the different ballistics of the 7.9mm and 20mm ammunition, which made using the smaller guns as 'sighters' problematic. The 7.9mm had a higher muzzle velocity, a shorter time of flight and a flatter trajectory, which could be compensated for only at a particular range and when firing at zero deflection; at other ranges, or against manoeuvring targets requiring deflection shooting, projectiles from both calibres of gun were unlikely to strike the target simultaneously.

The MG-FF's usual sixty-round drum feed also limited its combat persistence, although a compact ninety-round drum, the T 90-FF, was introduced much later, as well as a very small thirty-round drum for flexible mountings. The mechanism was

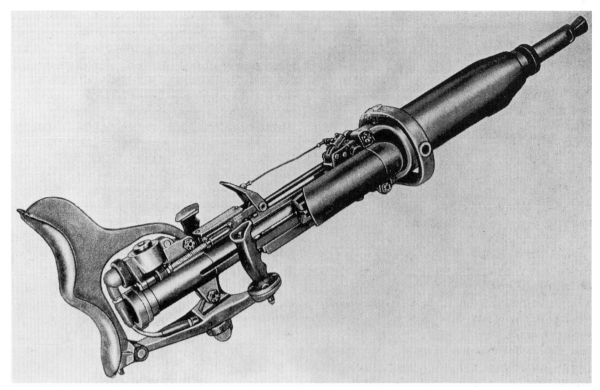

*2cm MG-FF for flexible mounting; note the barrel casing, handgrips and shoulder stock (BuOrd, USN)*

not suitable for driving a belt feed, but a complex electrically driven belt feed (GZ 1-FF, or *Gurtzuführer 1-FF*) was developed. It was mainly used in some night fighters and was capable of dealing with an astonishing 2,000-round capacity – enough for nearly four minutes' continuous firing!

Despite its limitations, the MG-FF survived in service until the end of the war. Its light weight made it popular for flexible mountings, and also for wing mounting as it minimised the impact on agility, which was presumably why most early Focke-Wulf Fw 190s had two MG-FF in the wings to supplement the inboard MG 151. The inherently recoil-absorbing nature of the mechanism also meant that simple mountings could be used (in contrast, the MG 151 had to be mounted to allow about 18mm of recoil movement). The Ikaria gun remained longest in night fighters and latterly in an upward-firing '*Schräge Musik*' (oblique or jazz music) installation in aircraft such as the Bf 110G-4/R3, in which its compactness was more important than its low muzzle velocity.

It is worth commenting on the *Schräge Musik* installation. There were basically three reasons for fitting guns in such a way. First, the RAF's night bombers were generally easier to see from below, with their full planform silhouetted against the night sky. Secondly, the night-fighters were less easy to spot from above, against the dark ground. Thirdly, unlike most *Luftwaffe* and USAAF bombers, few RAF aircraft were fitted with any downward-firing guns or even observation windows, so the fighters could creep close underneath them for an easy shot. On the other hand, some night-fighters were brought down by the falling aircraft they had just attacked. The Germans estimated that in 1943 and 1944 about 80% of night-fighter successes were achieved with *Schräge Musik* guns.

Tracer ammunition was not used in upward-firing guns to avoid alerting the bomber crew, and it took a long time for the RAF to realise that the *Luftwaffe* was using this technique. This is rather surprising, given that the British experience with upward-firing guns in the First World War had continued with the inter-war COW gun fighters and with early wartime experiments with upward-firing guns in a Blenheim (replacing the turret) and a Havoc (Douglas DB-7). It appears that British interest in such installations faded early in the war, with the introduction of AI (air interception) radar, which favoured a rear approach. Once the news broke, some bomber units fitted downward-firing guns and the H2S ground-mapping radar was adapted to spot aircraft flying underneath the bomber. The technical battle between bombers and night-fighters was intense and ever-evolving, but further comment is beyond the scope of this book.

Rheinmetall-Borsig were not discouraged by the failure of their MG C/30L and set about producing two other air-fighting cannon: the 2cm MG 204 and 3cm MK 101. In addition, their Swiss subsidiary Solothurn introduced an aircraft version of the S18-100 anti-tank rifle known as the S18-350. This was fitted in a flexible mounting in the nose of the Fokker T.V bomber in Dutch service, but it retained its semi-automatic mechanism and was not considered successful. By the beginning of the war the MG 204 (initially known as the Lb 204) was in limited service in some *Luftwaffe* seaplanes: the Do 18E, Bv 138A-1 and the ex-Dutch Do 24K-2. Two different ammunition types were used: initially the same belted $20 \times 105B$ (the 'short Solothurn') used in the S18-350, later a modified beltless version in an attempt to improve its dubious reliability. As it was intended for flexible mounting, in which role it must have been a handful, it was fed by a 20-round saddle-type drum magazine. Belt-fed and 100-round drum versions for fixed mounting were developed but not adopted. The gun was too heavy and too slow-firing to be a success.

The MK 101, a much larger cannon, was developed before the war as a long-range bomber-destroying gun for fitting to twin-engined aircraft such as the Bf 110. This massive weapon was designed around a new high-velocity $30 \times 184B$ cartridge. It saw action during the Battle of Britain, one shot-down Bf 110C-6 being found to have an externally mounted MK 101 instead of the usual pair of MG-FFs. It was also fitted experimentally to a Dornier Do 24T flying boat and to a dozen

Heinkel He 177A-1, intended as *Zerstörer* (bomber destroyers), in a steerable under-nose twin turret, the *Lafette* L101/1A. This big-gun concept was overtaken by the switch to the MG-FF, although the MK 101 later found a different and much more productive purpose in the anti-tank role, carried by the Henschel Hs 129B-1/R2.

A lot of other experimental work was carried out in Germany during the inter-war period, resulting in prototypes of gas-operated 2cm cannon by Lubbe and Krieghoff, neither of which was accepted. Instead, the German aircraft cannon and heavy machine guns which eventually replaced the rifle-calibre guns and the MG-FF during the Second World War became dominated by the designs of Mauser (in 15mm and 20mm calibre) and Rheinmetall-Borsig (in 13mm and 30mm).

Incidentally, the Germans used two different forms of aircraft gun nomenclature. Until 1942, the first number of the designation indicated the calibre, the next the gun model (e.g. the MG 131 was the first model of 13mm gun). After that date, the system was changed so that the first of the three numbers indicated the design firm (1 = Rheinmetall-Borsig, 2 = Mauser, 3 = Krieghoff, 4 = Krupp) with the next two identifying the model of gun. This system was not always applied, the MG-FF being the most obvious exception. There is also a minor mystery over the MK 101 designation, which complies with the post-1942 system; when initially used in the early part of the war, it should strictly have been called the MK 301, but this does not appear to have been the case.

The development of the wartime guns followed four priorities. First was the replacement of the MG-FF. This need was met by the Mauser MG 151. Next came a replacement for the RCMGs, which needed to be as compact as possible so that it could still be fitted into the restricted space within the engine cowlings of existing fighters; this led to the little Rheinmetall-Borsig MG 131. However, RCMGs, in the form of the compact and fast-firing MG 81 (often found in a twin flexible mounting) did remain in service throughout the war. Much later came a requirement for heavy cannon of 3cm and upwards in order to tackle the large four-engined bombers which were beginning to pound Germany. There was also a need for heavy, high-velocity cannon for airborne anti-tank purposes, and several of the large guns were developed to meet both purposes. Finally came a variety of attempts to improve the rate of fire, culminating in the Mauser MG 213C revolver cannon.

The MG 151 was first developed in 15 × 96 calibre, and in this form was considerably more powerful than any other aircraft HMG to see service. It was a contemporary of the 20mm Hispano, being developed in the mid-1930s, and fired a cartridge with a high-capacity case which was coincidentally virtually the same diameter as the Hispano's. As with all the later German aircraft guns, the MG 151 was available with electric priming to facilitate synchronisation (this version was sometimes referred to as the MG 151E), although percussion-primed versions were developed first. The 15mm gun was first fitted to the Bf 109F-2 in 1941 and was also used in a few other installations such as the nose mounting in the He 115C-1.

The MG 151 saw relatively little service in its original 15mm form. Wartime experience revealed that a larger explosive shell was more valuable than very high velocity, so the MG 151 cartridge case was 'necked out' and shortened (to preserve the same overall cartridge length with the longer 20mm projectiles) to 20 × 82, thus creating the MG 151/20. Projectile weight increased at the expense of muzzle velocity, but the gun weight and rate of fire of around 700 rpm remained the same. The armour penetration of the AP shot fell from 18mm/300m/60° to about 10–12mm, which was just about adequate to defeat aircraft armour. The gun retained the option of electrical priming and one of its first applications, the Focke-Wulf 190A, featured synchronised MG 151/20s in the wing roots.

The Bf 109 retained percussion-primed MG 151s throughout (the 20mm version being engine-mounted in the 109F-4 onwards), initially because the electrically primed versions were required for the Fw 190, later to avoid confusion over which type of ammunition was required. This consideration also complicated an abortive proposal to fit the Bf 109G-4 with an additional MG 151/20 in an underfuselage gondola, with far lower weight, drag and handling penalties than the two underwing gondola installation. The gun would have had to be synchronised and therefore needed to be electrical-ly primed, as the percussion-primed versions were not developed for this.

The Mauser was not particularly light, powerful or fast-firing but it was a sound design which rapid-ly became the most important *Luftwaffe* cannon of the war. It equipped most fighters and some bombers (latterly in the neat HD 151 single turret), was used in some *Schräge Musik* installations in heavy night-fighters such as the Ju 88, was also the principal Italian aircraft cannon and even saw some Japanese service. It is commonly reported that the gun was used in cowling-mounted synchronised installations in some German fighters, but it appears that this was only planned for the Focke-Wulf Ta 152C and Dornier Do 335, both of which were too late to see service.

The MG 151 was always belt-fed. Some wing-mounted installations on a few versions of the Messerschmitt Bf 109 appeared to be pan-fed, as the 135 rounds were arranged in three layers in a circular magazine, with the noses pointing inwards. However, the 'pan' was simply an unusual contain-er for a conventional belt, which was capable of being curved in a circle. The reason for this curi-ous arrangement was presumably to provide a reasonably shallow magazine in order to minimise aerodynamic drag.

The compact dimensions required of the MG 131, which replaced rifle-calibre machine guns in many bombers as well as fighters, dictated a small (13 × 64B) cartridge of modest power, resulting in a gun which weighed only 17kg yet could fire at 900 rpm. Armour penetration of the AP projectile was barely adequate at 10mm/100m/60°, and this fell to 7–8mm at 300m. By comparison, the best of the 7.92 × 57 AP loadings for the MG 17, the special high-velocity S.m.K-v (*Spitzgeschoss mit Stahlkern-verbesserte,* or improved pointed steel-cored bullet) could penetrate 8mm/100m/60° and 6mm/300m/60°.

As a defensive weapon the MG 131 started to replace the MG 15 in flexible mountings from 1941, in which form it was fitted with a pistol grip and conventional trigger. It was also installed in a neat, low-profile powered turret fitted, for example, to the cockpit roof of the Ju 188 and the rear dorsal position of the He 177. Twin and quadruple turrets were developed but these saw little or no use.

Remotely-controlled barbettes were used; a twin version was fitted in the forward dorsal position of the He 177, and two single barbettes were attached to the sides of the rear fuselage of the Me 210 and 410. Aimed by a gunner mounted in the cockpit, these could train up, down or to one side (although in the last case, obviously only one gun could fire at a time). Replacement of the synchronised MG 17 in fighter applications was surprisingly slow, the MG 131 first emerging in 1943 in the Bf 109 G-6 and later in the same year in the Fw 190A-7, both of which had two in cowling-mounted synchronised installations.

In an attempt to increase the destructive power of their cannon, German technicians developed a high-capacity 'mine' HE shell known as the *Minengeschoss* or *M-Geschoss*. This was manufactured by stamping out a thin-walled shell casing using the same technology used to make cartridge cases, instead of drilling out a solid projectile. The result was much more space for explosives and a much lighter weight, which also allowed a significant increase in muzzle velocity. The disadvantage was that the *M-Geschoss* was relatively ineffective against armour (no doubt accounting for RAF criticism of this aspect of its performance during the Battle of Britain), but this was evidently considered an acceptable trade-off for the greatly increased blast effect.

First to benefit from the mine shells was the MG-FF. The initial version was designed to use ammunition which fired 134g projectiles. In mid-1940 the 90–92g *M-Geschoss* was introduced, together with conventional 115–117g HE/T projectiles (apparently used because they were better suited to carrying tracer elements). The 115g projectiles were similar to the 134g but used light alloy instead of brass fuze bodies, and the velocity was reduced to match the momentum of the *M-Geschoss* in the interests of consistent gun functioning. These new cartridges generated less recoil than the 134g loading and required the gun mechanism to be slightly modified to compensate (with a lighter reciprocating mass and a weaker return spring), leading to the designation MG-FFM (or FF/M). Ammunition was therefore not interchangeable between the MG-FF and MG-FFM, despite being visibly similar. The first service application of the FFM appears to have

been in the Bf 109E-4, introduced in May 1940. Existing MG-FFs were then converted to the MG-FFM standard, which led to the two terms being used interchangeably thereafter. The *M-Geschoss* technology was applied to other German aircraft cannon such as the 2cm MG 151/20, the 3cm MK 108 and MK 103, and was widely adopted post-war.

The initial magazine loads for the MG-FFM had two *M-Geschoss* and two HE/I tracer rounds for every APHE or API (the AP loadings being capable of penetrating over 20mm of armour at normal fighting range). In the latter part of the war the *Luftwaffe* stopped using AP ammunition in air-to-air combat, partly because the armoured parts of an aircraft were too small to hit very often and partly because the flight of AP projectiles was often disturbed as they passed through the skin of the aircraft so they did not strike the armour point-first. The effect of penetrating a 3mm dural plate at a 20° angle was to reduce penetration of the armour behind it by up to 30%. It was also discovered that the most effective method of destroying aircraft was by the blast and incendiary effect of HE shells detonating within the structure, so the *M-Geschoss* became standard. Conventional HE/I projectiles with tracers (*mit Leuchtspur*) remained in service and were mixed with *M-Geschoss* in ammunition belts. The difference in muzzle velocity, and therefore time of flight and trajectory, was evidently considered to be within acceptable margins.

As we have seen, the *Luftwaffe* initially favoured high-velocity cannon but later switched to lighter and faster-firing guns. Later in the war, the need for large-calibre guns emerged in order to provide sufficient lethality against heavy bombers, and two very different 3cm weapons were developed. The introduction of these weapons, whose weight had a significant effect on the dogfighting ability of the single-engined aircraft which carried them, led the *Luftwaffe* to develop two versions of their day fighters: heavily armed and armoured 'Sturmgruppen' variants for attacking the bombers, and accompanying lighter and more agile aircraft to deal with escort fighters.

The more important of the new 3cm guns was the Rheinmetall-Borsig MK 108, a simple API blowback weapon which sacrificed muzzle velocity

*3cm MK 108 with blast tube attached (Courtesy: MoD Pattern Room)*

in the interests of destructive power, light weight and rate of fire. The *Luftwaffe* had calculated that it took an average of fifteen to twenty 2cm hits to down a heavy bomber, but only three or four 3cm hits. As an average only about 2% of shots fired hit their target, that meant that 750–1,000 2cm rounds had to be fired as opposed to 150–200 3cm rounds, so interest focused on the larger calibre. By comparison, Soviet calculations showed that about 150 20mm rounds were required to down a German opponent, possibly an indication that their targets were much smaller than the big Allied bombers. It is worth noting that the Germans found that only four or five 20mm hits were necessary in frontal attacks, where B-17s were relatively vulnerable, but such attacks were much more difficult to carry out.

The gun fired a low-velocity $30 \times 90RB$ cartridge and was compact enough to be fitted to the smallest fighters, being engine-mounted in the Bf 109K-4 (and an option in the G-6 and the G-10) together with two synchronised MG 131s. The K-4 could be equipped with two more of the MK 108 underwing in a *Rüstsatz* (field conversion set), a modification built in to the K-6 although it appears that few if any of these saw action before the end of the war. Four of the guns were fitted to the Me 262 jet fighter and they were used to equip some Fw 190 and night-fighters. The MK 108 was also used in upward-firing *Schräge Musik* installations in night-fighters such as the Heinkel He 219A-7 and B-3. The gun, nicknamed '*Presslufthammer*' as it looked and sounded like a pneumatic drill, was very effective but did suffer problems with the ammunition belts coming apart during violent manoeuvring – not the only aircraft gun to experience this. The pressure of war also led to its introduction in 1944, before development was complete. The original specification required 600 rpm, but an average of 650 rpm was reportedly achieved. At the end of the war, work on a modified version (referred to by one source as the MK 108A or MK 108 n A – presumably standing for *neuer Art*, or new type) was achieving around 900 rpm on test, but was too late to see service.

In complete contrast to the compact MK 108, Rheinmetall-Borsig also developed the MK 103 around essentially the same $30 \times 184B$ cartridge used in the earlier MK 101, but adapted to electric rather than percussion ignition, belt- instead of clip-fed, with a hybrid gas/recoil action instead of recoil operation, and using stamped-metal parts to simplify production. The MK 103 was no lightweight at 141kg, but was nonetheless significantly smaller, lighter and faster-firing than the MK 101. The ballistic performance using *M-Geschoss* was slightly worse than the MK 101 because the locking mechanism was not as strong, necessitating a slight down-loading of the ammunition to avoid overstressing the action.

From the start the MK 103, which entered production in 1943, was intended for dual anti-bomber and anti-tank roles, with appropriate ammunition developed for each. The anti-bomber round was a 330g *M-Geschoss* while the AP round was a tungsten-cored 355g *Hartkernmunition*, loaded to a higher velocity and pressure; presumably it was thought that the risk to the gun mechanism was worth taking in this case. Use of this AP ammunition lowered the rate of fire from 420 rpm to 360 rpm, because the gun mechanism unlocked more slowly as cartridge pressure increased. The gun was selected for some heavy fighters acting as bomber destroyers, including the He 219, Junkers Ju 188, various Me 410s and the experimental Me 262A-1a/U1, as well as the Do 335 and Ju 388J which were only produced at the end of the war.

Some mystery still surrounds the motor-cannon version of the MK 103, which has been referred to as the MK 103M, presumably standing for *Motorlafette*, or engine-mounted. The account which follows is the most likely explanation on the basis of the somewhat fragmentary available evidence. Two different approaches appear to have been tried: a radical redesign and (possibly) a minor modification.

The radical redesign was prompted by the fact that the MK 103 could not be mounted within the standard 7cm diameter blast tube which ran through the V-12 engines. Only about 80cm of the barrel length was able to fit within the tube; the rest

of the gun, 126cm long and up to 30cm wide, had to fit behind the engine, and in most aircraft (especially the Bf 109) there wasn't enough space between the engine and the cockpit. The MK 103M incorporated a modified layout which eliminated the wide barrel shroud as well as the standard muzzle brake so that the gun could be mounted further forward; a photograph exists of such a weapon, although it is not clear what changes to the operating cycle were involved. This was reportedly tested in a Bf 109 K-10 among others, but it proved unreliable and was not adopted as standard. In fact, contrary to many reports it seems clear that the Bf 109 never carried the MK 103 in action, the underwing 3cm mountings of the *Sturmgruppen* versions being MK 108 only.

There is some suggestion that a simpler modification might have been developed (whether previous or subsequent to the version described above is not clear), which merely deleted the muzzle brake and modified parts of the mechanism to cope with the heavier recoil. If so, it is possible that this might have been the version fitted to the Do 335 and the Ta 152C-3, which could have had enough room in their long noses to mount the gun between the engine and the cockpit, but these emerged too late to see action.

The MK 103 proved useful in ground attack, replacing the MK 101 which had achieved a good reputation but had been out of production for some time. The *Hartkernmunition* was able to penetrate 75–100mm of armour at 300m, dropping to a more realistic 40–60mm when impacting at 60°. The MK 103 was fitted to the Fw 190A-5/U11, A-6/R3 and A-8/R3 ground-attack variants and to more specialist aircraft such as the Henschel Hs 129B-2. The Henschel carried one, with 100 rounds, under the fuselage while the Focke-Wulfs carried two underwing FGB103 (*Flächengondelbewaffnung*) pods, each with thirty-two rounds. The pods were reportedly unsuccessful as accurate firing proved difficult. A shortage of tungsten, for which the machine tool industry had priority, limited the use of these weapons. Some reports (supported by Albert Speer's memoirs) suggest that this led to the use of uranium-cored ammunition on the Eastern Front, but no physical evidence of this has been found.

An earlier gun which saw service in both the

anti-bomber and anti-tank roles was the 37mm BK 3.7, a modified version of the FlaK 18 AA gun. Armour penetration with *Hartkernmunition* was quoted as 70mm/100m/60° or 140mm/100m/90°. The gun saw extensive use on the Eastern Front, fitted to such aircraft as the Henschel Hs 129B-2/R3 and Ju 88P-2 (a twin installation), and achieved particular fame when fitted, in pairs, to the Ju 87G version of the notorious *Stuka (Sturzkampfflugzeug* = dive bomber). This was by far the most important of the airborne anti-tank guns and the only one authorised to retain the use of *Hartkernmunition* after the summer of 1944 (along with the 5cm PaK 38 anti-tank gun, which needed it to stand any chance of penetrating Soviet tanks). It was also fitted in heavy fighters such as versions of the Bf 110G-2.

These weapons were supplemented by the BK 5 and BK 7.5, modified high-velocity anti-tank guns of great power and corresponding size and weight. The Rheinmetall-Borsig BK 5 used the same $50 \times 419R$ ammunition as the L/60 tank/anti-tank gun (it was basically the KwK 39 tank gun fitted with an autoloader and a twenty-two-round belt feed) which was claimed to penetrate up to 88mm armour at 250m. This might appear unimpressive in comparison with the smaller calibres but it was more reliable in that it was much less affected by the type of additional spaced armour plates on tanks which disrupted the HEAT and *Hartkern* rounds, and the destruction on penetration was greater. This was carried by the Ju 88P-4 and by some Hs 129B-2s as well as Me 410 A-1/U4 and B-2/U1. It was also fitted to or planned for the Ju 188S-1/U, Ju 288C, He 177A-3 and an Me 262A-1. A lightweight *M-Geschoss* loading was developed for air-to-air fighting. It was not popular because of reliability problems as well as its low rate of fire, so it saw far less use than the 3cm and 3.7cm weapons.

The BK 7.5 was likewise derived from the PaK 40 anti-tank gun and used its $75 \times 714R$ ammunition, but with a reduced propellant loading in order to moderate the heavy recoil. This did not affect AP performance as the speed of the aircraft added about 80 m/s to the velocity at 300 km/h. The muzzle velocity of the 6.8kg shot was around 700 m/s. The gun was fitted to the Ju 88P-1, with a twelve-round magazine, and to the Hs 129B-3, but it

appears that few aircraft were fitted with these large cannon and they saw very little action. As with the BK 5 (but even more so) these huge cannon had a crippling effect on aircraft performance and handling.

By the end of the war an astonishing range of large-calibre aircraft weapons was in the experimental stage, prompted by the calculation that a single direct hit by a shell of 5cm or 5.5cm calibre would be sufficient to destroy a heavy bomber. One was the 5.5cm Rheinmetall-Borsig MK 112, a compact, low-velocity API blowback gun which was in effect an enlarged MK 108, firing a $55 \times 175RB$ cartridge. It was planned to fit two into the nose of an Me 262, with twenty-five rounds each, a similar armament with 50 rpg in the Arado Ar 234 jet and two underwing guns on the Do 335. The Americans continued the post-war development of this weapon for a while as the 'Gun, 57mm, T78'.

At the other end of the large-calibre performance scale were the high-velocity 5cm and 5.5cm cannon which were intended to fit into the nose of heavy fighters such as the Me 410 and Me 262 jet in order to subject bomber formations to long-range artillery fire, a revival of the tactical thinking of the 1930s which had led to the MK 101. This was tried with a handful of Ju 88P-1s in the winter of 1942/3 and with BK 5-equipped Me 410s, which attacked a B-17 formation in May 1944. Neither experiment was a success, but despite this new weapons were developed.

The most promising of these large, high-velocity guns by the war's end was the 5cm Mauser MK 214 A, like the BK 5 based on the KwK 39 and using the same ammunition, but using a improved autoloader design to achieve 160 rpm while weighing 'only' 490kg. This was officially ready for use and there are some reports that it saw action, fitted to a Me 262 A-1a(V), but without success. A more adventurous weapon was the 5.5cm Rheinmetall-Borsig MK 114. This fired the large, high-velocity $55 \times 450B$ ammunition designed for the experimental FlaK 58 AA gun and was reportedly being developed for a stabilised mounting, to be aimed by a gunner, which was expected to improve the hit probability by at least five times. Performance was impressive, but the weapon was only at the development stage at the end of the war.

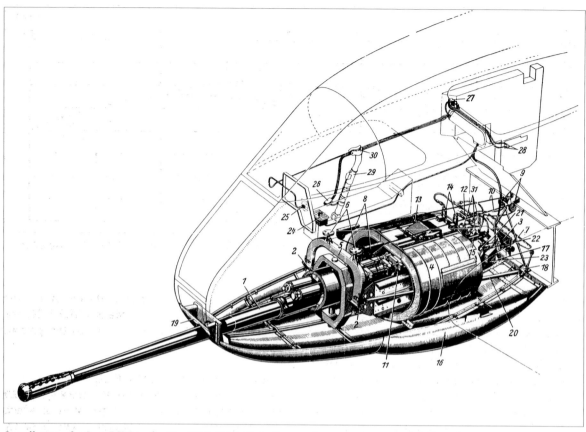

*Installation of a 5cm BK 5 in the Me 410A-1/U4. Note the annular magazine around the breech*

It is difficult to understand the *Luftwaffe's* obsession with long-range air-to-air artillery fire. The aiming problems were enormous and it was difficult to use smaller guns as 'sighters' because of the differences in trajectory. For example, the Me 410 A-1/U4 was equipped with a pair of MG 151/20 as well as the BK 5, but with the trajectories adjusted to coincide at 500m, the MG 151 projectiles varied from 65cm higher than the BK's at 200m to 65cm lower at 700m. The timing problem was just as bad: the MG 151 (*M-Geschoss*) projectiles took 0.952 seconds to reach 500m, by which time they had slowed to 363 m/s. Even the conventional HE round for the BK 5 took only 0.625 seconds and was still travelling at 736 m/s – the *M-Geschoss* would have been faster still. The Me 410 B-2/U-1 caused even more problems as this carried a pair of MG 131 as well; trajectories of the three types of gun did not coincide at any range. Even ignoring this problem,

the lack of proximity fuzes greatly limited long-range effectiveness and it is hard to see how even the Me 262 could have been expected to survive against the swarming USAAF escort fighters, given the need to fly a steady course for some time while aiming and firing.

On the other hand, the short-range, low-velocity MK 108 (and presumably even more so the MK 112) was well suited to the fast jet's ability to evade the escorts, get in amongst the bombers to fire at close range, then speed away. It must be realised that the effective velocity of the Me 262's weapons was much greater than gun performance would indicate, as an 800 km/h attack speed (around 500 km/h faster than the bombers) is equivalent to adding another 220 m/s to the muzzle velocity. In the case of the MK 108, this represents more than a 40% increase.

In their desperate efforts to obtain more

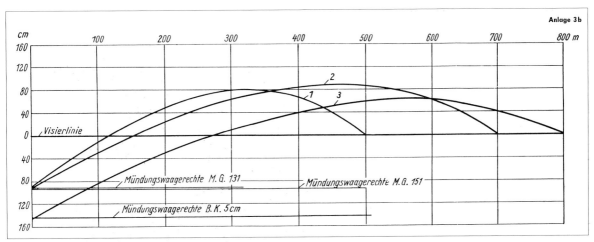

*Trajectory curves for weapons installed in an Me-410B-2/U1; 1 = 13mm MG 131, 2 = 15mm MG 151, 3 = 5cm BK 5 (M-Geschoss)*

destructive power, German designers pursued some novel and occasionally far-fetched concepts. These included such weapons as the Gustloff HF 15, which loaded between seven and nine 15mm projectiles in one chamber, driven by one propellant charge at an effective rate of fire of 36,000 rpm. A simpler approach to achieving a high-rate burst of fire was taken by the Rheinmetall-Borsig SG 117, 118 and 119, all of which consisted of a vertically mounted cluster of several 30mm MK 108 barrels, each only capable of firing a single shot, arranged to fire in rapid sequence equivalent to 10,000–12,000 rpm as the fighter passed under the target. To cancel out the recoil, the block of barrels was designed to recoil downwards out of the aircraft.

The Germans also experimented with squeeze-bore automatic guns with the aim of increasing muzzle velocity, for example the MG 131/14/9, in which the chamber calibre was 14mm and the muzzle calibre 9mm, and even automatic recoilless weapons such as the 5.5cm Rheinmetall MK 115, which used combustible cartridge cases and was designed to achieve 300 rpm. Most of this ingenuity was wasted as none of these weapons saw service and all proved to be conceptual dead ends. Design efforts continued with more conventional weapons. Mauser designed the MG 215, initially in 13mm and later in 15mm, but neither saw service. Of much more long-term significance was the work to

increase the rate of fire of aircraft cannon, leading to the literally revolutionary Mauser MG 213C, the forerunner of all revolver cannon to the present day.

## THE JAPANESE MISCELLANY

JAPANESE AIRCRAFT ARMAMENT WAS CHARACTERISED by a wide variety of different types most of which used their own unique ammunition. This is partly explained by the fact that the air forces were divided between the army and navy, although a similar situation did not prevent a high degree of commonality in US aircraft guns. Certainly the Imperial Japanese Army and Navy (IJA and IJN respectively) followed wilfully different procurement policies and seemed unconcerned about the benefits of standardisation. In the following, the names in brackets are the Allied code-names for the aircraft.

As with other air forces during the 1930s there was a great reliance on RCMGs, most of which were copies of old foreign designs. By the time Japan entered the war, these had been supplemented by HMGs and 20mm cannon. Later still, larger calibres were being developed under the pressure of attack by USAAF bombers; and towards the end of the war they had B-29 Superfortresses to deal with, which were even more of a challenge than the B-17s normally used in Europe. In this respect, the development of

Japanese air armament mirrored that of the Germans. There were differences, however: the relative unimportance of armoured warfare meant that airborne anti-tank guns were never a priority, and as we shall see there was even more interest in upward-firing guns.

Most of the weapons were based upon foreign designs, mainly Oerlikon and Browning (in some cases with improvements on the originals), but there was one talented Japanese engineer, Dr Masaya Kawamura of Japan Special Steel, who designed some very effective weapons.

The IJN adopted two weapons in the HMG class. The 13mm Type 2, used in flexible mountings for the defence of bombers and reconnaissance aircraft, was a copy of the German MG 131 except with percussion rather than electric priming for its $13 \times 64B$ cartridges. Later on, the much more powerful 13mm Type 3 (a version of the Browning M2 slightly modified to fire the Hotchkiss $13.2 \times 99$ ammunition already in naval service) was introduced as a fixed weapon in the Kawanishi Shiden (George) fighter from the N1K3-J version and the Mitsubishi Reisen (Zeke) fighter – better known as the Zero – from the A6M5 onwards. A flexible version of the 13mm Type 3 (*senkai kikanho* instead of *kotei kikanho*) was adopted as a replacement for the 13mm Type 2, with which the IJN apparently experienced problems. A scaled-down Oerlikon firing a $14 \times 101RB$ cartridge was developed but saw no service.

It appears that the IJN was particularly keen on Oerlikon designs. In the 20mm cannon class, the navy adopted (in 1939) and subsequently developed the Oerlikon FF and FFL guns, and was the only major user of the latter weapon. These were known as the Type 99-1 ($20 \times 72RB$) and Type 99-2 ($20 \times 101RB$) respectively, and differed considerably in length and power. The Type 99-1 bore a close resemblance to the immediately related *Luftwaffe* MG-FF, including the use of a barrel casing in the flexibly mounted version, although in this instance the casing was perforated to aid cooling and the gun was mounted upside-down so that the drum was underneath. Various versions of each weapon were made for both flexible and fixed mounting, all with drum feed except for the Model 4 (fixed) versions of both the Type 99-1 and 99-2,

which were adapted by Kawamura for self-powered belt feed (something the Germans failed to achieve with the MG-FF).

The Type 99-2 replaced the smaller gun in many applications as the need for higher muzzle velocity became evident (and aircraft became powerful enough to carry the extra weight), but the 99-1 remained in service throughout the war, particularly in defensive and upward-firing installations. Although information is incomplete, it appears that a few examples of a thoroughly revised version, the Type 99-2 Model 5, were produced by the end of the war. This had a bolt assembly lightened as much as possible which, together with additional buffer springs at the rear of the gun to accelerate the bolt's return stroke, enabled a rate of fire of between 620 and 750 rpm to be achieved. This was a much better performance than either Oerlikon or Ikaria managed with this type of gun.

The Type 99-1 was fitted as a defensive weapon in some versions of the Kawanishi H6K (Mavis) and H8K (Emily) flying boats (in turrets) and the Mitsubishi G3M (Nell) and G4M (Betty) bombers, but was mainly used as a fixed gun in IJN fighters such as the N1K Kyofu (Rex) floatplane fighter, early versions of the A6M (Zeke), the Nakajima J1N (Irving) and C6N Saiun (Myrt) reconnaissance/night-fighter and the Yokosuka P1Y Ginga (Frances) bomber/night-fighter. The Type 99-2 was fitted to the Kawanishi N1K1-J Shiden (George) fighter, the Aichi E16A (Paul) and B7A (Grace), later versions of the Mitsubishi A6M (Zeke) and G4M (Betty), the J2M Raiden (Jack) fighter, and also late versions of the J1N (Irving) and the Yokosuka D4Y Suisei (Judy) dive bomber/reconnaissance/night-fighter.

In larger calibres, the navy developed the 30mm Type 2, a scaled-up version of the Type 99 using a $30 \times 92RB$ cartridge, which was tried in the A6M3 (Zeke), J2M3/4 (Jack), P1Y1-S (Frances) and possibly the J1N1-S (Irving). It was not considered satisfactory, at least in part because of the limited (forty-two-round) magazine capacity, and saw little use. To replace it the navy adopted the Kawamura-designed Type 5, which used a new $30 \times 122$ cartridge giving a substantial increase in power over the Type 2. Unlike the earlier gun, it was not an API blowback weapon but used a combined gas and recoil action. It was fitted to one night-fighter version of the C6N1 (Myrt) (mounted in the rear cockpit to fire obliquely upwards), the P1Y2 (Frances) and the J2M5 (Jack). It was planned to become the navy's standard fighter weapon but appeared too late.

Typical armament installations of IJN fighters showed a steady increase in power. To give one example, the A6M2 (Zeke) commenced the war with two synchronised RCMGs and two 20mm Type 99-1s – virtually identical to the Bf 109E engaged in the Battle of Britain more than a year before. Initially, the pilots preferred to use just the RCMGs as they were easier to score hits with than the low-velocity cannon, but they had to learn to use the cannon as increasing US aircraft protection made the RCMGs less effective. The succeeding A6M3 saw the introduction of the more powerful Type 99-2 cannon, which in the A6M5 was fitted with belt feed (the Model 4) to increase the ammunition capacity to 125 rpg. Later A6M

versions saw the twin RCMGs replaced by a single 13mm Type 3; later still two Type 3s were added to the wings, outboard of the cannon. By now, the armament of three HMGs and two cannon was comparable with that of the USN fighters they faced, and probably more effective against bombers. Pressed into service as night-fighters, some A6M5d-S had an additional 20mm Type 99-1 cannon, with a 100-round drum magazine, installed behind the cockpit, firing obliquely upwards.

If the IJN was partial to Oerlikons, the Japanese Army Air Force was equally addicted to the Browning short-recoil mechanism, which was scaled up or down to use a wide variety of cartridges from 12.7mm to 37mm. Their heavy weapons started (in calibre terms) with their standard HMG – the Ho-103 or 12.7mm Type 1 (12.7 × 81SR), a scaled-down Browning M2 which was fitted to a wide range of aircraft in both fixed and flexible mountings.

Among the few weapons which did not use a

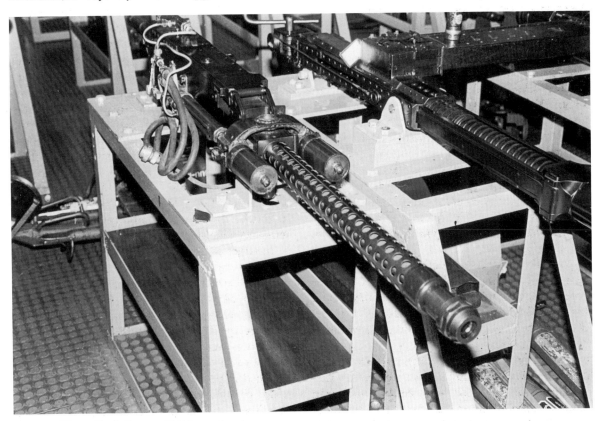

*Japanese 20mm Ho-5* (Courtesy: MoD Pattern Room)

Browning mechanism were the first of the 20mm cannon in regular service, the Kawamura-designed Ho-1 and Ho-3. These were modifications of the Type 97 gas/blowback anti-tank rifle and used the same $20 \times 125$ round. The Ho-1 was designed for flexible mounting and was fitted with a fifteen-round double-drum magazine, while the Ho-3 was used in fixed installations with the fifty-round magazine. Both were powerful but slow-firing weapons. The Ho-1 was carried by the Nakajima Ki-49 Donryu (Helen) bomber in a dorsal turret, while the Ho-3 was fitted to a version of the Kawasaki Ki-45 Toryu (Nick) heavy fighter.

Before the war some use was made of a 'Type 94 flexible gun' ($20 \times 99RB$) in the Ki-20 bomber. This was reportedly a modified version of the Oerlikon L, the predecessor of the FFL, but it does not appear to have been a success as no more was heard of it. The IJA later imported some 400 MG 151/20, only fitted to some Kawasaki Ki-61-I Hien (Tony) fighters, as a stop-gap until the development of the Ho-5.

The Ho-5 was yet another version of the Browning scaled up to take a $20 \times 94$ cartridge which was in effect a lengthened MG151/20 case (or a shortened Hispano!). The gun weighed only 37–45kg (depending on type) and achieved 850 rpm which made it, on paper at least, one of the best of the wartime cannon. Although it was adopted in 1942, development continued throughout the war and it suffered from poor quality towards the end of the conflict. The ammunition had to be steadily downloaded to avoid overstressing the mechanism, so it never achieved its performance potential. The gun equipped later versions of the Nakajima Ki-43 Hayabusa (Oscar) fighter and the Kawasaki Ki-45 (Nick) and Ki-61 (Tony) as well as the Nakajima Ki-84 Hayate (Frank) fighter, the Kawasaki Ki-100 fighter and Ki-102 (Randy) heavy fighter, the Mitsubishi Ki-46 (Dinah) – a reconnaissance aircraft converted to a bomber interceptor – and (as defensive armament) the Ki-67 Hiryu (Peggy) bomber.

After initial experiments with a Browning enlarged to take a $25 \times 115$ cartridge, the IJA decided that more power was needed and developed this into the 30mm Ho-155 (sometimes erroneously referred to as the Ho-105 or Ho-151), which used a $30 \times 114$ cartridge (case lengths of between 113mm and 115mm have been reported). Two versions of this gun were made, the Model II being a lightened version of the Model I. As with the Ho-5, the later version had a reduced performance to preserve reliability. Like the IJN's Type 5, it was intended to be a major weapon but development was still continuing at the end of the war and it only saw action in the Ki-61-I (Tony) and Ki-84-1c (Frank) fighters.

The IJA also used larger-calibre weapons in air fighting. The early 37mm Type 98, a version of the Type 94 tank gun using the same $37 \times 132R$ ammunition, was manually loaded. The long-recoil Ho-203 ($37 \times 112R$), yet another design by the prolific Dr Kawamura, fired automatically (if rather slowly) and was fed by a fifteen-round magazine. Initially, the cartridge was loaded with a 530g shell and only achieved a muzzle velocity of 430 m/s, but this was felt to be too low so the shell weight was reduced to 475g, permitting an increase to 570 m/s. The Ho-203 was fitted to later versions of the Kawasaki Ki-45 (Nick) and possibly other heavy fighters. The later Ho-204 used a new $37 \times 144$ rimless case which boosted muzzle velocity to 710 m/s, and the rate of fire also increased to 300–400 rpm by virtue of the usual Browning short-recoil action. It only reached service towards the end of the war in the Ki-46-III (Dinah), in an upward-firing installation, but was tested in other aircraft.

The IJA also used a 57mm aircraft gun, the Ho-401, a scaled-up version of the Ho-203 by the same designer. This was built around a $57 \times 121R$ cartridge, derived from a tank gun round, and was fitted to the Ki-102b (Randy) assault plane and the prototype Ki-93-1a heavy fighter. One even larger-calibre cannon also saw limited service: the manually loaded 75mm Type 88, which was fitted to the Mitsubishi Ki-109, a heavy fighter based on the Ki-67 (Peggy) bomber, and the prototype Ki-93-1b.

As with IJN aircraft, Japanese Army fighters steadily increased in hitting power. The Nakajima Ki-43 (Oscar), just entering service at the start of the war, was initially still armed with only two RCMGs. Later these were replaced by two 12.7mm Ho-103 and later still two 20mm Ho-5, still a light armament. The vee-engined Kawasaki Ki-61 (Tony), which had four Ho-103 in early versions, also replaced these with Ho-5 later on, with a few

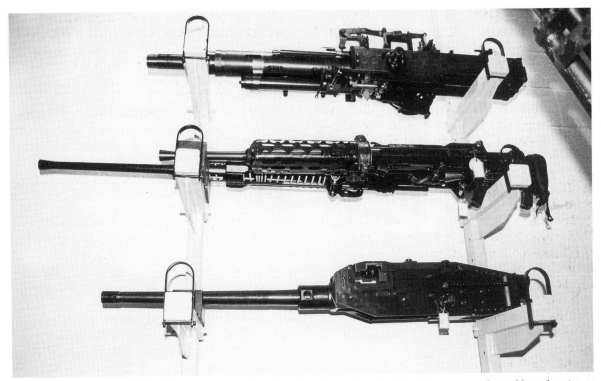

*Japanese aircraft guns: top = 37mm Ho-203, middle (front) = 20mm Type 99-1 flexible (note perforated barrel casing and forward-sloping grip), middle (rear) = 20mm Type 99-2, bottom = 30mm Ho-155 II (Courtesy: MoD Pattern Room)*

fitted with two Ho-103 and two of the powerful 30mm Ho-155. It appears that the Japanese were never interested in engine-mounted cannon, even though the Ki-61's engine was based on the DB601 and could therefore have been fitted with one.

Some accounts of upgunning have been exaggerated: the Nakajima Ki-44 (Tojo) which started with two RCMGs and two Ho-103 before graduating to four Ho-103, is claimed by some sources to have carried in later versions 20mm Ho-3 and Ho-5 cannon and even the massive 37mm Ho-203, but primary sources contradict this. However, a small number of Ki-44-II special versions (*tokubeti sobi*) did carry two of the remarkable 40mm Ho-301 in the wings. The rate of fire of the caseless ammunition was an impressive 450 rpm and the gun weight a reasonable 132kg, but the muzzle velocity was a very low 230 m/s and the ten-round magazine gave a firing time of just 1.3 seconds. These characteristics meant that the weapon could only be used for one attack, pressed home at a suicidally short range. It was not a success.

One unexplained aspect of Japanese aircraft ordnance was the difference in performance between the naval and army weapons. The IJN guns were generally quite powerful for their cartridge size, but the IJA guns noticeably less so, particularly towards the end of the war. While the IJA's Browning-pattern guns were evidently susceptible to the gradual reduction in manufacturing quality, forcing a reduction in ammunition power, it appears that the IJN's simpler Oerlikon-derived weapons were less affected by this problem.

It is worth noting that the Japanese took an early interest in upward-firing gun mountings for night-fighters and put these into service in 1942/3, in parallel with the German *Schräge Musik* system. The later prevalence of this type of mounting probably had much to do with the height and speed performance of the B-29, which many Japanese fighters had difficulty in intercepting.

Unlike German practice, aircraft so equipped included single-engined fighters such as versions of the IJN's A6M (Zeke) – one 20mm Type 99-1; C6N

*Japanese 40mm Ho-301 caseless. Note projectile standing on magazine* (Courtesy: MoD Pattern Room)

(Myrt) – two Type 99-2; or one 30mm Type 5, D4Y (Judy) – one Type 99-2; and J2M (Jack) – two Type 99-1, as well as the IJA's Ki-84 (Frank) – three 20mm Ho-5. Twin-engined naval aircraft with upward-firing guns included the J1N1 (Irving) – two Type 99, and P1Y1 (Frances) – four Type 99. The IJA aircraft were the Ki-45 (Nick) – two 20mm Ho-5; Ki-46 (Dinah) – one 37mm Ho-204; and Ki-102 (Randy) – two Ho-5. The J1N1-S (Irving) actually had four obliquely mounted 20mm cannon in the fuselage – two firing upwards, two downwards.

Complete information about which models of Type 99 were used in upward-firing installations is not available. The most common weapon was probably the Type 99-1 Model 3, which was fitted with a 100-round drum, but the belt-fed Model 4 and the Type 99-2 were used where there was space for them.

Perhaps the most remarkable armament fit belonged to the twin-engined Kawasaki Ki-45-Kai-C (Nick), which reportedly mounted one forward-

firing 37mm Ho-203 (with a fifteen-round belt feed) in the nose, a forward-firing Ho-3 in a ventral tunnel, two upward-firing Ho-5 inside the cockpit, and an RCMG for the observer! Other reports state that the Ho-3 was in practice removed when the Ho-5s were fitted.

The IJN also experimented with obliquely mounted guns for ground attack. The P1Y (Frances) was fitted with up to seventeen downward-firing Type 99 guns in the bomb bay, twelve angled forwards, five rearwards. Thirty of these aircraft were being prepared for attacking B-29 bases and for sweeping landing craft during amphibious assaults, but the war ended before they could see service.

## WEAPONS OF OTHER NATIONS

THE ITALIAN AIR FORCE WAS UNUSUAL IN CHANGING very early from RCMGs to HMGs, but rather threw away the lead this might have given them at the start of the war by typically fitting very few of

*12.7mm Breda-SAFAT (BuOrd, USN)*

them. As already stated, the Italians adopted the 12.7 × 81SR Vickers cartridge and produced two of their own weapons in this calibre, the Breda-SAFAT and the Scotti, the former being far more important and numerous. They also produced prototypes of two 20mm guns, the Breda CL20 and another design by Scotti, but neither saw service, the MG 151/20 being used instead.

When Italy entered the war in 1940, the main fighters were the FIAT CR32 and CR42 *Falco* biplanes, being supplemented by the FIAT G.50 *Freccia* and Macchi MC.200 *Saetta* monoplanes. The usual armament of all these aircraft consisted of two 12.7mm Breda-SAFATs in the traditional cowling-mounted and synchronised installations, although in some versions these were supplemented by another pair of wing-mounted guns, usually RCMGs. Even the first of the new inline-engined high-performance fighters, the MC.202 Veltro and Reggiane RE.2001 *Falco II*, were no better

equipped. The only adequately armed Italian fighters were the modified MC.205V, with two 12.7s and two MG 151/20s, and the FIAT G.55 *Centauro* which had two 12.7s and three MG 151s, but these were too late to have any impact before Italy's surrender in 1943.

Italian bombers were generally equipped with flexibly mounted defensive weapons, usually RCMGs, but some had one 12.7mm gun in a dorsal turret. The Savoia-Marchetti SM79 Sparviero and SM84 torpedo bomber were the only ones to feature more than one HMG, but even then had only three or four, most of which were flexibly mounted.

Like the British, the French had little time for HMGs, jumping straight from RCMGs to cannon. Hotchkiss did produce a belt-fed aircraft version of their 13.2mm HMG which was capable of 600 rpm, but its use is uncertain. Like the Germans, the French first experimented with large and powerful cannon, among them the 25mm Hotchkiss, a

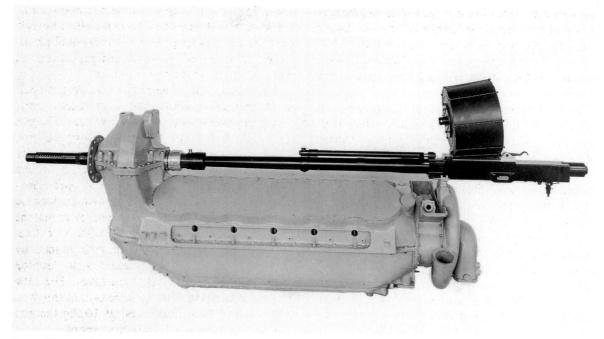

*20mm Hispano-Suiza HS 404 in engine mounting, with 60-round drum attached* (Courtesy: Ian Hogg)

gas-operated gun weighing 70kg but initially firing at only 180 rpm from a ten-round clip. By the late 1930s the performance had improved to 300 rpm from a thirty-five-round magazine and a visiting US delegation showed some interest, but the French claimed that it was secret and refused to sell. The first French cannon to see service, however, were versions of the Oerlikon FFS already described, adapted for engine mounting and made by Hispano-Suiza as the Types 7 and 9. Early inline-engined aircraft such as the Dewoitine D.501/510 and Morane-Saulnier MS405 carried one of these together with a pair of RCMGs.

The low rate of fire of the Oerlikon guns (around 400 rpm) was considered unsatisfactory, and as a result a much better weapon emerged (designed by a Swiss, Marc Birkigt), the famous 20mm Hispano-Suiza HS 404. This was used in the Dewoitine D.520 and MS406, but again only one engine-mounted cannon was fitted, supplemented by four or two RCMGs respectively. It appeared that Birkigt initially tried mounting the gun rigidly as had been achieved with the low-recoiling HS 7 and 9. However, the HS 404's action resulted in a much

sharper recoil blow so a recoiling mounting had to be devised, complicating the ammunition feed from the drum, which needed to remain stationary as its size and weight precluded its being rattled to and fro ten times per second.

The French were rightly proud of the HS 404 and were intending to rely increasingly on it had they remained in the war. Some versions of the radial-engined Bloch MB-152 and the MB-155 carried two wing-mounted cannon. It was even fitted as a defensive weapon in bombers such as the Farman (Centre) NC 223 and Lioré-et-Olivier LeO 451. While initial French interest was focused on a version firing a powerful $23 \times 122$ round (the HS 406), only the 20mm saw service. The gun even saw German service. Some versions of the Do 24, built on captured Dutch production lines, were equipped with the HS 404 in the dorsal cupola, and the gun was also used as an AA weapon.

Oerlikon were not the only Swiss company producing aircraft cannon. The Swiss adopted a version of the French MS406 fighter as the D-3800 series but fitted their own engine-mounted cannon, the recoil-operated FMK38, designed around a high-velocity 20 × 139 cartridge which was the precursor of the current Oerlikon KAD round. Rather bizarrely, the gun was also fitted to the C-35 biplane, thus combining an ancient aircraft concept with one of the most powerful 20mm aircraft guns ever to see service.

Finland produced a range of heavy weapons including the 12.7mm LKk/42, four of which were mounted in the cowling of the VL Myrsky fighter, in service between 1944 and 1947. Little information seems to have survived about this weapon, except that it was belt-fed and unpopular because of inaccuracy problems caused by a tendency to overheat. Cannon were also produced in Finland by Lahti, using his own 20 × 113 ammunition, but despite some reports that these saw airborne service in the Russo–Finnish wars it appears that they were only used by the navy, fitted to patrol boats. The Finns certainly used a wide variety of equipment including some 12.7mm Brownings converted for aircraft, 20mm MG-FF, MG 151 and ShVAK, and

according to one report some Oerlikon FFL. However, it is difficult to determine which aircraft used the guns, as it appears that individual planes received a variety of armament fittings, depending, presumably, on whatever was to hand.

The Danish firm Madsen also produced cannon which saw action, albeit mostly in German hands and in the AA rather than aircraft version. The gun was available in both 20mm and 23mm calibres, although it appears that only the former saw service despite considerable pre-war promotion of the 23mm, which was featured as the proposed armament of several aircraft of various nations. Madsen also produced a 'heavy' machine gun (to stretch the definition) which only saw service with Argentina, the 11.35mm. This was another attempt to increase the hitting power of air weapons while keeping weight and dimensions to a minimum. The little 11.35 × 62 cartridge had the same overall length as a .30'06 or 7.9mm round, and at 10.5kg the gun weighed the same as rifle-calibre weapons.

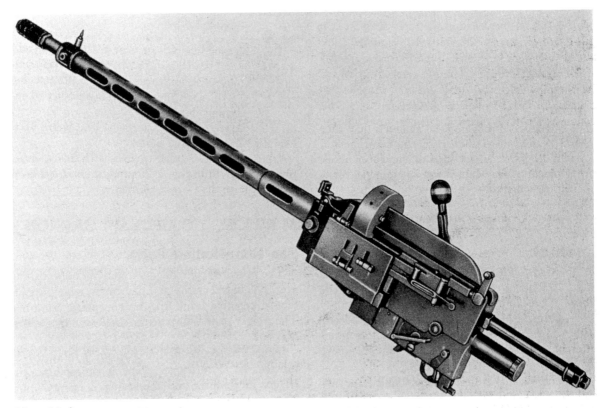

*23mm Madsen (BuOrd, USN)*

*57mm Bofors m/47 (BuOrd, USN)*

Sweden also used a version of the Browning HMG chambered for the $13.2 \times 99$ Hotchkiss round, a similar weapon to the IJN 13mm Type 3. Known as the m/39A, this was later converted to $12.7 \times 99$. At the other end of the heavy weapon spectrum, Bofors produced the 57mm m/47 airborne anti-shipping gun which was fitted to the SAAB T18B twin-engined attack bomber, but this was a post-war development.

Among the largest installations to see service was carried by the Italian Piaggio P.108A four-engined heavy bomber. This was fitted with an old naval gun of 4″ (102mm) calibre for anti-shipping purposes (not the Ansaldo 90/53 often mentioned; that was a high-velocity 90mm AA gun), but the gun was manually loaded.

## THE SECOND WORLD WAR:
### EXPERIENCE AND CONCLUSIONS
THE SECOND WORLD WAR COMMENCED WITH RCMGs dominating aircraft armament, supplemented by a few HMGs and low-powered 20mm cannon. It soon became evident that aircraft could be protected reasonably well against RCMG fire, which led to a rapid increase in the use of HMGs

and the introduction of more powerful and faster-firing 20mm guns. In the two nations which had to deal with massive onslaughts by heavy bombers – Germany and Japan – there was a growing interest in guns of 30mm or more by the end of the war.

Not all nations were willing to add armour to their aircraft. The Italians were slow to respond to the need for this and the Japanese Navy scorned it until the latter stages of the war, both unwilling to compromise the exceptional agility of their aircraft (and in the case of Japanese aircraft, their amazing range). Soviet fighters never had adequate protection, although ground-attack aircraft were heavily armoured. In contrast, the British, Germans and Americans rapidly adopted self-sealing tanks and armour protection, at least for pilots.

Bomber defensive armament saw much less development as it was much easier to bolt a bigger gun onto an existing fighter than it was for a bomber to be modified to accommodate a much larger turret. RCMGs were virtually standard at the beginning of the war, with rarely more than half-a-dozen guns carried. These were upgraded to HMGs in most air forces during the war, with the exception of the RAF which had planned no production of

*World War 2 fighter gun cartridges (from left to right): .50" Browning (12.7 × 99), Hispano HS 404/AN-M2 (20 × 110), 37mm M4/M10 (37 × 145R), IJN 13mm Type 3 (13.2 × 99), IJN Type 99-1 (20 × 72RB), IJN Type 99-2 (20 × 101RB), 12.7mm Breda-SAFAT/ Scotti/IJA Ho-103 (12.7 × 81SR), IJA Ho-5 (20 × 94), IJA Ho-1/Ho-3 (20 × 125), 12.7mm Beresin (12.7 × 108), ShVAK (20 × 99R), MG 131 (13 × 64B – also IJN 13mm Type 2), MG 151 (15 × 96), MG-FF (20 × 80RB), MG 151/20 (20 × 82), MG 204 (20 × 105), MK 108 (30 × 90RB), MK 103 (30 × 184B)*

HMGs. Later bomber designs in Germany, Japan and the Soviet Union featured defensive 20mm guns. The RAF and USAAF were handicapped in following suit by the great length of the unwieldy Hispano which they had both adopted as their standard cannon.

An aspect of Second World War armament which attracts little attention is that which is currently known as combat persistence – the ability to keep on fighting, which apart from aircraft fuel tankage was then very much connected with ammunition magazine capacity. During the Battle of Britain, the Spitfire I had a capacity of 300 rounds per gun, giving about sixteen seconds' firing (the Hurricane carried slightly more). Their main opponent, the Bf 109E, was in a curious position, in that the two MG-FF had only 60 rpg, around seven seconds' worth, but the two synchronised RCMGs had no less than 1,000 rounds each, enough for a whole minute's firing (this was reduced to 500 rpg in later versions with an engine-mounted cannon). On the other hand, sixty seconds of fire from two RCMGs delivered only the same weight of fire as fifteen seconds from the British planes' eight-gun installations.

The Germans stayed with *Trommel* (drum)

*World War 2 airborne ground-attack cartridges (left to right): ShVAK (20 × 99R), VYa (23 × 152B; this is actually the postwar ZU but the shape was almost identical), MK 101/MK 103 (30 × 184B; N.B. drawing in Appendix 3 shows the Hartkern projectile), 37mm M4/M10 (37 × 145R), 3.7cm BK 3.7 (37 × 263B), 40mm Vickers Class S (40 × 158R), 5cm BK 5 (50 × 419R), 6pdr Molins (57 × 441R). The NS-37 is shown in Appendix 3.*

Typical fighter armament fits, with an approximate comparison of their effectiveness, are shown below:

| Year | Aircraft | Weapons | KG | RPS | KPS |
|------|----------|---------|-----|-----|-----|
| 1940 | Hawker Hurricane I | 8 × 7.7mm Browning | 80 | 160 | 1.8 |
| 1940 | Messerschmitt Bf 109E-3 | 2 × 20mm MG-FF | 52 | 17 | 2.0 |
|      |          | 2 × 7.9mm MG 17 | 25 | 33 | 0.3 |
| 1941 | MiG-3 | 1 × 12.7mm UBS | 25 | 15 | 0.8 |
|      |       | 2 × 7.6mm ShKAS | 14 | 60 | 0.7 |
| 1941 | Focke-Wulf Fw 190A-2 | 2 × 20mm MG 151 | 84 | 23 | 2.6 |
|      |          | 2 × 20mm MG-FF | 52 | 17 | 2.0 |
|      |          | 2 × 7.9mm MG 17 | 25 | 33 | 0.3 |
| 1941 | Supermarine Spitfire VB | 2 × 20mm Hispano II | 100 | 20 | 2.6 |
|      |          | 4 × 7.7mm Browning | 40 | 80 | 0.9 |
| 1942 | Mitsubishi A6M2 (Zero) | 2 × 20mm Type 99-1 | 49 | 17 | 2.2 |
|      |          | 2 × 7.7mm Type 97 | 24 | 33 | 0.4 |
| 1942 | Curtiss P-40B | 2 × 12.7mm Browning | 58 | 15 | 0.7 |
|      |          | 2 × 7.6mm Browning | 20 | 40 | 0.4 |
| 1944 | Lavochkin La-7 | 3 × 20mm Beresin | 75 | 40 | 3.9 |
| 1944 | Hawker Tempest Mk V | 4 × 20mm Hispano V | 168 | 50 | 6.5 |
| 1944 | Nakajima Ki-84-1b | 4 × 20mm Ho-5 | 144 | 57 | 6.8 |
| 1944 | North American P-51D | 6 × 12.7mm Browning | 174 | 85 | 3.9 |
| 1944 | Messerschmitt Me 262A-1 | 4 × 30mm MK 108 | 240 | 43 | 14.2 |

KG = total weight of gun installation in kilograms
RPS = number of rounds fired per second
KPS = total weight in kilograms of projectiles fired per second

magazines for all applications of the MG-FF apart from the GZ 1-FF belt-drive, which could handle up to 2,000 rounds per gun. Later work raised the drum capacity to ninety rounds (the T 90-FF) without increasing the diameter, but this saw little service, as did other sizes of drum and magazine, varying from fifteen to a hundred rounds. The ammunition capacity of other *Luftwaffe* weapons varied considerably. The Bf 109G carried 150 rounds for its MG 151/20 (just over twelve seconds) and 300 rpg for its two synchronised MG 131 (twenty seconds) while the Fw 190D carried 250 rpg for each of its two MG 151/20 (twenty-one seconds) and 475 rpg for the two MG 131 (thirty-two seconds). Installation of the engine-mounted MK 108 in later versions of the Bf 109G reduced the capacity to

sixty rounds (six seconds), although each shell had far more hitting power. The Me 262 had 100 rpg for two of its MK 108s, 80 rpg for the other two.

The first 20mm Hispano guns also used a sixty-round drum (giving only six seconds' firing) which accounts for the RAF's keenness to introduce belt feeding. Fighter installations of belt-fed Hispanos typically provided 120–150 rpg (twelve to fifteen seconds), although the Beaufighter carried 240–283 rpg, providing almost half a minute's firing. These figures proved adequate in practice. Analysis of camera-gun film revealed that an average of seventeen rounds of 20mm were fired per burst, with three to five bursts per combat, at intervals of between three and ten seconds. Ammunition capacity for the American aircraft's .50″ calibre guns also varied, from 240–280 rpg in F4F, P-40 and most P-47 installations (around twenty seconds) to 400–500 rpg in P-38 and later P-47s (thirty to forty seconds).

Italian fighters typically carried 300–400 rounds of 12.7mm ammunition (twenty-five to thirty-five seconds) and an equally generous 200–250 rpg (seventeen to twenty-one seconds) for the MG 151/20 cannon fitted later on. Soviet fighters generally carried 120–200 20mm rounds (nine to fifteen seconds) and around 250–300 rpg for the 12.7mm guns (fifteen to eighteen seconds). Information about Japanese installations is less readily available, but RCMG capacity was typically 500 rpg, HMG 250 rpg and 20mm cannon, initially 50–60 rpg with drum feed, rose to 100–125 rpg when belt feed was introduced.

An interesting detail concerns the use of tracer ammunition. This was often favoured by bomber crews as they felt that it distracted attacking fighter pilots; the US Ordnance Department even developed a special .50″ tracer, the M21 'Headlight', which was three times more visible than usual from the front, and good results were reported. On the other hand, USAAF fighter units which did not use tracers reportedly achieved far more kills and suffered fewer losses than tracer-equipped units, presumably because the use of tracers warned enemy fighter pilots that they were being attacked.

In all cases, ammunition capacity for bomber defensive guns was considerable. The Avro Lancaster had an average of 1,750 rpg of RCMG rounds, enough for one and a half minutes' continuous firing. Operational Research revealed that the average expenditure per mission for mid-upper turrets in RAF aircraft was 235 rounds, while even for the rear gunner a total of 2,000 rounds was adequate for 99% of missions, in comparison with a capacity of up to 10,000 rounds.

The need for defensive fire for the RAF's night bombers was questionable as the main value of gunners was to give warning of approaching night-fighters early enough for the pilot to take the violent evasive action which gave the best chance of survival. Some 90% of Lancaster sorties were made without any contact being made with enemy fighters; of the 10% which were attacked, half were shot down despite their defensive armament. The

Mosquito bomber had no guns, relying on speed and stealth to evade the fighters, and had a loss rate one-twentieth that of the Lancaster.

American heavy bombers typically carried an average of 500 rpg of .50″ ammunition (the quantity per gun varied), but sometimes ran short of ammunition during their bitterly contested daylight raids. Despite the power of their HMGs the advantage still lay with the attacking fighters, against which the only effective defence proved to be escort fighters.

The war demonstrated that it was not the technically advanced concepts which achieved the most. The most successful weapons were those which were the most practical, in terms of being fully developed, easy to make and reliable in service. A good example of this is provided by a comparison between the 20mm Hispano, which was at first rather large and heavy for its class, and the Mauser MG 151. When the first MG 151/20 was recovered by the British, they were impressed by its compactness, light weight and high rate of fire, and considered copying it. However, on more detailed examination of the beautifully engineered rotary-locking bolt mechanism, British industrialists concluded that their equipment and workers were not capable of manufacturing it. Efforts were accordingly concentrated on improving the relatively simple Hispano instead, and the resulting Mark V was a close match for the Mauser.

Another interesting contrast is provided between the weapons turned out by the British, Germans and Americans on one hand, and the Soviets and Japanese on the other. The Soviet and Japanese guns commonly had a higher performance (in terms of rate of fire) and a significantly lighter weight than equivalent Western weapons, a tradition that the Russians have continued to this day. The Soviet 12.7mm Beresin, 20mm ShVAK and 20mm B-20, and the Japanese 12.7mm Ho-103 and 20mm Ho-5 are good examples.

How could they achieve this? It seems likely that they took a much more pragmatic attitude to weapon life than the Western nations. For example, the 20mm Hispano was initially designed for a life of 10,000 rounds. On investigation during the war, it was discovered that very few guns even managed 1,000 rounds before being destroyed in action or in a crash, and the majority never fired more than a few hundred rounds. In fact, the Hispano was later lightened but could still achieve 2,500 rounds even for the smaller components, with the main elements lasting for 5,000 rounds. A designed gun life of 500–1,000 rounds might well have permitted a much lighter construction and/or a higher rate of fire without any practical disadvantages.

## POST-WAR DEVELOPMENTS IN WESTERN NATIONS

AFTER THE SECOND WORLD WAR THERE WAS A lull in the previously rapid development of new weapons while the Allies absorbed the progress made by German weapon designers, debated the role of aircraft guns in the light of the prospect of guided missiles and (in the case of all except the USA) struggled to recover from the disastrous financial consequences of six years of war. The post-war period can therefore be divided into phases. Until the mid-1950s, weapons based on the wartime guns remained in service (with the Korean War of 1950–53 adding some useful experience), while the slow development of the new concepts of revolver and rotary cannon took place in parallel (and in rivalry) with that of guided missiles. By the late 1950s, the 'missile school' was in the ascendant, and it was not until experience of the Vietnam War in the late 1960s confirmed the value of an integral gun that the continued place of such a weapon was assured.

This did not prevent some unusual experimental work. One British line of investigation was into the *Luftwaffe*'s use of large airborne cannon to subject Allied bombers to artillery fire. It was felt that the use of VT (proximity) fuzes, not available to the *Luftwaffe*, would make this an interesting proposition and a 1947 feasibility study was therefore launched into fitting a suitably modified version of the army's 3.7″ AA gun into the long-suffering de Havilland Mosquito. An idea of the implications of this can be gained from the following statistics: the army gun fired a 12.7kg shell at 800 m/s, the barrel and breech alone weighed 1,770kg and measured 4.9m, and the air service version was to be fitted with a Galliot muzzle brake which was 1.22m long, 610mm in diameter and weighed 118kg!

A slightly saner if still mind-boggling scheme was to fit a 4.50″ (114mm) recoilless gun (RCL) to fighter aircraft (the Gloster Javelin was a possible host). It was to be fitted with a seven-round rotary magazine and due to the usual lightweight construction possible with RCLs was to weigh 'only' 650kg. This idea was overtaken by the prospect of the guided air-to-air missile.

To return to service weapons, the British, Americans and French fitted versions of the HS 404 to many of their early jets, with the Americans also using the .50″ Browning in fighters and for bomber defence (a quad tail mounting being fitted to the B52C to G models). The Browning is still in use today, mainly in gun pods but it is currently offered mounted in the wings of the Embraer EMB-314 Super Tucano. The French even continued the use of the Mauser MG 151, initially as an AA gun but later as a helicopter weapon, and it remained in service in that guise until the 1970s.

The Americans were reluctant to give up the well-tried .50″ Browning, standardised in April 1945 in the M3 version, which achieved a remarkable 1,200 rpm. Versions of the 20mm Hispano did, however, increasingly find their way into American aircraft, initially USN and later USAF fighters, until the new generation of American weapons was ready. This was prompted by battle experience in the Korean War when it was discovered that Sabre pilots were having to fire an average of 1,000 .50″ calibre rounds to shoot down each enemy aircraft. The USN used the M3 version of the Hispano, uprated to 750 rpm, in the F2H-1, F9F-2 and F9F-6. The armament was probably the best compromise in Korea between rate of fire and destructive effect, but these older aircraft were not as good as the USAF's Sabre (or, more crucially, the MiG-15). The 20mm M3 was also used in the FJ-2 Fury from January 1954.

From the late 1940s the USAF used the 20mm M24, which was essentially the same as the M3 except for its electric ignition (which meant that it required different ammunition, although this confusingly retained the same M90 series designations). The M24 saw service in some versions of the F-86 and F-89 and also for bomber defence (B-36B, B-47E, B-52B), before being replaced in service by the M39 and M61. The B-36 was one of the most heavily defended aircraft ever to see service, mounting no fewer than sixteen M24 cannon in twin turrets.

The HS 404 design was ultimately developed into the USN's Mk 12. The origin of this weapon was for a wartime fast-firing (1,000 rpm) AA gun to counter kamikaze attacks, but it was cancelled at the end of the war. Work recommenced in 1948, initially for the electrically-primed 20 × 110 M24 cartridge, then modified for the new 20 × 102, before finally being modified again to take the navy's powerful new 20 × 110 (Mk 100 series) cartridge.

The Mk 12 was fitted to a number of aircraft including later models of the North American FJ-1 Fury, the Douglas F4D Skyray and A4D Skyhawk, the McDonnell F3H Demon and the Vought F8U Crusader. It saw considerable action in the Crusader during the Vietnam War but proved inaccurate and unreliable, persuading the USN to adopt the air force's M61 in future aircraft. The reliability problem was caused by the feed from the ammunition cans, which were located directly behind the cockpit. From there, flexible chutes guided the belts a considerable distance down to the guns. In violent manoeuvres, the chutes would flex, causing the belts to jam and pull apart.

Development of the basic HS 404 design was continued by the parent company, Hispano-Suiza, but mainly for army and naval AA guns. Some unsuccessful attempts were, however, made to produce larger-calibre aircraft cannon. Following abortive wartime experiments by BMARCO (the British Hispano subsidiary) with a 30mm aircraft cannon using a necked-up 25mm Hotchkiss case, in the early 1950s Hispano themselves competed with Aden for the Fleet Air Arm contract with the HS 825. This used a unique bottleneck 30 × 136 cartridge combining a relatively light shell with a high muzzle velocity (ideal for air combat) but the type of linear mechanism chosen suffered insoluble technical problems in trying to compete with the Aden's rate of fire – it was designed to reach 950–1,000rpm. Hispano persevered with this gun and eventually succeeded in having it selected for service in the Swiss FFA P-16 fighter-bomber. However, production of the aircraft was cancelled following several accidents.

A much longer life has been achieved by developments of the Mauser MG 213C revolver cannon, largely achieved with the aid of engineers who formerly worked for Mauser. As already described in Chapter 2, this wartime German design was developed in Britain (where Werner Jungerman worked for Aden), France (Anton Politzer worked on DEFA designs between 1947 and 1967), Switzerland (Fredrick Linder worked for Oerlikon) and the USA (Otto von Lossnitzer). The high-velocity 20mm version of the Mauser gun was intended by the *Luftwaffe* for two roles: bomber defence and ground attack. The low-velocity 30mm MK 213/30 was planned for fighters, to replace the MK 108.

In Europe, the 30mm version was the preferred basis for development post-war, the RAF as ever concerned with destroying heavy bombers. At first, the original MK 213/30 case length of about 85mm was used, with some modifications to the rim; this Aden 3M (Armament Development Enfield) cartridge briefly saw British service, and was subsequently referred to as the 'low-velocity' (LV) round. The French adopted a longer 97mm case in the DEFA 541 series to achieve a higher muzzle velocity for their Vautour and Mystère IV installations of 1954/5.

In the mid-1950s, Britain and France agreed on common chamber dimensions for the Aden Mk 4 and DEFA 550 series guns. The 30 × 113B, which has now become standard, is also used in various American cannon. The 30M552 DEFA (and the very similar -553) was used in such aircraft as the Super Mystère, Mirage III and F1, Etendard, Jaguar and Alpha Jet, and has been built in South Africa as the 55C5, which incorporates modifications to increase the rate of fire from 1,300 to 1,800 rpm. The Aden was the standard British fighter gun from the late 1950s up to the introduction of the Mauser BK 27 in the Panavia Tornado over twenty years later (with some use of the American M61A1 in Phantom aircraft). Introduced in the Hawker Hunter it saw service in the Gloster Javelin, Supermarine Swift and Scimitar, Folland Gnat and English Electric Lightning, as well as the Saab Draken, the Commonwealth CA-27 (Avon Sabre) and HAL Marut, and is still in service in versions of the Harrier, Hawk and Jaguar.

The guns required relatively little modification

*30mm Aden 'gunpack' for the Hawker Hunter* (RAF Museum)

through all these cartridge changes, as the overall length of all the cartridges remained the same at 200mm. It is worth noting that the straight case design means that case length is not particularly critical, and the 30 × 113B cases often measure around 111mm. The guns fired at about 1,200–1,400 rpm, although the final development of the French series, the 30-554 GIAT used in the Mirage 2000, can achieve 1,800 rpm. Despite the identical appearance, ammunition for weapons of different nationalities is not necessarily interchangeable as it can vary in the gas pressure generated and the voltage required by the electric ignition system. Furthermore, British and French ammunition belts, although superficially almost identical, differ in link strength and belt flexibility. Barrel lengths also vary, affecting muzzle velocities.

Oerlikon took a different route developing their range of revolver cannon, altering the basic design more than the British and French. After offering

various models without any sales they eventually achieved success in 1970 with the massive KCA, designed around an extremely powerful 30 × 173 cartridge. This outclasses the Aden/DEFA in muzzle velocity and hitting power while still achieving 1,350 rpm, but its size is such that it has only been fitted as standard to one aircraft, the SAAB Viggen (in Swedish service the KCA is known as the m/1975). It can also be installed in the Hughes Model 34 gun pod, which weighs 475kg including 125 rounds of ammunition. The KCA was considered in the USA as a fall-back in case of the GAU-8/A rotary's failure, which uses an alloy-cased and percussion-primed version of the same cartridge; known as the GAU-9/A, two would have been fitted to the A-10 aircraft. It was also planned to fit two of these guns to the Taiwanese AIDC A-3 single-seat attack version of their AT-3 trainer, but this did not progress beyond prototype status. If the aircraft had reached production, it would

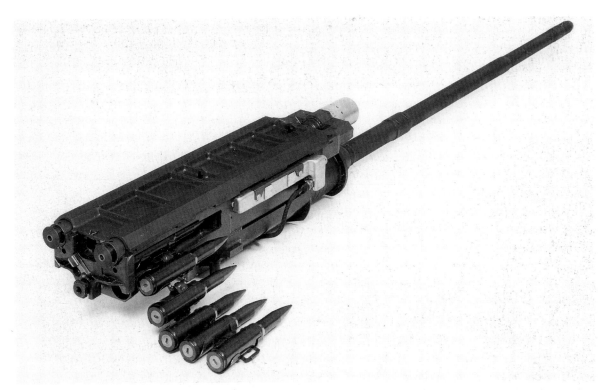

*30mm Oerlikon KCA revolver cannon* (Courtesy: Oerlikon/Ian Hogg)

*SAAB Viggen; the only aircraft with an integral 30mm Oerlikon KCA, fitted in the fairing underneath the fuselage*
(Courtesy: Oerlikon-Contraves)

have carried one of the heaviest gun armaments of modern times.

In America, work took place on rotary as well as revolver designs but generally in smaller calibres. Most of the new guns were designed around the .60″ (15.2 × 114) T17 anti-tank gun cartridge (which never actually saw service), its necked-out, electrically primed 20 × 102 variant, or the lengthened navy Mk 100 (20 × 110). However, there were various fruitless experiments with 30mm revolver cannon, culminating in the T182 gun whose cartridge had a lengthened version of the Aden/DEFA case (30 × 126B) for improved performance, and in the remarkable front-loading T168 described in Chapter 2.

The 20 × 102 cartridge (known as the M50 series) was introduced into service in the Pontiac M39 revolver cannon, which was capable of 1,700 rpm. A few F-86F-2s Sabres, experimentally fitted with four 20mm T-160 cannon (the prototype of the M39), arrived in Korea in 1953, in time to be tested in action. Results were promising, but airframe stress and other unreliability problems meant that some years of continuing development were required before the gun was considered entirely satisfactory. It saw widespread service in the F-86H, F-100, F-101, B-57B and latterly in the Northrop F-5 series.

The Navy's Mk 11 gun, which used the Mk 100 series cartridge, was a twin-barrelled revolver cannon with a rate of fire of up to 4,200 rpm, whose only application was in the Mk 4 gun pod. The USA experimented with even larger 20mm cartridges for the T33 series of aircraft guns, achieving a muzzle velocity of 1,150 m/s, but these were not adopted.

These revolver weapons were completely overshadowed by the six-barrel General Electric M61 rotary cannon, which emerged in 1957 from 'Project Vulcan' (which basically started from the nineteenth-century Gatling gun with an electric motor attached). This rapidly became the classic

*20mm GAU-4 in the SUU23A gun pod; the only service version of the 20mm Vulcan family to be gas-operated*
(*Courtesy: R.W. Clarke*)

188

American fighter gun of the second half of the twentieth century. It was originally belt-fed, which limited its maximum rate of fire to 4,000 rpm, but in 1964 the M61A1 was introduced, with various improvements including a linkless feed system which permitted a reliable 6,000 rpm to be achieved. Ammunition is the same $20 \times 102$ as the M39. Despite its ubiquity, there are drawbacks: the appetite for ammunition requires a large magazine and both magazine and gun are very bulky, the latter having a diameter of 34cm.

The M61 was first fitted to the F-104 Starfighter, and also equipped the F-105, F-106, F-4, F-111, F-14, F-15, F-16, F/A-18, A-7, the Italian AMX and (for rear defence) the B-52H and B-58 bombers. The first use of the M61A1 version was in the F-105D. The drum magazines used for the linkless feed are power-driven with the capacity varying according to the installation. The F/A-18 drum is 53cm long and 57cm in diameter and contains 570 rounds. To the gun weight of 114kg is added the drum and feed system weight of 122kg, while a full load of ammunition adds a further 145kg, giving a grand total of 381kg. This is considered to be the 'compact' version. At the other extreme was the F-111 installation, housing 2,084 rounds, which had a total weight of 790kg. The rear installation in the

*20mm M61A1 in F-16 aircraft* (*Courtesy: Oerlikon-Contraves*)

*HS 804 20mm cannon with 200-round wing magazine* (*BuOrd, USN*)

B52H used a sophisticated radar system with track-while-scan capabilities.

The major nations were not the only ones to design new aircraft cannon. Despite making some use of the HS 404 (known as the m/41) and HS 804 (m/47), Sweden also used Bofors weapons for their initial post-war generations of aircraft. These short-recoil guns, the m/45 and a modified version, the m/49, were designed around the Hispano's 20 × 110 ammunition and were fitted to most versions of the SAAB 21 and early jets, until replaced by the 30mm Aden (m/55) in later versions of the A32 Lansen.

## POST-WAR DEVELOPMENTS IN THE SOVIET UNION

THE POST-WAR SOVIET DESIGNERS AGREED WITH the British and French that the priority was the ability to shoot down nuclear-armed heavy bombers and thus chose to develop large-calibre cannon. The NS-23 (*Nudelman-Suranov*), which first appeared in 1944, was a logical replacement for the 20mm ShVAK and the B-20; it was effectively an NS-37 scaled-down to use a new 23 × 115 cartridge. This short-recoil gun was very light at 37kg, but could fire at only 550 rpm. It saw initial use in propeller-driven aircraft (Il-10, La-7, La-9 – which had four synchronised guns – and La-11) before arming the first generation of jet fighters. A few years later, the much better NR-23 (this time designed by Nudelman and Rikhter) increased the rate of fire to 950 rpm while only weighing 2kg more. The line of linear-action guns to see service ended with the AM-23 (designed by Afanasev and Makarov), adopted in 1954, which achieved 1,300 rpm. At the end of the decade the TKB-513 used 'impact-free ramming' to achieve an impressive 2,000 rpm, but no applications are reported, although the experience gained with this may have been put to good use in the later GSh-301. A revised 23 × 115 cartridge loading with a lighter projectile and a higher muzzle velocity was

*Fierce face; the MiG-9 with one N-37 and two NS-23* (*Courtesy: Russian Aviation Research Trust*)

introduced for the AM-23 and subsequent weapons.

As well as equipping the early jet fighters, the 23mm guns were used for bomber defence. It is not easy to determine which of the several different 23mm guns were used with which aircraft (different marks of some aircraft appeared to use different guns), but it appears that the later versions of the Tu-4 and the Il-28 were equipped with NS-23s (early Tu-4s being fitted with 20mm B-20s), while the Tu-16, M-4 'Bison', most types of Tu-22 and Tu-95 used NR-23s, as did the An-12 transport. The AM-23 is mentioned in association with versions of the Tu-16, Tu-95, M4 (also known as the M-6 and 3M), Il-54, Il-76, Be-6, Be-12, An-8 and An-12B.

Not satisfied with the 23mm, the Soviets also introduced a massive 37mm cannon, the only post-war air-fighting gun of more than 30mm to see service. The gas-operated N-37 was something of a committee gun, being designed under Nudelman's direction by Nemenov, Suranov, Rikhter and Gribkov. Despite being scaled down in size and performance from the wartime NS-37 anti-tank gun, it was an impressive weapon as it combined great hitting power with a weight of only 103kg, but rate of fire was limited to 400 rpm. It was first tested in the Yak-9UT piston-engined fighter in 1944 but saw most service in the early jet fighters. The MiG-15 and -17 carried one each (with 40 rounds of ammunition); initial versions of the Yak-25 were fitted with two (100 rounds each). Even larger guns, the N-45 and N-57 (a Nudelman design based on the NS-37), were developed and tested, the latter in the prototype MiG-9, but not adopted for service. The N-57 (also known as the OKB-16-57 and 100P) used a 57 × 160 cartridge which was much less powerful than that for the OKB-15-57 airborne anti-tank gun under development at the end of the war.

Rather surprisingly, the Soviet Union also developed a new aircraft HMG in the early 1950s, the A-12.7, designed by Afanasev. The reasoning behind this weapon is not obvious as its performance was no better than the wartime UB; in fact it weighed the same as the much more powerful 20mm B-20. It saw most use in helicopters and fighter-trainers.

Like the Americans, the Soviets learned some

*Gunpack for MiG-15 (it could be lowered from the fuselage for easy maintenance); one N-37 and two NS-23 (Courtesy: Russian Aviation Research Trust)*

hard lessons in Korea. The USAF's F-86 and the MiG-15 were closely comparable aircraft, but their gun armament could hardly be more different. The Sabre's six .50" M3s fired at a combined rate of 7,200 rpm, while the MiG's two NS-23s and one N-37 could manage only 1,500 rpm. While the Americans found the hitting power of the HMG bullets inadequate, the Soviet pilots found it difficult to hit the agile Sabres with their slow-firing, low-velocity cannon, a problem exacerbated by inferior gunsights.

The introduction of the MiG-15bis and the MiG-17 in the 1950s saw some improvement in rate of fire, as they were fitted with the NR-23. The real answer, however, was to replace the N-37 with a faster-firing but still hard-hitting weapon, and this was achieved in the mid-1950s with the introduction of the NR-30 (Nudelman and Rikhter again), firing a new 30 × 155B cartridge. This was a potent combination of hitting power and rate of fire and became the standard fighter weapon for some years, being fitted to the MiG-19 (and Chinese-built derivatives), the Sukhoi Su-7 and Su-17 families and some early versions of the Yak-28 and MiG-21 – the 21F (Fishbed-C) and 21F-13 (Fishbed E).

The most remarkable of the 23mm guns was the R-23, a Rikhter-designed revolver cannon which used unique front-loading 23 × 260 ammunition and achieved an impressive 2,500 rpm for a weight of only 58kg. First produced in 1957, it suffered considerable teething problems and was not officially adopted for service until 1963. It appears that it was only used in the DK-20 turret fitted to the Tu-22B and Tu-22K, presumably because the GSh-23 came out in 1959 and offered an even higher rate of fire for a slightly lighter weight, as well as using conventional 23mm ammunition.

## MODERN WESTERN WEAPONS

THERE WAS A PERIOD IN THE 1950S AND 1960S WHEN most nations felt that guns would no longer be required, and several fighters were designed to use only missiles. Most of these, such as the USAF's F-102A and F-106A, were intended for intercepting strategic bombers. Naval fighters such as the RN's Sea Vixen and the USN's F-4 Phantom II were also introduced without guns.

The US realised its mistake in the Vietnam War and accordingly fitted the USAF's F-4E with an M61A1 cannon. This version achieved half of its kills with the gun rather than its missiles. Some F-106As were also modified to carry an M61A1 in the missile bay. Where guns could not be retrofitted, gun pods were used as an expedient, but they were not as rigid (and therefore as accurate) as internal cannon, besides increasing aerodynamic drag.

The experience of the Americans, Europeans and Russians in developing their current range of aircraft cannon has been markedly different. After an attempt at updating the M-39 (the Ford Tigerclaws, intended for the abortive F-20 Tigershark) the Americans have remained true to the rotary cannon. This is despite the development of an impressive twin-barrel 25mm gun, the GE 225. This chambers the NATO 25 × 137 cartridge and while using the Gast-type alternating fire principle, was tried in two versions: gas-operated (to achieve 2,000 rpm) and externally driven (variable rate up to 750 rpm).

The Americans at one time attempted to produce an advanced 25mm rotary cannon (the Philco-Ford GAU-7/A being the chosen version) intended for the F-15 fighter. The projectile was buried within a cylindrical combustible case which resembled an oversized shotgun cartridge. This was defeated by technical problems and the 20mm M61A1 has remained in US service ever since. Now produced by General Dynamics, it has even been selected for the new F-22 fighter, albeit in an improved M61A2 version, with a 480-round magazine. Ammunition performance has been improved by the adoption of the PGU-28 series, which combines a chemical fuze with a different shape to reduce aerodynamic drag by 33%.

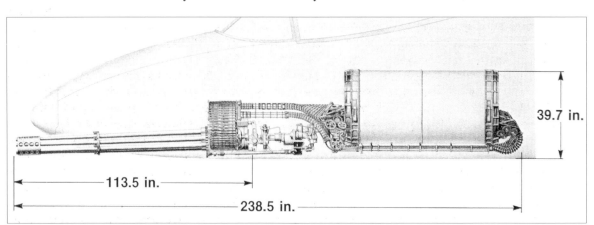

*Installation of 30mm GAU-8/A with magazine. The entire installation is over six metres long and the ammunition drum is one metre in diameter* (Courtesy: General Electric/Ian Hogg)

A 25mm cannon is seeing US airborne service, but with the Marines, in the five-barrel GAU-12/U rotary cannon fitted externally to the AV-8B (American Harrier). This uses the conventional 25 × 137 NATO cartridge, is powered by a pneumatic drive using gas bled from the engine and has a 300-round magazine (in the form of a linear linkless feed rather than the usual helical drum, to keep down the frontal area).

Two larger guns have seen USAF service, but only in the ground-attack role. These are the massive seven-barrel General Electric GAU-8/A rotary cannon fitted to the Fairchild A-10 'tankbuster' (which was designed around the gun) and a four-barrel version of the same gun, the GAU-13/A. The 30 × 173 cartridge used by both is dimensionally identical to that of the Oerlikon KCA but uses a light-alloy instead of steel case. The GAU-8/A weighs 281kg, but the complete installation with a full magazine of 1,350 rounds crunches the scales at 1,828kg. The GAU-13/A is only available in the GPU-5A gun pod, for fitting to aircraft with only an occasional need for such firepower. It uses a pneumatic drive via a storage bottle and the pod weighs 862kg including 353 rounds of ammunition. In this case the helical magazine is arranged to store the ammunition points-forwards rather than points-inwards, again to minimise frontal area.

In contrast, Western Europe has remained wedded to the revolver. In addition to the Aden, DEFA and Oerlikon developments, Mauser re-entered the market with the BK 27, a 100kg weapon capable of firing its 27 × 145B cartridges at 1,700 rpm. Introduced in the Panavia Tornado and the Alpha Jet light strike aircraft in the early 1970s, it has been selected for the SAAB Gripen (as the m/85). Although early reports indicated that a new 27mm rotary cannon was to be developed for the EFA2000 'Eurofighter', it will actually be equipped with a version of the BK 27, modified for a linkless feed.

The French have been primarily concerned with the low muzzle velocity of their 30mm cannon, which they have remedied by developing a longer case (which also differs slightly in other dimensional details) to create the 30 × 150B. The associated GIAT 30M791 cannon, intended to be fitted to the Dassault Rafale, is heavier than earlier models at

*GSh-23 in Tu-22M (Courtesy: Russian Aviation Research Trust)*

120kg but can achieve a remarkable 2,500 rpm. However, technical problems have led to many changes in the detailed specification of the gun and ammunition, which at the time of writing were still continuing.

The British rather surprisingly decided to develop a new weapon, the Aden 25, to equip the latest marks of Harrier, instead of staying with the very similar BK 27 which was already in RAF service and seems likely to be selected for the American Joint Strike Fighter, in which Britain has a close interest. The Aden is essentially similar to the earlier models but is designed to use the standard 25 × 137 NATO round, which it fires at up to 1,850 rpm. Like the 30M791, it experienced considerable development problems which eventually led to its cancellation in 1999.

## Modern Soviet and Russian armament

THE SOVIET AIR FORCE ALSO WENT THROUGH A crisis in confidence over guns (or perhaps a bout of over-confidence in the capabilities of missiles) and the Su-9, -11, -15 and -21, the Yak-28P and the Tu-128 fighters were all produced without integral cannon. The development of guns did not cease, however, and Soviet designers responded to the limitations of their early post-war weapons in two stages: the first was to achieve a dramatic increase in rate of fire by adopting multi-barrel cannon while keeping to the established 23 × 115 cartridge; the second was to scale up the weapons to take the new tri-service 30 × 165 round.

The 23mm guns include the famous twin-barrel GSh-23. This was developed in the late 1950s and was for a time the standard aircraft cannon. It was fitted to later versions of the MiG-21 and the MiG-23, as well as being used for defence (Tu-22M3, Tu-142, Il-76M, Il-78 and Tu-95MS) and available in gun pods, in one of which (the 260-round, 320kg SPPU-22-01 for use with the MiG-27, Su-25 and Su-17 family) the gun can be angled downwards by 30° to facilitate ground attack. Development of this gun has not finished; in the Czech Republic it has been redesigned to chamber the American 20 × 102 ammunition, for fitting into a light gun pod. The gun is known as the ZPL-20 and the gun pod is called the *Plamen* (flame). This is an interesting concept, trading the GSh-23's projectile weight for a high muzzle velocity, and results in a very compact, lightweight and fast-firing gun. The gun pod, which weighs 215kg when loaded with 224 rounds, has been tested in the new Aero Vodochody L159 trainer/light strike aircraft.

The six-barrel rotary GSh-6-23, adopted in 1974, achieves a remarkable 9,000 rpm and is fitted to the MiG-31 interceptor. It is also available in the Su-24 (NPU-19 system) and in the 500-round, 500kg SPPU-6 gun pod carried by the Su-27UB bomber, in which the gun is not only capable of being angled downwards by 45° but also traversed horizontally by the same amount. This has interesting implications for sighting the gun, which is achieved by the gunner rather than the pilot.

The new 30 × 165 Russian cartridge, originally developed for the naval AO-18 six-barrel rotary

cannon, is also available in a variety of different guns. The GSh-6-30 is an air-cooled version of the navy cannon, developed in parallel with the GSh-6-23 and also accepted into service in 1974. It equips the MiG-27 ground-attack aircraft and reportedly some versions of the Su-25 and MiG-31. There is also a twin-barrelled gun, the GSh-30, a Gast-type weapon similar to the GSh-23 which can fire at up to 3,000 rpm. This is fitted to the Su-25 ground-attack aircraft and is available in the NNPU-8M gun pod.

The latest 30mm aircraft cannon is a remarkable weapon: the GSh-301. It is a single-barrelled gun weighing only 44kg and firing at 1,500–1,800 rpm, continuing the Soviet tradition of combining remarkably low weight with high rates of fire. Amazingly, it has an 'old-fashioned' recoil-operated linear action rather than the revolver mechanism frequently attributed to it by Western sources, but handsomely beats all other aircraft guns in terms of hitting power for its modest weight and size. To make an historical comparison with the Second World War weapons, it is approximately the same size and weight as a 2cm MG 151 but has the hitting power of a battery of *four* 3cm MK 103s – which weighed twelve times as much! It is now the standard Russian fighter weapon, being fitted to the

*Postwar fighter gun cartridges (from left to right): .50" M3 (12.7 × 99), 20mm Hispano/M3/M24 (20 × 110), Soviet NS-23/NR-23/GSh-23 (23 × 115), Soviet N-37 (37 × 155), US M39/M61 (20 × 102), USN Mk 11/Mk 12 (20 × 110), 30mm Aden/DEFA + M230 chain gun (30 × 113B), Soviet NR-30 (30 × 155B), Oerlikon KCA (30 × 173), Mauser BK 27 (27 × 145B), Soviet GSh-30/GSh-6-30/GSh-301 + 2A42 helicopter gun (30 × 165)*

MiG-29 and Su-27 families, and is also offered in the 9A-4273 gun pod (weighing 480kg including 150 rounds) which has the now traditional ability to pivot within the pod, this time by 30° downwards and 15° in the horizontal plane.

Incidentally, it is curious that in the 'collectivist' USSR, successful gun designers were generally honoured in the designations of their guns, as with Gryazev and Shipunov in the current 'GSh-' range, whereas in the 'individualist' West this tradition largely died with John Browning. It is tempting to speculate that this might have a bearing on the remarkable performance of Russian guns.

## DESTRUCTIVE POWER AND COMBAT PERSISTENCE

ONE TYPICALLY RUSSIAN CHARACTERISTIC IS THE tendency to favour heavy projectiles at the expense of muzzle velocity. The 23 × 115 round fires a 170g or 200g projectile, in comparison with the 102g of the 20 × 102 M61 and the 180g of the much bigger NATO 25 × 137. Similarly, the 390g 30 × 165 projectile compares with around 270g for the 30 × 113B (Aden) and 30 × 150B (GIAT). If the Russian cartridge were loaded with 270g projectiles, muzzle velocity in the GSh-301 could be expected to increase, for the same muzzle energy, from 860 m/s to around 1,030 m/s. This preference is surprising, as muzzle velocity is generally considered to be of paramount importance in air fighting because it minimises the time of flight and therefore reduces the problems of deflection shooting. The Russians are apparently content to accept a lower velocity in return for greater destructive effect.

The effective range of modern aircraft guns is aided by sophisticated sighting and fire control systems. The 20mm M61A1, for example, has a normal air-fighting range of about 500m but in favourable circumstances (a fast closing speed), or for ground attack, this can be more than doubled.

Despite the retention of the fighter gun, it is worth noting that while its technology and performance has continued to develop (although in rather more subtle ways than in the past, concerned with better materials and careful design analysis) its relative fall in importance is reflected in reduced magazine capacities. A typical revolver cannon installation includes space for only about 150 rounds;

enough for just five or six seconds' firing. The MiG-29 carries only 100 rounds. Even the apparently generous 570 rounds in the F/A-18 lasts for only six seconds, while the GSh-6-23 installation in the MiG-31 reportedly can hold only 260 rounds, which would be expended in less than two seconds. On the other hand, some modern fire control systems can prevent a gun from firing until a hit is certain, so wasted ammunition is far less of a problem than in the past.

In the specialised field of ground attack, the GAU-8/A of the American A-10 'tankbuster' has a clear lead in hitting power over the GSh-6-30 used in the MiG-27, even if its rate of fire is lower. The A-10 also has a huge advantage in combat persistence. Its massive ammunition capacity lasts for about twenty seconds' firing; the MiG's 265 rounds for less than three seconds and the slower-firing GSh-30 in the Su 25 just five seconds.

## HELICOPTER GUNS

THE VIETNAM WAR WAS THE FIRST CONFLICT IN which helicopters played a major role, initially for rapid troop deployment in a country in which other forms of transport were slow and subject to guerrilla attack. The necessarily low-flying helicopters were vulnerable to ground fire, particularly when landing or picking up troops, so some were fitted with machine guns. These were initially mounted in the windows or doorways of transport helicopters on simple pintle mounts, a practice which continues to this day with weapons of up to 20mm calibre.

It was not long before the advantages of a purpose-designed ground-attack helicopter became apparent. A smaller, two-man fuselage made it possible to fit armour protection and allowed for a more powerful gun, usually mounted in an under-nose turret. Rockets, bombs and anti-tank missiles could be carried under stub wings. The first of these was the Bell AH-1, which arrived in time to see service in Vietnam.

Subsequent Western attack helicopters have kept to the same formula, but the first Soviet model – the Mil Mi-24 Hind – took a different approach, being much bigger and with a cabin capable of carrying eight troops – in effect, an airborne infantry combat vehicle. More recently, the Mi-28 two-seater and

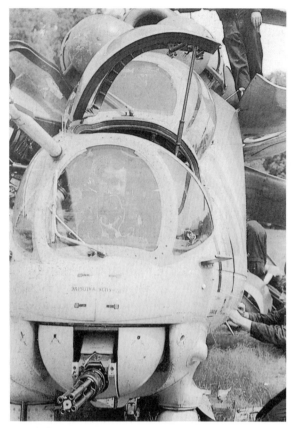

*Yak B-12.7 four-barrel rotary gun in Mi-24 Hind-D*
(*Courtesy: MoD Pattern Room*)

Kamov Ka-50 have emerged, although these are still larger and heavier than their Western equivalents.

The gun armament of these helicopters has developed in different ways from that of fighter aircraft. It is almost entirely optimised for ground-strafing and therefore usually flexibly mounted so it can be rapidly traversed onto new targets. In modern applications, the mountings are computer-controlled and may be aimed by helmet-mounted sights; the gun will point wherever the gunner looks. However, most attack helicopters can be fitted with additional fixed gun pods, and there is a tendency in some cases to fit more powerful cannon for the anti-helicopter role.

There is much more variety of gun armament in helicopters than there is in fighter aircraft. Targets vary from unprotected troops to armoured vehicles and other helicopters, so weapon fits available include rifle-calibre and heavy machine guns, cannon of 20–30mm and 40mm grenade launchers.

This gives designers something of a headache. Should they optimise the flexibly mounted gun for dealing with troops, which would suggest a rapid-firing machine gun possibly combined with a grenade launcher, and leave the anti-armour role to missiles or fixed gun pods? Alternatively, should they choose a powerful anti-armour cannon, or

*GSh-30K twin-barrel 30mm gun on Mi-24P Hind-F* (*Courtesy: Russian Aviation Research Trust*)

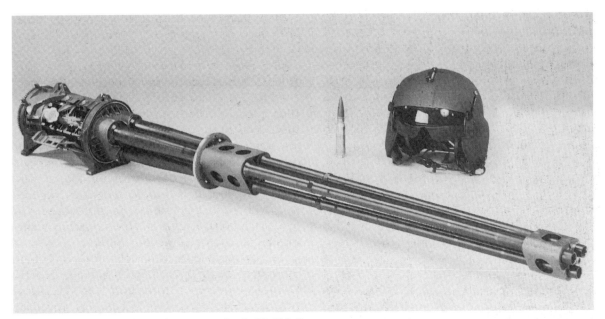

*GE 20mm XM-301 three-barrel rotary gun for RAH-66 helicopter* (*Courtesy: General Electric*)

perhaps something in between? If they choose a powerful weapon, how do they cope with the recoil effects, which when firing to one side might well deflect the helicopter enough to move the gun off aim?

The smallest weapon normally fitted to the turrets of attack helicopters is the HMG. The rate of fire of the usual army weapons was judged insufficient for this role, so new rotary guns have been developed in both the Soviet Union and the USA.

The four-barrel Soviet YakB-12.7 (*Yakushev-Borzov*) – the complete mounting being known as the 9A624 or USPU-24 – uses the usual 12.7 × 108 round and was introduced in the 1970s for mounting in an under-nose turret in the Mi-24 Hind-D attack helicopter. However, experience in Afghanistan indicated the need for longer range; the Mi-24VP (Hind-E) turret was accordingly fitted with the 23mm twin-barrel GSh-23 cannon in the NPPU-24 mounting and the Mi-24P (Hind-F) was given the powerful, fuselage-mounted, twin-barrel 30mm GSh-30K, with longer barrels than the GSh-30, in the NPPU-30 mount.

The General Electric company developed two versions of their GECAL 50 with a choice of three or six barrels, the smaller of which has now been adopted as the GAU-19A. Ammunition is the standard 12.7 × 99. Interestingly, the GECALs were originally offered with either externally driven or gas operation, but the GAU-19A retains the American preference for external power.

Most Western attack helicopters are fitted with cannon. These use the same ammunition as fighter guns, but do not require such a high rate of fire; in fact, that would be a disadvantage because helicopter guns tend to be used for much longer bursts of fire, so barrel cooling and ammunition supply are important factors. Recoil is also a problem made worse by a high rate of fire. As it is, modern mountings often incorporate sophisticated recoil control mechanisms. The survival of the MG 151 in French helicopters up to the 1970s was presumably due to its modest power and therefore light recoil, although in pintle-mounted form a recoil-absorbing mounting was still found to be necessary.

The first version of the M61 for helicopters, the belt-fed M195, featured shorter barrels (100cm) fitted with blast deflectors and was fitted to the stub wing of the AH-1G (Cobra). It was capable of 850 rpm. The first purpose-designed nose turret gun, the GE M197 fitted to the Bell AH-1J, is similar but with only three barrels of standard length and a 750 rpm rate of fire. The weapon has been retained in the current AH-1W SuperCobra and an improved version, the XM-301, has been developed for the RAH-66 Comanche.

Although the requirements of modern air fighting are such that the 30mm Aden's relatively low muzzle velocity is a handicap, the $30 \times 113B$ cartridge's combination of compact size, modest recoil and highly destructive shells is still useful and it is enjoying a new lease of life in weapons designed for helicopters. The Americans experimented with a shorter ($30 \times 100B$) cartridge for the Philco-Ford XM140 (popularly known as the WECOM after the US Army Weapons Command) but adopted the Aden round in the interests of NATO commonality.

This development led to the McDonnell Douglas M230 chain gun, an externally powered weapon limited to 625 rpm, which is fitted to the AH-64 Apache attack helicopter. A three-barrel revolver cannon using the same ammunition, the GE XM-188, can fire at anything between 200 and 2,000 rpm but has so far not seen service. Incidentally, it is useful to be able to vary the firing rate in helicopter installations in order to avoid resonant vibration frequencies, which affect accuracy.

The South Africans have produced two weapons for their Rooivalk attack helicopter: the 39kg XC-F2, which is a development of the Vektor GA-1, and the XC-30, which fires the $30 \times 113B$ Aden/DEFA ammunition.

The French HAP (*Helicoptère d'Appui et de Protection*) version of the Eurocopter Tiger is intended to use the GIAT 30M781, an externally powered turret-mounted weapon firing the usual $30 \times 113B$ cartridge, which is therefore a direct equivalent of the M230. In by far the most radical development in cannon to be announced in decades, the German version of the Tiger (now known as the UHT, for *Unterstützungshubschrauber Tiger*) could be equipped with a new recoilless Mauser weapon, the RMK 30, which is described in more detail in Chapter 6.

All the above weapons are designed for turret mounting. This causes problems in coping with high-powered guns (RMK 30 excepted), which can be surmounted in forward-firing installations. These may be built into the helicopter (in the interests of maximum rigidity and therefore accuracy) or fitted to detachable pods, to achieve more tactical flexibility, at the likely expense of some accuracy.

*30mm 2A42 gun on Kaman Ka-50 Werewolf helicopter. Note the GSh-23 gunpod under the stub wing* (*Courtesy: Russian Aviation Research Trust*).

*Russian 30mm AG-17A helicopter automatic grenade launcher, with round of ammunition standing on it*
*(Courtesy: MoD Pattern Room)*

Recent Russian developments appear to favour built-in mountings. While the Mi-28 Havoc is fitted with a turret-mounted cannon (the NPPU-28 mounting being fitted with the army's 30mm 2A42), the Mi-24P Hind F has the GSh-30K twin-barrel 30mm cannon fitted to one side of the fuselage, and the Ka-50 Werewolf attack helicopter, as befits its 'fighter' status, carries its 30mm 2A42 in the same location. However, these are not rigidly fixed as they can be depressed by up to 40° and traversed 5–6°. All of these weapons use the Russian 30 × 165 cartridge, significantly more powerful than the 30 × 113B used in Western helicopter guns, although it should be noted that the army guns use percussion-primed ammunition, the GSh-30K electric.

At the bottom end of the scale in size and weight, although at the top end for calibre, comes the 40mm MDHC M129 automatic grenade launcher. This is electrically driven and fires the usual 'high-velocity' 40 × 53SR cartridge used in automatic army grenade launchers. The M129 is sometimes combined with a 7.62mm rotary machine gun in a lightweight chin turret suitable for

*Low-velocity cartridge development (from left to right): 37mm Hotchkiss/Maxim (37 × 94R), 1pdr Vickers Mk III (37 × 69R), 1.59" Crayford (40 × 79R), 40mm LV grenade (40 × 46SR), 40mm HV grenade (40 × 53SR, with belt link still attached), 30mm AGS-17/AG-17A (30 × 29B)*

smaller helicopters. The Russians have an equivalent: an aircraft version of the 30mm AGS-17, known as the AG-17A, which weighs just 20kg, has a 300-round magazine and a rate of fire increased to 420–500 rpm.

# Chapter Six

# THE FUTURE

THE DEVELOPMENT OF HEAVY AUTOMATIC WEAPONS over the past century has seen great technical advances, which have shifted in emphasis over time. The first pressures came from navies anxious to find a counter to the agile new torpedo boats which were beginning to pose a threat to large warships. They found answers initially in large-calibre, manually operated repeaters from Gatling, Nordenfelt and Hotchkiss, and later in Maxim-type automatic cannon. Similar weapons proved themselves useful to armies as light, fast-firing artillery pieces until they were eclipsed by the development of improved conventional artillery.

The First World War saw the introduction of new threats – military aircraft and armoured fighting vehicles – and the development of fast-firing HMGs and cannon to counter them. The desirability of a high muzzle velocity in these roles drove up cartridge and gun size, and several weapon types reached a virtual peak of design during the inter-war period. While the current generation of 40mm Bofors guns has much superior performance to the originals, this has been achieved by gradual development rather than the adoption of any radical new principles. The .50″ Browning M2 has changed even less, and must be one of the very few military weapons still in front-line service with major armies that is over seventy-five years old.

The period of twenty years starting from the mid-1930s saw the most rapid technical developments, this time driven by the need to arm aircraft with weapons capable of destroying their own kind. In the ammunition field, thin-walled mine shells and tungsten-cored armour-piercing projectiles

made their appearance. New gun mechanisms such as the revolver and rotary cannon also emerged, dramatically increasing the destructive power of aircraft guns. This was in many ways the golden age of the heavy automatic weapon.

From the mid-1950s the pace of development greatly slowed. Emphasis shifted to guided missiles, both for the anti-aircraft and aircraft armament roles, and guns were seen as a backup of secondary importance, sometimes dispensed with altogether. Despite this, guns retained a niche as light AA weapons in most (but not all) armies and navies.

In the last quarter of the twentieth century, interest in heavy automatic weapons was renewed to counter two very different new threats: anti-ship missiles and armoured infantry fighting vehicles. The former threat generated a need for very fast-reacting, fast-firing, radar-controlled guns to act as a last-ditch ship defence. To meet this need, technology originally developed for aircraft guns has proved most suitable. The latter problem led to the development of much slower-firing weapons of great reliability, accuracy and penetrative power. The smaller versions of these weapons have also proved themselves well-suited to arming the new breed of attack helicopters, alongside other guns such as HMGs and grenade launchers. Finally, those same grenade launchers are finding a place as light infantry weapons, thereby returning to one of the original uses of the weapon.

Throughout all this there have been few radical changes in either ammunition or operating mechanisms. A gun designer of a century ago would instantly recognise and quickly understand our current heavy automatic weapon systems in almost all respects, with only a few concepts such as proximity fuzes and radar-directed mountings being beyond him. This situation might well change in the foreseeable future, with new developments in both ammunition and weapons, although the essential conservatism of military procurement processes (which usually demand proof of overwhelming advantages, with no disadvantages, before adopting a new technology) mean that rapid changes are unlikely.

## NEW PROJECTILES

PERHAPS THE MOST SIGNIFICANT AREA FOR current developments is in the field of projectile design. Conventional HE shells have probably been taken to their design limits as have conventional APDS rounds, but the solving of the technical problem associated with firing APFSDS projectiles from rifled barrels has led to a substantial improvement in armour penetration. Projectiles for AA weapons have also shown several notable developments, with the use of FAPDS in smaller calibres and shrapnel-type shells with sophisticated fuzing options in larger ones.

The current emphasis is on developing steerable projectiles. This is not a new idea – the American laser-homing Copperhead artillery round was in service decades ago – but the conventional flip-out fins occupy a lot of space and are best applied to larger calibres. An alternative which has been tried with some experimental success in calibres as small as 20mm is the use of minute charges ringing the projectile's circumference. These can be fired at a critical moment in order to correct the trajectory if the weapon system's sensors detect that the projectile is going to miss, significantly increasing the maximum effective range – i.e. the maximum engagement range at which there is a reasonable chance of connecting with the target. The potential advantages in the AA and anti-missile roles in particular are obvious.

Exotic terminal effects are also being considered. One side-effect of a nuclear explosion is the intense electromagnetic pulse which can disrupt or destroy electronic devices within its range. It is in principle possible to produce a small-scale version of this effect by using conventional explosive to compress a piezo-electrical material or to compress a magnetic field. Various organisations are currently studying this concept, including Bofors and the US Los Alamos laboratories, which if successful is more likely to be applied to larger artillery projectiles.

## THE PLASTIC CARTRIDGE CASE

CARTRIDGE CASE DESIGN HAS SO FAR CHANGED much less than projectiles. Despite the practical advantages of the cartridge case it has always been regarded as something of a nuisance by weapon designers. It adds greatly to the weight of ammunition and complicates weapon design because of the need for mechanisms to extract and eject the fired case from the gun.

Other types of cartridge case have occasionally been tried, many of them making use of modern plastics. Attempts to produce entirely plastic versions of conventional cartridges have not worked, because in most guns the head of the case is unsupported, with the rim and extractor groove protruding from the chamber to enable the extractor claw to hook on. The problem with plastic as a case material is that it cannot withstand the pressures and temperatures associated with high-pressure cartridges without being totally supported by the chamber. Conventional cartridge shapes using plastic therefore need composite construction, with metal head, shoulder and neck. Composite cartridges in $20 \times 102$ have been made experimentally; they work in the M61 (which handles ammunition quite gently) but are not strong enough for use in the M39 (which gives them much rougher treatment).

For all-plastic cases to work, a different approach to gun and cartridge design is required. One of the most radical was the Dardick Tround, a plastic case of triangular cross-section in which the primer, propellant and projectile were completely buried. It was intended for a radical form of revolver gun in which the chambers were open on one side, permitting a simpler loading system, although the cartridge was obviously firmly supported at the instant of firing. Small-arms versions saw limited commercial production, but 12.7mm and larger military versions, although extensively tested (the US Navy has been carrying out trials of a 25mm version), have so far not been adopted.

The need to take a new look at cartridge design for plastic cases has led many designers to incorporate the benefits of telescoped ammunition, burying the projectile within the case with the propellant wrapped around it. The much more compact dimensions have obvious benefits in reducing the magazine space needed and enabling gun actions to be smaller and faster-acting. In such designs it is clearly necessary to ensure that the projectile is on its way and providing a gas-tight seal in the barrel before the gun gas can escape past it. This has been achieved in some designs (e.g. the Hughes Lockless) by using a two-stage propellant: a small charge behind the projectile launches it into the barrel, followed by ignition of the main charge.

This two-stage ignition has the advantage that firing the first charge creates space behind the projectile in which the main charge can expand. This enables compressed propellant to be used (in a normal cartridge, there are air spaces between the propellant grains), permitting a dramatic reduction in case volume. This can be judged by comparing the size of the ARES TARG (telescoped ammunition revolver gun), which used plastic-cased telescoped ammunition, with the Tround or the conventional $12.7 \times 99$. The gas-operated TARG was claimed to weigh only 20.4kg yet have the potential to achieve up to 2,000 rpm, while the cylindrical $12.7 \times 88$ cartridge had a muzzle velocity of 900 m/s.

A variation on the same theme, and an even more radical departure from the traditional cartridge shape, was demonstrated by the Hughes Lockless in the late 1960s. The cartridge for this weapon (made in various calibres up to 30mm) used a flat square plastic box enclosing the projectile, with the compressed propellant fitting on each side. The ammunition was designed to slot sideways into the breech, which was then enclosed by a pressure sleeve before firing. The benefits in terms of compactness are illustrated by the dimensions of the 30mm cartridge: just 158mm long by 78mm wide and 35mm thick.

Even more peculiar in appearance are the examples of 'folded path' ammunition. In these, the cartridge case is set alongside the projectile, giving a much more compact round but clearly enforcing some interesting new concepts in loading and

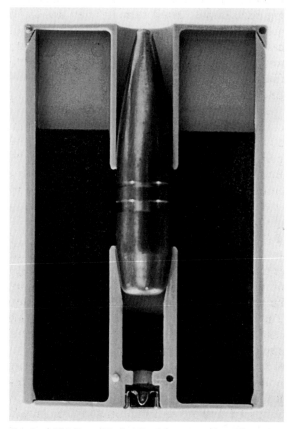

*Different shapes in 12.7mm cartridges (from left to right): .50" Browning (for comparison), Hughes Lockless, Tround, ARES TARG*

*Sectioned 12.7mm Hughes Lockless cartridge. The case is wide but not much thicker than the bullet. Note that the main charge cannot be ignited until the projectile is moving*

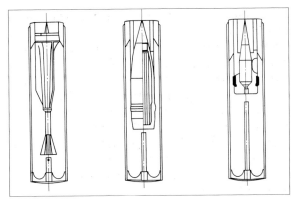

*Section through typical cased telescopic rounds (from left to right): APFSDS, HE, APDS (Courtesy: D.F. Allsop)*

extracting the ammunition. Despite the fact that many of these unusual designs have shown promising performance on test, none of them has so far achieved any production success. However, the cased telescopic principle might at last be on the way towards service use (at some point in the future) as a result of the COMVAT studies described below.

It is worth pointing out that the cased telescopic concept does not depend on new case materials; the $50 \times 330$ 'Supershot' round for the Rh 503 AFV gun (now being developed by Boeing as the Bushmaster III), in which the projectiles are almost entirely buried within the case, uses a conventional steel case.

## THE CASELESS CARTRIDGE

IF IT IS A GOOD IDEA TO USE PLASTIC-CASED telescoped cartridges to reduce the size and weight of the ammunition load, surely it would be even better to dispose of the cartridge case altogether? This would not only save more weight, it would remove the need for the case to be extracted and ejected, thereby simplifying gun design.

In larger artillery calibres cartridge cases are not normally used. The projectile and propellant are loaded separately and priming arrangements are contained within the mechanism of the breechblock. Obturation – the sealing of the rear of the chamber against gas escape – is achieved by the design of the breechblock.

The artillery solution is not suitable for auto-

matic weapons, which require the projectile and propellant to be handled as a unit. Various attempts have been made to overcome this problem. There are three basic approaches (all loosely known as 'caseless'): combustible cases, either with or without metal heads, and entirely caseless cartridges, with the projectile fixed within rigidly moulded propellant. In larger cannon calibres such as tank armament, developments have mainly concentrated on cartridge cases made from combustible material which is burned away as the cartridge fires. This is lighter than metal and greatly reduces the ejection problem, but it is usually still necessary to form the head of the case out of metal in order to achieve obturation.

The completely combustible telescoped case came very close to adoption in the early 1970s, as part of the 25mm GAU-7/A rotary cannon intended for the F-15 fighter. Several years of development were ended when the project finally ran out of time with the introduction of the F-15. The gun worked well enough, but the ammunition suffered from inconsistent performance because it proved impossible to isolate the propellant from variations in atmospheric temperature and humidity conditions.

The most radical development for a very long time is the new Mauser RMK 30, which uses combustible-cased telescoped 30mm rounds which are front-loaded into a three-chamber revolver cannon, whose design allows for much of the gun gas to be deflected to the rear thereby cancelling most of the recoil. This enables a powerful weapon to be mounted in light helicopters and AFVs which would find it difficult to cope with the recoil forces of a conventional weapon of equivalent power. In the past, most recoilless weapons have been less powerful than their conventional equivalents, but by using advanced propellant technology Mauser have demonstrated muzzle energy comparable with that of the redoubtable GAU-8/A. The gun is intended for the German version of the new European attack helicopter.

There have been many attempts to achieve a different approach in which the cartridge case is dispensed with entirely, the propellant being formed into a hard substance in which are buried the projectile and primer. There are many problems with this approach: how to obtain obturation, how to make the cartridge tough and weatherproof, how to stop it 'cooking off' (i.e. being fired by the heat in the chamber after a long firing session). In the small-arms field, Heckler and Koch of Germany overcame all of them and their caseless 4.7mm G11 rifle was being prepared for production when the end of the Cold War put a brake on military expenditure. While there has so far been no comparable success in larger calibres, there can be little doubt that the future will see the first major change to the military cartridge case in over a century, and may eventually witness its disappearance.

A possible final stage of the process may be to dispose of the concept of a cartridge altogether, in favour of injecting liquid propellant into the chamber the instant before firing. This will permit even simpler ammunition handling, with only the projectiles to be loaded. Its attractions are such that active development work is proceeding with the aim of introducing it into next-generation artillery systems. However, there are currently considerable technical problems.

## GUN DESIGN

THE CURRENT EMPHASIS IN GUN DESIGN IS ON externally powered weapons for arming light AFVs and helicopters, as this provides several advantages: compactness, reliability and a rate of fire which can be varied to suit the tactical circumstances. The introduction of new ammunition concepts such as those described above does, however, have implications for gun mechanisms. In particular, caseless cartridges offer the promise of considerable simplification. The Russians have experimented with guns using combustible cartridge cases and liquid propellants, the latter including the 23mm AO-23 prototype aircraft gun, although no details are available.

Even more radical concepts will be needed to achieve muzzle velocities in excess of 1,800 m/s (around 2,500 m/s has been calculated to be necessary to defeat the best modern armour). Among those being examined are electromagnetic or rail guns. These use a powerful electromagnetic field to accelerate projectiles up to very high velocities without the need for any cartridge case or propellant. The compactness of the ammunition

and the lack of visual or aural signature on firing are clearly attractive, but the current drawback is the massive electrical power required. Some form of breakthrough in generating intense pulses of electricity by means of light and compact batteries or machinery will be required before this becomes feasible even for ships and AFVs, let alone other applications.

A less radical alternative is to use electrothermal-chemical technology. This uses a (relatively) conventional cartridge case and propellant, but the primer is replaced by a plasma generator extending into the propellant. When a strong pulse of electricity is applied to the generator, temperatures of up to 10,000K can be developed. More importantly, the temperature and therefore the burning rate of the propellant are variable, enabling a much better control of the pressure being generated. In a conventional cartridge, it is difficult to achieve a theoretically ideal pressure curve; the plasma generator allows a careful rise in initial pressure to start the projectile safely on its way, building up to achieve the maximum temperature, pressure and velocity which the gun can accept. Test firings have been demonstrated by Bofors using a modified 40mm gun, with the cartridge case being made of synthetic material to achieve electrical isolation. Replacement of the conventional propellant with a material whose gasses have a lower molecular weight would permit even higher velocities. The main problem is the electrical power needed by the plasma generator, not as great as with a rail gun but still too much for current military use.

## THE FUTURE OF
## NAVAL APPLICATIONS

THE RELATIVE ADVANTAGES AND DISADVANTAGES of gun and missile air defence systems for warships is a complex issue, the balance of which shifts from time to time depending on technological developments both in the systems themselves and in the threats with which they have to cope.

The major advantage held by missiles (at least up to the present) is that they can be steered all the way to the target. By contrast, the hit probability of a projectile from a gun decreases very rapidly with increasing distance, partly because of aiming errors or other ballistic influences (winds, barrel wear, variation in muzzle velocity) and partly because aircraft can manoeuvre and missiles are small and hence difficult to hit.

On the other hand, guns have their own advantages. Ammunition is small and cheap, can be stored in great quantity and fired at a high rate, making up to some extent for the system's inherent inaccuracy. Their minimum range is virtually zero, whereas all current AA missiles (except small, man-portable systems) take time to come under full control after launching and thus have a minimum range which can be as much as 1km.

On balance, missiles can be said to be clearly more effective in the anti-aircraft role at ranges of 5km or more, guns preferable for ranges of under 2km, with a grey area in between. Against missiles, the effective range of all systems is sharply reduced. Developments such as the Russian *Kashtan*, which combines guns and missiles on one mount, appears to offer the most comprehensive anti-aircraft and anti-missile protection which will be available for the foreseeable future.

A particular pressure on the gun element of CIWS is to increase effectiveness in order to be able to cope with the next generation of supersonic anti-ship missiles. Both calibre and rate of fire are therefore being pushed up, with rotary guns in 30mm being the norm. Somewhat surprisingly, the USN

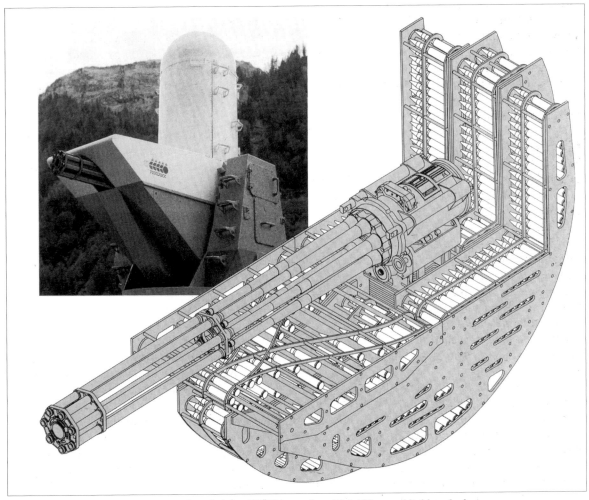

*25mm Oerlikon KBD rotary cannon for Phalanx CIWS upgrade, with 1,000-round linkless feed*
*(Courtesy: Oerlikon-Contraves)*

has chosen to replace its Phalanx CIWS with RAM AA missiles in many of the Ticonderoga class cruisers, albeit in a modified version also capable of engaging surface targets. However, this may be more of a comment about the long-term effectiveness of the small-calibre Phalanx rather than of CIWS in general. Phalanx continues to be developed, the latest Block 1B version has barrels that are 46cm longer and thicker, to achieve a greater effective range, coupled with improved fire control systems. A different solution to this problem is offered by Oerlikon-Contraves, in the form of a 25mm KBD gun to replace the M61A1 in the Phalanx.

All but the most specialised CIWS are also more versatile than missiles. They can be fired against surface vessels and land targets as well as aircraft, and can also fire warning shots in a display of determination – hardly economic, even if feasible, with missiles. It was this final factor which really preserved the Oerlikon and Bofors guns in RN service after the introduction of the short-range Seacat missile, and it has also led to the retention of larger-calibre naval weapons.

Modern warships sent to deal with terrorist insurrections in the Far East, a job which involved much stopping and searching of small vessels, found light cannon to be the most useful weapons. The involvement of NATO forces in the Persian Gulf during the Iran–Iraq war, which saw terrorist attacks using grenade launchers from small boats, underlined the message. It also emphasised the advantage of manually aimed over radar-directed guns in dealing with terrorist craft which may be manoeuvring within an innocent fishing fleet.

The lesson is clear. Every warship needs at least one 'old-fashioned' manually aimed light cannon for dealing with low-level threats, and their more sophisticated CIWS cousins are also currently unrivalled (although under long-term threat) as a last-ditch defence against missile attack. Larger-calibre guns have also proved their worth in limited warfare, leading, for example, to the Batch 3 versions of the Royal Navy's Type 22 frigates to be fitted for the 4.5″ Mk 8 (omitted from earlier batches) following experience in the Falklands conflict.

While every destroyer or frigate class built or planned is equipped with a medium-calibre gun of

at least 57mm, there is some debate about the ideal calibre. If a shore bombardment role is likely to be significant, a gun of at least 100mm and preferably 127mm is the obvious choice. In fact, the US Marines like gunfire support to be as large as possible – they were among the strongest supporters of retaining the 16″ (406mm) gun Iowa class battleships in service and have encouraged the development of various guns of 155–203mm calibre. On the other hand, the spread to developing nations of long range anti-ship missiles, capable of being fired from the shore, is undoubtedly increasing the risk of the shore bombardment role. It seems likely that guns will be supplemented by longer-range missiles (apart from the very expensive Tomahawk cruise missiles) in the future. For the short term, the USN is working on a land attack version of the SM-2 AA missile, using GPS and inertial guidance. An accurate range in excess of seventy miles (112 km) has been demonstrated.

In the meantime, the USN has developed a Mk 45 Mod 4 version of its 5″ (127mm) gun, fitted with a 62 calibre barrel and firing Extended Range Guided Munitions out to sixty-three nautical miles (117km) with a claimed CEP (Circular Error Probable) of twenty metres. A more radical propos-

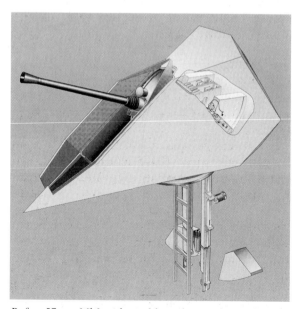

*Bofors 57mm Mk3 with stealth gunhouse; the gun barrel retracts into the housing when not required*
*(Courtesy: Celsius)*

al was the fixed, vertically firing 155mm gun being developed by the US Navy, designed to fire its projectiles high into the stratosphere, from where they extend fins and glide down, guided to targets 100nm (185km) or more away. This results in a very simple and inexpensive weapon, with the guidance being achieved by the projectiles (typically using GPS systems, which have already been proved to function when fired in conventional shells) rather than the gun.

Smaller-calibre guns such as the 57mm Bofors or 76mm OtoBreda have the advantage of very high rates of fire, which makes them much more credible as AA and even anti-missile weapons. Practical combat experience is no guide in deciding the right calibre to meet all circumstances; the Falklands conflict saw extensive use of 4.5″ (114mm) guns for shore bombardment, with over 8,000 rounds being fired. On the other hand, those ships subjected to intense air attack in San Carlos Water would doubtless have benefited from a gun biased more towards the AA role.

For the future, the effectiveness of guns will be further enhanced by the continued development of ammunition, both with sophisticated fuzing technology, such as the Bofors 3P round, and with steerable capability. The automatic cannon, in various guises, is not going to disappear from warships in the foreseeable future.

## ARMY USES

FOR TERRESTRIAL ANTI-AIRCRAFT DEFENCE, THERE are the same kind of gun-versus-missile arguments as in naval applications, with the additional point that features such as hills, trees and buildings can greatly reduce the range at which low-flying aircraft are detected, giving quick-reacting, gun-based systems an advantage. On the other hand, the increasing range of the anti-armour missiles carried by attack helicopters is taking them beyond effective gun engagement range, with the possible exception of the largest calibres such as the 76mm OTOMAT-IC. The ideal solution is the same as the naval one: combine guns and missiles on one mounting. Once again the Russians are in the lead with the powerful *Tunguska*, the US Blazer equivalent being much less impressive in terms of both gun and missile effectiveness.

Gun calibre escalation is even more acute in surface fire roles, driven by the increasing armour protection of MICVs. The standard US calibre of 25mm is now the smallest being considered for new developments, with 30mm being common and 35mm and even 40mm being offered.

To give an example of current trends, Rheinmetall developed the Rh503 cannon for the next generation of MICVs, a project now taken on by Boeing as the Bushmaster III. Like most of the modern AFV weapons, it is externally driven, with a rate of fire variable between 150 rpm and 400 rpm, and weighs around 500kg. It is initially offered in 35 × 228 Oerlikon calibre, but designed to convert easily to a new 50 × 330 'Supershot' cartridge which is based on the 35mm case, but has the neck expanded to the larger calibre, effectively making it entirely straight. The reason for this is that the larger the calibre of the barrel, the more power can be pushed down it. Given that the diameter of the main anti-armour projectile, the APFSDS, is unrelated to the gun calibre, it therefore makes sense to adopt as wide a calibre as possible. For the same overall length and width as the 35mm cartridge (the projectile is almost entirely buried within the case), the 50mm has 75% more muzzle energy. A very similar weapon in the same calibres is the South African EMAK 35, now offered in the LCT-35 turret.

A similar approach has been adopted for the proposed 'Super Forty' version of the Bushmaster II, in which the 30 × 173 cartridge has been necked up to 40mm. This should not be confused with the much bigger 40mm Bushmaster IV, designed around the Bofors 40 × 364R ammunition.

France, the UK and the USA are taking a different route to the same objective, by developing revolutionary cased telescopic ammunition (CTA) weapons. The American COMVAT and Franco-British experimental 45 M911 both use a 45 × 305 cartridge in which the projectiles are entirely contained within the lightweight case. The result is a very compact and light cartridge, optimised for APFSDS ammunition. The M911 gun can achieve 400 rpm, although 200 rpm is considered adequate for ground fighting. French and British interest has more recently focused on the slightly smaller (40 × 225) CTA 2000 weapon.

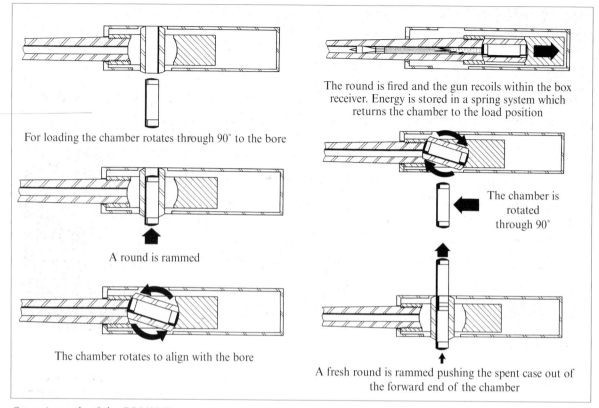

For loading the chamber rotates through 90° to the bore

A round is rammed

The chamber rotates to align with the bore

The round is fired and the gun recoils within the box receiver. Energy is stored in a spring system which returns the chamber to the load position

The chamber is rotated through 90°

A fresh round is rammed pushing the spent case out of the forward end of the chamber

*Operating cycle of the COMVAT cannon* (*Courtesy: D.F. Allsop*)

A 12.7mm Gatling-type four-barrel HMG is also being developed using the CTA principle. Weighing 26kg, it is capable of 4,000 rpm. The USA has established the JMAT (joint medium-calibre automatic) programme, initially concentrating on rotary guns in 20mm and 25mm calibre – effectively a second attempt at the abortive GAU-7/A.

Options for mounting AFV guns have also been affected by the development of optronics. The need to be able to fight at night and in all weathers had led to a great increase in the number of light intensifying and thermal-imaging observation and sighting systems. As these detach the gunner and commander from the need to be placed close to the gun, it is now feasible to dispense with a large and vulnerable turret. Instead, the crew can be located in the relative safety of the hull of the AFV, with only the gun mounting and optronics sensors protruding above.

It is clear that the externally powered single-barrel gun is beginning to dominate in vehicle- or heli-copter-mounted applications in which reliability, compactness and controllability are more important than a high rate of fire, albeit with strong competition from long-recoil designs.

In artillery calibres, automatic loading (first introduced in the Bofors 155mm *Bandkanon* SPG of the 1960s) is now becoming standard for two separate reasons. First, the danger from artillery-locating radar means that guns cannot stay long in one position before being subject to counter-battery fire, so they need to fire several shots very quickly then move to a new location. Secondly, the first few rounds from artillery are the most effective, before the enemy has time to take cover or scatter, so a rapid burst of fire is desirable. A further advantage can be gained by firing each shot at a different muzzle velocity and angle of elevation, calculated so that all of the rounds of a burst arrive simultaneously. This is possible to some extent by adjusting the propellant charges but would obviously be much easier to arrange given a finer control of

*25mm OCSW prototype (Courtesy: Primex Technologies)*

muzzle velocity, which helps to account for the current interest in liquid propellants.

As with naval weapons, heavy automatic guns are not just useful in their main roles. Wartime experience has shown that they can be very effective in dealing with infantry attacks which may be too far away, or under too much cover, to be affected by small-arms fire. Infantry engagements, however, are normally more efficiently countered by using smaller, man-portable weapons. In this role the HMG, and the specialised rifles using the same ammunition, appear to have a continuing future.

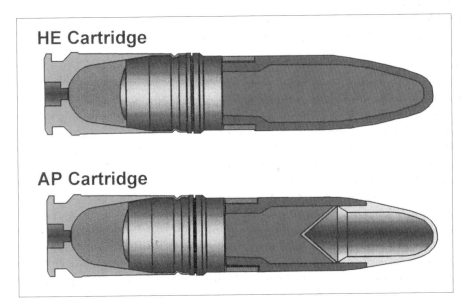

*Early version of ammunition for the 25mm OCSW (Courtesy: Primex Technologies)*

Today, they are not only highly effective long-range anti-personnel weapons, with the ability to punch through walls and other types of cover favoured by infantrymen, but with the use of advanced ammunition types are also effective against soft-skinned or lightly armoured vehicles.

An alternative approach to the anti-personnel role is represented by the OCSW (objective crew served weapon) programme which is intended to enter US Army service by 2008. The 25mm gun, which fires at 220 rpm, weighs only 10.4kg (around 17kg with mount and fire control system and 29kg with 60 rounds of ammunition) and is intended to be carried and operated by a crew of two. The effective range of 2,000m is not much further than the 40mm AGL's, but the OCSW's major advantage is the fire control system, which incorporates a rangefinder and electronic fuze setter. The time fuze is set as the projectile leaves the gun to ensure that the HE shell is detonated directly above the target. This airburst facility dramatically increases the lethality, especially against troops in defilade (i.e. out of line of sight) who have taken cover against direct-fire weapons. Effectiveness in comparison with the 40mm AGL is calculated to be four times greater against standing troops but nearly fifty times greater in defilade. In addition, a HEAT round is being developed to penetrate up to 51mm of armour.

## AIR FORCE EQUIPMENT

THE FIRST AND MOST OBVIOUS CONCLUSION IS THAT after a period in the 1950s and 1960s of believing that aircraft-mounted guns would be made obsolete by missiles, all fighter aircraft are now fitted with them.

The main reason for this is the flexibility of the gun. It can be used for air-to-air and air-to-ground fighting, will not be deflected by the electronic or thermal countermeasures used against missiles and provides a backup for when the missiles run out. The lack of range in comparison with missiles is less significant than was imagined, because most modern conflicts are carefully limited, with rules of engagement which require visual verification of the target before opening fire. The enormous ranges achievable by many air-to-air missiles can therefore rarely be used. Also, while the size and weight of

combat aircraft has tended to increase, that of aircraft cannon has not, so fitting one of the modern single-barrel cannon carries only a small payload penalty.

Fighter guns have therefore continued to flourish, albeit in various different directions. It is puzzling that the USA has retained both the 20mm calibre (with the exception of the primarily ground-attack weapons) and the rotary cannon, which together with its ammunition feed arrangements is a very bulky package to accommodate. All other fighter-producing nations have selected compact single-barrel cannon in much harder-hitting 25–30mm calibres (with up to four times the projectile weight of the 20mm) as the most appropriate equipment for such aircraft. The theoretically lower rate of fire of these cannon, ranging in current models from 1,600 rpm to 2,500 rpm, is compensated to some extent by the instant acceleration, while even the best externally powered rotary guns take time to reach the maximum rate of fire.

To give an example, the M61A1 reportedly fires only eighteen rounds in the first half-second (the lighter, but so far not in service, M61A2 can double this). This amounts to a total weight of projectiles fired of 1.8kg (3.6kg for the A2). In comparison, the BK 27 fires fourteen rounds weighing 3.7kg, while the new GIAT 30M791, a little heavier but far more compact than the M61A2, fires twenty-one rounds in the same time for a weight of 5.7kg. Even more remarkable is the Russian GSh-301; this may only fire thirteen rounds in the first half-second but each projectile is nearly four times the weight of the 20mm, giving a total weight of fire of over 5kg, from a gun which is significantly smaller than the GIAT and less than half the weight. Even once they have accelerated to full speed, neither M61 version can beat the Russian gun in firepower, yet they weigh over twice as much and occupy many times the volume. The USA is reportedly developing rotary cannon using cased telescopic ammunition for the possible replacement of the 20mm guns in the F-22 and RAH-66, but that is unlikely to happen for some time.

A different approach is being promoted for the US Joint Strike Fighter. A version of the Mauser BK 27 developed jointly by Mauser, Boeing and Primex, featuring linkless feed and intended to use

HEDP ammunition, has been selected by the Boeing-led team and at the time of writing was a possible choice for the Lockheed Martin competitor.

Logically, the future of fighter guns should be secure. Not only will the widespread use of stealth technology reduce target acquisition and therefore combat ranges, but the introduction of thrust vectoring means that aircraft attitude will no longer be tied to the direction of travel. This will make it much easier to aim the gun, as the aircraft can rapidly be pointed in the right direction. However, some recent decisions by the RAF give cause for concern. First, the failure of the Aden 25 means that the Harrier GR.7s are likely to remain gunless (although there seems no technical reason why the BK 27 should not be used instead). Second, it was announced in May 2000 that for reasons of cost, the RAF's Eurofighter Typhoons would not utilise the planned BK 27 installation. It is hoped that the RAF does not have cause to regret these decisions in future conflicts.

For ground attack, both Russia and the USA have specialised aircraft fitted with high-velocity 30mm guns to supplement their missiles and bombs, although the USAF's future commitment to this type of aircraft is in question. During the Gulf War, the USAF's A-10 aircraft reportedly made relatively little use of their formidable GAU-8/A cannon, preferring to use guided missiles because their much greater stand-off distance minimised the risk from Iraqi AA fire. The claimed penetration of the 30mm DU round is 76mm at 700m, which is marginal against the ever-thickening top armour of modern battle tanks. The Russians have tried larger-calibre weapons for ground attack, tests having been conducted with a 45mm TKB-700 smooth-bore automatic cannon designed for the Su-25, but so far without result.

The most varied range of weapons is in the field of helicopter armament, with every type of gun up to a high-powered 30mm being available, in flexibly mounted, turreted, fixed or podded forms. The reason for such variety is probably the relative lack of major combat experience with attack helicopters, those occasions when they have been used being rather one-sided affairs. One must hope that our air forces do not have the opportunity to acquire such experience in the foreseeable future. It seems evident, however, that a quickly responding cannon will remain of value as attack helicopters inevitably evolve to fight each other as well as their original ground targets. Pilots are trained to keep low and make full use of cover, so engagement opportunities are likely to be fleeting and at short range.

The introduction of the new Mauser RMK 30 recoilless gun may well alter the limits which normally apply to such powerful weapons, as it appears to be ideal for helicopter installations. The design permits a relatively light and compact weapon, with a light and simple mounting as recoil does not have to be absorbed. Furthermore, the lack of recoil movement also permits a high degree of accuracy, which means that a lower rate of fire can produce the same effect, and less ammunition therefore has to be carried, saving yet more weight. It is, of course, less suited to internal mounting in fighter aircraft because of the low rate of fire and the problems of dispersing the gas ejected from the rear, but podded versions could make an interesting underwing load for light, propeller-driven COIN aircraft.

Finally, it is worth noting that the large-calibre (over 30mm) airborne cannon concept is not quite dead. They were never an unqualified success, except for limited periods when circumstances favoured them, such as anti-tank use on the Eastern Front in Second World War. Despite this, the idea refused to go away and has led to the sporadic reappearance of such weapons.

Undoubtedly the most spectacular modern example is the Lockheed AC130 Hercules gunship, fitted for special operations with a variety of ground-attack guns including 40mm Bofors and even 105mm howitzers. Parallels can be drawn between these and the First World War and inter-war 'battleplane' concept.

Those who believe that nothing is really new but is merely reinvented in different forms will enjoy the thought that the US Army's M129 40mm automatic grenade launcher, flexibly mounted in various attack helicopters, is remarkably similar in purpose and broad performance specification to the Vickers 37mm 1pdr Mk 111, one of the first automatic cannon ever to see airborne service.

# *Appendix One*

## ANTI-TANK AND MODERN HEAVY RIFLES

THE FIRST ANTI-TANK (AT) RIFLE, THE MAUSER *Tank-Gewehr* M1918, was developed towards the end of the First World War in parallel with the MG TuF machine gun which used the same 13 × 92SR ammunition. It was rushed into service to provide infantry with some protection against the Allied tanks until the TuF could be introduced. The M1918 was conceptually very simple: a bolt-action weapon just like a scaled-up infantry rifle but 1.68m long and weighing 17.7kg.

The steel-cored projectile was claimed to be capable of penetrating 20mm of armour plate at 100m range and 15mm at 300m, provided it hit at 90° (performance dropped off sharply with more

glancing hits). Given that the thickest armour on contemporary British tanks measured just 12mm, the gun was quite effective. The disadvantages were those which handicapped AT rifles throughout their existence; size, weight and recoil.

The two nations which provided the lineal successors to the Mauser were Britain and the Soviet Union. In Britain, the first experimental AT rifle, the .600/500″ Godsal, was actually a contemporary of the Mauser M1918, but was not proceeded with. Little then happened until the mid-1930s, when much experimentation resulted in the Boys Rifle, a bolt-action weapon of brutally functional appearance, chambered for a new .55″ (13.9 × 99B) round

*Mauser Tank-Gewehr M1918 (with M16 rifle for comparison)* (Courtesy: *MoD Pattern Room*)

*.500" Godsal experimental (Courtesy: MoD Pattern Room)*

which was similar in dimensions to the .50″ Browning cartridge except for the larger calibre and the belted case.

The cartridge was available in two service AP loadings, the W Mark 1 and the improved W Mark 2. Even the performance of the latter was not a great deal better than the Mauser's, with penetration of 20mm at 100m range and 70° striking angle. Later in the war a 45.5g tungsten-cored shot was developed which was fired at 945 m/s. It was far more effective, but came too late for service use.

The Boys saw extensive use, with BSA producing nearly 69,000 of them. They were fitted to light armoured vehicles as well as available in a shortened version for paratroops. Despite their ubiquity, their unpleasant firing characteristics and ineffectiveness against all but the thinnest armour meant that they were never popular.

The Soviet Union paid even greater homage to the Mauser in that their first effort, the Sholoklov M39, was simply a Mauser copy chambered for their 12.7 × 108 heavy machine gun round. Performance was disappointing, leading to the rapid development of a considerably more powerful 14.5 × 114 cartridge, with armour penetration leaping from 10mm to 30mm (both at 100m/60°), and after some abortive experiments in 1939–40, two very different guns to fire it.

The PTRS (*Protivotankovoe Ruzh'ye* = anti-tank rifle) of 1941, a Simonov design, was a sophisticated semi-automatic gas-operated weapon fed by a five-round clip. It was relatively fragile and expensive and far less common than Degtyarev's rival PTRD. This was an extremely simple bolt-action single-shot rifle whose appearance rather resembled a piece of plumbing. Its one refinement was a recoiling barrel/breech assembly, which as well as helping to absorb the brutal recoil of the massive cartridge incorporated automatic breech opening and case ejection.

These weapons' combination of portability and power made them the most useful of the AT rifles and they remained in service even after 1945, being used by the North Koreans in the Korean War, albeit primarily for long-range sniping. The cartridge lives on in the post-war KPV heavy machine gun.

Another nation which produced an AT rifle in this class was Czechoslovakia. The 15mm vz 41, known to the Germans as the PzB 41(t), was a single-shot bolt-action rifle designed around the 15 × 104 cartridge for the big ZB machine gun (which saw British service as the 15mm Besa). Armour penetration was midway between the two Soviet rounds. In German hands, production concentrated on a version modified to accept the 7.92 × 94 *Panzerbüsche* round, but the original was supplied in small numbers to Italy and Croatia.

The USA developed the largest of the HMG-class AT rifles, the T1E1 Cal .60″. The 15.2 × 114

*.55" Boys rifle (Courtesy: MoD Pattern Room)*

cartridge was even bigger than the Soviet 14.5mm round and featured impressive ballistics, with target armour penetration of 32mm at 450m. The gun was a gas-operated semi-automatic weapon designed to be fired from a low tripod. It was tested in 1942, by which time the futility of any anti-tank rifle had become apparent and it never saw service. The cartridge was used in several experimental machine guns but was not adopted until it was necked out to 20mm, in which form it became the $20 \times 102$ round used in the M39 and M61 Vulcan aircraft cannon.

Even the 13mm Mauser was adequate to deal with the great majority of tanks in service in the 1930s, most of which were only designed to keep out standard rifle ammunition. There were already signs, however, that tanks were getting tougher. The French had some massive heavy tanks in service and the first of the British infantry tanks, the A11 (better known as the Matilda 1), boasted armour up to 60mm thick. Even in standard cruiser tanks, frontal armour of up to 30mm was beginning to appear.

The problem was that to follow the conventional route and increase the calibre of AT rifles would result in a significant increase in the size, weight and recoil of the weapon, thus greatly reducing its usefulness to front-line troops. Some nations accepted these disadvantages nonetheless, but others took a different route.

As we have seen, the British and Soviet AT rifles were in a direct line of development from the Mauser M1918 in that they retained a similar calibre (12.7–15mm) and often used cartridges shared with HMGs. The .55" Boys round was actually the subject of various attempts to design a machine gun around it (by Vickers and Rolls-Royce, and even in Italy!). There were two alternative approaches also used: the small-calibre, high-velocity weapons and the big 20mm guns.

## THE SMALL BORES

DESIGNERS IN GERMANY AND POLAND WERE aware that penetration was improved much more by increases in striking velocity than it was by increases in projectile weight or calibre. They therefore independently designed weapons using their standard military rifle calibre of 7.92mm, but firing massively oversized cartridges to achieve the highest possible muzzle velocity.

The Polish weapon, known as the *Kb Ur wz 35* (the 'Ur' being short for Uruguay, as for security reasons the gun was stored in cases labelled 'rifles for Uruguay'), the PzB 35 (to the Germans) and the *Maroszec* (after the leader of the design team), was the neatest AT rifle ever produced: a slim, conventional bolt-action rifle weighing only 9kg and designed around a long, thin $7.9 \times 107$ cartridge.

*Anti-tank rifles at the Pattern Room 1 (from left to right): 20mm Type 97 (with box magazine), 14.5mm PTRD, 14.5mm PTRS, 20mm Solothurn S18-1000, 20mm Solothurn S18-100 (Courtesy: MoD Pattern Room)*

The muzzle velocity of 1,200 m/s gave armour penetration variously quoted as 33mm, 20mm or 15mm at 100m (the last being at a striking angle of 60°). It was effective against most of the invading German tanks but had been kept so secret that it was only possible to put a small number into action. Captured examples were used by Finland, who also used several other types of ATR as well as developing their own, as we shall see.

The German equivalent was a shorter but much fatter 7.9 × 94 cartridge derived from a necked-down Mauser M1918, technically called the *Patronen 318* and generally known as the *Panzerbüsche*. There is some debate about the actual ballistics. Although officially the muzzle velocity was about 1,200 m/s, the measured muzzle velocity in US tests was only 1,080 m/s. This reduced performance might have been a consequence of

barrel wear, which was a major problem. Armour penetration of the tungsten-cored bullet was very similar to the Polish round (30mm/100m/90°) but it was available in a variety of weapons: the PzB 38, PzB 39 and M.SS 41.

The first of these was similar to the PTRD in that the barrel recoiled, automatically ejecting the spent cartridge, which was manually replaced. It was expensive to make and soon replaced by the simplified, manually operated PzB 39. The M.SS 41 (sometimes referred to as the SS 41, MS 41 or even MPzB 41) was an adaptation of the Czech 15mm gun already described. It was of bullpup design (with the magazine behind the pistol grip) and manually operated by rotating and sliding the grip. Despite the small-calibre cartridge, the guns were not particularly light.

The performance of these weapons was, by most

accounts, significantly better than the .55″ Boys or the 12.7mm Sholoklov. However, it was still not enough against the rapidly improving Soviet tanks so some of the PzB 39s were converted to grenade launchers, in which form they were known as GrB 39. The barrel was reduced in length from 117cm to 58cm and fitted with a cup to take two different shaped-charge projectiles. The No.41 weighed 425g and could penetrate around 90mm of armour; the No.61 weighed 580g and could penetrate 125mm. Range was about 100m and the low launching velocity made hitting the target relatively difficult.

Most remarkably, an AFV machine gun was devised to fire the *Patronen 318*, the MG 141. This followed the development of the experimental EW 141 (*Einbau Waffe*), which was semi-auto only. The MG 141 was reportedly produced in small numbers, but the barrel wear, bad enough in the single-shot rifles, must have been extremely severe. It was a Mauser design (similar to the MG 151) which fired at 900 rpm, weighed 22.5kg, was 174cm long and had a 100cm barrel.

Mention should be made of other nations' experiments in producing 7.9mm AT rifles. The French tried necking down a 13.2mm Hotchkiss HMG round; the Spanish produced an $8 \times 87$ round similar to a short *Maroszec* for a prototype rifle which reportedly saw action in their civil war; and after experiments with a .55/.303″ intended for training, the British considered a .55/7.9mm. None was adopted.

The problem with the 7.9mm AT rifles was that only a limited amount of energy could be pushed down the narrow bore; the big cartridges were already 'over-bore' and highly inefficient, causing severe barrel wear with a life of only about 200 rounds. Velocity could not be increased further without a radically different approach. This led to some experimentation with squeeze- or taper-bore guns, but these only saw service in larger calibres and were not adopted for AT rifles.

## THE BIG CANNON

THE ALTERNATIVE APPROACH TO ACHIEVING improved penetration was simply to increase the calibre. In practice, the maximum before reaching the artillery category was around 20mm and weapons in this class were developed and adopted by several nations. Nearly all of them used existing cartridges developed for aircraft or AA use and also used similar mechanisms, although usually semi rather than fully automatic.

In comparison with the smaller calibres, the more powerful 20mm cannon suffered disadvantages of size, weight and recoil (requiring at least two men to handle them) but benefited from less sensitivity to range; small projectiles tended to lose velocity, and therefore penetration, at a much higher rate. To illustrate this, a typical 7.9mm AP bullet of 14.3g has a sectional density ratio of .32 while a 20mm projectile of 150g has an SDR of .53, and (projectile shapes being equal) the SDR is directly

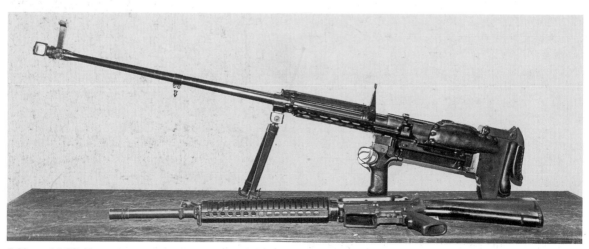

*7.92mm M.SS 41 (Courtesy: MoD Pattern Room)*

related to the ballistic coefficient which determines the velocity loss; the higher the SDR, the lower the velocity loss with range.

The first of the AT cannon was developed from the 20mm Becker aircraft cannon. By the 1930s the design had been developed by Oerlikon and was offered in various versions, still principally for the same roles. However, the firm also offered anti-tank rifles using the same API blow-back mechanism, in semi-automatic form: the SSG and SSG36, chambered for the $20 \times 72RB$ and $20 \times 110RB$ cartridges respectively (although the shorter barrels reduced the muzzle velocities in comparison with the aircraft and AA guns). SSG stood for *Schweres Selbstladegewehr*, or heavy self-loading rifle.

The guns were relatively compact but heavy. Even the low-velocity SSG was credited with penetrating 20mm of armour at 100m/90° (and 11mm at 1,000m); the SSG36, with a much higher muzzle velocity (750 m/s instead of 550 m/s), was appreciably more effective. The problem was that the API blowback mechanism required the gun to fire as the heavy bolt was moving forward, which inevitably affected the gunners' accuracy.

Oerlikon's main Swiss competition was Solothurn, a subsidiary of the German Rheinmetall-Borsig firm which was not allowed to develop AT rifles under the provisions of the Treaty of Versailles. Solothurn also developed 20mm guns, but these fired from a locked breech and were derived from the Erhardt aircraft cannon first conceived in the First World War. This enabled the use of more powerful cartridges as well as a much shorter lock time for more accurate shooting. For complex political and commercial reasons, the Erhardt was actually offered as an AT gun around 1930 by the Dutch firm HAIHA (*Hollandische Artillerie Industrie und Handelsmaatschappij*), another subsidiary of Rheinmetall.

Further development led to the introduction of the Solothurn S18-100, a purpose-designed, recoil-operated, self-loading AT weapon using the short, belted $20 \times 105B$ Solothurn round also used in aircraft cannon. It was bought by Hungary and Finland, the version for the latter being known as the S18-154. The relatively low velocity limited its effectiveness, although it was still capable of penetrating over 30mm/100m/90°.

The S18-100 was replaced by the much larger S18-1000, chambered for the long $20 \times 138B$ Solothurn cartridge also used in the standard German AA cannon, the FlaK 30 and 38. This was a far more powerful weapon which was capable of penetrating 40mm at short range. Power had its price, however: it was 2.17m long and weighed 44kg. The S18-1100 was identical but offered fully automatic fire, a feature of somewhat dubious value as the heavy recoil would have made it difficult to hold an automatic weapon on target. These weapons were mainly deployed by the Italian Army but also saw service with Switzerland and the Netherlands. Incidentally there is some confusion surrounding the nomenclature of this weapon, as it has been reported that a few were tried in German

*The 20mm anti-tank rifles, like this Solothurn S18-1000, were too heavy to pick up and carry*
(*Courtesy: Verlag Stocker-Schmid, Dietikon-Zürich*)

service as the PzB 41. This should not be confused with the Czech PzB 41 already referred to.

A very similar but gas-operated weapon, also using the long Solothurn round, was the Finnish Lahti L39 (popularly known as the *Norsupyssy*, or elephant gun). This saw service against the Soviet forces in the Winter War of 1939–40 and proved quite successful, aided no doubt by its chief novelty: a small pair of skis to enable the big gun to be towed across snow. It also featured a large muzzle brake of distinctive shape, in an attempt to reduce recoil to manageable levels. Surprisingly, it fired from an open bolt, but this must have been useful later when a fully automatic version was adapted for AA use. This was not the first attempt by Lahti to produce an AT rifle. The L38 was initially developed in 13.2mm calibre but it appears (the facts are not entirely clear) that it was later adapted to take Lahti's own $20 \times 113$ cartridge used in the naval

AA cannon. Neither rifle appears to have seen service.

Like the Lahti and the Oerlikons, the 20mm Madsen AT rifle was developed from an aircraft cannon. Using Madsen's own large $20 \times 120$ cartridge, this was the bulkiest of the AT guns, weighing 60kg and firing semi-auto from a thirty-round drum magazine. Introduced into Danish service, it was taken over post-1940 by the *Wehrmacht*, who reportedly did not like it very much.

Sweden also produced AT rifles, the more conventional being the massive Bofors m/40, which was a multi-purpose weapon also used in AA and AFV roles. The Bofors fired the company's own long, rimmed $20 \times 145R$ cartridge and was mounted on a tripod. It used a long-recoil system capable of automatic fire from an odd twenty-five-round rotary magazine (like a drum only with the cartridges exposed to the elements) sitting above the breech.

*Anti-tank rifles at the Pattern Room 2: Swedish m/42 recoilless in the foreground, with its huge cartridge standing in front (Courtesy: MoD Pattern Room)*

*The massive 24mm Tb.41 in firing position* (Courtesy: Verlag Stocker-Schmid, Dietikon-Zürich)

*Another solution to the problem of transporting large anti-tank rifles; this is the Swiss 24mm Tankbüsche 41*
(Courtesy: Verlag Stocker-Schmid, Dietikon-Zürich)

*Anti-tank rifle cartridges (from left to right): 7.92 × 57 (for scale), 7.92mm Panzerbüsche (7.92 × 94), 7.92mm Maroszek (7.92 × 107), modern .50" Browning SLAP APDS (12.7 × 99), 13mm Mauser T-Gewehr (13 × 92SR), .55" Boys (13.9 × 99B), 14.5mm PTRD/PTRS (14.5 × 114), Oerlikon SSG (20 × 72B), Solothurn S18-100 (20 × 105B), Oerlikon SSG-36 (20 × 110RB), Japanese Type 97 (20 × 125), Solothurn S18-1000/Lahti L39 (20 × 138B), Swiss Tankbüsche 41 (24 × 138)*

The other Swedish weapon was the exception to the rule and the most remarkable of the European AT rifles, the 20mm Carl Gustav m/42 recoilless. Such weapons are profligate in their use of propellant as most of the charge is used to generate the back-blast needed to counteract the recoil. The cartridge is therefore simply gigantic, with a case 180mm long and with a rim diameter of 48mm. The light and handy gun was necessarily single-shot, with an artillery-type breech.

The Japanese also adopted the 20mm calibre for their only AT rifle, the Type 97. The 20 × 125 cartridge was a large and powerful item and the gun used a gas-unlocked delayed blowback mechanism similar to the Hispano's. Provision was also made for the barrel and receiver to recoil in order to steady the weapon. However, reports that the gun could fire full-auto are incorrect; the armourer's manual for the gun shows no means of achieving selective fire and the Japanese nomenclature is *Jidoho* (autoloading gun) instead of *Kikanho* (automatic cannon). This gun's claim to fame is that it was available with an armoured shield which helped to raise the travelling weight to 68kg. The gun was probably of more value when converted for use as an aircraft cannon, in which form it was renamed the IJA 20mm Ho-3 (fixed) and Ho-1 (for flexible mounting).

The largest of the AT rifles (although approaching the light artillery category) was the Swiss Tb 41 (*Tankbüsche 41*). This short-recoil self-loading weapon was designed around the 24 × 138 cartridge and was essentially the same gun as the Pzw-Kan 38 AFV cannon. It weighed 53kg empty and was available on tripod or wheeled mountings. The calibre may be only a fraction less than the 25mm

Hotchkiss AT gun, but the French weapon was much bigger and heavier, and definitely out of the AT rifle class.

## ANTI-TANK RIFLES: THE VERDICT

THE MAIN CONCLUSION IN STUDYING THE HISTORY of AT rifles is that they were a considerable waste of time and resources. They seemed like a good idea during the rearmament boom of the mid- to late 1930s, offering the power to defeat most contemporary tanks in a package handy enough to make them infantry weapons, but no sooner had the fighting started than the deficiencies became apparent.

Even the best of the weapons was only marginally effective against early Second World War tanks and AT riflemen soon found that they had to wait until they were suicidally close, or until they could shoot at the thinner side armour. As tank armour rapidly increased in thickness, the AT rifles could not keep up. A weapon which was primarily devised to assist the morale of front-line troops began to have the opposite effect. They reportedly saw some use as long-range sniping rifles, starting as early as the First World War when the M1918 was used in the counter-sniper role as it had the ability to punch through the armoured shields sometimes used by snipers. This hardly justified the sums spent on them.

It is sometimes, not unreasonably, asked whether AT rifles were effective even when they were able to penetrate the armour of an AFV. It is admittedly unlikely that the small projectiles would do much damage to the vehicle; the most they could hope for would be to disable one or two of the crew as the shot bounced around inside. This concern might have lain behind the rather optimistic addition to the base of the *Patronen 318* cartridge of a small tear-gas capsule. The main effect of AT rifles may have been psychological: the knowledge that their armour could be penetrated might be enough to make AFV crews more cautious about pushing forwards and exposing their vehicles to fire. At any rate, armies still find it worthwhile providing AP projectiles for HMGs and modern versions of the AT rifle.

With the benefit of hindsight, AT rifles could have remained effective for longer if they had made use of some of the ammunition developments stimulated by the war. APCR projectiles offered huge improvements in short-range penetration. The later APDS ammunition was at least as good at short range and much better at longer distances. While proving highly effective in anti-tank artillery, such projectiles never saw service in AT rifles.

## MODERN RIFLES

THE NEW FORMS OF AMMUNITION DEVELOPED for HMGs, such as multi-purpose and SLAP (APDS) rounds, have helped to restore interest in the concept of a large-calibre, shoulder-fired rifle as a combination long-range sniping/anti-sniping and

*Barrett M82A1; a modern .50" calibre rifle, with M16 for scale (Courtesy: MoD Pattern Room)*

anti-materiel weapon. Light armoured vehicles are generally vulnerable to SLAP rounds and soft-skinned vehicles (including parked aircraft) can be severely damaged by the new APHEI shells. Furthermore, even main battle tanks can have their effectiveness reduced by hits on their relatively vulnerable externally mounted equipment such as night-sights. Such weapons are also useful in disposing at a safe distance of unexploded battlefield ordnance such as mines, and they are even attracting interest as vehicle-mounted HMG replacements in circumstances in which weight is at a premium.

New rifles in .50″ Browning, $12.7 \times 108$ and even $14.5 \times 114$ have been introduced in many countries in recent years. Most of these are bolt-action weapons but some, such as the Barrett M82, are semi-automatic and one, the Czech LCZ B-30, even offers selective fire. Efficient recoil-reduction techniques make the new weapons much lighter and handier than the old AT rifles, at around 10–16kg. Precision shooting is possible at 1,500m, with the maximum effective range being around 2,000m.

A less extreme approach to long-range sniping is offered by rifles designed around the .338″ Lapua Magnum cartridge ($8.58 \times 71$), such as the Accuracy International bolt-action and the Barrett Model 98A autoloader. These weapons extend the accurate sniping range from about 850m for $7.62 \times 51$ NATO sniping rifles out to 1,400+m. The British Army recently selected the .338 Accuracy International as the L115A1.

US forces have deployed more than one type of .50″ calibre rifle in recent years, particularly those by Barrett and Harris, and at least thirty other nations have also purchased quantities of rifles of this type.

Most of the rifles use standard HMG ammunition, but there are some exceptions. Steyr has developed a specialised IWS 2000 anti-materiel rifle, designed around a plastic-cased 15.2mm round intended to fire a fin-stabilised APFSDS projectile of 5.5mm calibre. This is launched at an extremely high muzzle velocity and is capable of penetrating 40mm of armour at 1,000m. A simpler development with a similar purpose is the South African Mechem NTW 20/14.5 AMR. It is designed around the $20 \times 82$ cartridge used in the Vektor GA-1 automatic cannon. While relatively low-powered for a modern 20mm, it is claimed to penetrate 20mm (AP projectile) or 15mm (SAP) at 'normal battle ranges'. A barrel chambered for the Russian $14.5 \times 114$ cartridge is available when greater effective range is required. The gun is a simple bolt-action weapon weighing 26kg and can be broken down into two sections for easier carrying. Finland has produced the Helenius 20mm APH RK20 using the old ShVAK rimmed cartridge, while Croatia has developed the semi-recoilless RT20 AMR around the $20 \times 110$ HS 404 cartridge; part of the gun gas is ducted backwards, over the gunner's shoulder.

## SILENCED HEAVY RIFLES

ANOTHER TYPE OF SPECIAL-PURPOSE LARGE-CALIBRE weapon is the silenced sniping rifle. Apart from the need to fit a large silencer to the barrel (or preferably design the barrel with an integral silencer) it is also necessary to hold the muzzle velocity down to subsonic speeds of around 320 m/s in order to avoid the revealing 'crack' of a supersonic bullet passing by. Conventional large-calibre machine gun rounds are therefore far too powerful for this purpose.

Perhaps the most famous of the early weapons of this type was the British De Lisle carbine of the Second World War. This fired a standard .45″ ACP pistol ($11.5 \times 23$) round from a bolt-action rifle. It was certainly silent, but the light, round-nosed bullet quickly lost velocity, limiting the maximum range.

The next attempt was an experimental American weapon tested in Vietnam. It was similar in principle to the De Lisle but chambered for a much more effective cartridge, the specially developed .458 × $1\frac{1}{2}$″ Barnes ($11.5 \times 38B$), which was made by shortening the .458″ Winchester Magnum big-game round. The solid bullet was still round-nosed but was twice the weight of the De Lisle's, which in conjunction with its higher muzzle velocity extended its useful range. The gun was long and heavy, however, and was not popular in service.

The idea has been revived in modern weapons such as the Whisper range of rifles. These are chambered for special cartridges based on commercial hunting ammunition, modified to take bullets which are very heavy for their calibre and highly streamlined to retain as much velocity and range as possible. Most of these fit into the small-arms category, but the .458″ (11.6 × 44B), based on a cut-down .458″ Winchester big-game cartridge, and the .500″ (12.7 × 57B), which uses a cut-down and expanded .460″ Weatherby case, qualify for our heavy weapons class. The rifles in which they are used are adapted versions of normal commercial bolt-action hunting weapons, with weights in the region of 5kg.

## POSTSCRIPT

FINALLY, THE US ARMY HAS SELECTED ALLIANT Techsystems to develop a future infantry rifle called the Objective Individual Combat Weapon (OICW).

This is planned to combine 5.56mm and 20mm weapons in a gun no heavier than the current 5.56mm M16 rifle with M203 grenade launcher. By means of extremely sophisticated but highly automated sighting and computing systems, the low-velocity, low-recoil 20mm ammunition can be set to air-burst over a target at a range of up to 1,000 metres, although impact and delay modes are also available. The effect is a claimed 500% improvement in effectiveness over the M16 at 300m. Not surprisingly, the concept has already prompted the development of a fully automatic light cannon, the 25mm Objective Crew Served Weapon (OCSW).

*Cartridges used in sniper rifles (from left to right): .45" pistol round used in De Lisle carbine (11.5 × 23), .458 × 1½" silent sniper (11.5 × 38B), .458" Whisper (11.5 × 44B), .500" Whisper (12.7 × 57B), .50" Browning (12.7 × 99), .338" Lapua (8.58 × 71), .300" Winchester Magnum (7.62 × 67B), 7.62mm NATO (7.62 × 51)*

# *Appendix Two*

## DATA TABLES

THE FOLLOWING TABLES list the key data about the heavy automatic weapons and ammunition described in this book. In addition, information is given about other selected cartridges and weapons for comparison purposes.

### NOTES ON THE TABLES

THE 'COUNTRY OF ORIGIN' ABBREVIATIONS ARE THE usual international motor vehicle letters, except for UK and PRC (China). Both Soviet and Russian equipment are listed as 'SU'. Entries are normally limited to the country of origin or principal production, but may be duplicated where there is major production in other countries.

Cartridge case measurements are taken from individual examples and there may in practice be some variations from those given. Many other loadings of some cartridges have seen service. The loading given is the most typical; additional loadings are given where significant. Some confusion is possible over APDS and APFSDS loadings, concerning whether the projectile weight includes the sabot; published information is frequently vague on this point. An indication is given in the tables by the muzzle energy figure; where this is significantly lower than other loadings of the cartridge, it is likely that the figure concerns the projectile only.

Gun specifications could also change considerably as weapons developed, with variations in weight, barrel length and rate of fire. The rate of fire was also reduced (usually by 10–20%) by synchronisation, and generally varied by around 10% anyway.

Other abbreviations used are as follows:

| | |
|---|---|
| *AA* | anti-aircraft |
| *AAC* | American Armament Corporation |
| *AFV* | armoured fighting vehicle |
| *AGL* | automatic grenade launcher |
| *air* | for aircraft use |
| *AT* | anti-tank |
| *ATR* | anti-tank rifle |
| *bbl* | barrel |
| *CL* | caseless |
| *CTA* | cased telescopic (consumable case) |
| *(e)* | gun uses electrical priming – others are percussion; (?) indicates not known |
| *exp* | experimental use only |
| *GD* | General Dynamics |
| *GE* | General Electric |
| *HS* | Hispano-Suiza |
| *IJA* | Imperial Japanese Army |
| *IJN* | Imperial Japanese Navy |
| *MDHC* | McDonnell Douglas Helicopters (Hughes), now Boeing |
| *Oe* | Oerlikon |
| *Rh* | Rheinmetall |
| *RhB* | Rheinmetall-Borsig |
| *(w)* | gun fitted with water-cooled barrel – all others are air-cooled (NB: gun weight is without water) |

# APPENDIX TWO

## *TABLE 1:* CARTRIDGES USED IN AUTOMATIC WEAPONS 11.35MM – 57MM

| Metric calibre | Rim diam. mm | Body diam. mm | Country of origin/main use | Projectile type/ weight gm | Muzzle velocity m/sec | Muzzle energy joules | Name/Weapons chambered in |
|---|---|---|---|---|---|---|---|
| 11.35 × 62 | 16.0 | 16.0 | DK | 20 | 850 | 7,200 | 11.35mm Madsen aircraft gun (Argentina) |
| 12.7 × 81 | 18.3 | 18.4 | UK | SAP/37.6 | 753 | 10,700 | .5″ Vickers V/580: AA/AFV |
| 12.7 × 81SR | 19.7 | 18.4 | UK/I/J | 36.7 | 760 | 10,600 | .5″ Vickers V/565: 12.7mm Breda-Safat, Scotti, IJA 12.7mm Type 1 (Ho-103) aircraft guns |
| 12.7 × 99 | 20.3 | 20.3 | USA | AP/46 | 880 | 17,800 | .50″ Browning M2, M3, M85, GAU-19/A, CIS 50MG, |
| " M23 | | | | I/32 | 1,067 | 18,200 | Barrett, LCZ and other rifles |
| " SLAP | | | | APDS/27 | 1,215 | 19,900 | (APDS (SLAP) penetrates 25mm/1,000m) |
| 12.7 × 108 | 21.8 | 21.8 | SU/PRC | API/52 | 860 | 19,200 | DShK 38/46, UB, NSV, YakB-12.7, PRC Type 77 & W-85; |
| " | | | | APDS/22.5 | 1,150 | 14,900 | Sholoklov ATR, Gepard M1, LCZ & OSV-96 rifles |
| " duplex | | | | 30+31 | 750 | 17,200 | |
| 13 × 64B | 17.1 | 17.1 | D/J | HET/34 | 750 | 9,600 | Rheinmetall-Borsig MG 131 (electric), IJN 13mm Type 2 |
| | | | | AP/38.5 | 710 | 9,700 | aircraft (percussion) |
| 13.2 × 99 | 20.2 | 20.2 | F/I/J | 52 | 790 | 16,200 | Hotchkiss, Breda M31, IJN 13mm Type 3 + Type 93. (93 and 96mm case lengths also used) |
| 14.5 × 114 | 26.9 | 26.9 | SU/PRC | AP/64 | 1,000 | 32,000 | KPV (PRC Type 75): PTRD, PTRS ATRs, Gepard M3 and Mechem NTW-14.5 rifles |
| 15 × 96 | 25.2 | 25.1 | D | HET/57 | 960 | 26,300 | Mauser MG151 aircraft (percussion and electric versions |
| | | | | APT/72 | 850 | 26,000 | both used). |
| | | | | APCR/52 | 1,030 | 27,600 | APCR = *Hartkernmunition* |
| 15 × 104 | 24.9 | 24.8 | CZ/UK | 75 | 880 | 29,000 | ZB vz/60 (BESA) AFV/AA: MPzB M41 ATR. 101mm case length used in German service. |
| 20 × 70RB | 20.2 | 21.9 | D | AP/130 | 490 | 15,600 | Becker aircraft, early Oerlikon F |
| 20 × 72RB | 19.0 | 21.9 | CH/J | HE/128 | 550–600 | 19–23,000 | Oerlikon FF, Japanese Navy Type 99–1, Oerlikon SSG ATR (550 m/s) |
| 20 × 80RB | 19.0 | 22.0 | D | HE/134 | 600 | 24,100 | MG-FF aircraft |
| | | | | HEI/115 | 585 | 19,700 | MG-FFM aircraft |
| | | | | HE/92 | 700 | 22,500 | " *M-Geschoss* |

| Metric calibre | Rim diam. mm | Body diam. mm | Country of origin/main use | Projectile type/ weight gm | Muzzle velocity m/sec | Muzzle energy joules | Name/Weapons chambered in |
|---|---|---|---|---|---|---|---|
| 20 × 82 | 25.2 | 25.2 | D | HE/115 | 710 | 29,000 | Mauser MG 151/20 (electric or percussion) |
| | | | | HE/92 | 800 | 29,400 | " *M-Geschoss* (92g) |
| | | | SA | HE/111 | 720 | 28,800 | Vektor GA-1, Mechem NTW-20 rifle (SA) |
| 20 × 94 | 24.9 | 25.0 | J | HEI/79 | 730 | 21,000 | IJA 20mm Type 1 (Ho-5) aircraft |
| | | | | APT/120 | 700 | 29,400 | (these are final loadings; earlier ones were c. 820 m/s, 33,300 j) |
| 20 × 99R | 25.2 | 21.8 | SU | HE/97 | 860 | 35,900 | ShVAK, B-20 aircraft (+ subcalibre training), Helenius rifle |
| 20 × 101RB | 19.0 | 21.9 | CH/J | HE/127 | 675 | 28,900 | Oerlikon L(675 m/s)/FFL (100mm case length); |
| | | | | HE/128 | 750 | 36,000 | IJN Type 99-2 (101mm) |
| 20 × 102 | 29.5 | 29.1 | USA | HE/101 | 1,030 | 53,600 | M39, M61 (Vulcan), M197, GIAT M 621, Ford Tigerclaws, |
| | | | | APDS/100 | 1,100 | 60,500 | (APDS is M149 Phalanx round) (M50 series ammunition) |
| 20 × 105B | 25.0 | 25.0 | D | AP/140 | 730 | 37,300 | Solothurn (Short): S18-100 ATR & S18-350 aircraft, Lb/MG 204 (early) |
| 20 × 105 | 25 | 26.2 | D | HE/134 | 750 | 37,700 | MG 204 aircraft (late) |
| 20 × 110RB | 21.9 | 24.9 | CH/UK/ USA | HE/122 | 830 | 42,000 | Oerlikon FFS + SS series, Polsten AA, (SSG-36 ATR-750m/s) |
| 20 × 110 | 24.8 | 24.8 | F/UK/USA | HE/130 | 880 | 50,300 | HS404/804; AN/M2+M3 (US), m/45+49 (S), M1955 (YU), |
| | | | | " | 850 | 46,900 | G 360 (IS) RT20 rifle (Croatia). 850 m/s = UK Mark V (short barrel) |
| | | | | HE/102 | 945 | 45,500 | 945 m/s = US M24 (electric primed) |
| 20 × 110 | 29.5 | 29.3 | USA | 110 | 1010 | 56,100 | Mark 11 + Mark 12 aircraft. (Mk 100 USN series ammunition) |
| 20 × 113 | 28.0 | 28.0 | SF | 156 | ? | ? | 20mm Lahti L34 naval (exp. belted version also) |
| 20 × 120 | 28.9 | 29.0 | DK | AP/154 | 780 | 46,800 | 20mm Madsen AA/AT/aircraft |
| | | | | HE/126–112 | 840–890 | 44,400 | |
| 20 × 125 | 28.5 | 28.7 | J | AP/162 | 790 | 50,500 | IJA 20mm Type 97 AT rifle |
| | | | | HEI/127 | 820 | 42,700 | IJA 20mm Ho-1, Ho-3 aircraft |
| 20 × 128 | 32.0 | 32.3 | CH | HE/120 | 1,050 | 66,100 | Oerlikon KAA, KAB (add 50m/s for KAB) |
| | | | | APCR/102 | 1,300 | 86,200 | (APCR (e) is for Meroka CIWS) |

| Metric calibre | Rim diam. mm | Body diam. mm | Country of origin/main use | Projectile type/ weight gm | Muzzle velocity m/sec | Muzzle energy joules | Name/Weapons chambered in |
|---|---|---|---|---|---|---|---|
| 20 × 138B | 27.0 | 27.0 | D/I | HE/119<br>AP/147<br><br>AP/101<br>HE/134 | 900<br>795<br><br>975<br>950 | 47,000<br>46,500<br><br>48,000<br>60,500 | Solothurn (Long): FlaK 30+38 AA, KwK 30+38 AFV, MG C/30 L air, Breda M 35, Scotti and Lahti L40 AA, plus S18-1000/1100 and Lahti ATRs 134g loading was for MG C/30 L |
| 20 × 139 FMK | 28.5 | 28.5 | CH | HE/131<br><br>AP/147 | 1,010<br><br>930 | 66,800<br><br>63,800 | WW2 FMK aircraft and WW2+ post-war Flab Kan 38 AA. (Rim 2.6mm thick) |
| 20 × 139 | 28.5 | 28.5 | CH/D/F | HE/120<br>APDS/108 | 1,100<br>1,250 | 72,600<br>84,400 | HS 820/Oerlikon KAD (US M139), Rheinmetall Rh 202, GIAT M 693, Mauser MK20, HS 827 exp. (Rim 3.5mm thick) |
| 20 × 142 | 33.4 | 33.5 | J | HET/132 | 950 | 59,600 | IJA 20mm Type 98 AA |
| 20 × 145R | 29.5 | 25.4 | S | AP/145 | 815 | 48,200 | 20mm Bofors m/40 AA/AT (+ sub-calibre training) |
| 23 × 115 | 27.0 | 27.0 | SU/PRC | 200<br>175 | 690<br>740 | 47,600<br>47,900 | 23mm NS/NR 23 (690 m/s loading) 23mm AM: GSh23/6-23, Norinco Type 2 (740 m/s) |
| 23 × 152B VYa | 33.4 | 33.2 | SU | API/200 | 880 | 77,400 | aircraft gun (brass case) (+ sub-calibre training) |
| 23 × 152B ZU | 33.3 | 33.2 | SU/PRC | HEI/185 | 970 | 87,000 | AA gun+2A14 AFV (steel case) |
| 23 × 260 | 15.0 | 30.0 | SU | HEI/174 | 885 | 68,100 | R-23 aircraft (post-war frontloading revolver) |
| 24 × 138 | 31.4 | 32.0 | CH | AP/225 | 900 | 91,000 | Pzw.Kan 38 AFV and TB.41 ATR |
| 25 × 87R | 31.5 | 28.1 | UK/I/S | HE/200 | 470 | 22,100 | Vickers-Terni (Akan m/22) |
| 25 × 87 | 30.2 | 30.2 | I | HE/200 | 440 | 19,400 | FIAT/Revelli Modello 1917 |
| 25 × 137 | 38.0 | 38.2 | CH/USA | HE/180<br>APDS/128<br>FAPDS/150<br>APFSDS/ 140 | 1,100<br>1,360<br>1,335<br>1,370 | 109,000<br>118,000<br>134,000<br>131,000 | Oerlikon KBA, MDHC 242, Mauser E, GE GAU-12/U GE 225, Aden 25, GIAT 25 M 811 APDS penetrates 30mm/1,000m/60° APFSDS penetrates 30mm/1,400m/60° |
| 25 × 163 | 42.6 | 42.7 | F/J | HE/250<br>AP/300 | 900<br>875 | 101,000<br>115,000 | Hotchkiss Mle 1938 AA, IJN Type 96 AA |
| 25 × 184 | 38.0 | 38.2 | CH | HE/250<br>FAPDS/230<br>APDS/150 | 1,160<br>1,160<br>1,400 | 168,000<br>155,000<br>147,000 | Oerlikon KBB/KBD (181mm case length also used, depending on projectile type) |

| Metric calibre | Rim diam. mm | Body diam. mm | Country of origin/main use | Projectile type/ weight gm | Muzzle velocity m/sec | Muzzle energy joules | Name/Weapons chambered in |
|---|---|---|---|---|---|---|---|
| 25 × 205R | 42.0 | 37.0 | S | HE/250 | 850 | 90,300 | Bofors m/32 AA |
| 25 × 218R | 40.0 | 34.7 | SU | HE/280 | 900 | 113,000 | Soviet M1940 naval AA |
| 25 × 218 | 34.8 | 34.7 | SU/PRC | HE/288 | 900 | 117,000 | 2-M3, 2-M8 naval AA |
| 27 × 145B | 34.0 | 33.1 | D/UK/I | HE/260 | 1,025 | 137,000 | Mauser BK 27 |
| 28 × 199SR | 43.5 | 41.4 | USA | HE/416 | 823 | 141,000 | 1.1″ USN naval AA |
| 30 × 29B | 31.5 | 31.5 | SU | HE/275 | 185 | 4,700 | AGS-17, AG-17, AGS-30 AGLs |
| 30 × 86B | 33.2 | 32.3 | UK | HE/273 | 604 | 49,800 | Aden 3M (Low Velocity) |
| 30 × 90RB | 24.9 | 32.3 | D | HE/330 | 505 | 42,100 | Rheinmetall-Borsig MK 108 aircraft (*M-Geschoss*) |
| | | | | HEI/470 | 440 | 45,500 | 470g loading adopted but use unconfirmed |
| 30 × 92RB | 27.8 | 33.0 | J | HE/264 | 710 | 66,500 | IJN 30mm Type 2 aircraft |
| 30 × 97B | 33.2 | 32.0 | F | HE/296 | 670 | 66,400 | DEFA 30M541 aircraft |
| 30 × 113B | 33.3 | 32.3 | UK/F/USA | AP/275 | 790 | 85,800 | (brass or steel case) 30mm |
| | | | | HEI/247 | 810 | 81,000 | Aden/DEFA M 552/3/4 GIAT 30M781, Vektor 55C5 and XC-30 aircraft |
| | | | | HEI/237 | 800 | 75,800 | (alloy case) MDHC M230, ASP-30, GE M188, |
| 30 × 114 | 37.5 | 38.0 | J | HE/235 | 700 | 57,600 | IJA 30mm Ho-155 aircraft |
| 30 × 122 | 40.0 | 41.0 | J | HE/345 | 710 | 87,000 | IJN 30mm Type 5 aircraft |
| 30 × 155B | 39.9 | 39.9 | SU/PRC | HE/410 | 780 | 125,000 | NR-30 aircraft, Norinco Type 1 |
| 30 × 165 | 40.0 | 40.0 | SU | HE/390 | 860 | 144,000 | AO18 cartridge in three versions: electric primed for |
| | | | | HE/390 | 900 | 158,000 | GSh aircraft (860–890 m/s) and naval (900 m/s), percussion |
| | | | | HE/390 | 960 | 180,000 | for 2A42, 2A72 and 2A38M |
| | | | | APDS/304 | 1,120 | 191,000 | (960 m/s and 1,120 m/s) |
| 30 × 170 | 42.8 | 43.0 | CH/UK | HE/420 | 1,000 | 210,000 | HS 831A (brass case) = 420g, |
| | | | | HE/360 | 1,080 | 210,000 | HS 831L/Oe KCB (steel case) = 360g |
| | | | | APDS/300 | 1,175 | 207,000 | Rarden L21 AFV (brass case) (APDS loading) |
| 30 × 173 | 44.0 | 43.6 | CH/USA/D | HE/360 | 1,080 | 210,000 | (steel case) Oerlikon KCA aircraft (e) |
| | | | | API/425 | 988 | 207,000 | (alloy case)GE GAU-8/A airborne |
| | | | | FMPDS/234 | 1,150 | 155,000 | AT (425g) and Goalkeeper naval AM (234g), GAU-13/A, MDHC Bushmaster II AFV |

| Metric calibre | Rim diam. mm | Body diam. mm | Country of origin/main use | Projectile type/ weight gm | Muzzle velocity m/sec | Muzzle energy joules | Name/Weapons chambered in |
|---|---|---|---|---|---|---|---|
| 30 × 173 (continued) | | | | HEI/360 | 1,040 | 195,000 | Mauser MK 30 (HEI) |
| | | | | FAPDS/202 | 1,300 | 171,000 | FAPDS and APDS for Mauser |
| | | | | APDS/225 | 1,225 | 168,800 | MK30 |
| 30 × 184B | 37.8 | 37.9 | D | HE/447 | 800 | 143,000 | Rheinmetall-Borsig MK 101 (percussion) + MK 103 |
| | | | | AP(HE)/500 | 725 | 131,500 | (electric) + FlaK 38. APCR=*Hartkernmunition* |
| | | | | APCR/355 | 960 | 163,600 | (M) = *M-Geschoss*; MK 103 |
| | | | | HE(M)/330 | 920 | 139,700 | reduced to 860 m/s, 122,000 j |
| 30 × 210 | 47.7 | 47.7 | D/CZ | HE-T/435 | 1,000 | 217,500 | Czech M53 AA (Krieghoff MK 303 exp.) |
| 30 × 210B | 45.9 | 45.9 | SU/YU | AP-T/350 | 1,050 | 193,000 | NN-30 naval+Romanian army AA, Zastava M86/89 |
| 34 × 239 | 47.8 | 47.8 | CH | HE/720 | 900 | 292,000 | Flab Kan 38 WW2+post-war AA |
| | | | | AP/720 | 930 | 311,000 | |
| 35 × 228 | 54.5 | 55.1 | CH | HE/550 | 1,180 | 383,000 | Oerlikon KD Series and 35/1000, |
| | | | | APDS/294 | 1,385 | 282,000 | ARES Talon, Vektor GA-35, |
| | | | | AHEAD/ 750 | 1,050 | 413,000 | Rheinmetall Rh503/Bushmaster III, |
| | | | | FAPDS/375 | 1,440 | 389,000 | EMAK 35 AFV |
| | | | | HET/610 | 1,150 | 403,000 | HET and APFSDS intended for Rh |
| | | | | APFSDS/ 446 | 1,400 | 437,000 | 503/Bushmaster III |
| 37 × 69R | 44.0 | 39.5 | UK | HE/450 | 365 | 30,000 | Vickers 1 pdr Mk III/V aircraft |
| 37 × 94R | 44.1 | 39.7 | F | HE/555 | 367 | 37,400 | Hotchkiss manual rotary and Maxim 'Pom-pom', Puteaux |
| | | | +many others | HE/450 | 400 | 36,000 | m1918 |
| | | | | API/390 | 600 | 70,200 | API loading = French 1935 tank gun round |
| 37 × 101SR | 42.9 | 39.9 | D | 465 | ? | ? | 3.7cm Sockelflak WW1 AA |
| 37 × 112R | 47.0 | 43.5 | J | HE/475 | 570 | 77,200 | IJA 37mm Ho-203 aircraft |
| 37 × 123R | 47.6 | 43.7 | UK | HE/680 | 365–395 | 45– 53,000 | WW1 1½ pdr naval (also first aircraft trials) |
| 37 × 137R | 44.7 | 40.6 | USA | HE/476 | 640 | 97,500 | pre-WW1 naval 'heavy one-pounder'/Maxim 1¼ pdr |
| 37 × 144 | 44.0 | 44.0 | J | HE/475 | 710 | 120,000 | IJA 37mm Ho-204 aircraft |
| 37 × 145R | 45.0 | 40.6 | USA/SU | HE/608 | 610 | 113,000 | M4 + M10 aircraft |
| | | | | AP/753 | 556 | 116,000 | |

| Metric calibre | Rim diam. mm | Body diam. mm | Country of origin/main use | Projectile type/ weight gm | Muzzle velocity m/sec | Muzzle energy joules | Name/Weapons chambered in |
|---|---|---|---|---|---|---|---|
| 37 × 155 | 46.0 | 45.8 | SU/PRC | HE/735 | 690 | 175,000 | N-37 aircraft |
| 37 × 190 | 46.5 | 47.0 | UK | HE/680 | 610 | 126,000 | 1¹/₂ pdr COW gun aircraft/AA |
| 37 × 195 | 53.3 | 53.3 | SU | AP/735 | 900 | 298,000 | NS-37 aircraft |
| 37 × 223SR | 51.1 | 50.3 | USA | M54 HE/608 | 800 | 195,000 | M1 AA; M9 aircraft |
| | | | | M59 AP/870 | 625 | 170,000 | M1 (M9 loaded to 853 m/s, 317,000 joules) |
| | | | | M80 AP/753 | 930 | 326,000 | M9 only |
| 37 × 230SR | 51.5 | 50.0 | I | HE/799 | 800 | 256,000 | Breda M39 AA |
| 37 × 240 | 54 | 54 | PRC | HE/741 | 1,000 | 370,000 | Type 76 naval AA |
| 37 × 249R | 51.4 | 45.9 | D | HE(M)/? | 925 | ? | RhB FlaK M 42 WW2 naval AA. (M) = M-Geschoss |
| | | | | HE/? | 850 | ? | (cartridge also used in KwK AFV/PaK 36 AT gun; |
| | | | | AP/? | 815 | ? | see Table 2 for loadings) |
| 37 × 250R | 51.9 | 45.8 | SU/PRC | HE/732 | 880 | 283,000 | Model 1939 AA, PRC Type 55 |
| 37 × 263B | 46.8 | 45.9 | D | HE/640 | 820 | 215,000 | Rheinmetall-Borsig FlaK |
| | | | | APT/685 | 780 | 208,000 | 18/36/37/43, BK 3.7 |
| | | | | APCR/380 | 1,170 | 260,000 | APCR is BK 3.7 Hartkern loading |
| 40mm CL | - | - | J | HE/585 | 246 | 17,700 | IJA 40mm Ho-301 caseless aircraft |
| 40 × 53SR | 43.6 | 41.3 | USA | HE/245 | 240 | 7,050 | 40mm HV for AGLs: MDHC M129, Mark 19, CIS 40–AGL, LAG-40, Vektor Striker, HK GMG. |
| 40 × 158R | 48.1 | 43.9 | UK | HE/900 | 620 | 173,000 | –Vickers 2 pdr Pom-pom AA |
| | | | | HE/760 | 730 | 203,000 | –Vickers High Velocity AA |
| | | | | AP/1,130 | 615 | 214,000 | –Vickers Class S aircraft |
| | | | | AP/1,360 | 570 | 221,000 | –Vickers Class S MkVI AP shot |
| 40 × 311R | 61.8 | 55.8 | S/UK/USA | HE/955 | 850 | 345,000 | Bofors L56/L60 AA |
| 40 × 364R | 65.0 | 57.9 | S/I | HE/870 | 1,030 | 461,000 | Bofors L70 AA/AFV, OtoBreda 40L70N |
| | | | | APFSDS/ 200 | 1,475 | 218,000 | APFSDS penetrates 100+mm at 1,000m |
| 45 × 386SR | 83 | 79 | SU | HE/1,500 | 900 | 607,000 | Naval AA |
| 50 × 346B | 68 | 68 | D | HE/2,200 | 840 | 776,000 | Rheinmetall-Borsig 5cm FlaK 41 AA |
| 50 × 419R | 78.4 | 70.4 | D | AP/2,060 | 835 | 718,000 | RhB 5cm BK 5; Mauser MK 214A exp. |
| | | | | AP/1,540 | 920 | 652,000 | PaK 38 AT and KwK L60 AFV guns |
| | | | | APCR/1,250 | 1,200 | 900,000 | APCR is Hartkern loading |
| | | | | HE/1,100 | 960 | 507,000 | HE is M-Geschoss for BK 5 and MK 214A |

| Metric calibre | Rim diam. mm | Body diam. mm | Country of origin/main use | Projectile type/ weight gm | Muzzle velocity m/sec | Muzzle energy joules | Name/Weapons chambered in |
|---|---|---|---|---|---|---|---|
| 57 × 121R | 68.4 | 60.8 | J | HE/1,500 | 495 | 184,000 | IJA 57mm Ho-401 aircraft |
| 57 × 230R | 79.7 | 73.0 | S | AP/2,450 | 686 | 576,000 | 57mm Bofors m/47 airborne |
| | | | | HE/2,230 | 744 | 617,000 | anti-ship |
| 57 × 347SR | 95.7 | 91.0 | SU/PRC | HE/2,800 | 1,000 | 1,400K | S60 AA, ZIF-31+72 |
| 57 × 438R | 93.0 | 83.0 | S | HE/2,400 | 1,020 | 1,250K | 57mm Bofors m/54 army and naval SAK-57 AA |
| | | | | HCER/2,500 | 950 | 1,142K | high capacity extended range |
| 57 × 441R | 90.0 | 82.0 | UK | AP/3,170 | 790 | 989,000 | Molins 6 pdr 7 cwt aircraft + naval (+AFV and AT) |

## TABLE 2: MISCELLANEOUS MILITARY CARTRIDGES

This list contains information about selected additional cartridges in the following categories:
- new developments which are not yet in service;
- used in HMGs and cannon which saw little or no service;
- used in manually cranked machine guns;
- used in heavy shoulder-fired weapons; principally anti-tank or other heavy rifles;
- used in the principal rifle-calibre machine guns;
- some service cartridges from well-known manually loaded cannon for comparative and identification purposes.

| Metric calibre | Rim diam. mm | Body diam. mm | Country of origin/main use | Projectile type/ weight gm | Muzzle velocity m/sec | Muzzle energy joules | Name/Weapons chambered in |
|---|---|---|---|---|---|---|---|
| **CARTRIDGES FOR WEAPONS CURRENTLY UNDER DEVELOPMENT** | | | | | | | |
| 25 × 53B | 27 | 26.5 | USA | HE/132 | 425 | 11,900 | OCSW Army system (early type) |
| 30 × 150B | 34.7 | 33.9 | F | HE/275 | 1,025 | 144,000 | GIAT 30M791 aircraft |
| 30 × 280 | ? | ? | D | 300 | 1,200 | 200,000 | Mauser RMK 30 cased telescopic recoilless |
| 40 × 74.5 | ? | ? | ROM | HE/290 | 220 | 7,020 | RATMIL AGL |
| 40 × 255 | 65 | 65 | UK/F | HE/950 | 1,000+ | 475,000+ | CTA 2000 AFV |
| | | | | APFSDS/ 250 | 1,600+ | 320,000+ | APFSDS total projectile weight = 490 g |
| 45 × 305 | 70 | 70 | US/F/UK | HE/1,095 | ? | ? | COMVAT AFV (also European 45 M 911) |
| | | | | APFSDS/ 421 | 1,600+ | 539,000+ | APFSDS total projectile weight = 754 g |
| 50 × 330 | 54.5 | 55.1 | D | APDS/440 | 1,600 | 563,000 | Rh 503/ Bushmaster III AFV 'Supershot', also available for EMAK-35 |

| Metric calibre | Rim diam. mm | Body diam. mm | Country of origin/main use | Projectile type/ weight gm | Muzzle velocity m/sec | Muzzle energy joules | Name/Weapons chambered in |
|---|---|---|---|---|---|---|---|
| **EXPERIMENTAL/LIMITED SERVICE MACHINE GUN AND CANNON CARTRIDGES** | | | | | | | |
| 11 × 59R | 16.9 | 13.8 | F | 17.51 | 610 | 3,250 | 11mm Gras-Vickers WWI aircraft |
| 12.7 × 81 BSA | 18.3 | 18.4 | UK | 37.4 | 785 | 11,500 | .5″ BSA Mod 24 inter-war exp. aircraft gun |
| 12.7 × 88 | 25.0 | 25.0 | USA | 46 | 900 | 18,600 | ARES TARG exp. post-war (plastic telescoped case) |
| 12.7 × 108R | 25.2 | 21.8 | SU | 48 | 810 | 15,700 | 12.7mm ShVAK inter-war air gun |
| 12.7 × 110SR | 25.0 | 24.0 | UK | 63.6 | 716 | 16,300 | .50″ Colt-Kynoch (North) exp HMG, 1901+ |
| 12.7 × 114 | 29.5 | 29.2 | USA | API/32.4 API/42.8 | 1,340 1,200 | 29,100 30,800 | .50/60″: T17 series WW2 exp. aircraft gun |
| 12.7 × 120SR | 22.1 | 20.9 | UK/J | 45 | 927 | 19,300 | .5″ Vickers High Velocity V690 (Class D) inter-war AA |
| 12.7 × 127 | – | 28.0 | USA | 42 | 975 | 20,000 | .50″ Tround post-war exp. (plastic triangular case) |
| 13 × 92B | 19.0 | 21.2 | D | 32 | 1,000 | 16,000 | MG 215 aircraft gun, 1944 |
| 15 × 115 | 24.7 | 24.7 | B | 70 APDS/48 | 1,050 1,340 | 38,600 43,100 | FN BRG-15 post-war exp. AFV (first pattern) |
| 15 × 83B | 19.0 | 21.2 | D | 57 | 870 | 21,600 | MG 215/15 aircraft gun, 1944 |
| 15.2 × 114 | 29.5 | 29.2 | USA | AP/76.5 I/45.1 | 1,097 1,250 | 46,000 35,500 | .60″: WW2 T17 series exp. aircraft guns (originally developed for experimental ATR) |
| 15.5 × 106 | 26.9 | 26.9 | B | 70 | 1,050 | 38,600 | FN BRG-15 post-war exp. AFV (final pattern) |
| 16.8 × 149SR | 29.1 | 26.6 | UK | 85 | 1,000 | 42,500 | .661″ Vickers inter-war exp. naval AA |
| 20 × 70RB (E) | 21.0 | 23.0 | D | ? | 670 | ? | Erhardt WW1 aircraft cannon |
| 20 × 135 | 32.0 | 32.0 | D | 112 | 1,050 | 61,700 | WW2 Mauser MG 213C exp. aircraft |
| 23 × 106 | 29.0 | 29.0 | DK | HE/175 | 730 | 46,600 | inter-war 23mm Madsen exp. aircraft |
| 23 × 122 | 34.5 | 34.5 | F | 200 | 900 | 81,000 | HS 406/407 WW2 exp. aircraft |
| 23 × 133 | 31.5 | 32.5 | CH | HE/160 APDS/60 | 1,050 1,300 | 88,200 50,700 | Hispano-Suiza HS 827 post-war exp. AFV gun APDS penetrates 27mm/45°/1,000m |
| 23 × 139SR | 30.9 | 29.3 | USA | ? | 823 | ? | .90″ for T1-4 series inter-war exp aircraft |

| Metric calibre | Rim diam. mm | Body diam. mm | Country of origin/main use | Projectile type/ weight gm | Muzzle velocity m/sec | Muzzle energy joules | Name/Weapons chambered in |
|---|---|---|---|---|---|---|---|
| 25 × 152 | 40.3 | 40.3 | USA | 194 | 1,200 | 140,000 | cased telescopic for GAU-7/A post-war exp aircraft |
| 30 × 85B | 31.7 | 32.0 | D | HE/330 | 530 | 46,300 | Mauser MK 213/30 WW2 exp. aircraft |
| 30 × 100B | 34.5 | 32.5 | USA | ? | 670 | ? | XM140 WECOM post-war exp. heli |
| 30 × 126B | 33.3 | 32.3 | USA | 250 | 850 | 90,300 | T239 round for T182 post-war exp aircraft (revolver) |
| 30 × 136 (B) | 39.5 | 39.5 | CH | 225 | 1,050 | 124,000 | HS 825 post-war exp aircraft (belted version later) |
| 30 × 138 | 42.7 | 42.7 | CH | HE/230 APDS/110 | 1,150 1,350 | 152,000 100,000 | Hispano-Suiza HS 836 postwar exp AFV |
| 37 × 87R | 44.0 | 39.5 | USA | HE/500 | 380 | 36,100 | AAC Type M inter-war exp aircraft |
| 37 × ? | ? | ? | USA | HE/500 | 823 | 169,300 | AAC Type F inter-war exp aircraft |
| 37 × 218R | 60.0 | 54.0 | F | HE/831 | 825 | 283,000 | Hotchkiss M1935 inter-war naval AA (trials use) |
| 37 × ? | ? | ? | F | ? | 800 | ? | Schneider M1930 inter-war army AA |
| 45 × 185 | 53.3 | 53.3 | SU | HE/1,065 | 850 | 385,000 | NS-45 WW2 exp. aircraft (trials use) |
| 55 × 175RB | 45.8 | 59.3 | D | HE/1,485 | 600 | 267,000 | RhB MK112 WW2 exp. aircraft (M-Geschoss) |
| 55 × 450B | 75.0 | 78.2 | D | HE/2,030 | 1,050 | 1,119K | RhB WW2 FlaK 58 + MK 114 exp. aircraft |
| 57 × 160RB | 61 | 64 | SU | HE/2,000 | 600 | 360,000 | N-57 post-war exp. aircraft (OKB-16-57) (dimensions approx) |
| 57 × 514R | 89.5 | 82.0 | UK | HE/2,720 | 945 | 1,215K | 6 pdr 6 cwt WW2 exp. AA |
| 57 × ? | ? | ? | SU | AP/2,780 | 980 | 1,335K | OKB-15–57 WW2 exp. airborne AT |

**MANUALLY OPERATED REPEATING MACHINE GUN AND CANNON CARTRIDGES**

| | | | | | | | |
|---|---|---|---|---|---|---|---|
| 16.5 × 97R | 24.3 | 20.5 | USA | lead/92 | ? | ? | 19th century .65″ Gatling naval |
| 25 × 94R | 31.1 | 27.8 | S | iron/steel/206 | 470 | 22,750 | 1″ Nordenfelt 4-bbl 19th century naval |
| 47 × 139R | 60.0 | 55.0 | F | HE/1,075 | 425 | 97,000 | 19th century Hotchkiss rotary |
| 53 × c.180R | 64 | 58 | F | HE/1,630 | 450 | 165,000 | 19th century Hotchkiss rotary |

**CARTRIDGES FOR SHOULDER-FIRED HEAVY WEAPONS: ANTI-TANK RIFLES, SNIPER RIFLES AND GRENADE LAUNCHERS**

| | | | | | | | |
|---|---|---|---|---|---|---|---|
| 7.62 × 67B | 13.5 | 13.0 | USA | 11.7 | 900 | 4,740 | .300″ Winchester Magnum: current sniper round |
| 7.92 × 94 | 20.9 | 21.1 | D | 14.3 | 1,210 | 10,500 | WW2 Panzerbüsche: PzB38/39, M.SS41 ATR |

| Metric calibre | Rim diam. mm | Body diam. mm | Country of origin/main use | Projectile type/ weight gm | Muzzle velocity m/sec | Muzzle energy joules | Name/Weapons chambered in |
|---|---|---|---|---|---|---|---|
| 7.92 × 107 | 16.4 | 16.5 | P | 12.8 | 1,220 | 9,500 | WW2 Maroszek: Kb Ur wz 35 ATR |
| 8.58 × 71 | 15.0 | 15.0 | SF | 16.2 | 900 | 6,560 | .338″ Lapua Magnum: current sniper round |
| 11.5 × 23 | 12.0 | 12.0 | UK | 14.9 | 260 | 500 | .45″ ACP used in WW2 De Lisle silent carbine |
| 11.5 × 38B | 13.3 | 12.9 | USA | 32.4 | 320 | 1,700 | .458 × 1$^{1}/_{2}$″ used in post-war silent sniping rifle |
| 11.5 × 44B | 13.3 | 12.9 | USA | 39 | 320 | 2,000 | .458″ Whisper silent sniping rifle (current) |
| 12.7 × 57B | 14.6 | 14.7 | USA | 58 | 320 | 3,000 | .500″ Whisper silent sniping rifle (current) |
| 13 × 92SR | 23.1 | 20.9 | D | AP/52 | 770 | 15,400 | Mauser M1918 ATR (+ MG TuF exp. HMG) |
| 13.9 × 99B | 20.3 | 20.4 | UK | AP/60 | 747 | 16,700 | WW2 Boys .55″ ATR; W Mk I loading |
|  |  |  |  | AP/47.6 | 884 | 18,600 | WW2 Boys .55″ ATR; W Mk II loading |
| 15.2 × 169 | 25.7 | 25.7 | A | APFSDS/20 | 1,450 | 21,000 | Steyr IWS 2000 (composite case) (under development) N.B. sabot weighs 15g; total projectile. wt 35g |
| 20 × 180R | 47.9 | 42.6 | S | AP/108 | 950 | 48,700 | Carl Gustav Model 1942 recoilless ATR |
| 40 × 46SR | 43.6 | 41.3 | USA | HE/170 | 76 | 490 | current low-velocity grenade launcher |
| **RIFLE CALIBRE MACHINE GUN CARTRIDGES** | | | | | | | |
| 5.45 × 39 | 10.0 | 10.0 | USSR | 3.44 | 900 | 1,390 | 5.45mm Russian: current assault rifle/LMG |
| 5.56 × 45 | 9.5 | 9.5 | USA/NATO | 3.56 | 975 | 1,690 | 5.56mm NATO: current assault rifle/LMG |
|  |  |  |  | 3.95 | 930 | 1,710 | 3.56g loading is US M193; 3.95 g is NATO SS109 |
| 6.5 × 50SR | 12.1 | 11.4 | J | 8.94 | 762 | 2,590 | 6.5mm Arisaka: WW1/2 |
| 6.5 × 52 | 11.35 | 11.30 | I | 10.5 | 700 | 2,570 | 6.5mm Mannlicher Carcano: WW1/2 |
| 7.62 × 39 | 11.3 | 11.2 | USSR | 7.97 | 710 | 2,010 | 7.62mm M1943 (Kalashnikov): post-war |
| 7.62 × 51 | 11.9 | 11.8 | USA/NATO | 9.33 | 823 | 3,160 | 7.62mm NATO: current GPMG |
| 7.62 × 54R | 14.4 | 12.3 | USSR | 11.8 | 818 | 3,950 | 7.62mm Russian: late 19th century–current MG/sniper |
|  |  |  |  | 9.7 | 870 | 3,670 |  |

| Metric calibre | Rim diam. mm | Body diam. mm | Country of origin/main use | Projectile type/ weight gm | Muzzle velocity m/sec | Muzzle energy joules | Name/Weapons chambered in |
|---|---|---|---|---|---|---|---|
| 7.62 × 63 | 12.0 | 12.0 | USA | 9.85 | 837 | 3,450 | .30–06 Springfield: WW1–mid 20th century |
| 7.7 × 56R | 13.5 | 11.5 | UK | 13.9 | 610 | 2,590 | .303″ British: late 19th–mid 20th century |
| | | | | 11.27 | 744 | 3,120 | 610 m/s loading = Mk 2 ball, 744 m/s = Mk 7 ball, |
| | | | | 11.27 | 777 | 3,400 | 777 m/s = Mk 8 boat-tailed ball for Vickers MG |
| 7.92 × 57 | 11.9 | 11.9 | D | 10.00 | 854 | 3,620 | 7.9mm Mauser: late 19th–mid-20th century (velocities |
| | | | | 11.53 | 837 | 4,040 | varied with loading and barrel length. 10.0g WW2 'v' |
| | | | | 12.83 | 808 | 4,190 | aircraft loading 905 m/s) |
| 8 × 50R | 16.0 | 13.6 | F | 12.96 | 725 | 3,410 | 8mm Lebel: late 19th century–WW2 |

**MANUALLY LOADED SINGLE-SHOT CANNON CARTRIDGES**

| Metric calibre | Rim diam. mm | Body diam. mm | Country of origin/main use | Projectile type/ weight gm | Muzzle velocity m/sec | Muzzle energy joules | Name/Weapons chambered in |
|---|---|---|---|---|---|---|---|
| 25 × 194R | 47.2 | 42.8 | F | 320 | 960 | 147,000 | Hotchkiss Mle 1934 WW2 AT/AFV gun |
| 37 × 132R | 46.0 | 43.5 | J | 460–595 | 640 | 94–122,000 | Type 94 tank gun, Type 98 aircraft (WW2) |
| 37 × 223R | 55.3 | 50.0 | USA | AP/870 | 884 | 340,000 | M3 AT+M5/6 WW2 AFV gun |
| 37 × 249R | 51.4 | 45.9 | D | AP/680 | 762 | 200,000 | KwK AFV/PaK 36 WW2 AT gun (also used in FlaK M42 in |
| | | | | APCR/350 | 1030 | 186,000 | Table 1) |
| 37 × 277R | 61.6 | 56.7 | F | HE/725 | 850 | 262,000 | Hotchkiss M1925 naval AA |
| 37 × 380R | 57.8 | 49.6 | D | HE/750 | 1,000 | 375,000 | 3.7cm SKC/30 WW2 naval AA |
| 40 × 79R | 47.9 | 43.8 | UK | HE/540 | 240 | 15,500 | 1.59 inch Vickers Crayford |
| | | | | AP/540 | 300 | 24,300 | WW1 aircraft |
| 40 × 304R | 56.9 | 52.0 | UK | AP/1,077 | 853 | 392,000 | 2pdr WW2 AFV/AT |
| | | | | APCBC/1,219 | 792 | 382,000 | SV = Littlejohn squeezebore shot (emergent calibre 30mm): |
| | | | | APSV/454 | 1,280 | 372,000 | 454g = Mk 1; 567g = Mk 2 |
| | | | | APSV/567 | 1,143 | 370,000 | |
| 45 × 310R | 57.8 | 52.9 | SU | APCBC/1,400 | 760 | 404,000 | WW2 AFV/AT gun |
| | | | | APCR/850 | 1,067 | 484,000 | APCR is 'arrowhead' shot |
| 47 × 376R | 63.9 | 57.7 | UK | 1,474 | 560 | 231,000 | 3 pdr naval and inter-war AFV gun |
| 50 × 288R | 78.6 | 70.5 | D | APC/2,040 | 745 | 566,000 | KwK 38 L42 WW2 AFV gun |
| | | | | APCR/950 | 1,050 | 524,000 | |

| Metric calibre | Rim diam. mm | Body diam. mm | Country of origin/main use | Projectile type/ weight gm | Muzzle velocity m/sec | Muzzle energy joules | Name/Weapons chambered in |
|---|---|---|---|---|---|---|---|
| 57 × 306R | 76.0 | 67.3 | UK | 2,720 | 540 | 397,000 | naval+WW1 AFV gun (lower velocity is for short- |
|  |  |  |  | 2,720 | 411 | 230,000 | barrelled gun used in later tanks) |
| 57 × 464R | 78.8 | 70.8 | UK | HE/2,830 | 719 | 731,000 | 6 pdr 10 cwt Twin Six WW2 coast defence gun |
| 57 × 480R | 89.9 | 83.4 | SU | 3,100 | 1,000 | 1,550K | WW2+post-war AFV/AT gun |

*TABLE 3:* **SERVICE HEAVY AUTOMATIC WEAPONS 11.35MM – 57MM**

| Name | Metric calibre | Gun kg | Length cm | Barrel cm | Method of operation | Cartridge feed | Rate of fire rpm | Notes |
|---|---|---|---|---|---|---|---|---|
| **CHINA** (SEE ALSO SOVIET/RUSSIAN WEAPONS) | | | | | | | | |
| Type 77 | 12.7 × 108 | 40.6 | 215 | 102 | gas | belt | 650–750 | current army: weight = 56kg inc tripod |
| Type W-85 | 12.7 × 108 | 18.5 | 199 | 102 | gas | belt | 750 | current army |
| NORINCO Type 2 | 23 × 115 | 43 | ? | ? | gas | belt | 1,200 | current aircraft (AM-23?) |
| NORINCO Type 1 | 30 × 155B | 66 | ? | ? | gas | belt | 850 | current aircraft (NR-30) |
| NORINCO Type 76A | 37 × 240 | ? | ? | 233 | recoil | ? | 380 | current naval AA |
| **FRANCE** | | | | | | | | |
| Hotchkiss | 13.2 × 99 | 37.5 | 170 | 129 | gas | box-30 or strip-15 | 450 | WW2 AA |
| GIAT M 621 | 20 × 102 | 49 | 221 | 150 | gas | belt | 800 | current; AA/heli (e) |
| HS Type 9 | 20 × 110RB | 48 | 207 | ? | API blowback | drum-60 | 400 | inter-war air (Oerlikon FFS; Type 7 similar) |
| HS 404 | 20 × 110 | 50 | 250 | 170 | gas/blowback | various | 700 | WW2 aircraft/AA |
| GIAT M 693 | 20 × 139 | 72 | 270 | 206 | gas | dual belt | 900 | current; mainly AA |
| Hotchkiss M 1938/9 | 25 × 163 | 115 | 245 | 150 | gas | box-15 | 220 | WW2 AA (IJN Type 96) |

| Name | Metric calibre | Gun kg | Length cm | Barrel cm | Method of operation | Cartridge feed | Rate of fire rpm | Notes |
|---|---|---|---|---|---|---|---|---|
| 30M541 DEFA | 30 × 97B | 84 | 166 | 110 | gas revolver | belt | 1,200–1,400 | post-war aircraft (e) |
| 30M552/3/4 DEFA | 30 × 113B | 80 | 170 | 140 | gas revolver | belt | 1,100–1,500 | post-war aircraft (e) |
| 30–554 GIAT | 30 × 113B | 85 | 201 | ? | gas revolver | belt | 1,800 | current aircraft (e) |
| **GERMANY** | | | | | | | | |
| RhB MG 131 | 13 × 64B | 17 | 117 | 55 | short recoil | belt | 900 | WW2 aircraft (e) |
| Mauser MG 151 | 15 × 96 | 42 | 193 | 125 | short recoil | belt | 700 | WW2 aircraft: some (e) |
| Becker | 20 × 70RB | 30 | 137 | 80 | API blowback | box-15 | 300 | WW1 aircraft |
| MG-FF/MG-FFM | 20 × 80RB | 24–28 | 134 | 82 | API blowback | drum-60 | 520–540 | WW2 aircraft |
| Mauser MG 151/20 | 20 × 82 | 42 | 177 | 110 | short recoil | belt | 700 | WW2 aircraft: some (e) |
| Lb/MG 204 | 20 × 105(B) | 55 | c.160 | c.110 | short recoil | drum-20 | 400 | WW2 aircraft. Drum-100 also |
| RhB FlaK 30 | 20 × 138B | 64 | 230 | 130 | short recoil | box-20 | 280 | WW2 AA |
| RhB KwK 30 | " | 63 | 194 | 110 | " | box-10 | 280 | WW2 AFV |
| RhB MG C/30L | " | 64 | c.280 | 180 | " | drum-100 | 300–350 | inter-war aircraft |
| Mauser FlaK 38 | " | 57–71 | 225 | 130 | " | box-20 | 450 | WW2 AA |
| Mauser KwK 38 | " | 56 | 194 | 110 | " | box-10 | 420–480 | WW2 AFV |
| Rh202 | 20 × 139 | 75–83 | 261 | 184 | gas/blowback | dual belt | 800–1,000 | current AA+AFV mainly |
| Mauser Model E | 25 × 137 | 112 | 286 | 210 | gas | dual belt | 60–600 | current AA+AFV |
| Mauser BK 27 | 27 × 145B | 100 | 231 | 170 | gas revolver | belt | 1,700–1,800 | current aircraft (e) |
| RhB MK 108 | 30 × 90RB | 60 | 105 | 44 | API blowback | belt | 600–650 | WW2 aircraft (e) |
| Mauser MK30 | 30 × 173 | 141 | 322 | 246 | gas | dual belt | 800 | current AA/AFV |
| RhB MK 101 | 30 × 184B | 180 | 259 | 155 | short recoil | box-6/ drum30 | 250 | WW2 aircraft |

| Name | Metric calibre | Gun kg | Length cm | Barrel cm | Method of operation | Cartridge feed | Rate of fire rpm | Notes |
|---|---|---|---|---|---|---|---|---|
| RhB MK 103 | 30 × 184B | 141 | 235 | 134 | recoil+gas | belt | 360–420 | WW2 aircraft (e) |
| RhB 3cm FlaK 38 | 30 × 184B | ? | 232 | 134 | recoil+gas | belt | 400 | WW2 AA (MK 103) (e) |
| 3.7cm Sockelflak | 37 × 101SR | ? | ? | 54 | short recoil | ? | ? | WW1 AA |
| RhB FlaK M 42 | 37 × 249R | 300 | ? | 256 | recoil | clip-5 | 160–180 | WW2 naval AA |
| RhB FlaK 18 | 37 × 263B | 278 | 363 | 211 | short recoil | strip-6 | 160 | WW2 AA |
| RhB BK 3.7 | 37 × 263B | 295 | 363 | 211 | short recoil | strip-6 | 160 | WW2 aircraft |
| RhB FlaK 36 | 37 × 263B | ? | 363 | 211 | short recoil | strip-6 | 160 | WW2 AA. FlaK 37 similar |
| RhB FlaK 43 | 37 × 263B | 265 | 330 | 211 | gas | strip-8 | 250 | WW2 AA |
| RhB 5cm FlaK 41 | 50 × 346B | 570 | 469 | 342 | gas | clip-5 | 130 | WW2 AA |
| RhB BK 5 | 50 × 419R | 540 | 434 | 304 | long recoil | belt | 45–50 | WW2 aircraft |
| **ITALY** | | | | | | | | |
| 12.7mm Breda-SAFAT | 12.7 × 81SR | 29 | 139 | 80 | short recoil | belt | 700 | WW2 aircraft |
| 12.7mm Scotti | 12.7 × 81SR | 23 | 141 | 86 | gas/blowback | belt | 700 | WW2 aircraft |
| 13.2mm Breda M31 | 13.2 × 99 | 19.3 | 166 | 110 | gas | box-20 | 450–500 | WW2 AFV |
| 20mm Breda M35 | 20 × 138B | 67 | 209 | 130 | gas | strip-12 | 220 | WW2 AA+AT |
| 20mm Scotti | 20 × 138B | ? | 226 | 154 | gas/blowback | drum-60/ belt | 250 | WW2 AA (strip-12 also) |
| FIAT M1917 | 25 × 87 | 45 | 133 | 67 | long recoil | box-8 | 150 | WW1 aircraft (Revelli) |
| 37mm Breda M39 | 37 × 230SR | ? | ? | 200 | gas | clip-6 | 130 | WW2 AA |
| OtoBreda 40L70N | 40 × 364R | ? | ? | 280 | recoil | linkless | 450 | current AA 'Fast Forty' |
| **JAPAN (ALL USED IN WW2 PERIOD)** | | | | | | | | |
| Ho-103 | 12.7 × 81SR | 22 | 124 | 81 | short recoil | belt | 900 | Army aircraft (12.7mm Type 1) |
| 13mm Type 2 | 13 × 63B | 17 | 117 | 55 | short recoil | belt | 900 | Navy aircraft; percussion-primed version of MG 131 |

| Name | Metric calibre | Gun kg | Length cm | Barrel cm | Method of operation | Cartridge feed | Rate of fire rpm | Notes |
|------|------|------|------|------|------|------|------|------|
| 13mm Type 93 | 13.2 × 99 | 42 | 170 | 129 | gas | box-30 | 450 | Navy AA (Hotchkiss) |
| 13mm Type 3 | 13.2 × 99 | 30 | 142 | 91 | short recoil | belt | 800 | Navy aircraft (Browning) |
| 20mm Type 99–1 | 20 × 72RB | 23–26 | 133 | 81 | API blowback | drum-60/100 | 500 | Navy aircraft. Mod 4=belt |
| Ho-5 | 20 × 94 | 35–37 | 145 | 90 | short recoil | belt | 700–850 | Army aircraft (Type 2) |
| 20mm Type 99–2 | 20 × 101RB | 34–38 | 189 | 125 | API blowback | drum-60/100 | 490 | Navy aircraft. Mod 4=belt |
| Ho-1 | 20 × 125 | 45 | 175 | 120 | gas/blowback | drum-15 | 400 | Army aircraft (flexible) |
| Ho-3 | 20 × 125 | 45 | 175 | 120 | gas/blowback | drum-50 | 400 | Army aircraft (fixed) |
| 20mm Type 98 | 20 × 142 | 69 | 201 | 126 | gas/blowback | box-20 | 450 | Army AA (some AT use) |
| 25mm Type 96 | 25 × 163 | 115 | 230 | 150 | gas | box-15 | 220 | Navy AA (Hotchkiss) |
| 30mm Type 2 | 30 × 92RB | 50 | 210 | 135 | API blowback | drum-42 | 400 | Navy aircraft |
| Ho-155 | 30 × 114 | 60 | 186 | 114 | short recoil | belt | 450–600 | Army aircraft |
| 30mm Type 5 | 30 × 122 | 70 | 207 | 144 | recoil+gas | belt | 450 | Navy aircraft |
| Ho-203 | 37 × 112R | 89 | 154 | 87 | long recoil | belt-15 | 120 | Army aircraft |
| Ho-204 | 37 × 144 | 130 | 247 | 130 | short recoil | belt | 300–400 | Army aircraft (Type 4) |
| Ho-301 | 40mm CL | 132 | 148 | 78 | API blowback | box-10 | 450 | Army aircraft |
| Ho-401 | 57 × 121R | 150 | 204 | 100 | long recoil | belt-17 | 80 | Army aircraft |
| **SOVIET UNION/RUSSIA (N.B. Many of which also made in PRC (China) under different designations)** | | | | | | | | |
| DShK-38/46 | 12.7 × 108 | 36 | 159 | 107 | gas | belt-50 (DShK-38) belt (-38/46) | 550–600 | DShK-38 WW2 army: DShK-38/46 post-war PRC Type 54 post-war |
| UB (Beresin) | 12.7 × 108 | 25 | 135 | 101 | gas | belt | 900–1,050 | WW2 aircraft |
| A-12.7 | 12.7 × 108 | 25 | 135 | 101 | gas | belt | 800–1,100 | post-war aircraft |
| NSV | 12.7 × 108 | 25 | 156 | 99 | gas | belt | 700–800 | current army |

| Name | Metric calibre | Gun kg | Length cm | Barrel cm | Method of operation | Cartridge feed | Rate of fire rpm | Notes |
|---|---|---|---|---|---|---|---|---|
| YakB-12.7 | 12.7 × 108 | 28 | 134 | 97 | gas rotary | belt | 4,000–5,000 | current 4-bbl: heli |
| KPV | 14.5 × 114 | 49 | 200 | 135 | short recoil | belt | 600 | post-war AFV/AA: PRC Type 75 |
| ShVAK | 20 × 99R | 42 | 168 | 124 | gas | belt | 800 | WW2 aircraft (barrel length varied) |
| B-20 (Beresin) | 20 × 99R | 25 | 138 | ? | gas | belt | 800 | WW2 aircraft (barrel length varied) |
| NS-23 | 23 × 115 | 37–55 | 199 | 145 | short recoil | belt | 550–700 | post-war aircraft |
| NR-23 | 23 × 115 | 39 | 202 | 145 | gas (?) | belt | 850–950 | post-war aircraft |
| AM-23 | 23 × 115 | 43 | 217 | ? | gas | belt | 1,300 | post-war aircraft (PRC Type 2?) |
| GSh-23 | 23 × 115 | 50 | 139–154 | 85–100 | gas twin bbl | belt | 3,000–3,500 | current Gast type aircraft |
| GSh-6-23 | 23 × 115 | 76 | 152 | ? | gas rotary | belt | 9,000 | current 6-bbl. aircraft |
| VYa | 23 × 152B | 68 | 214 | 165 | gas | belt | 500–700 | WW2 aircraft |
| ZU | 23 × 152B | 75 | 255 | 200 | gas | belt | 800–1,000 | post-war AA: (w) in SP |
| Rikhter R-23 | 23 × 260 | 58 | c.175 | c.140 | gas revolver | belt | 2,500 | post-war aircraft |
| M1940 naval | 25 × 218R | 125 | 180 | 145 | long recoil | clip-6 | ? | WW2 naval AA |
| M-110 + 110-PM naval (2M3 + 2M8) | 25 × 218 | ? | 285 | 184 | recoil | clip-5 or belt | 250 | post-war naval AA: PRC Type 61 |
| AGS-17 | 30 × 29B | 18 | 84 | 29 | API blowback | belt | 350–400 | current AGL (AG-17A heli version) |
| AGS-30 | 30 × 29B | 16* | 110 | ? | " | " | 425 | current AGL: *incl.tripod |
| NR-30 | 30 × 155B | 66 | 216 | 181 | gas | belt | 900 | post-war aircraft (PRC Type 1) |

| Name | Metric calibre | Gun kg | Length cm | Barrel cm | Method of operation | Cartridge feed | Rate of fire rpm | Notes |
|------|------|------|------|------|------|------|------|------|
| 2A42 | 30 × 165 | 115 | 303 | ? | gas/recoil | dual belt | 250–650 | current AFV/heli. |
| 2A72 | 30 × 165 | 84 | 301 | ? | long recoil | dual belt | 330 | current AFV/AA (*Pantsyr*) |
| GSh-301 | 30 × 165 | 45 | 197 | ? | short recoil | belt | 1,500–1,800 | current aircraft and AA (e) |
| GSh-30 | 30 × 165 | 105 | 205–295 | 141–231 | gas twin bbl | belt | 2,000–3,000 | current aircraft (e). GSh-30K has longer barrels |
| 2A38M | 30 × 165 | 195 | 345 | ? | gas twin bbl | belt | 2,000–2,500 | current AA (*Tunguska*) (w) |
| GSh-6-30 | 30 × 165 | 160 | 204 | ? | gas rotary | belt | 4,500–5,000 | current 6-bbl aircraft (e) |
| GSh-6-30K (AK630) | 30 × 165 | 200 | 218 | ? | gas rotary | belt | 4,000–6,000 | current naval 6-bbl AA (w) (e) |
| AO18L (AK 306) | 30 × 165 | 180 | 217 | ? | power rotary | belt | 1,000–3,000 | current naval 6-bbl AA (e) |
| NN-30 (AK230) | 30 × 210B | 155 | 267 | 193 | gas revolver | belt | 1,000 | post-war naval AA (e) (w): PRC Type 69, Romanian Army AA |
| N-37 | 37 × 155 | 103 | 246 | 131 | gas | belt | 400 | post-war aircraft |
| NS-37 | 37 × 195 | 170 | 341 | 230 | short recoil | belt | 250–350 | WW2 aircraft: Yak-9T, Il-2 type 3M |
| M39 | 37 × 250R | ? | ? | 232 | recoil | clip-5 | 170 | WW2+post-war AA: PRC Type 55 |
| 70K/W-11–M | 37 × 250R | ? | ? | 232 | recoil | clip-5 | 170 | post-war naval AA |
| 45mm naval | 45 × 386SR | ? | ? | 382 | recoil | clip-5 | 200 | post-war naval AA |
| S-60 | 57 × 347SR | ? | ? | 439 | recoil | clip-4 | 120 | post-war army AA/SPAAG |

| Name | Metric calibre | Gun kg | Length cm | Barrel cm | Method of operation | Cartridge feed | Rate of fire rpm | Notes |
|------|----------------|--------|-----------|-----------|---------------------|----------------|------------------|-------|
| ZIF-31 (AK 725 single mounting) | 57 × 347SR | ? | ? | 439 | recoil | clip-4 | 120 | post-war naval AA. PRC Type 66 (single barrel) |
| ZIF-72 (twin) | 57 × 347SR | ? | ? | 427 | recoil | belt | 120 | post-war naval AA (twin) |
| **SWEDEN** | | | | | | | | |
| Bofors 20mm m/45 | 20 × 110 | 49 | 214 | 130 | recoil | belt | 700 | post-war aircraft (A21) |
| Bofors 20mm m/49 | 20 × 110 | 59 | 211 | 140 | recoil | belt | 775 | post-war aircraft (A32A) |
| Bofors 20mm m/40 | 20 × 145R | 42 | 205 | 132 | recoil | drum-25 | 360 | WW2 AA/AT |
| 25mm m/22 | 25 × 87R | 50 | 137 | 76 | long recoil | belt-25 | 150 | inter-war submarine AA (Vickers-Terni) |
| Bofors 25mm m/32 | 25 × 205R | 125 | 180 | 145 | recoil | clip-6 | ? | inter-war AA |
| Bofors 40mm L56/60 | 40 × 311R | ? | 340 | 224 | recoil | clip-4 | 120–150 | inter-war–post-war AA: some naval (w) |
| Bofors 40mm L70 | 40 × 364R | 560 | 405 | 280 | recoil | clip-4 or mags | 240–330 | current AA + AFV |
| Bofors 57mm m/47 | 57 × 230R | 570 | 384 | 274 | recoil | drum-41 | 180 | post-war Saab T18B aircraft |
| Bofors 57mm m/54 | 57 × 438R | ? | ? | 342 | recoil | clip | 160 | post-war AA |
| Bofors SAK 57 L/60 | 57 × 438R | ? | ? | 342 | recoil | linkless | 130 | post-war naval (w) |
| Bofors SAK 57 L/70 | 57 × 438R | ? | ? | 400 | recoil | linkless | 200–220 | current naval |
| **SWITZERLAND** | | | | | | | | |
| Oerlikon F/FF | 20 × 72RB | 30/24 | 135 | 76 | API blowback | drum-45–100 | 450/520 | inter-war aircraft |
| Oerlikon L/FFL | 20 × 101RB | 43/30 | 188 | 120 | " | drum-45–100 | 350/500 | inter-war aircraft |
| Solothurn S18–350 | 20 × 105B | 40 | 176 | 90 | short recoil | box-10 | semi-auto | inter-war aircraft |

| Name | Metric calibre | Gun kg | Length cm | Barrel cm | Method of operation | Cartridge feed | Rate of fire rpm | Notes |
|---|---|---|---|---|---|---|---|---|
| Oerlikon S/FFS | 20 × 110RB | 62/39 | 212 | 140 | API blowback | drum-45–100 | 280/470 | inter-war aircraft |
| Oerlikon SS | 20 × 110RB | 67 | 216 | 140 | " | drum-60 | 450 | WW2+post-war naval AA |
| HS 804 | 20 × 110 | 45 | 254 | 170 | gas/blowback | various | 750–800 | post-war aircraft/AA |
| Oerlikon KAA (204GK) | 20 × 128 | 87 | 263 | 170 | gas | belt | 1,000 | current, mainly AA |
| Oerlikon KAB (5TG) | 20 × 128 | 109 | 335 | 240 | gas | box or drum | 1,000 | current, mainly AFV |
| 20mm FMK38 | 20 × 139 FMK | 57 | 255 | 183 | short recoil | belt | 400 | WW2 aircraft; also WW2+post-war Flab Kan 38 AA |
| HS820/Oe KAD | 20 × 139 | 57–66 | 257–298 | 190–231 | gas/blowback | various | 1,000 | current, mainly AA. US=M139 |
| Pzw.-Kan 38 | 24 × 138 | 77 | 259 | 188 | short recoil | box-6 | 30–40 | WW2 AFV |
| Oerlikon KBA | 25 × 137 | 108 | 289 | 217 | gas | dual belt | 600 | current, mainly AA, AFV |
| Oerlikon KBB | 25 × 184 | 146 | 319 | 230 | gas | dual belt | 800 | current, mainly AA, AFV |
| HSS 831/Oe KCB | 30 × 170 | 158 | 352 | 256 | gas/blowback | strip-5, drum or belt | 600–650 | current, mainly AA |
| Oerlikon KCA | 30 × 173 | 136 | 269 | 198 | gas revolver | belt | 1,350 | current aircraft (e) |
| 34mm Flab K38 | 34 × 239 | 280 | ? | 272 | short recoil | belt | 250–270 | WW2+ post-war AA (w) |
| Oerlikon KDA/B/C/F | 35 × 228 | 430–670 | 437–474 | 315 | gas | various | 550–600 | current army and naval AA |
| Oerlikon KDE | 35 × 228 | 510 | 409 | 315 | long recoil | various mag | 200 | current AFV |
| **UK** | | | | | | | | |
| Vickers .5″ Mk III | 12.7 × 81 | 26 | 119 | 79 | short recoil | belt | 700 | WW2 naval AA (w) |

| Name | Metric calibre | Gun kg | Length cm | Barrel cm | Method of operation | Cartridge feed | Rate of fire rpm | Notes |
|---|---|---|---|---|---|---|---|---|
| Vickers .5″ Mk V | 12.7 × 81 | 26 | 119 | 79 | short recoil | belt | 450 | WW2 AFV (w) |
| 15mm BESA | 15 × 104 | 55 | 205 | 146 | gas | belt-40 | 420 | WW2 AFV (ZB vz/60) |
| Hispano Mk I /II | 20 × 110 | 50 | 250 | 170 | gas/blowback | drum-60, belt | 600 | WW2 aircraft (HS 404) |
| Hispano Mk V | 20 × 110 | 42 | 220 | 140 | gas/blowback | belt | 750 | WW2+post-war aircraft |
| Oerlikon Mk 1 | 20 × 110RB | 67 | 216 | 140 | API blowback | drum-60 | 450 | WW2+post-war naval AA |
| Polsten | 20 × 110RB | 55 | 218 | 145 | API blowback | box-30 | 450 | WW2 AA+AFV |
| Aden 3M (LV) | 30 × 86B | 87 | 159 | 108 | gas revolver | belt | 1,200 | post-war aircraft (e) |
| Aden Mk 4 | 30 × 113B | 87 | 159 | 108 | gas revolver | belt | 1,200–1,400 | current aircraft (e) |
| Rarden L21 | 30 × 170 | 113 | 295 | 244 | long recoil | clip-3 | 90 | current AFV |
| Vickers Mk III/V | 37 × 69R | 62 | 143 | 81 | short recoil | belt | 300 | WW1 aircraft |
| 1¹/₂ pdr Vickers | 37 × 123R | 250 | 231 | 157 | short recoil | belt | 150 | WW1 naval |
| 1¹/₂ pdr COW gun | 37 × 190 | 64 | 234 | 190 | long recoil | clip-5 | 60–100 | WW1+inter-war aircraft |
| Vickers 2 pdr | 40 × 158R | 356–416 | 294 | 157 | short recoil | belt | 90–115 | WW1+WW2 naval AA (w) |
| Vickers Class S | 40 × 158R | 134 | 297 | 170 | long recoil | drum-15 | 100 | WW2 aircraft |
| Bofors 40mm L56/60 | 40 × 311R | ? | 340 | 224 | long recoil | clip-4 | 120–150 | WW2+post-war AA: some naval (w) |
| Molins 6 pdr 7 cwt | 57 × 441R | 816 | 360 | 244 | long recoil | mag-22 | 60 | WW2 aircraft/naval |
| **USA** | | | | | | | | |
| Browning M2 | 12.7 × 99 | 45 | 165 | 114 | short recoil | belt-110 (web) | 650 | inter-war–WW2 navy AA (w) |
| M2 HB | 12.7 × 99 | 38 | 165 | 114 | short recoil | or steel link | 450 | inter-war–post-war army |
| M2 | 12.7 × 99 | 29 | 146 | 91 | short recoil | or steel link | 600–800 | inter-war–WW2 aircraft |
| M3 | 12.7 × 99 | 29 | 152 | 91 | short recoil | or steel link | 1,200 | post-war aircraft |

| Name | Metric calibre | Gun kg | Length cm | Barrel cm | Method of operation | Cartridge feed | Rate of fire rpm | Notes |
|---|---|---|---|---|---|---|---|---|
| Saco 50/Ramo M2 Lightweight | 12.7 × 99 | 27 | 152 | 91 | short recoil | belt | 500–750 | current army |
| M85 | 12.7 × 99 | 28 | 138 | 91 | short recoil | | 450–1,050 | post-war AFV |
| GAU-19A | 12.7 × 99 | 34 | 118 | 91 | power | linkless or belt | 1,000 or 2,000 | current 3-bbl rotary |
| Pontiac M39 | 20 × 102 | 81 | 183 | 136 | gas revolver | belt | 1,700 | post-war aircraft (e) |
| GE M61A1 Vulcan | 20 × 102 | 114 | 187 | 152 | power rotary | linkless | 3,000–7,200 | current 6-bbl aircraft/AA (e) |
| GAU-4 | 20 × 102 | 125 | 187 | 152 | gas rotary | linkless | 6,000 | SUU-23/A gunpod |
| GE M195 | 20 × 102 | ? | 137 | 102 | power rotary | belt | 750–850 | post-war 6-bbl heli (e) |
| GE M197 | 20 × 102 | 66 | 183 | 152 | power rotary | belt or linkless | 750 | current 3-bbl: helis (e) |
| Oerlikon SS | 20 × 110RB | 67 | 216 | 140 | API blowback | drum-60 | 450 | WW2 naval AA |
| 20mm AN/M2 | 20 × 110 | 51 | 238 | 171 | gas/blowback | drum-60 /belt | 600–700 | WW2+post-war aircraft (HS 404). M24 = (e). Mk 16 = shipboard version |
| 20mm M3/M24 | 20 × 110 | 45 | 197 | 133 | gas/blowback | belt | 700–800 | |
| Navy Mark 11 | 20 × 110 USN Mk 100 series | 109 | 199 | 143 | gas/recoil twin revolver | twin belt | 700 or 4,200 | post-war aircraft: Mk 4 pod (e) |
| Navy Mark 12 | 20 × 110 USN | 46 | 190 | 122 | gas/blowback | belt | 1,000–1,200 | post-war (HS 404 type) (e) |
| MDHC M242 | 25 × 137 | 110 | 276 | 230 | power | dual belt | 100–500 | current chain gun; AFV |
| GE GAU-12/U | 25 × 137 | 123 | 211 | ? | power rotary | belt | 1,800–4,200 | current AA+aircraft. 5-bbl |
| USN 1.1″ | 28 × 199SR | ? | 304 | 208 | long recoil | clip-8 | 150 | WW2 naval AA (w) |
| MDHC M230 | 30 × 113B | 59 | 164 | 107 | power | linkless | 100–650 | current heli chain gun (e) |
| GE GAU-8/A | 30 × 173 | 281 | 290 | 230 | power rotary | linkless | 4,200 | current aircraft, naval AA |

| Name | Metric calibre | Gun kg | Length cm | Barrel cm | Method of operation | Cartridge feed | Rate of fire rpm | Notes |
|---|---|---|---|---|---|---|---|---|
| GE GAU-13/A | 30 × 173 | 154 | 279 | 214 | power rotary | linkless | 2,400–3,000 | current 4-bbl: aircraft GPU-5/A pod |
| 'Heavy 1-pounder' | 37 × 137R | 259 | 268 | 157 | short recoil | belt | ? | pre-WW1 naval |
| 37mm M4 | 37 × 145R | 96 | 226 | 165 | long recoil | endless belt 15 or 30 | 140–150 | WW2 aircraft (P-39, P-63) + PT boats |
| 37mm M10 | 37 × 145R | 109 | 226 | 165 | long recoil | belt | 150–170 | WW2 aircraft (P-63A-9 +) |
| 37mm M1 | 37 × 223SR | 166 | ? | 198 | long recoil | clip-10 | 120 | WW2 AA |
| Mk 19 | 40 × 53SR | 33 | 110 | 41 | API blowback | belt | 325–385 | current AFV AGL |
| MDHC M129 | 40 × 53SR | 20.4 | 60 | 42 | power | belt | 230–450 | current heli AGL |
| Bofors 40mm L56/60 | 40 × 311R | ? | 340 | 224 | long recoil | clip-4 | 120–150 | WW2 AA: some naval (w) |

## OTHER NATIONS

| Name | Metric calibre | Gun kg | Length cm | Barrel cm | Method of operation | Cartridge feed | Rate of fire rpm | Notes |
|---|---|---|---|---|---|---|---|---|
| Madsen (DK) | 11.35 × 62 | 10.5 | 128 | 75 | short recoil | belt | 900–1,050 | WW2 aircraft |
| Madsen (DK) | 20 × 120 | 53 | 200 | 120 | short recoil | belt, box-10, drum-60 | 400 | WW2 AA/AT and aircraft |
| CIS 50MG (SGP) | 12.7 × 99 | 30 | 178 | 114 | gas | dual belt | 600 | current army |
| CIS 40–AGL (SGP) | 40 × 53SR | 33 | 97 | 35 | API blowback | belt | 350 | current army AGL |
| Santa Barbera LAG-40 (E) | 40 × 53SR | 34 | 100 | 41 | long recoil | belt 24–33 | 215 | current army AGL |
| Meroka (E) | 20 × 128 | 295 | ? | ? | power | belt | salvo | current 12-bbl naval AA (e) |
| ZB vz/60 (CZ) | 15 × 104 | 55 | 205 | 146 | gas | belt-40 | 420 | WW2 AFV+AA |
| M53 (CZ) | 30 × 210 | 200 | 300 | 243 | gas | strip-10 or box-50 | 450–500 | post-war AA: (MK 303) |
| MBT G360 (IL) | 20 × 110 | 48 | 204 | ? | ? | belt | 600 | current AFV |
| Vektor GA-1 (SA) | 20 × 82 | 39 | 177 | 110 | short recoil | belt | 600–700 | current (MG 151); XC-F2 helicopter version |

| Name | Metric calibre | Gun kg | Length cm | Barrel cm | Method of operation | Cartridge feed | Rate of fire rpm | Notes |
|---|---|---|---|---|---|---|---|---|
| Vektor G1–2 (SA) | 20 × 139 | 73 | 269 | ? | gas/blowback | dual belt | 740 | current |
| Vektor 55C5 (SA) | 30 × 113B | 82 | 166 | 140 | gas revolver | belt | 1,800 | current aircraft (DEFA 550) (e); XC-30 is heli version (700–900 rpm) |
| Vektor GA-35 (SA) | 35 × 228 | 429 | 434 | 315 | gas | single or dual belt | 500–600 | current AA/AFV |
| Zastava M1955 (YU) | 20 × 110 | ? | ? | 140 | gas/blowback | drum | 800 | post-war M55 (triple mount) |
| Zastava M86/89 (YU) | 30 × 210B | 200 | 300 | 210 | gas | single or dual belt | 650–750 | current AA+AFV (e) M89 has dual belt feed |
| Lahti L34 (SF) | 20 × 113 | ? | 168 | 100 | recoil | box-15 or drum-45 | 350 | inter-war naval |
| Lahti L40 (SF) | 20 × 138B | 40 | ? | 130 | gas | box-32 | 250 | WW2 AA (used in twin mounting) |
| Maxim Pom-pom | 37 × 94R | 186 | 187 | 110 | short recoil | belt | 200–300 | 19th century: (w) effectively international |

*TABLE 4:* **OTHER HEAVY AUTOMATIC WEAPONS**

This includes information about some of the weapons referred to in the text which saw little or no service, or have completed development but have not yet been officially adopted, or are still under development. Weapons in the latter two categories are described as 'current'. It is by no means a comprehensive list of experimental weapons – this would run to hundreds of entries.

| Name | Metric calibre | Gun kg | Length cm | Barrel cm | Method of operation | Cartridge feed | Rate of fire rpm | Notes |
|---|---|---|---|---|---|---|---|---|
| **FRANCE** | | | | | | | | |
| HS 407 | 23 × 122 | 56.5 | 258 | 172 | gas/blowback | drum-20 | ? | WW2 exp. aircraft/AA |
| Puteaux M1918 | 37 × 94R | 90 | ? | ? | long recoil | strip-5 | 60 | inter-war aircraft |
| Hotchkiss M 1935 | 37 × 218R | ? | ? | 178 | ? | clip-6 | 165 | WW2 naval AA |

| Name | Metric calibre | Gun kg | Length cm | Barrel cm | Method of operation | Cartridge feed | Rate of fire rpm | Notes |
|---|---|---|---|---|---|---|---|---|
| Schneider M 1930 | 37 × ? | ? | ? | ? | ? | strip-8 | 175 | inter-war AA |
| GIAT 25M811 | 25 × 137 | 109 | 264 | ? | electric | dual belt | 125–650 | current; AFV/heli |
| GIAT 30M781 | 30 × 113B | 65 | 187 | 140 | electric | belt | up to 720 | current heli+AFV (e) |
| GIAT 30M791 | 30 × 150B | 120 | 240 | ? | gas revolver | belt | 2,500 | current aircraft (e) |
| **GERMANY** | | | | | | | | |
| MG TuF | 13 × 92SR | 38 | ? | ? | short recoil | belt | 400 | WW1 army (w) |
| 2cm Erhardt | 20 × 70RB (E) | 36 | 150 | 101 | short recoil | box | 250–300 | WW1 aircraft |
| Mauser MG 213C | 20 × 135 | 75 | 193 | 160 | gas revolver | belt | 1,200–1,400 | WW2 aircraft (e) |
| Mauser MK 213/30 | 30 × 85B | 75 | 163 | 130 | gas revolver | belt | 1,100–1,200 | WW2 aircraft (e) |
| Mauser RMK 30 | 30 × 280 | 100 | 234 | 170 | power revolver | linkless | 300 | current caseless/ recoilless heli |
| 35mm Rh 503 | 35 × 227 | 510 | 471 | 315 | electric | dual linkless | 150–400 | post-war AFV (now Boeing) |
| Heckler and Koch GMG | 40 × 53SR | 29 | 118 | 41 | API blowback | belt | 350 | current AGL |
| 50mm Rh 503 | 50 × 330 | 540 | 581 | 425 | electric | dual linkless | 150–400 | post-war AFV (now Boeing) |
| Mauser MK 214A | 50 × 419R | 490 | 416 | 282 | recoil | belt | 160 | WW2 aircraft (e) |
| RhB 5.5cm MK 112 | 55 × 175RB | 275 | 200 | 105 | API blowback | belt | 300 | WW2 aircraft (e) |
| RhB 5.5cm MK 114 | 55 × 448B | 700 | ? | 421 | gas | ? | 150 | WW2 aircraft (?) |
| RhB 5.5cm Flak 58 | 55 × 448B | 600 | 615 | 421 | gas | clip-4 | 140 | WW2 AA (?) |
| **SOVIET UNION/RUSSIA** | | | | | | | | |
| NS-45 (OKB-16-45) | 45 × 185 | 150–170 | 252 | ? | short recoil | belt | 250 | WW2 aircraft (Yak-9K) |
| RShR-57 (OKB-16–57) | 57 × 160RB | 135 | ? | ? | gas | belt | 230 | post-war aircraft |

| Name | Metric calibre | Gun kg | Length cm | Barrel cm | Method of operation | Cartridge feed | Rate of fire rpm | Notes |
|---|---|---|---|---|---|---|---|---|
| RShR-57 (OKB-15-57) | 57 × ? | 290 | 290 | ? | ? | ? | 180 | WW2 airborne AT |
| **SWITZERLAND** | | | | | | | | |
| HS 827B Hurricane | 20 × 139 | 56 | 251 | 170 | short recoil | dual belt | variable | post-war AFV |
| HS 827C MC-23 | 23 × 133 | 58 | 251 | 170 | short recoil | dual belt | variable | post-war AFV |
| HS 837 Thunderball | 30 × 170 | 105 | 329 | 225 | short recoil | dual belt | variable | post-war AFV |
| HS 825 | 30 × 136 (B) | 103–112 | 238–289 | 174–224 | gas | belt | 950–1,000 | post-war aircraft |
| HS 836 Spitfire | 30 × 138 | 89 | 274 | 180 | short recoil | dual belt | 720 | post-war AFV |
| Oerlikon KBD | 25 × 184 | 290 | 276 | 230 | electric rotary | linkless | 5,000 | current 7-bbl: naval AA |
| Oerlikon 35/1000 | 35 × 228 | 450 | 411 | 276 | gas revolver | linkless | 1,000 | current AA/AFV/ aircraft |
| **UK** | | | | | | | | |
| Vickers .5" Class B | 12.7 × 81 | 24 | 119 | 79 | short recoil | belt | 700 | inter-war aircraft |
| .5" BSA Mod 24 | 12.7 × 81 (BSA) | 21 | 137 | 96 | long recoil | pan-37 | 400 | inter-war aircraft (flexible) |
| Vickers Class D | 12.7 × 120 SR | 46 | 179 | 114 | short recoil | belt | 350–450 | inter-war (w): service with J and China? |
| .661" Vickers | 16.8 × 149 SR | ? | ? | ? | short recoil | feed rails | 300 | inter-war naval AA |
| 1" Vickers | 25 × 87R | 50 | 137 | 76 | long recoil | belt-25 | 150 | WW1 (Vickers-Terni) |
| Aden 25 | 25 × 137 | 92 | 229 | 170 | gas revolver | belt | 1,650–1,850 | current aircraft |
| Rolls-Royce BH | 40 × 158R | 152 | 358 | 203 | long recoil | hopper-8 | 120 | WW2 aircraft |
| 6pdr 6cwt | 57 × 514R | ? | ? | 319 | recoil | ? | ? | WW2 AA |
| **USA** | | | | | | | | |
| ARES TARG | 12.7 × 88 | 20.4 | 113 | 93 | revolver | linkless | 1,400–2,000 | post-war exp. heli gun |
| .50" Tround | 12.7 × 127 | 54 | ? | ? | electric | drum-100 | 1,250 | modern concept test gun |

| Name | Metric calibre | Gun kg | Length cm | Barrel cm | Method of operation | Cartridge feed | Rate of fire rpm | Notes |
|---|---|---|---|---|---|---|---|---|
| T17 Series | 15.2 × 114 | 61 | 234 | ? | short recoil | belt | 600–800 | WW2 aircraft (also 12.7 × 114) |
| Ford 'Tigerclaws' | 20 × 102 | 58 | ? | ? | gas revolver | belt | 2,300 | post-war aircraft; developed M39 (e) |
| GD M61A2 | 20 × 102 | 93 | 187 | 152 | power rotary | linkless | up to 7,200 | current: for F-22 (e) |
| GD XM301 | 20 × 102 | 34.5 | 183 | 152 | power rotary | " | 750–1,500 | current: for RAH-66 (e) |
| .90" T2 | 23 × 139SR | 109 | ? | ? | API blowback | drum-48 | 400–450 | inter-war aircraft |
| OCSW | 25 × 53B | 10.4 | ? | ? | ? | ? | 220 | current infantry |
| GE-225 | 25 × 137 | 82 | 221 | ? | gas or power | belt | 2,500 or 750 | post-war aircraft. Gast type |
| Philco-Ford GAU-7/A | 25 × 152 | 193 | 229 | 213 | power rotary | linkless feed | 6,000 | post-war 5-bbl aircraft (CTA) |
| XM-140 WECOM | 30 × 100B | 63.5 | 154 | 107 | power | belt | 405 | post-war heli (AH-56) |
| GE XM188 | 30 × 113B | 53 | 156 | 107 | power rotary | linkless | 200–2,000 | post-war 3-bbl heli (e) |
| MDHC ASP-30 | 30 × 113B | 52 | 216 | 132 | gas | belt | 450 | current army (e) |
| Bushmaster II | 30 × 173 | 147 | 339 | 241 | power | belt | 200 or 400 | current chain gun AFV |
| Bushmaster III | 35 × 228 | 218 | 402 | 279 | power | belt | 1 or 200 | current chain gun (50 × 330 version also available) |
| ARES Talon | 35 × 228 | 270 | 419 | 315 | gas | dual belt | 550 | current AFV/AA |
| 37mm AAC Type M | 37 × 87R | 61 | 76 | ? | recoil | clip-5 | 125 | inter-war aircraft (turret mount) |
| 37mm M9 | 37 × 223SR | 181 | 264 | 198 | long recoil | belt | 140 | WW2 exp. aircraft + PT boats |

| Name | Metric calibre | Gun kg | Length cm | Barrel cm | Method of operation | Cartridge feed | Rate of fire rpm | Notes |
|---|---|---|---|---|---|---|---|---|
| 37mm AAC Type F | 37 × ? | 163 | 190 | ? | recoil | clip | 90 | inter-war aircraft (fixed) |
| COMVAT (+F, UK) | 45 × 305 | ? | ? | ? | power | linkless | 200–400 | current AFV (cased telescopic): M911 (F+UK) |
| **OTHER NATIONS** | | | | | | | | |
| FN BRG-15 (B) | 15.5 × 106 | 60 | 215 | ? | gas | dual belt | 600 | post-war AFV (15 × 115 first pattern) |
| ZPL-20 (CZ) | 20 × 102 | 64 | 200 | ? | gas twin bbl | belt-224 | 700–2,600 | current aircraft gun pod (*Plamen*) (GSh-23 rechambered) |
| Type 94 flexible (J) | 20 × 99RB | 43 | 173 | 120 | API blowback | drum-60 | 380 | interwar aircraft (Oe L) |
| Madsen-Saetter (DK) | 12.7 × 99 | 28 | 163 | 100 | gas | belt | 1,000 | post-war army AA |
| Madsen (DK) | 23 × 106 | 53 | 200 | 120 | short recoil | belt | 400 | interwar aircraft |
| EMAK 35 (SA) | 35 × 228 | 380 | 418 | ? | electric | belt | 1–120 | current AFV (50 × 330 also) |
| Vektor Striker (SA) | 40 × 53SR | 41 | ? | ? | ? | belt | 425 | current AGL |
| RATMIL AGA-40 (ROM) | 40 × 74.5 | 23 | 89 | 50 | API blowback | drum-10 | 300–400 | current AGL |
| CTA 2000 (UK/F) | 40 × 255 | ? | ? | ? | power | linkless | c.200 | current AFV (cased telescopic) |

*TABLE 5:* **ANTI-TANK AND CURRENT HEAVY RIFLES**

| Name | Country of origin | Metric calibre | Weight kg | Length cm | Barrel cm | Method of operation | Cartridge feed/rounds | Notes |
|---|---|---|---|---|---|---|---|---|
| **ANTI-TANK RIFLES** | | | | | | | | |
| PzB 38 | D | 7.92 × 94 | 16.2 | 161 | 109 | manual | single | WW2 auto eject AT |
| PzB 39 | D | 7.92 × 94 | 12.6 | 159 | 109 | manual | single | WW2 AT |

| Name | Country of origin | Metric calibre | Weight kg | Length cm | Barrel cm | Method of operation | Cartridge feed/rounds | Notes |
|---|---|---|---|---|---|---|---|---|
| 7.92mm M.SS 41 | CZ/D | 7.92 × 94 | 18.1 | 134 | 84 | manual | box-10 | WW2: from 15mm M41 |
| Maroszek | P | 7.92 × 107 | 9 | 177 | 119 | manual | box-4 | WW2: also used by Finland |
| Sholoklov | SU | 12.7 × 108 | 19.5 | 191 | 115 | manual | box-5 | inter-war Mauser copy |
| Mauser M1918 | D | 13 × 92SR | 17.3 | 168 | 99 | manual | single (box-5) | WW1 original AT rifle |
| .55″ Boys Rifle | UK | 13.9 × 99B | 16.6 | 161 | 91 | manual | box-5 | WW2: only British AT rifle |
| PTRS | SU | 14.5 × 114 | 20 | 212 | 122 | gas | box-5 | WW2 Simonov design |
| PTRD | SU | 14.5 × 114 | 16 | 198 | 117 | manual | single | WW2 Degtyarev design |
| 15mm MPzB M41 | CZ | 15 × 104 | 18.5 | 171 | 150 | manual | single | WW2: limited use |
| Oerlikon SSG | CH | 20 × 72RB | 32 | 145 | 75 | API blowback | box-5/10 | inter-war AT: limited use |
| Oerlikon SSG 36 | CH | 20 × 110RB | 38.5 | 173 | 90 | API blowback | box | WW2 AT: Swiss use |
| Solothurn S18-100 | CH | 20 × 105B | 45 | 161 | 90 | short-recoil | box-5/10 | Finland used S18-154 |
| Madsen AT | DK | 20 × 120 | 60 | 182 | 120 | long-recoil | drum-15/30 | WW2: version of AA gun |
| Type 97 | J | 20 × 125 | 68 | 202 | 119 | gas | box-7 | WW2 |
| Solothurn S18-1000/1100 | CH | 20 × 138B | 44 | 217 | 130 | short recoil | box-5/10 | WW2: S18-1100 = full auto. Italy main user |
| Lahti L39 | SF | 20 × 138B | 42 | 223 | 130 | gas | box-10 | WW2 (L39/44 for AA use) |
| Bofors m/40 | S | 20 × 145R | 63.5 | 205 | 140 | long recoil | drum-25 | WW2: version of AA gun |
| Carl Gustav m/42 | S | 20 × 180R | 11.2 | 140 | 108 | manual | single | WW2: recoilless |

| Name | Country of origin | Metric calibre | Weight kg | Length cm | Barrel cm | Method of operation | Cartridge feed/rounds | Notes |
|---|---|---|---|---|---|---|---|---|
| Tankbüsche 41 | CH | 24 × 138 | 131.5 | 259 | 151 | short recoil | box-6 | WW2: wheeled mount also |

## CURRENT RIFLES (SELECTED)

| Name | Country of origin | Metric calibre | Weight kg | Length cm | Barrel cm | Method of operation | Cartridge feed/rounds | Notes |
|---|---|---|---|---|---|---|---|---|
| Barrett Model 98 | USA | 8.58 × 71 | 7.0 | 117 | 61 | gas | box-10 | |
| Barrett M82A1 | USA | 12.7 × 99 | 12.9 | 155 | 84 | short recoil | box-11 | |
| Harris 0.50 M-93 | USA | 12.7 × 99 | 9.5 | 135 | 737 | manual | box-5 | bolt action |
| Harris 0.50 M-96 | USA | 12.7 × 99 | 13.6 | 142 | 737 | gas | box-5 | |
| Stoner SR-50 | USA | 12.7 × 99 | 14.2 | 148 | 90 | gas | box-10 | |
| PGM Hecate II | F | 12.7 × 99 | 13.5 | 138 | 70 | manual | box-7 | bolt action |
| KBP OSV-96 | SU | 12.7 × 108 | 11.7 | 170 | 102 | gas | box-5 | can fold to 110cm |
| LCZ B-30 AMR | CZ | 12.7 × 108 / 12.7 × 99 | 13.2 | 145 | 75 | delayed blowback | box-16 | selective fire (700 rpm) |
| Gepard M1 | H | 12.7 × 108 | 18 | 152 | 114 | manual | single | bolt action |
| Gepard M2 | H | 12.7 × 108 | 15–16 | 127–134 | 83–110 | long recoil | box-5/10 | shorter/lighter version is M2A1 for airborne troops |
| Gepard M3 | H | 14.5 × 114 | 21 | 188 | 163 | long recoil | box-5/10 | |
| Steyr IWS 2000 | A· | 15.2 × 169 | 18 | 180 | 120 | long recoil | box-5/8 | smooth-bore rifle (APFSDS) |
| Mechem NTW-20/14.5 | SA | 20 × 82 / 14.5 × 114 | 26 / 29 | 179 / 201 | 100 / 122 | manual | box-3 | bolt-action, can break down into two loads |
| Helenius APH RK97 | Finland | 20 × 99R | 22.5 | 140 | 86 | manual | single | vertical breechblock |
| RT20 20mm AMR | Croatia | 20 × 110 | 17 | 133 | 92 | manual | single | bolt-action, semi-recoilless |

*TABLE 6:* **SELECTED RIFLE-CALIBRE MACHINE GUNS**

| Name | Country of origin | Metric calibre | Weight kg | Length cm | Barrel cm | Method of operation | Cartridge feed | Rate of fire rpm | Notes |
|---|---|---|---|---|---|---|---|---|---|
| **MEDIUM MACHINE GUNS** | | | | | | | | | |
| Maxim MG08 | D | 7.92 × 57 | 26.4 | 117 | 72 | recoil | fabric belt | 300–450 | WW1, water-cooled |
| Vickers | UK | 7.7 × 56R | 18 | 115 | 72 | recoil | fabric belt | 450–550 | WW1/2, water-cooled |
| Fiat-Revelli M 14 | I | 6.5 × 52 | 17 | 118 | 65 | delayed blowback | strip-feed box (50) | 400 | WW1/2, water-cooled |
| Hotchkiss M 1914 | F | 8 × 50R | 23.6 | 127 | 77 | gas | strip-24 | 600 | WW1/2, air-cooled |
| Goryunov | SU | 7.62 × 54R | 13.6 | 112 | 72 | gas | belt | 650 | WW2, air-cooled |
| Browning M 1917/1919 | USA | 7.62 × 63 | 14–15 | 98–104 | 61 | recoil | belt | 500 | WW1/2, air or water-cooled |
| **AIRCRAFT MACHINE GUNS** | | | | | | | | | |
| Vickers | UK | 7.7 × 56R | 10–12.5 | 117 | 63 | recoil | belt | 450–750 | WW1–inter-war |
| Parabellum | D | 7.92 × 57 | 10 | 117 | 56 | recoil | belt | 700 | WW1 |
| Lewis | UK | 7.7 × 56R | 10.4 | 128 | 67 | gas | pan-47 | 500–600 | WW1/2 |
| Browning | USA/UK | 7.62 × 63 / 7.7 × 56R | 9.7–10.9 | 101 | 61 | recoil | belt | 1,000–1,350 | inter-war–WW2. .303″ calibre (UK) |
| MG 15 | D | 7.92 × 57 | 7.1 | 108 | 60 | recoil | saddle drum-75 | 1,000 | WW2 flexible |
| MG 17 | D | 7.92 × 57 | 12.6 | 121 | 60 | recoil | belt | 1,000–1,100 | WW2 fixed |
| MG 81 | D | 7.92 × 57 | 6.3 | 89 | 48 | recoil | belt | 1,200–1,500 | WW2 flexible |
| ShKAS | SU | 7.62 × 54R | 7.1 | 80 | 51 | gas | belt | 1,800 | WW2–post-war |
| **GENERAL-PURPOSE MACHINE GUNS** | | | | | | | | | |
| MG 34 | D | 7.92 × 57 | 12.1 | 122 | 63 | recoil | belt | 800–900 | WW2 |
| MG 42 | D | 7.92 × 57 | 11.5 | 122 | 53 | recoil | belt | 1,200 | WW2 (post-war versions in 7.62 × 51 NATO) |
| M60 | USA | 7.62 × 51 | 10.5 | 110 | 56 | gas | belt | 550 | post-war |

# APPENDIX TWO

| Name | Country of origin | Metric calibre | Weight kg | Length cm | Barrel cm | Method of operation | Cartridge feed | Rate of fire rpm | Notes |
|------|----|----|----|----|----|----|----|----|----|
| FN MAG | B | 7.62 × 51 | 10.15 | 125 | 55 | gas | belt | 850 | post-war |
| **LIGHT MACHINE GUNS/SQUAD AUTOMATIC WEAPONS** | | | | | | | | | |
| Madsen | DK | many | 9.1 | 114 | 58 | recoil | box-25/40 | 450 | WW1/2 |
| BAR | USA | 7.62 × 63 | 7.3–9.5 | 122 | 61 | gas | box-20 | 400–500 | inter-war–post-war |
| Taisho 11th Year | J | 6.5 × 50SR | 10.2 | 110 | 48 | gas | hopper-30 | 500 | inter-war–WW2 |
| ZB30/Bren | CZ/UK | 7.92 × 57 <br> 7.7 × 56R | 8.7–10.5 | 108–115 | 56–63 | gas | box-30 | 500–550 | inter-war–post-war |
| Degtyarev DP | SU | 7.62 × 54R | 9.1 | 129 | 60 | gas | pan-47 | 500–550 | inter-war–post-war |
| RPK | SU | 7.62 × 39 | 4.8 | 104 | 59 | gas | box-40 or drum-75 | 600 | post-war (Kalashnikov action and ammunition) |
| RPK 74 | SU | 5.45 × 39 | 4.6 | 109 | 59 | gas | box-45 | 600 | current |
| FN Minimi | B/USA | 5.56 × 45 | 6.8 | 104 | 47 | gas | box-30 or belt | 750–1,000 | current |
| **EXTERNALLY POWERED GUNS** | | | | | | | | | |
| GE Minigun M134 | USA | 7.62 × 51 | 15.9 | 80 | 56 | electric | belt | 6,000 | current 6-bbl rotary |
| Hughes Chain Gun EX-34 | USA | 7.62 × 51 | 13.2 | 89 | 56 | electric | belt | 1–600 | current AFV |

# *Appendix Three*

## COMPARATIVE SCALE DRAWINGS OF CARTRIDGES

THE FOLLOWING DRAWINGS, PREPARED BY DR JEAN-François Legendre, represent cartridges used in service automatic weapons between the calibres of 11.35mm and 57mm. Some which may have seen only very limited use have been excluded. One cartridge has so far eluded all efforts to trace it; that for the 37mm Schneider M1930 AA gun.

The measurements are mainly taken directly from examples of cartridges. In some cases, they have been based upon reliable secondary sources. The cartridges on any one page are drawn to the same scale, but the scales are not the same on every page. To enable quick comparisons, a scale bar of constant relative size to the cartridges (representing 20cm long by 1cm wide) has been included on each page. Measurements of case length and rim and body diameter are included in Appendix 2 in Table 1 (and Table 2 for experimental and other comparable cartridges).

No attempt has been made to show the variety of projectile types used in these cartridges. In most cases a typical AP or HE has been drawn, but in some cases an interesting but less common projectile is shown (e.g. the early HE round for the 20 × 70RB, the APDS for the 25 × 184 and the *Hartkernmunition* for the 30 × 184B). Detailed and sectioned drawings of many different projectiles are included in other works, particularly those by Labbett and Lenselink/de Hek.

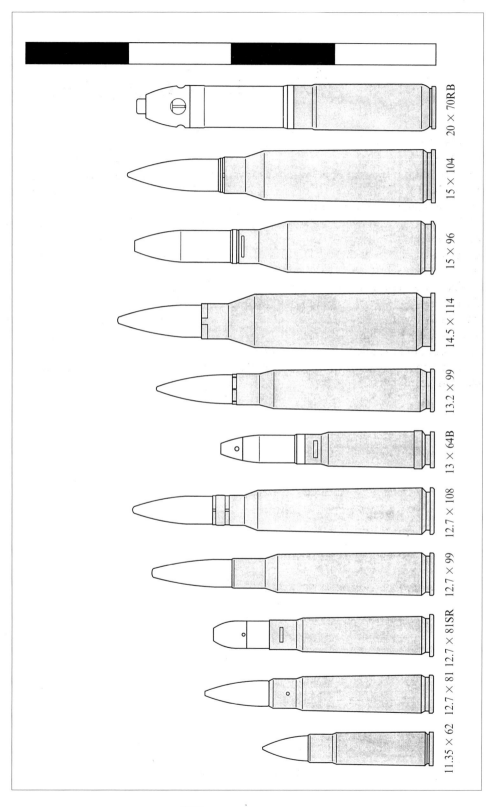

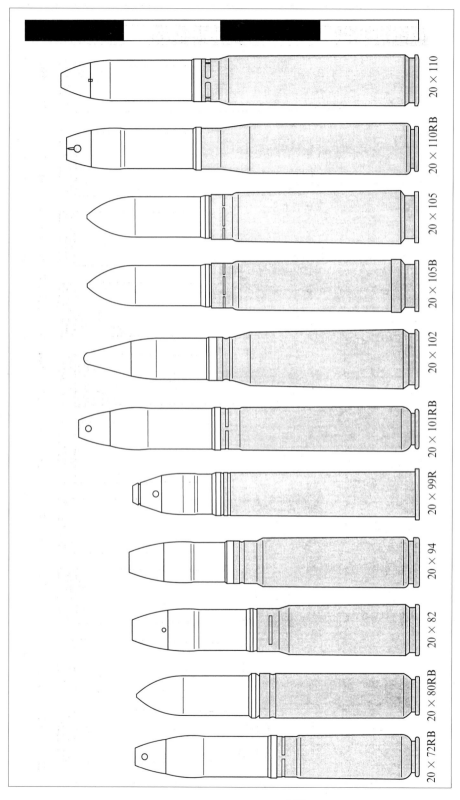

20 × 110
20 × 110RB
20 × 105
20 × 105B
20 × 102
20 × 101RB
20 × 99R
20 × 94
20 × 82
20 × 80RB
20 × 72RB

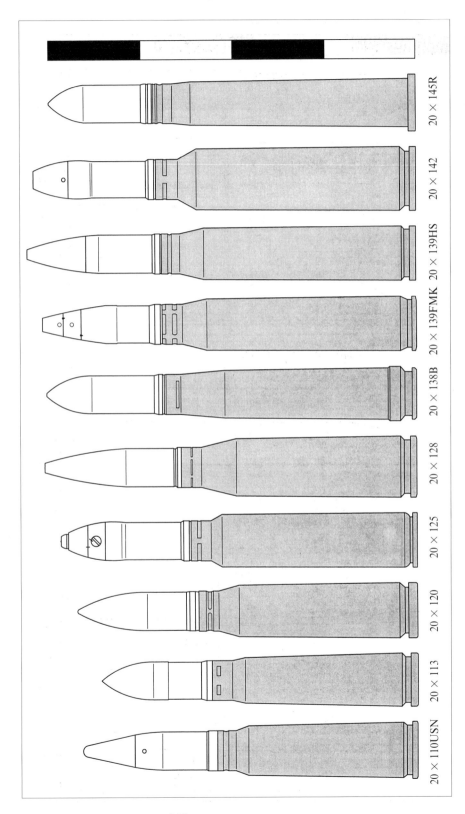

20 × 145R

20 × 142

20 × 139HS

20 × 139FMK

20 × 138B

20 × 128

20 × 125

20 × 120

20 × 113

20 × 110USN

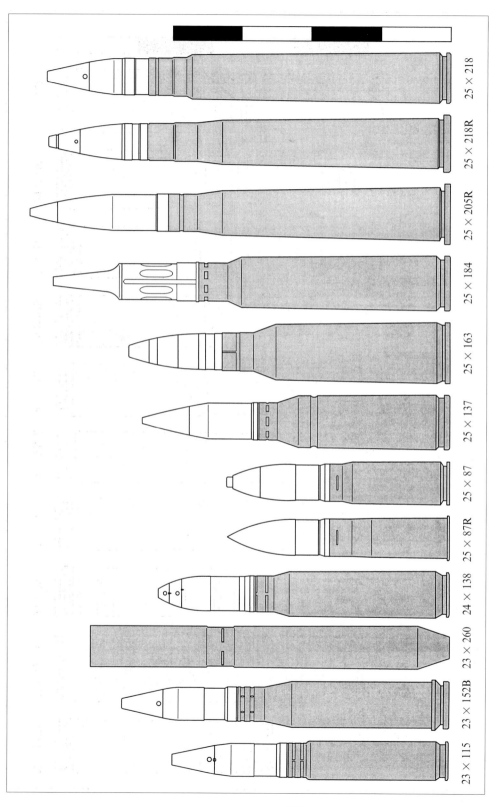

25 × 218
25 × 218R
25 × 205R
25 × 184
25 × 163
25 × 137
25 × 87
25 × 87R
24 × 138
23 × 260
23 × 152B
23 × 115

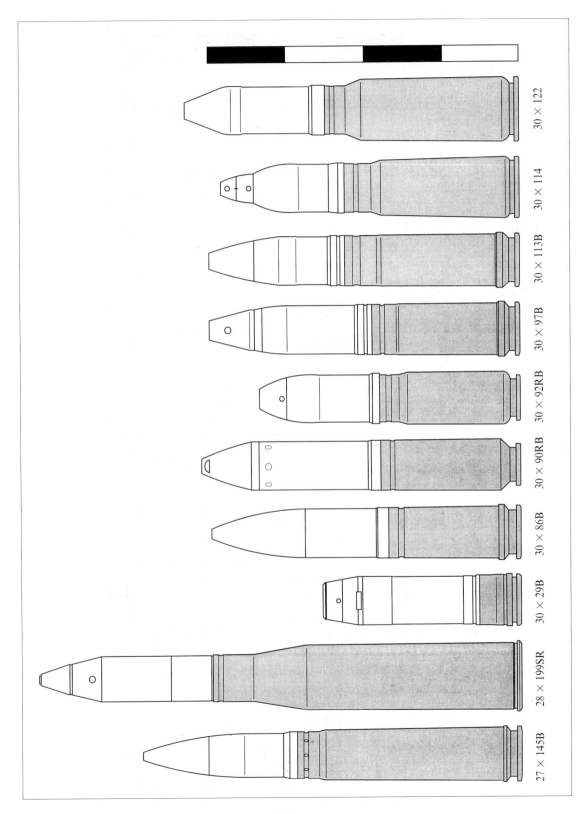

30 × 122

30 × 114

30 × 113B

30 × 97B

30 × 92RB

30 × 90RB

30 × 86B

30 × 29B

28 × 199SR

27 × 145B

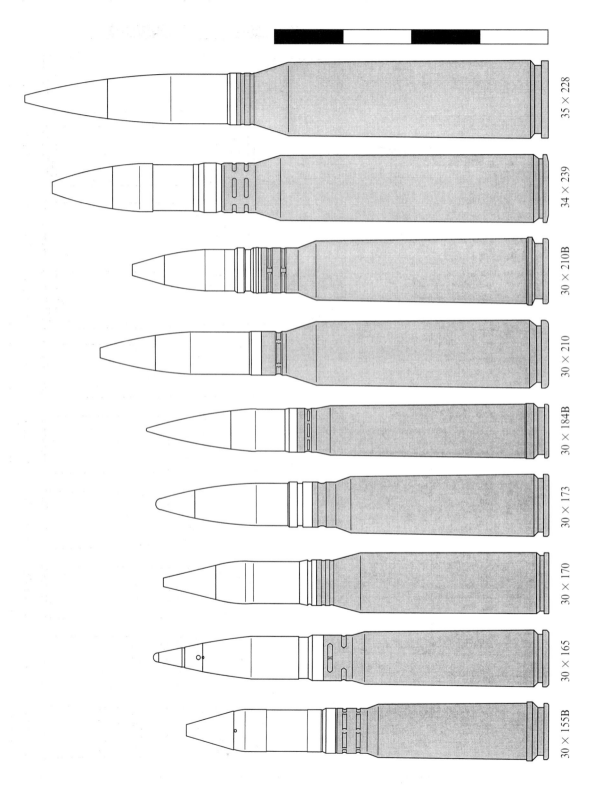

35 × 228

34 × 239

30 × 210B

30 × 210

30 × 184B

30 × 173

30 × 170

30 × 165

30 × 155B

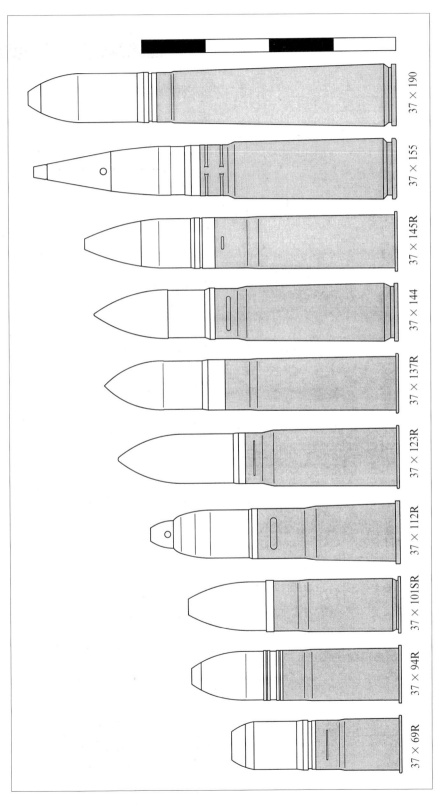

37 × 190

37 × 155

37 × 145R

37 × 144

37 × 137R

37 × 123R

37 × 112R

37 × 101SR

37 × 94R

37 × 69R

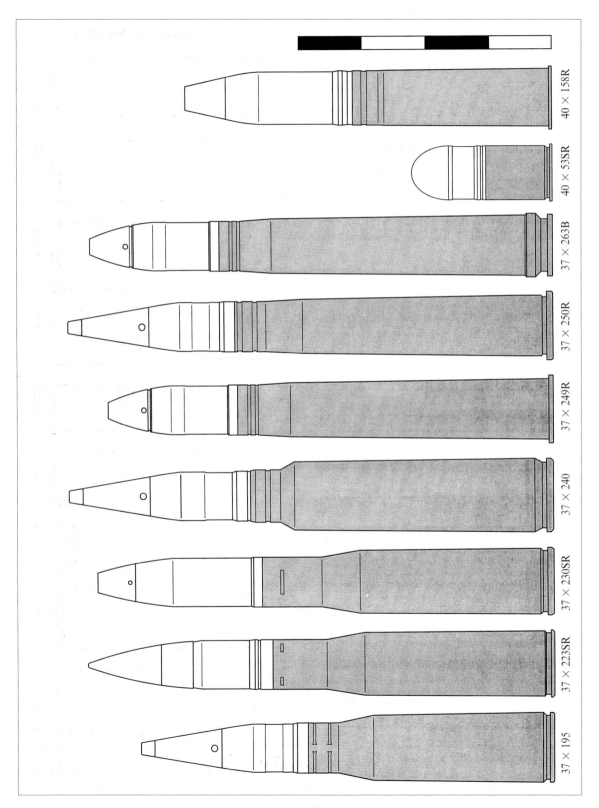

40 × 158R

40 × 53SR

37 × 263B

37 × 250R

37 × 249R

37 × 240

37 × 230SR

37 × 223SR

37 × 195

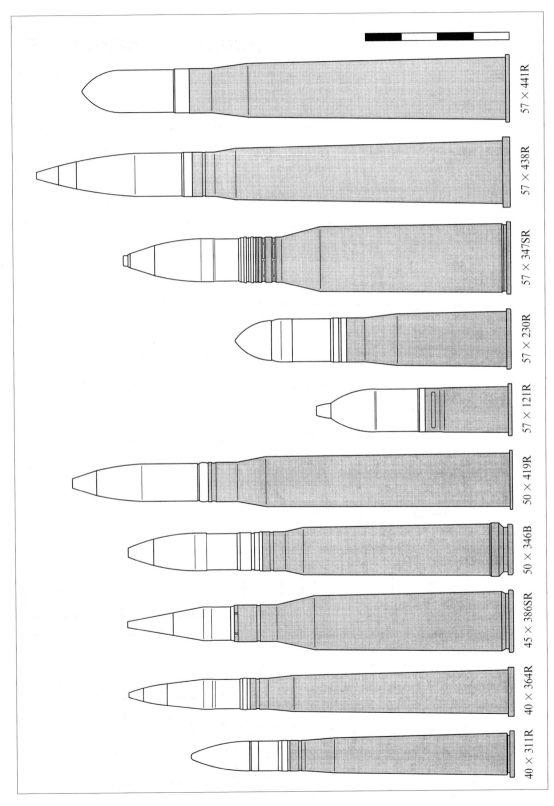

57 × 441R

57 × 438R

57 × 347SR

57 × 230R

57 × 121R

50 × 419R

50 × 346B

45 × 386SR

40 × 364R

40 × 311R

# *Appendix Four*

## COMPARATIVE DRAWINGS OF SECOND WORLD WAR AIRCRAFT GUNS

THE FOLLOWING DRAWINGS REPRESENT AIRCRAFT guns of between 12.7 and 57mm calibre which saw service in the Second World War, together with some models which saw only experimental use. They have been compiled from a wide range of sources, mainly photographic and of varying quality. They are therefore not precise scale drawings, and detailed measurements should not be taken from them. They are included here to give an impression of the general appearance and relative size, as they have all been drawn to approximately the same scale (a one-metre scale bar is included on each page). It should be noted that the detailed appearance could alter between different versions of a gun, and some had significant variations in barrel length. All guns are drawn in side view unless otherwise stated. All guns are belt-fed unless otherwise stated. Magazine-fed guns are sometimes shown with the magazine (where the shape is known), sometimes not.

Particular thanks are expressed to Ted Bradstreet for providing illustrations of the 20mm MG 204 and of three Japanese guns: the 20mm Ho-1 and Ho-3 and the 30mm Type 5.

1. Browning .303" (7.7 × 56R) UK. Included for comparative purposes. Version for turret mounting (note the cocking lever and the flash hider).
2. MG 131 (13 × 64B) Germany. Observer version with a pistol grip. IJN 13mm Type 2 was the same, except for ignition method.
3. Ho-103 (12.7 × 81SR) Japan (IJA). Also known as the 12.7mm Type 1. Browning type action.
4. 12.7mm Breda-SAFAT (12.7 × 81SR) Italy.
5. 12.7mm Scotti (12.7 × 81SR) Italy. Note gas duct under barrel.

6. Browning .50" M2 (12.7 × 99) USA. IJN 13mm Type 3 was the same, except chambered for the 13.2 × 99 cartridge.
7. 12.7mm Beresin UB (12.7 × 108) USSR. Note gas duct above barrel, with charging cylinder above that. Different versions were built for different installations.
8. Mauser MG 151 (15 × 96) Germany. Note the long, slim barrel, designed for engine mounting.
9. Oerlikon FFF (20 × 72RB) Switzerland. Note 60-round drum in place. IJN Type 99-1 was initially identical, but developed in service.
10. Ikaria MG-FF (20 × 80RB) Germany. Developed from Oerlikon FFF. Drawn from above, without magazine, to show the pneumatic charging cylinder alongside the gun.
11. Oerlikon FFL (20 × 101RB) Switzerland. IJN Type 99-2 was initially identical, but developed in service. This version is drum-fed (without magazine). Belt-fed versions were developed later.
12. Oerlikon FFS (20 × 110RB) Switzerland. Drawn without drum magazine. Note charging cylinder above barrel.
13. Hispano-Suiza Type 9 (20 × 110RB) France. Note 60-round drum and charger. Version of Oerlikon FFS adapted for engine mounting. Type 7 was similar.
14. Mauser MG 151/20 (20 × 82) Germany. Note barrel shorter than 15mm version.
15. Ho-1 (20 × 125) Japan (IJA). Designed for flexible mounting, in which the recoil was absorbed by the mounting. Used a 15-round double-drum magazine (not shown). Directly derived from Type 97 anti-tank rifle. Kawamura design.
16. Ho-3 (20 × 125) Japan (IJA). Version of Ho-1 for fixed mounting. Note 50-round double-drum magazine and recoil cylinder mounted underneath the gun.

17. Ho-5 (20 × 94) Japan (IJA). Browning type action.

18. ShVAK (20 × 99R) USSR. Designed by Shpitalnyi and Vladimirov. Observer version with both pistol and spade grips. Engine mounted version had much longer barrel.

19. Beresin B-20 (20 × 99R) USSR. Engine mounted version had much longer barrel.

20. Rheinmetall-Borsig MG C/30L (20 × 138B) Germany. Designed for engine mounting. Saw action in Spanish Civil War, but not WW2. Used very large (100-round) drum magazine underneath the gun (not shown).

21. Solothurn S18-350 (20 × 105B) Switzerland. Version of S18-100 anti-tank rifle. Side-loading box magazine (not shown).

22. Rheinmetall-Borsig MG 204 (20 × 105) Germany. Used 20-round double-drum magazine (not shown). A complex 100-round drum was also developed but might not have been used.

23. Hispano-Suiza HS 404 (20 × 110) France. Note 60-round drum (smaller capacity magazines were available for flexible mountings). British Hispano Mk 1 and US AN/M1 and M2 virtually identical.

24. Hispano Mk 5 (20 × 110) UK. Drum-shaped feature over barrel is the belt feed. US AN/M3 was similar but differed in detail.

25. VYa (23 × 152B) USSR. Designed by Volkov and Yartsev.

26. NS-23 (23 × 115) USSR. Scaled-down version of NS-37. Designed by Nudelman and Suranov.

27. Ho-155 (30 × 114) Japan (IJA). Browning type action.

28. 30mm Type 2 (30 × 92RB) Japan (IJN). Oerlikon type action. Fed by 42-round magazine (not shown). Gun appears to be pictured from above.

29. 30mm Type 5 (30 × 122) Japan (IJN). Kawamura design.

30. Rheinmetall-Borsig MK 101 (30 × 184B) Germany. Initially a 6-round magazine, subsequently a 30-round drum (not shown).

31. Rheinmetall-Borsig MK 108 (30 × 90RB) Germany. Shown without blast tube.

32. Rheinmetall-Borsig MK 103 (30 × 184B) Germany.

33. Rheinmetall-Borsig MK 103M (30 × 184B) Germany. Version for engine mounting; note lack of muzzle brake and slimmer barrel casing with no gas duct. Probably saw no combat.

34. 37mm M4 (37 × 145R) USA. Long-recoil Browning action. Initially a 15-round magazine, subsequently a 30-round continuous-loop belt (not shown). M10 was similar, but adapted for disintegrating link belt feed.

35. 37mm M9 (37 × 223SR) USA. Long-recoil Browning action. Adopted for service, but no actual aircraft use. Adapted from US Army's M1 AA gun.

36. Ho-204 (37 × 144) Japan (IJA). Also known as 37mm Type 4. Browning type action.

37. Ho-203 (37 × 112R) Japan (IJA). Note cage enclosing fixed-length belt feed. Kawamura design.

38. Ho-301 (40mm caseless) Japan (IJA). Viewed slightly from above, to show horizontal box magazine. Oerlikon type action.

39. Ho-401 (57 × 121R) Japan (IJA). Scaled-up version of Ho-203 with 17-round belt feed.

40. NS-37 (37 × 195) USSR. Nudelman and Suranov design. Experimental NS-45 was identical except for 45 × 185 chambering and bulbous muzzle brake.

41. Vickers 40mm Class 'S' Gun (40 × 158R) UK. Note 15-round drum in place.

42. 57mm Molins gun (57 × 441R) UK. Properly known as the QF 6 pdr 7cwt Class M with Molins autoloader. The framework above and behind the gun is the magazine. Feed was by a combination of electrical power and gravity.

43. Rheinmetall-Borsig BK 3.7 (37 × 263B) Germany. Derived from FlaK 18 AA gun. Fed by a 6-round clip (not shown).

44. Rheinmetall-Borsig BK 5 (50 × 419R) Germany. Note annular magazine surrounding gun breech.

45. Mauser MK 214A (50 × 419R) Germany. Experimental use only.

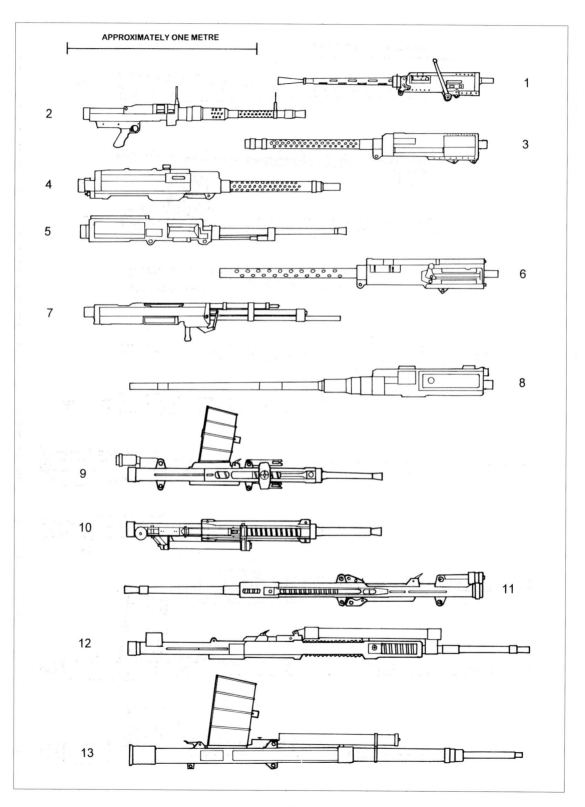

APPROXIMATELY ONE METRE

1

2

3

4

5

6

7

8

9

10

11

12

13

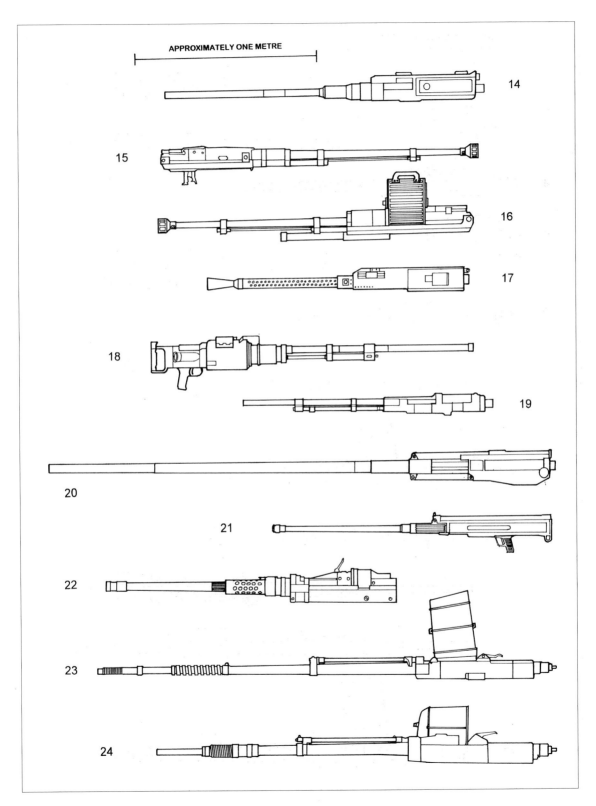

APPROXIMATELY ONE METRE

14

15

16

17

18

19

20

21

22

23

24

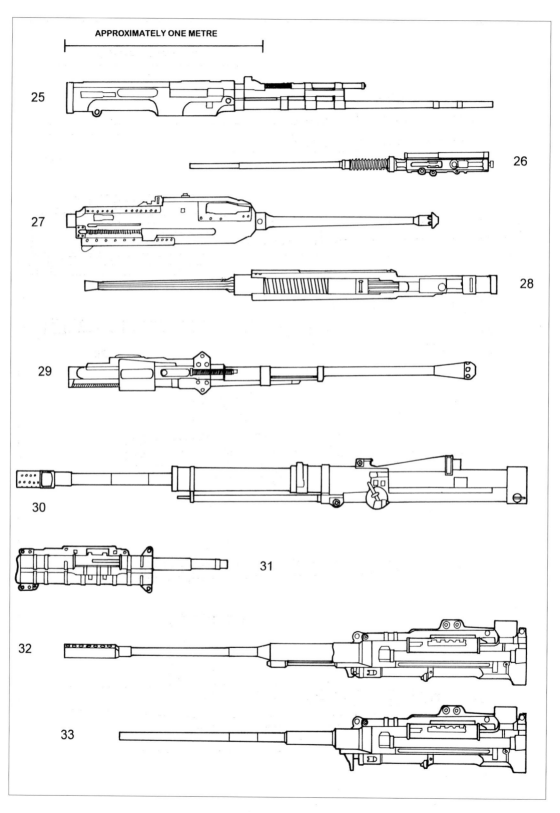

APPROXIMATELY ONE METRE

25

26

27

28

29

30

31

32

33

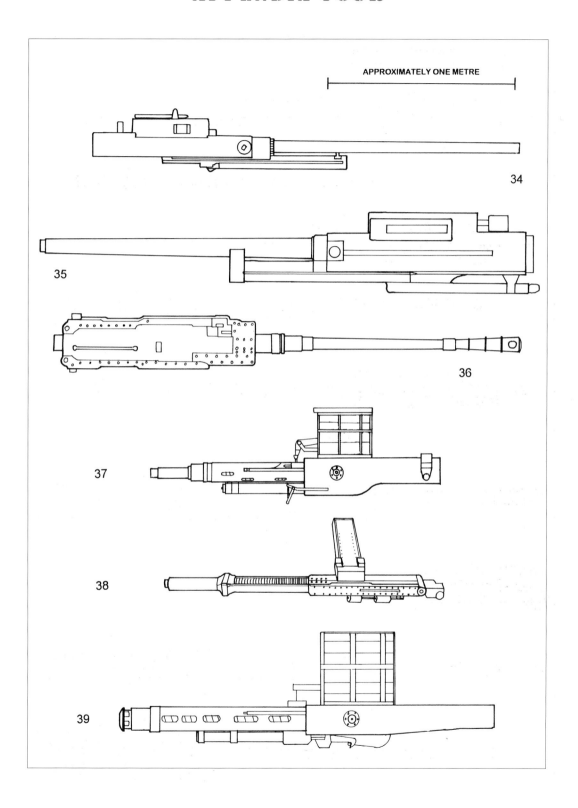

APPROXIMATELY ONE METRE

34

35

36

37

38

39

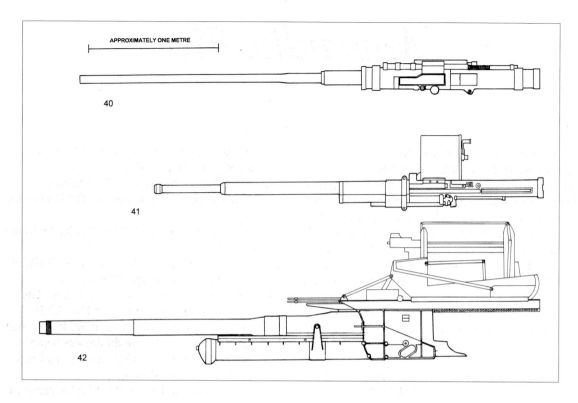

APPROXIMATELY ONE METRE

40

41

42

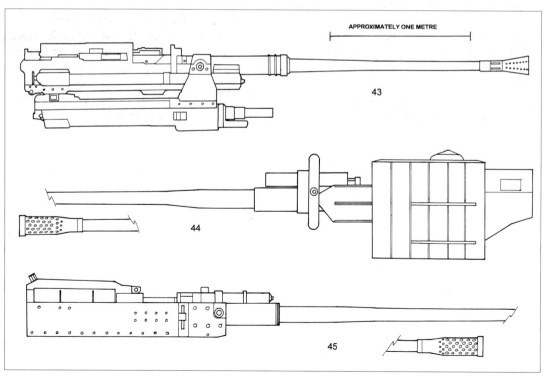

APPROXIMATELY ONE METRE

43

44

45

# *Appendix Five*

## COMPARATIVE DRAWINGS OF POST-WAR FIGHTER GUNS

THE FOLLOWING DRAWINGS REPRESENT FIGHTER aircraft guns which have been introduced into service since World War 2. As with the drawings in Appendix 4, they are not all drawn to precise scale so measurements should not be scaled from them. The approximate scale used is the same as in Annex 4, so the general size of the guns may be compared.

Particular thanks are expressed to the Russian Aviation Research Trust for making material available from which most of the Soviet guns have been drawn.

1. Nudelman-Rikhter NR-23 (23 × 115) USSR.
2. Nudelman N-37 (37 × 155) USSR. The largest calibre post-war fighter gun to see service.
3. Nudelman-Rikhter NR-30 (30 × 155B) USSR. A version with a different-shaped barrel casing and a bulbous muzzle brake also exists.
4. 20mm Mark 12 (20 × 110 USN) USA. The ultimate service derivative of the Hispano-Suiza HS 404, chambered for a more powerful cartridge.
5. 20mm M39 (20 × 102) USA. The only revolver cannon to be adopted for US service (so far).
6. 20mm M61 (20 × 102) USA. Six-barrel rotary cannon.
7. Gryazev-Shipunov GSh-23 (23 × 115) USSR. Twin-barrel gun, drawn from above.
8. 30mm Aden Mark 4 (30 × 113B) UK. The various Aden and the French DEFA/GIAT 540-550 series revolver cannon all looked very similar, the main visible differences being in barrel length (later GIAT guns having longer barrels than that shown).
9. 30mm Oerlikon KCA (30 × 173) Switzerland. Revolver cannon.
10. Mauser BK 27 (27 × 145B) Germany. Revolver cannon. Different muzzle attachments are used according to the installation.
11. Gryazev-Shipunov GSh-6-23 (23 × 115) Russia. Six-barrel rotary cannon.
12. Gryazev-Shipunov GSh-301 (30 × 165) Russia. Recoil-operated.

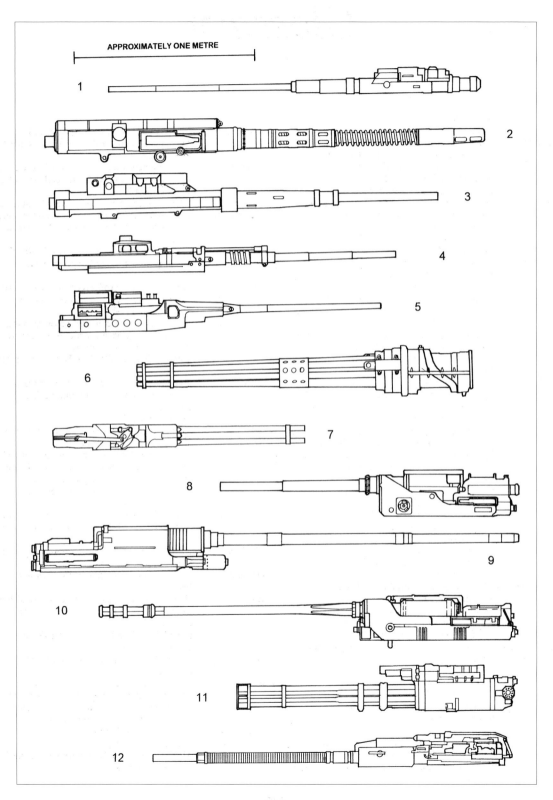

APPROXIMATELY ONE METRE

1

2

3

4

5

6

7

8

9

10

11

12

# *Glossary*

**AA**    anti-aircraft

**AC**    armoured car

**accelerator**    a pivoting lever inside a short-recoil mechanism which acts to accelerate the rearward movement of the bolt

**AFV**    armoured fighting vehicle

**AGL**    automatic grenade launcher

**AHEAD**    advanced hit efficiency and destruction (a proprietary Oerlikon ammunition development)

**AIFV**    armoured infantry fighting vehicle; also known as *MICV*

**air-cooled**    a weapon which achieves barrel cooling by radiation direct to the atmosphere

**ammunition**    collective name for cartridges (or equivalent)

**AP**    armour-piercing; a projectile designed to penetrate armour, or a cartridge loaded with such a projectile

**APC(BC)**    armour-piercing, capped (ballistic capped): an AP shot with a softer cap to aid penetration of face-hardened armour (and a streamlined cap to reduce air resistance)

**APCR**    armour-piercing, composite, rigid: shot consisting of a penetrating core (usually of tungsten alloy) enclosed within a light-alloy body, which travels as a unit to the target

**APDS**    armour-piercing, discarding-sabot: similar to APCR except that the body (which may be light alloy or plastic) breaks up and falls away from the penetrating core when the shot leaves the muzzle

**APFSDS**    armour-piercing, fin-stabilised, discarding-sabot: similar to APDS except that the penetrating core is long and narrow and is stabilised in flight by fins

**APHC**    armour-piercing, hard-core: an alternative designation for APCR

**APHE**    armour-piercing, high-explosive

**API**    armour-piercing incendiary

**API blowback**    advanced primer ignition blowback: a type of automatic mechanism

**APSV**    armour-piercing super velocity; British term for Littlejohn squeezebore ammunition (also initially used to describe APDS)

**arrowhead shot**    APCR with reduced-diameter alloy body in centre

**AT**    anti-tank

**ATGW**    anti-tank guided weapon

**automatic**    a weapon which continues to fire and reload automatically for as long as the trigger or firing button is pressed

**B**    added to a cartridge designation to identify a belted case (e.g. 20 × 105B)

**ball (round)**    a small-arms projectile or bullet, i.e. not *AP, I,*

*HE,* or *T*

**ballistics**    the science concerning the passage of a projectile from the instant of firing to the end of its flight

**ballistic cap**    a streamlined (usually light alloy) nose cone used to improve the ballistic coefficient of a blunt projectile

**ballistic coefficient**    a factor which measures the aerodynamic drag of a projectile and therefore the rate at which it loses the velocity; the higher the number, the lower the drag

**barrel**    the tube connected to (or integral with) the chamber, down which the projectile is accelerated

**barrel extension**    the part of the barrel which extends behind the chamber, usually to accommodate a locking mechanism

**base bleed**    a projectile which contains a slow-burning chemical in the base in order to reduce air resistance and extend range

**base fuze**    a detonating fuze fitted to the base of an HE shell

**battery**    a gun is 'in battery' when it is at rest in a forward position in the mounting (i.e. not recoiling)

**BB**    see *base bleed*

**belt**    (1) a raised strip around a cartridge case, in front of the extractor groove
(2) a strip of fabric or (more usually) metal, into which cartridges are fitted to facilitate feeding them into a weapon. Metal belts may be disintegrating, non-disintegrating or a continuous loop

**belted case**    a cartridge case with a raised section in front of the extractor groove to aid location in the chamber

**belt feed**    the use of a belt to supply ammunition to a gun mechanism

**belt link**    a piece of metal which constitutes a part of a belt

**BK**    *Bordkanone* (German): a large-calibre airborne cannon for ground attack (also used for current BK 27)

**blank**    a cartridge which has a primer and propellant but no projectile

**blowback**    a type of automatic weapon operating mechanism

**bolt**    a part of the operating system, containing the firing mechanism, which slides in line with the barrel, pushing a cartridge into the chamber and holding it there during firing

**bore**    the inside of the barrel

**bottlenecked cartridge**    a cartridge with a case whose diameter reduces sharply to the neck, creating a shoulder

**box magazine** — a type of magazine in which the cartridges are stacked on top of each other (they may be single or double stacked)

***Brandgranate*** — (German) incendiary shell

***Brandspreng granate*** — (German) high-explosive/ incendiary shell

**breech** — the opening at the rear of the chamber which allows cartridges to be loaded and fired cases extracted

**breechblock** — alternative term for bolt, normally used when its operating movement involves pivoting, or sliding vertically or horizontally

**breech face** — the part of the barrel surrounding the breech

**bullet** — see ball

**bullpup design** — a rifle in which the action and magazine are behind the trigger

**calibre** — (1) the diameter of a projectile, or of the inside of a barrel
(2) designation of the cartridge a weapon is designed for

**calibre length** — the barrel length divided by the calibre, usually prefixed with 'L'; e.g. a 40mm L/70 indicates a barrel ($40 \times 70 =$) 280 cm long

**cannelure** — a groove around a small-arms bullet for receiving a crimp

**cannon** — (modern) a large-calibre, fast-firing automatic weapon, generally taken to be between 20mm and around 57mm calibre

**cartridge** — a unit or round of ammunition, normally comprising the cartridge case, projectile, propellant and primer

**cartridge case** — the part of the cartridge which contains the propellant and holds the projectile and primer firmly in place

**caseless ammunition** — ammunition which does not have a cartridge case but uses solid propellant to hold the projectile and primer

**centrefire** — cartridge fired by a primer located in the centre of the head

**chain gun** — an externally powered automatic weapon which uses a chain to drive the operating cycle

**chamber** — the space at the rear of the barrel in which the cartridge is positioned and supported during firing

**chemical fuze** — a contact fuze on an HE shell which operates by percussion

**chromium plating** — used to protect the barrel bore and chamber

**CIWS** — close-in weapon system; a naval short-range AA/anti-missile system, usually with automatic aiming and firing

**clip** — a piece of metal which holds together several cartridges (normally by the case heads) for feeding into a weapon; or several cartridges held together by a clip

**closed bolt** — an automatic weapon designed to commence the firing cycle with the cartridge already loaded into the chamber (see open bolt)

**closed loop** — a CIWS control system which uses radar to track both target and projectiles and corrects the aim accordingly

**coaxial mounting** — a means of mounting a secondary gun in parallel with a primary gun so that both weapons can be aimed using the same sights

**COIN** — counter-insurgency

**combustible case** — a cartridge case which is designed to burn with the propellant

**contact fuze** — a fuze which is initiated by impact with the target

**cook-off** — the unwanted ignition of a cartridge by heat in a gun chamber

**cordite** — a type of propellant

**counter-recoil** — a type of gun mounting in which the gun is fired as it returns to battery, so the initial recoil force is expended in arresting the forward movement of the gun – see *floating mounting* and *soft recoil*

**cowling mounting** — an automatic weapon mounted in the cowling of a propeller-driven fighter and synchronised to fire through the propeller disc

**crimp** — a depression in the neck of a cartridge case, intended to hold the projectile firmly in place prior to firing

**CTA** — cased telescoped ammunition: in which the projectile is contained with the cartridge case (which is often combustible)

**dark trace** — the initial burn of a tracer, designed to give no light

**deflection** — the angle between the position of a crossing target (usually an aircraft) and the required aiming point, which will be ahead of it

**detonation** — the explosion of an HE projectile

**disintegrating link** — a type of ammunition belt consisting of metal links, which fall apart as each cartridge is chambered

**double base** — a type of propellant

**drill round** — a cartridge which is totally inert, used to practise loading and unloading drills; it is always made easily recognisable

**driving band** — a strip of soft metal or plastic around a projectile, which is intended to be gripped by the rifling in order to induce spin

**drum** — a type of circular magazine in which the cartridges are held parallel to each other (sometimes used to describe a pan magazine) – see helical drum and pan magazine.

**DU** — depleted uranium; a heavy metal used in some AP shot

**dual belt feed** — a gun with two belt feeds

**dummy round** — a cartridge which is completely inert (i.e. no primer or propellant)

**duplex loading** — a cartridge loaded with two full-calibre projectiles, intended to follow each other down the barrel – see *multiball, triplex*

**ejection** — the act of throwing an extracted cartridge case clear of the gun

**electric ignition** — a method of igniting cartridges by passing an electrical current through the primer

**electromagnetic gun** — a gun which uses electromagnetic force to accelerate a projectile (also known as a rail gun)

**electrothermal (chemical)** — a system which uses a plasma generator instead of a primer

**elevation** — the movement of a gun in its mounting through a vertical arc

**ER** — extended range

**ERFB** — extended range, full bore

**erosion** — wear on the inside of a barrel caused by hot propellant gases and friction generated by projectiles

**external ballistics** — the science of projectile flight from the muzzle of a gun

**extended chamber** — see *hooded chamber*

**externally powered** — a gun mechanism which requires an external source of power to operate; this is usually electric but may be hydraulic or manual, or in aircraft powered by engine gas or the slipstream

**extraction** — the act of pulling a fired cartridge case from the chamber

**extractor claw** — a hook, attached to the bolt, which fits into the extractor groove in order to pull the cartridge out of the chamber

**extractor groove** — a groove around the head of a cartridge case, into which the extractor claw fits

**FAA** — (British) Fleet Air Arm (1924 onwards)

**FAPDS** — frangible armour-piercing discarding-sabot

**feed** — the method of delivering ammunition to the gun

**FGB** — *Flächengondelbewaffnung* (German), an aircraft gun pod

**fin stabilised** — a projectile whose flight is stabilised by fins rather than by being spun by rifling

**firing cycle** — the sequence of loading, firing, extracting, ejecting and reloading

**firing pin** — a spring-loaded steel pin which strikes a primer to cause ignition

**FlaK** — *Fliegerabwehrkanone* (German), AA artillery; also sometimes given as *Flugabwehrkanone* or *Flugzeugabwehrkanone*

**flat trajectory** — the flight of a projectile which involves minimal drop due to gravity; associated with high velocity

**flexible mounting** — a simple, unpowered gun mounting in which the gun can be moved in traverse and elevation by the gunner's hands

**floating firing** — see *counter-recoil*

**floating mounting** — see *counter-recoil*

**fluted chamber** — longitudinal grooves in the chamber to permit gun gas to seep back around the cartridge case to prevent it from sticking

**FMPDS** — frangible missile-piercing discarding-sabot

**frangible** — a projectile designed to break up on hitting the target

**full-calibre** — a projectile which fills the bore of a gun – see *sub-calibre*

**fuze** — a device for initiating the detonation of an HE shell

**gas operated** — a type of gun mechanism using gas tapped from the barrel to drive the firing cycle

**gas-unlocked blowback** — a type of gun mechanism using gas tapped from the barrel to unlock the breechblock; the remainder of the firing cycle being blowback

**Gast** — a type of twin-barrel automatic gun mechanism

**Gatling** — an early type of manually powered rotary gun; sometimes used to refer to any rotary weapon

**GAU** — (American) gun aircraft unit

**Glimmspur** — (German) often written *Gl'spur*; a dimly glowing tracer for night use

**GPMG** — general-purpose machine gun

**grain** — measure of weight used in UK and USA for propellant charges and (in smaller calibres) projectiles; 1 gram = 15.432 grains

**gravity feed** — the use of gravity to supply ammunition to the gun mechanism

**grenade launcher** — a low-velocity gun designed to fire small HE projectiles

**grooves** — the larger interior diameter of a rifled barrel; between the lands

**gun gas** — gas generated by ignition of the propellant in a cartridge

**gun pod** — a detachable pod, containing a gun (or guns) and ammunition, which is carried by aircraft

**gyro gunsight** — a simple type of lead-computing gunsight to aid deflection shooting

**half-track** — a vehicle with tracks replacing the rear wheels

**hang fire** — a delay in the ignition of a cartridge after the primer has been struck

**Hartkern-munition** — (German, WW2) an APCR shot used in aircraft cannon

**HC** — high-capacity; a shell with an unusually large (HE) capacity

**HE** — high-explosive; the normal filling of cannon shells

**head** — the rear of the cartridge, into which is fitted the primer

**headspace** — the accurate location of a cartridge in the chamber ready for ignition

**headstamp** — information about the cartridge, stamped into the head

**HEAT** — high-explosive, anti-tank – see hollow charge

**heavy machine-gun** — a machine gun with a calibre significantly larger than a military rifle cartridge but smaller than a cannon; in effect, 12.7–15 mm

**HEDP** — high-explosive dual-purpose; a modern projectile which combines hollow-charge with general HE effect

**helical drum** — a magazine in which all rounds point inwards, following a spiral track

**high-angle mounting** — a mounting which permits a weapon to be elevated at or close to the vertical for AA fire

**hollow charge** — an explosive projectile with a cone-shaped hollow, lined with metal, in the nose, which generates an intense armour-piercing jet

**hooded chamber** — a chamber which is longer than necessary to contain a cartridge; associated with API blowback designs

**HMG** — heavy machine gun

**HV** — high-velocity

**HVAP** — high-velocity, armour-piercing; US description for APCR, also used to describe early APDS

**hybrid** — a mechanism which uses more than one operating principle

**igniter charge** — intermediate charge which ignites the primer burn, helping to ignite the propellant

**ignition** — the igniting of propellant by a primer

**IJA** — Imperial Japanese Army

| | |
|---|---|
| **IJN** | Imperial Japanese Navy |
| **inert** | a cartridge or explosive which cannot fire or detonate |
| **internal ballistics** | the science of the passage of a projectile down a gun barrel |
| **kamikaze** | (Japanese) 'Divine Wind'; name given to suicide attacks |
| *Kriegsmarine* | German Navy |
| **KwK** | *Kampfwagenkanone* (German), tank gun |
| *Lafette* | (German) gun mounting |
| **LAFV** | light AFV; typically, an armoured car or light tank |
| **lands** | the smaller interior diameter of a rifled barrel; between the grooves |
| **lead computing gunsight** | a gunsight which calculates the correct point of aim for deflection shooting |
| *Leuchtspur* | (German) tracer; often written *L'Spur* |
| **linear action** | a gun mechanism in which the elements reciprocate in line with the gun barrel |
| **link** | an element of an ammunition belt |
| **linkless feed** | a method of supplying ammunition to a gun in which the cartridges are not linked together |
| **LMG** | light machine gun |
| **lock time** | the period of time between pressing the trigger or gun button and the first shot being fired |
| **long recoil** | a type of gun operating mechanism |
| *Luftwaffe* | German Air Force |
| **LV** | low-velocity |
| **machine gun** | an automatic weapon of less than 20mm calibre |
| **magazine** | a container which holds ammunition ready for loading into a gun |
| **manually operated** | a gun in which the firing cycle is operated by a manual crank or lever |
| **MG** | machine gun (German: *Maschinengewehr*) |
| **MGB** | motor gun boat: a small, fast, naval vessel armed with guns |
| **MICV** | mechanised infantry combat vehicle (also known as AIFV) |
| *Minengeschoss* or *M-Geschoss* | (German) mine shell |
| **mine shell** | a thin-walled, lightweight type of HE projectile |
| **MK** | (German) *Maschinenkanone*, automatic cannon |
| **MMG** | medium machine gun: a heavy gun of rifle calibre |
| *moteur-canon* | (French) motor cannon; an aircraft cannon designed for mounting between the cylinder banks of a vee-engine, firing through a hollow propeller hub. |
| **mounting** | the method of supporting a gun ready for firing |
| **MTB** | motor torpedo boat: a small, fast, naval vessel armed with torpedoes |
| **multiball** | a cartridge which contains several projectiles – see *duplex, triplex* |
| **multipurpose ammunition** | ammunition with a mixture of capabilities (AP, HE, I); associated with the Norwegian firm Raufoss |
| **muzzle** | the end of the barrel from which the projectile emerges |
| **muzzle blast** | the violent escape of gun gas from the muzzle as a projectile leaves the barrel |
| **muzzle booster** | a device fitted to the muzzle to use some of the muzzle blast to increase recoil, to assist the action of recoil-operated guns |
| **muzzle brake** | a device fitted to the muzzle which deflects part of the muzzle blast to the side or rear in order to reduce recoil |
| **muzzle energy** | a calculation of the energy of a projectile as it leaves the muzzle; a function of projectile velocity and weight |
| **muzzle velocity** | the speed of a projectile as it leaves the muzzle |
| **NATO** | North Atlantic Treaty Organisation |
| **neck** | the part of a cartridge case which holds the projectile |
| **necked-down** | a cartridge case which has its neck reduced in diameter to accept a smaller-calibre projectile than the case was designed for |
| **necked-up** | (or necked-out) a cartridge case which has its neck increased in diameter to accept a larger calibre projectile than the case was designed for |
| **obturation** | the sealing of a gun breech to prevent the escape of gun gas on firing (in automatic weapons, normally achieved by the cartridge case); also forward obturation achieved by the driving bands |
| *obus* | (French) shell |
| **OCSW** | Objective Crew Served Weapon; US programme for a light automatic 25mm support weapon |
| **OICW** | Objective Individual Combat Weapon; US programme for a new infantry weapon combining 5.56mm and 20mm calibres |
| **open bolt** | an automatic weapon designed to commence the firing cycle without a cartridge loaded into the chamber – see *closed bolt* |
| **optronics** | the combination of optical and electronic systems to provide day/night/all-weather sights |
| **ounce (oz)** | UK and USA measure of weight; 1oz = 28.35g |
| **over-bore** | a cartridge which has a case capacity too large for all of the propellant to be efficiently utilised |
| **PaK** | *Panzerabwehrkanone* (German), anti-tank gun |
| **pan magazine** | a flat, circular magazine in which the cartridges are held pointing inwards – see *drum* and *helical drum* |
| *Panzerbrand-spreng granat-patrone L'spur m. Zerl* | (German) armour-piercing high-explosive incendiary cartridge with tracer and self-destruct |
| *Panzergranat patrone* | (German) armour-piercing cartridge |
| *Patrone* | (German) cartridge |
| **penetration** | the ability of an AP shot to penetrate armour |
| **percussion ignition** | a method of igniting cartridges by striking a percussion primer with a firing pin |
| **PFHE** | pre-fragmented high-explosive |
| *Pfeilgeschoss* | (German) arrow shell; a long, fin-stabilised HE projectile |
| **pintle mounting** | a type of flexible mounting in which the gun is |

| | |
|---|---|
| | mounted at the top of a vertical rod |
| **pivoting block** | a gun mechanism in which the breechblock movement is pivoted |
| **Pom-pom** | unofficial name for a slow-firing automatic weapon, usually of 37mm or 40mm calibre |
| **primer** | a percussion cap fitted into the head of a cartridge case, used to ignite the propellant |
| **primer pocket** | the part of a cartridge case into which the primer fits |
| **progressive rifling** | rifling which commences with a gentle or zero twist, which gradually increases in twist down the length of the barrel |
| **projectile** | any bullet, shot or shell fired from a gun |
| **propellant** | the chemical which burns rapidly to generate gas which accelerates the projectile up the gun barrel |
| **propeller disc** | the area swept by the blades of an aircraft propeller |
| **propeller hub or boss** | the central part of an aircraft propeller, which may be made hollow to allow an engine-mounted gun to fire through it |
| **proximity fuze** | a shell fuze which is triggered by the close proximity of a target |
| **PT boat** | (American) a small, fast naval vessel |
| **pyrophoric** | gives off sparks on impact and/or ignites spontaneously at high temperature |
| **Pzgr** | *Panzergranate* (German): AP Projectile |
| **R** | rimmed cartridge case (when it occurs at the end of a cartridge designation, as in 20 × 99R) |
| **radial engine** | an engine in which the cylinders are arranged radially, with the crankshaft in the centre |
| **rail gun** | see electromagnetic gun |
| **railway gun** | a gun mounted on a railway wagon |
| **rate of fire** | frequency with which individual shots are fired in an automatic weapon, usually measured in rpm |
| **rebated rim** | a cartridge case with a rim of smaller diameter than the case body |
| **RAF** | (British) Royal Air Force (since 1918) |
| **RB** | rebated rim (case description, added to the end of a cartridge designation, also given as RR) |
| **RCMG** | rifle-calibre machine gun, typically of 7.5–8mm calibre |
| **receiver** | the body of the gun, to which the barrel and operating mechanism are attached |
| **recoil-operated** | a gun mechanism operated by the recoiling gun barrel |
| **reflector sight** | a gunsight in which the aiming marks are reflected onto an angled glass plate through which the gunner views the target |
| **revolver cannon** | a normally single-barrel gun with a rotating cylinder containing several chambers, each of which is loaded and unloaded in stages, and fired as it comes into line with the barrel |
| **RFC** | (British) Royal Flying Corps (1912–1918) |
| **rifling** | the spiral grooving within a gun barrel which grips the projectile and spins it in order to ensure its stability – see progressive rifling |
| **rimfire** | a cartridge which is ignited by means of a percussion compound contained within the rim – see *centrefire* |
| **rimless (case)** | a cartridge case in which the rim is the same diameter as the case body, separated from it by an extractor groove |
| **rimmed (case)** | a cartridge case with a rim which has a larger diameter than the case body |
| **RN** | (British) Royal Navy |
| **RNAS** | (British) Royal Naval Air Service (1914–1918) |
| **rotary cannon** | a multi-barrel gun with several parallel barrels rotating around a common axis, each barrel being loaded and fired in turn |
| **rotary lock** | the locking of the bolt to the barrel extension by a rotary movement |
| **round (of ammunition)** | a single cartridge (or equivalent) |
| **RP** | rocket projectile |
| **rpg** | rounds per gun |
| **RR** | rebated rim (also given as RB) |
| **rpm** | rounds per minute; the usual measure of rate of fire |
| ***Rüstsatz, Rüstsätze*** | field conversion set(s) (German); not fitted at the factory |
| ***S-Boot*** | *Schnell-boot* (German): a small, fast, naval vessel commonly but inexplicably known to the Allies as an E-boat |
| **sabot** | a sleeve into which a sub-calibre projectile is fitted, to enable it to be fired from a larger-calibre weapon; the sabot breaks up and falls away after the projectile leaves the muzzle |
| **saddle drum** | a type of drum magazine in which the cartridges are held in two small connected drums on either side of the action, from each of which rounds are fed in turn |
| **salvo squeezebore** | a multiball system in which the projectiles are of the squeezebore type |
| **SAP(HE)** | semi-armour-piercing (high-explosive) |
| ***Schräge Musik*** | jazz or oblique music (German); a type of gun mounting used by night-fighters, in which the barrels point upwards and forwards |
| **SD** | self-destruct; an HE projectile which is designed to detonate a few seconds after firing |
| **SDR** | sectional density ratio: the ratio between calibre and projectile weight; together with the projectile shape this determines the ballistic coefficient |
| **selective fire** | can fire semi or fully automatically |
| **semi-automatic** | a rifle which automatically fires, ejects and reloads each time the trigger is pulled; also used to describe artillery in which the fired case is automatically ejected but a new round is manually loaded |
| **semi-rimmed (case)** | a cartridge case which has a rim only slightly larger in diameter than the case body, separated from it by an extractor groove; also known as semi-rimless |
| **shaped charge** | see *hollow charge* |
| **shell** | a projectile which is hollow in order to contain HE or other contents |
| **short recoil** | a type of recoil-operated gun mechanism |
| **shot** | any solid armour-piercing projectile (i.e. contains no HE) |
| **shoulder** | the part of a cartridge case where the diameter reduces sharply from the case body to the neck |
| **shrapnel** | a type of anti-personnel artillery ammunition which consists of a shell containing metal balls in the forward part and a small bursting |

charge at the rear, detonated by a time fuze to explode just before reaching the target; named after its nineteenth-century inventor (nowadays loosely used to describe shell fragments)

| | |
|---|---|
| **sights** | the devices used to aim a gun |
| **single base** | a type of propellant |
| **slant range** | line-of-sight range from an AA position to a target aircraft |
| **sliding block** | a type of gun action locking mechanism which moves across the breech face |
| **smooth-bored** | a barrel which is not rifled (used with fin-stabilised ammunition) |
| **soft recoil** | see *counter-recoil* |
| **SPAAG** | self-propelled anti-aircraft gun; usually mounted on an AFV chassis |
| **spin-stabilised** | a projectile whose flight is stabilised by being rotated by rifling |
| *Sprenggranate* | (German) HE shell |
| **squeeze bore** | a gun in which special projectiles are fired down a tapered barrel, or fitment to the end of the barrel, thereby reducing their diameter |
| **SR** | semi-rimmed (or semi-rimless); a type of cartridge case |
| **stabilised mounting** | a mounting in which the gun is kept to a constant point of aim regardless of the movement of the vehicle or ship which carries it |
| **STANAG** | Standardisation Agreement; applies to NATO equipment |
| **Stellite** | a heat-resistant material used to line gun barrels |
| **straight-cased cartridge** | a cartridge case which has little or no taper between the head and the neck; which therefore has no shoulder |
| **striking angle** | the angle at which an AP projectile strikes armour plate – two different conventions have applied: in one, a strike perpendicular to the plate is called 0°, in NATO it is called 90° |
| **strip** | a number of cartridges linked rigidly together for ease of loading |
| *Sturmgruppe* | attack group (German), consisting of aircraft which were heavily armed to attack daylight heavy bombers at the end of WW2 |
| **sub-calibre** | a projectile which is smaller than the bore of the gun; for firing, it is supported by a sabot – see *APDS, APFSDS* and *full calibre* |
| **sub-calibre training** | a cartridge used for training purposes in a much larger-calibre (usually artillery) weapon via an adaptor |
| **sub-machine-gun** | a portable machine gun normally designed to use pistol ammunition |
| **sub-projectiles** | projectiles which are carried by a larger projectile |
| **SV** | super velocity; implies a lighter than standard projectile |
| **synchronised** | a gun mounting fitted to a piston-engined fighter in which the gun is designed to fire through the propeller disc; each shot has to be precisely timed (synchronised) to avoid hitting a propeller blade |
| **T** | tracer (when attached to a projectile designation) |
| **taboo zone** | restriction on the freedom of movement of a flexible gun mounting to prevent firing at own |

| | |
|---|---|
| | ship or aircraft |
| **taper bore** | see *squeeze bore* |
| **telescoped ammunition** | ammunition in which the projectile is buried within the cartridge case |
| **terminal ballistics** | the science concerning the performance of projectiles on striking the target |
| **time fuze** | a fuze fitted to an HE shell which detonates it a predetermined time after firing |
| **time of flight** | the time taken for a projectile to reach its target |
| **toggle joint** | a type of elbow joint used in some short-recoil gun mechanisms |
| **TP** | target practice; a type of projectile or cartridge used for training |
| **tracer** | a chemical compound in the base of a projectile which burns slowly, giving a visible indication of its trajectory |
| **trajectory** | the curve traced by a projectile in flight |
| **traverse** | the movement of a gun in its mounting through a horizontal arc |
| **triple base** | a type of propellant |
| **triplex loading** | a cartridge which contains three projectiles – see *duplex, multiball* |
| **tripod** | a type of gun mounting used with light portable weapons |
| *Trommel* | (German) a drum magazine |
| **Trunnion** | projection from a gun body used to mount the gun, traditionally at the point of balance |
| *Übungsmunition* | (German) often written *Üb*; practice ammunition |
| **USAAC** | United States Army Air Corps (1926–1947) |
| **USAAF** | United States Army Air Force (1941–1947) |
| **USAF** | United States Air Force (1947 onwards) |
| **USMC** | United States Marine Corps |
| **USN** | United States Navy |
| **vee-engine** | a piston engine in which the cylinders are arranged in two banks, set at an angle to each other, driving a common crankshaft |
| *Vierling* | quadruple (German); a four-barrel gun mounting |
| **VT** | WW2 code letters for a proximity fuze |
| **water-cooled** | a weapon which achieves barrel cooling by means of a water jacket |
| *Wolfram* | (German) tungsten |
| *Zerleger* | (German) self-destroying (fuze), often written *Zerl*; *m. Zerl* means *mit Zerl* (with self-destruct), *o. Zerl* means *ohne Zerl* (without self-destruct) |

## CONVERSION FACTORS

The following approximate conversion factors will convert metric to Imperial measures:

To convert millimetres to inches .........................divide by 25.4
To convert centimetres to inches.........................divide by 2.54
To convert metres to feet...............................multiply by 3.28
To convert metres to yards...............................multiply by 1.1
To convert kilometres to miles...........................divide by 1.61
To convert grams to grains..........................multiply by 15.432
To convert grams to ounces ..............................divide by 28.35
To convert kilograms to pounds ......................multiply by 2.2

# *Sources*

THE MOST COMPREHENSIVE AND AUTHORITATIVE SOURCES OF INFORMATION FOR ALL MODERN WEAPONS AND ammunition are the various Jane's annuals. This information has been supplemented by various manufacturers' published data. In addition, the following publications, covering current and historical equipment, were consulted in the preparation of this book:

## AMMUNITION – KEY TEXTS

Courtney-Green, P. R. *Ammunition for the Land Battle.* Brassey's (UK, 1991)

Davis, D. M. *Historical Development Summary of Automatic Cannon Calibre Ammunition: 20–30 Millimeter.* Air Force Armament Laboratory (USA, 1984)

Hogg, I. V. *The Illustrated Encyclopedia of Ammunition.* Quarto (London, 1985)

Hogg, I. V. *Jane's Directory of Military Small Arms Ammunition.* Jane's Publishing Company (London, 1985)

### Other Books

Anon. *Small-Caliber Ammunition Identification Guide.* US Army Material Development and Readiness Command (1981)

Anon. *Oerlikon Pocket Book.* Oerlikon-Bührle AG (Zurich, 1981)

Braun, M. *Handbuch der Flugzeug Bordwaffenmunition.* (1977)

Hackley, F. W., Woodin, W. H. and Scranton, E. L. *History of Modern US Military Small Arms Ammunition, Volumes I and II.* The Macmillan Company (New York, 1967) and The Gun Room Press (USA, 1978)

Hogg, I.V. (introduction) *The American Arsenal: The World War II Official Standard Ordnance Catalogue.* Greenhill Books (London, 1996)

Huon, J. *Military Rifle and Machine Gun Cartridges.* Arms & Armour Press (London, 1986)

Kent, D. W. *German 7.9mm Military Ammunition 1888–1945.* Privately published (USA)

Labbett, P. *British Small Arms Ammunition 1864–1938.* Privately published (UK, 1993)

Lenselink, J. and de Hek, W. D. *Notes on Small and Medium Calibre Military Cartridges.* Delfia Press (Rijswijk, 1986)

Lenselink, J. and de Hek, W. D. *Military Cartridges Part 1 3.5 × 45> 20 × 138B.* Privately published (Netherlands, 1995)

Lippert, J. *Deutsche Bordwaffen Munition Bis 1945.* Privately published (München, 1989)

## GUN DESIGN – KEY TEXTS

Allsop, D. F. *Cannons.* Brassey's (UK, 1995)

Chinn, G. M. *The Machine Gun.* (5 volumes) Vols I–IV Bureau of Ordnance, Department of the Navy (USA, 1951–55); Vol V RAMP Inc. 1987

Musgrave, D. D. *German Machineguns.* Greenhill Books (London, 1992)

Richardson, D. *The History of the Revolver Cannon.* Oerlikon-Contraves (Zurich, 1994)

### Other Books

Anon. *Oerlikon Pocket Book.* Oerlikon-Bührle AG (Zurich, 1981)

Hobart F.W.A., *Pictorial History of the Machine Gun.* Ian Allan (Shepperton, 1971)

Gander, T. *The Machine Gun: A Modern Survey.* Patrick Stephens (Yeovil, 1993)

Reinhart, C. am Rhyn, M. *Automatwaffen II.* Verlag Stocker-Schmid, Dietikon-Zürich (1983)

Schreier, K. *Guide to the United States Machine Guns.* Normount Technical Publications (Oregon, 1971)

## ARMY WEAPONS INC. ANTI-TANK RIFLES – KEY TEXTS

Archer, D. *Jane's Heavy Automatic Weapons.* Macdonald and Jane's (London, 1978)

Chinn, G. M. *The Machine Gun.* (5 volumes)
Bureau of Ordnance, Department of the Navy
(USA, 1951–87)

Hoffschmidt, E. J. *Know Your Antitank Rifles.*
Blacksmith Corp (USA, 1977)

Musgrave, D. D. *German Machineguns.* Greenhill
Books (London, 1992)

*Other Books*

Allsop, D. F. *Cannons.* Brassey's (UK, 1995)

Anon. *100 Jahre Eidg. Waffenfabrik Bern.* (ND)

Anon. *Technisches Reglement No. 16 Die schwere
Tankbüsche Tb. 41.* (1941)

Chamberlain, P. and Gander, T. *WW2 Fact Files:
Anti-Aircraft Guns.* Macdonald and Jane's
(London, 1975)

Chamberlain, P. and Gander, T. *WW2 Fact Files:
Anti-Tank Weapons.* Macdonald and Jane's
(London, 1974)

Foss, C. F. *Artillery of the World.* Ian Allan
(London, 1981)

Gander, T. *The 40mm Bofors Gun.* Patrick Stephens
(UK, 1990)

Gander, T. *The Machine Gun: A Modern Survey.*
Patrick Stephens (Yeovil, 1993)

Hogg, I.V. (introduction) *The American Arsenal:
The World War II Official Standard Ordnance
Catalogue.* Greenhill Books (London, 1996)

Hogg, I.V. *Anti-Aircraft: A History of Air Defence.*
Macdonald and Jane's (London, 1978)

Hogg, I. V. *German Artillery of World War Two.*
Arms and Armour Press (London)

Hogg, I. V. *British & American Artillery of World
War Two.* Arms and Armour Press (London, 1978)

Hogg, I. V. *Infantry Support Weapons.* Greenhill
Books (London, 1995)

Hogg, I. V. *The Greenhill Military Small Arms Data
Book.* Greenhill Books (London 1999)

Hogg, I.V. and Thurston, L.F. *British Artillery
Weapons & Ammunition 1914–18.* Ian Allan
(London, 1972)

Hogg, I.V. and Weeks, J. *Military Small Arms of the
20th Century.* Arms and Armour Press
(London, 1991)

Jessen, H. *Automatic Standard Arms of Modern
Warfare: Madsen machine guns and machine
cannon.* Dansk Industri Syndikat (Copenhagen,
1946)

Nicholson, C. and Hughes, B.P. *The History of the
Royal Artillery 1919–1939.* Royal Artillery
Institution, 1978

Pile, Sir F. P. *Ack-Ack: Britain's Defence Against Air
Attack During the Second World War.* George G.
Harrap (London, 1949)

Reinhart, C. and Rhyn, M. *Automat Waffen II.*
Verlag Stocker-Schmid, Dietikon-Zürich (1983)

Sallaz, K. and Riklin, P. *Bewaffnung und Ausrüstung
der Schweizer Armee seit 1917: Panzer und
Panzerabwehr.* Verlag Stocker-Schmid (Dietikon-
Zürich, 1982)

Schild, H. *Bewaffnung und Ausrüstung der Schweizer
Armee seit 1917: Fliegerabwehr.* Verlag Stocker-
Schmid (Dietikon-Zürich, 1982)

Skennerton, I. *British Small Arms of World War 2.*
Greenhill Books (London, 1988)

Tantum, W. H. and Hoffschmidt, E. J., (eds.) *Second
World War Combat Weapons: Japanese.* WE Inc.
(Connecticut, 1968)

Weeks, J. *World War II Small Arms.* Macdonald &
Co. (London, 1988)

Weeks, J. *Small Arms Profile 21: Recoilless Anti-
Tank Weapons.* Profile Publications (Windsor,
1973)

Werrel, K. P. *Archie, Flak, AAA and SAM.* Air
University Press (USA, 1988)

Zaloga, S. *ZSU-23–4 Shilka and Soviet Air Defense
Gun Vehicles.* Concord Publications
(Hong Kong, 1993)

Zaloga, S. & Madej, V. *The Polish Campaign 1939.*
Hippocrene Books (New York, 1991)

## NAVAL EQUIPMENT – KEY TEXTS

Campbell, J. *Naval Weapons of World War 2.*
Conway Maritime Press (London, 1985)

Friedman, N. *The Naval Institute Guide to World
Naval Weapon Systems.* US Naval Institute
(1989 and 1994 update)

Friedman, N. *US Naval Weapons.* Naval Institute
Press (Annapolis)

*Other Books*

Allsop, D. F. *Cannons.* Brassey's (UK, 1995)

Chinn, G. M. *The Machine Gun.* (5 volumes)
Bureau of Ordnance, Department of the Navy
(USA, 1951–87)

Hodges, P. and Friedman, N. *Destroyer Weapons of*

*World War 2.* Conway (London, 1979)

Nordenfelt, T. *The Nordenfelt Machine Guns.* Griffin & Co. (Portsmouth, 1884)

Richardson, R. *Naval Armament.* Jane's (London, 1981)

Werrel, K. P. *Archie, Flak, AAA and SAM.* Air University Press (USA, 1988)

## AIR FORCE EQUIPMENT – KEY TEXTS

Chant, C. *World Encyclopaedia of Modern Air Weapons.* Patrick Stephens (UK, 1988)

Chinn, G. M. *The Machine Gun.* (5 volumes) Bureau of Ordnance, Department of the Navy (USA, 1951–87)

Gunston, W. *Encyclopedia of Aircraft Armament.* Salamander Books (London, 1987)

Price, A. *Combat Development in World War Two: Fighter Aircraft.* Arms and Armour Press (UK, 1989)

Richardson, D. *The History of the Revolver Cannon.* Oerlikon-Contraves (Zurich, 1994)

Woodman, H. *Early Aircraft Armament.* Arms & Armour Press (London, 1989)

### Other Books

Anderton, D. A. and Watanabe, R. *Aggressors Volume 3; Interceptor vs. Heavy Bomber.* Airlife (UK, 1991)

Bruchiss, L. *Aircraft Armament.* Aerosphere (New York, 1945)

Bürli, A. *Flugzeug-bewaffnung: Die Schusswaffen der Scweizerischen Militärflugzeug.* Verlag Stocker-Schmid (Dietikon-Zürich, 1994)

Fozard, J. W. (ed) *Sydney Camm and the Hurricane. Perspectives on the master fighter designer and his finest achievement.* Smithsonian (1991)

Francillon, R. J. *Japanese Aircraft of the Pacific War.* Putnam (London, 1979)

Gooderson, I. *Air Power at the Battlefront: Allied Close Air Support in Europe 1939–45.* Frank Cass (London 1998)

Goulding, J. *Interceptor.* Ian Allan (UK, 1986)

Griehl, M. and Dressel, J. *German Anti-Tank Aircraft.* Schiffer (1993).

Green, W. *War Planes of the Second World War* (10 volumes). Macdonald & Co. (London, 1960–1968)

Gunston, W. *Encyclopedia of Russian Aircraft 1875–1995.* Osprey (London, 1995)

Gunston, W. and Gordon, Y. *Yakovlev Aircraft Since 1924.* Putnam (London, 1997)

Hahn, F. *Deutsche Geheimwaffen 1939–45.* Erich Hoffman Verlag (Heidenheim, 1963)

Hoffschmidt, E. J. *German Aircraft Guns and Cannons.* WE Inc (Greenwich, USA)

Hogg, I. V. (introduction) *The American Arsenal: The World War II Official Standard Ordnance Catalogue.* Greenhill Books (London, 1996)

Jarrett, P. (ed) *Aircraft of the Second World War: The Development of the Warplane 1939–45.* Putnam (UK, 1997)

Keith, C. H. *I Hold My Aim.* Tinling & Co. (UK, 1946)

King, H. F. *Armament of British Aircraft 1909–39.* Putnam (London, 1971)

Kosin, R. *The German Fighter since 1915.* Putnam (UK, 1988)

Mason, T. *The Secret Years. Flight Testing at Boscombe Down 1939–45.* Hikoki (UK 1998)

Merrick, K. *German Aircraft Interiors 1939–45. Vol. 1 – Day Fighters.* Monogram Aviation Publications (Massachusetts, 1996)

Musgrave, D. D. *German Machineguns.* Greenhill Books (London, 1992)

Nemecek, V. *The History of Soviet Aircraft.* Williams Collins (London, 1986)

Postan, M., Hay, D. and Scott, J. *Design and Development of Weapons.* HMSO (1964)

Schliephake, H. *Die Bordwaffen der Luftwaffe von deb Anfängen bis zur Gegenwart.* Motorbuch Verlag (Stuttgart, 1977)

Tanner, J (ed.) *British Aircraft Guns of World War Two.* Arms and Armour Press (London, 1979)

Vanags-Baginskis, A. and Watanabe, R. *Aggressors Volume 1: Tank Buster vs. Combat Vehicle.* Airlife (UK, 1990)

Wallace, G. F. *Guns of the Royal Air Force 1939–1945.* William Kimber and Co. (London, 1972)

Wallace Clarke, R. *British Aircraft Armament.* (two volumes) Patrick Stephens Ltd (UK, 1993 and 1994)

## JOURNAL AND MAGAZINE ARTICLES

Anon. 'Die 3,7-cm-Flak M 42 der Deutschen Kriegsmarine', *Waffen-Revue 106–107*

Anon. 'Paths of Destruction – NWM De Kruithoorn Demonstration of Frangible Medium Calibre Ammunition', *Military Technology* (12/94)

Barnes, S. 'Helicopter Gunnery: Options and Tactics', *Military Technology* (8/94)

Boulay, P. 'Comment L'Helicoptère de combat naquit en France', *Le Fana de l'Aviation* (2/96)

Broden, D. 'Revolutionising Combat Capability', *Global Defence Review, 1999*

Bustin, I. 'Getting to the Point – Cased Telescopic Ammunition Development in Europe', *Military Technology* (3/96)

Carlin, J. 'Ordnance Collecting', a regular column in *The Armourer*.

Frommer, H. 'Status and Trends in Automatic Cannons', *Military Technology* (3/85)

Gryazev, V. and Zelenko, V. 'Russia's Modern Aircraft Gun Armament' *Military Parade* (July–August 1997)

James, F. W. 'Lahti 20mm Anti-Tank Rifle', *Guns & Weapons* (March/April, 1990)

Johansson, S. 'Pulsed Power in Weapon Applications', *Celsius Defence News, Naval Issue 99*

Kaiser, H and Schmucker, G. 'Military Fuzes', *Military Technology* (4/85)

Kontis, G. 'Special Application Rifles', *Global Defence Review* (1999)

Labbett, P. 'Anti-Tank Rifle Ammunition', *Guns Review* (Jan 1967)

Labbett, P. 'Anti-Tank Rifle Ammunition', *Guns Review* (Feb 1984)

Labbett, P. 'Cannon Ammunition 15mm to 35mm, 1945–1990', *Guns Review* (two parts: November and December 1990)

Labbett, P. 'Russian 20mm ShVAK Aircraft Ammunition', *Guns Review* (June 1993)

Labbett, P. 'Russian 23 × 115mm Aircraft Ammunition', *Guns Review* (July 1993)

Labbett, P. 'Russian 23 × 152mm Cannon Ammunition', *Guns Review* (August 1993)

Labbett, P. 'Russian 30mm and 37mm Cannon Ammunition', *Guns Review* (September 1993)

Labbett, P. 'The .661″ Vickers Cartridge', *Guns Review* (July 1981)

Labbett, P. '30mm Hispano-Suiza Type 825 Ammunition', *Guns Review* (June 1989)

Petersen, D. 'Bofors 57 Mk3 Naval All-Target Gun', *Celsius Defence News, Naval Issue 99*

Simpkin, R. 'Light Armoured Vehicle Armaments', *Military Technology* (3/85)

Steadman, N. 'Large Calibre Sniping', *Military Technology* (11/91)

Strandli, K. R. 'Multipurpose Ammunition', *Military Technology* (9/91)

Whitford, R. 'Fundamentals of Fighter Design: Armament and Tactics', *Air International* (1 and 3/98)

Zhirnikh, G. 'The Development of Soviet Aircraft Armament', *Aviatsiya I Kosmonavtika* (8/1967)

Various contributors: many items in *The Cartridge Researcher,* the Official Bulletin of the European Cartridge Research Association.

## OTHER PUBLICATIONS

Bruderlin, E. B. and Nelson, R. S. *Research, Development and Production of Small Arms and Aircraft Armament of the Japanese Army.* Ordnance Technical Intelligence Report Number 19, 1946 (reprinted in USA, 1971)

Elks, K. *Japanese Ammunition 1880–1945*

Labbett, P. and Brown, F. A. *British Anti-Tank Rifle Ammunition 1917–1945*

Labbett, P. and Brown, F. A. *British Service .50 inch Browning Ammunition*

Labbett, P. and Brown, F. A. *German 2cm Cannon Ammunition 1935–1945*

Labbett, P. and Brown, F. A. *British-Made .5 inch and 13mm Machine Gun Ammunition, not for British Service*

Labbett, P. and Brown, F. A. *12.7mm × 108 and 14.5mm × 114 Ammunition (Communist)*

Labbett, P. and Brown, F. A. *British Service 20mm Oerlikon Ammunition*

Labbett, P. and Brown, F. A. *British 30mm & 30/20mm Ammunition*

Labbett, P. and Mead P. J. F. *British 20mm Hispano Ammunition*

Labbett, P. and Mead P. J. F. *British Madsen Ammunition*

Legendre, J-F. *Soviet Union Machine Gun Belt Links* (1998)

Legendre, J-F. *Atelier de Fabrication de Mulhouse:*

*CEAM-AME 1947–1967: Munitions de Moyen Calibre* (1998)

Newport W.H.A. *Evolution of American Fighter Aircraft Armament 1910–1964 – Barrelled Weapons from the 1903 Springfield Rifle to the M61A1 Vulcan Cannon.* UMI Dissertation Services, 1998.

## UNPUBLISHED DOCUMENTS

### (MAINLY HELD IN THE MINISTRY OF DEFENCE PATTERN ROOM)

Ackers, T. *General Survey of Main Problems Connected with Installation, Functioning and Accuracy of Aircraft Gun Armament During the War.* Technical Note Arm. 383, A&AEE Monograph No. 4.08 (Royal Aircraft Establishment, 1947)

Anon. *The Second World War 1939–1945 Royal Air Force Armament Volume II: Guns, Gunsights, Turrets, Ammunition and Pyrotechnics.* S.D. 737 Air Ministry (1954)

Anon. *Me 410 A-1/U4 Flugzeug-Handbuch* (1944)

Anon. *Development of German Fighter Armament.* Air Ministry (UK) 1944

Anon. *German Aircraft Armament and Ammunition During the War of 1939–45.* A.D.I. (K) Report No. 11/1946

Anon. *New Japanese Aircraft Types and Miscellaneous Armament Development.* Technical Air Intelligence Summary #14, DNI (1944)

Anon. *Japanese Air Weapons and Tactics.* The US Strategic Bombing Survey (1947)

Anon. *Gun Ammunition in 37mm Calibre.* D. of A. (India) Japanese Ammunition Leaflets Section E, Leaflet E11 (1945)

Anon. *Preliminary Notes on the Ammunition for Vickers Class 'S' Mk.I Gun.* (Official British publication, status unclear)

Anon. *Japanese Ammunition.* Military Intelligence Division, War Department (USA)

Anon. *Report of Naval Anti-Aircraft Gunnery Committee 1931* (UK)

Anon. *Renseignments sur les Munitions de Petits Calibres.* P.R.R.E.M. de Bourges (France) 1940

Bradstreet, T. *Checklist of German Disintegrating Links Used in Automatic and Semi-Automatic Weapons to 1945* (1998)

Bradstreet, T. *The Luftwaffe MG-FF* (1998)

Bradstreet, T. *Notes on Japanese Aircraft Guns and Cartridges Over 13.2mm* (1998)

Bühler, Dipl. Ing. and Sörensen, Ing. *Table of German Armament Equipment (Approved and Experimental) Small Arms, Automatic Arms and Guns up to 55 mm Calibre.* Unterlüss Report 295/I (1948)

Bühler, Dipl. Ing. Burgmueller, Dr. and Sörensen, Ing. *Table of German Armament Equipment (Approved and Experimental) Ammunition up to 55 mm Calibre.* Unterlüss Report 295/II (1948)

Burney, D. *Letter to the Broadway Trust Company to the Ministry of Supply Armaments Design Department* (25 November 1943)

Cabeen, C. *The Calibre Ninety Aircraft Gun.* Lafayette College, Easton, Pennsylvania

Mix, Dipl. Ing. (late Director of Aircraft Weapon Development, R.L.M.) *Development of Aircraft Weapons, Munitions and Installations – A comprehensive review of the German position at the end of the War.* Unterlüss Report 376 T (1948)

Smithurst, P. *Machine Guns before Maxim.* The Royal Armouries (1998)

Various: *Reich Ministry of Armaments and War Production: Interrogation of Speer, Saur, Mommen and Bosch.* Combined Intelligence Objectives Sub-committee, G-8 Division, SHAEF (May/June 1945)

N.B. The 'Unterlüss Reports' (named after a Rheinmetall establishment) were written immediately after the end of the Second World War following interrogation of German technical staff by the British. They provide detailed information about the state of German armament developments at the end of the war. Copies are kept at the Pattern Room.

# Index

The index is divided into five different parts in order to facilitate browsing as well as locating specific items:

1. Cartridges and guns, by metric calibre
2. Gun index by designation: designer, manufacturer and name
3. Gun mountings, self-propelled guns & vehicles
4. Aircraft index
5. Warship index
6. General index

The following conventions have been followed:

**123** = numbers in bold are page references to significant information about the item
123 = ordinary numbers indicate other references to the item
*123* = numbers in italics are page references to illustrations of the item
C = an illustration of the item is included in the colour plate section
*A3, A4, A5* = a drawing of the cartridge or gun is contained within Appendix 3,4 or 5
T1, T2, T3 etc = data about the cartridge or gun is contained within Table 1, 2, 3 etc.
G = information about this item is included within the Glossary
References in brackets indicate information about a closely related item

## Cartridges & guns, by metric calibre

Where only one gun is mentioned in relation to a particular cartridge, the cartridge and gun references are combined. Where more than one gun is referred to, the cartridge references are given first followed by the gun references on separate lines.

# INDEX